CHALLENGED BORDERLANDS

BORDER REGIONS SERIES

Series Editor: Doris Wastl-Walter

In recent years, borders have taken on an immense significance. Throughout the world they have shifted, been constructed and dismantled, and become physical barriers between socio-political ideologies. They may separate societies with very different cultures, histories, national identities or economic power, or divide people of the same ethnic or cultural identity.

As manifestations of some of the world's key political, economic, societal and cultural issues, borders and border regions have received much academic attention over the past decade. This valuable series publishes high quality research monographs and edited comparative volumes that deal with all aspects of border regions, both empirically and theoretically. It will appeal to scholars interested in border regions and geopolitical issues across the whole range of social sciences.

Challenged Borderlands
Transcending Political and Cultural Boundaries

Edited by

VERA PAVLAKOVICH-KOCHI
University of Arizona, USA

BARBARA J. MOREHOUSE
University of Arizona, USA

DORIS WASTL-WALTER
University of Berne, Switzerland

ASHGATE

Published by
Ashgate Publishing Limited
Gower House
Croft Road
Aldershot
Hants GU11 3HR
England

Ashgate Publishing Company
Suite 420
101 Cherry Street
Burlington, VT 05401-4405
USA

Ashgate website: http://www.ashgate.com

British Library Cataloguing in Publication Data
Challenged borderlands : transcending political and
   cultural boundaries. - (Border regions series)
   1. Regional economics 2. Balkan Peninsula - Boundaries -
   European Union countries 3. European Union countries -
   Boundaries - Balkan Peninsula 4. Mexico - Boundaries -
   United States 5. United States - Boundaries - Mexico
   6. Europe - Economic conditions 7. Europe - Social conditions
   8. Mexican-American Border Region - Economic conditions
   9. Mexican-American Border Region - Social conditions
   I. Pavlakovich-Kochi, Vera
   II. Morehouse, Barbara J. (Barbara Jo), 1945- III. Wastl-Walter, Doris
   330.9'4

Library of Congress Cataloging-in-Publication Data
Challenged borderlands : transcending political and cultural boundaries / edited by Vera
   Pavlakovich-Kochi, Barbara J. Morehouse, Doris Wastl-Walter.
      p. cm. -- (Border regions series)
   Includes bibliographical references and index.
   ISBN 0-7546-4093-0
      1. Boundaries. 2. Europe--Boundaries. 3. Mexican-American Border Region. 4.
   Regionalism. I. Pavlakovich-Kochi, Vera. II. Morehouse, Barbara J. (Barbara Jo), 1945-
   III. Wastl-Walter, Doris, 1953- IV. Series.

   JC323.C33 2004
   320.1'2--dc22   2004046264

ISBN 0 7546 4093 0

Printed and bound in Great Britain by MPG Books Ltd, Bodmin, Cornwall

Contents

List of Figures

List of Tables

List of Contributors

Ana Barbič

Ana Barbič is a Professor of Rural Sociology at the University of Ljubljana, Slovenia. She has been awarded several prestigious scholarships. She was a vice-president of the European Society of Rural Sociology (1988-1993) and has been a member of advisory/editorial boards for several foreign journals. Her bibliography contains some 200 works, among which are two books and 24 chapters (a few co-authored) in 23 Slovenian and 19 foreign books.

Norris C. Clement

Norris C. Clement received his Ph.D. in economics from the University of Colorado in 1968. Since that time he has taught and carried out research and consulting projects related to border-regional development in Latin and North America, Europe and Africa. An accomplished jazz pianist and composer, he is developing a multi-media project, 'Al Norte', that portrays the saga of undocumented immigrants through integrated musical, photographic and verbal images.

Zoltán Hajdú

Zoltán Hajdú is the Deputy Director of the Transdanubian Reseach Institute of the Centre for Regional Studies of the Hungarian Academy of Sciences. He teaches political and historical geography at the University of Pécs. He is the author of three books and 90 papers in Hungarian and foreign languages, and he has edited or co-edited seven books.

Susanne Janschitz

Susanne Janschitz received her M.A. and Ph.D. degrees in geography and mathematics, respectively, at the University of Klagenfurt, Austria. Since 1998 she has been a research fellow in the Institute of Geography and Regional Science at the University of Graz, Austria. Her research involves application of GIS in tourism and regional development.

Mladen Klemenčić

Mladen Klemenčić is a Croatian political geographer. He is a senior researcher and editor at the Lexicographic Institute, Zagreb. He edited *Atlas Europe* (1997) and the *Concise Atlas of the Republic of Croatia* (1993). A lecturer in political geography for the Geography Department, University of Zagreb, he has authored and co-authored more than 80 articles and book chapters in Croatia and abroad.

Andrea Ch. Kofler

Andrea Ch. Kofler received her M.A. degree in geography and history at the University of Klagenfurt, Austria, and she is a Ph.D. candidate at the University of Bern, Switzerland. In her research, she focuses on the question of how to overcome borders acting as barriers to the interactions and exchanges of people across borders. Specifically, she examines the manifestations of identity and space.

Francisco J. Llera Pacheco

Francisco J. Llera Pacheco obtained his Ph.D. degree in geography and regional development at the University of Arizona, U.S.A. Currently he is the Director for Research at the Universidad Autónoma de Ciudad Juárez in México. In addition, he is a professor at the Department of Business Administration at the same university. His field of research is border and political and urban geography.

Barbara J. Morehouse

Barbara J. Morehouse, Associate Research Scientist at the University of Arizona's Institute for the Study of Planet Earth, U.S.A., holds a B.A. degree in music and M.A. and Ph.D. degrees in geography. She specializes in border studies and boundary theory, broadly defined. Her research interests include the implications of borders and boundaries in natural resource management and climate impacts on human and natural systems.

Vera Pavlakovich-Kochi

Vera Pavlakovich-Kochi is the Director of the Regional Development Program in the Office of Economic Development and an adjunct faculty in the Department of

Geography and Regional Development at the University of Arizona, U.S.A. She has participated in a number of international research teams investigating cross-border cooperation and regional responses to globalization. Her research focuses on border economy and transboundary region building in the United States-Mexico borderlands and southeast Europe.

Patricia L. Salido

Patricia L. Salido is a researcher at the Centro de Investigación en Alimentación y Desarrollo, A.C. (CIAD), in Sonora, Mexico. She is an economist trained at the Universidad de Sonora and University College London, U.K. Her main research interests are related to regional specialization processes, particularly in the services sector. She has participated in binational research teams on cross-border health issues.

Clive Schofield

Clive Schofield is a Research Fellow at the School of Surveying and Spatial Information at the University of New South Wales in Sydney, Australia. Prior to this appointment, he was Director of Research at the International Boundaries Research Unit (IBRU) at the University of Durham, U.K. His research remains focused on international boundary issues.

Arthur L. Silvers

Arthur L. Silvers is Associate Dean and Director of the School of Public Administration and Policy, and Professor of Public Administration and Policy at the University of Arizona, U.S.A. He also serves as an Adjunct Professor of geography and regional development and of planning. He holds a Ph.D. in regional science and an M.B.A. from the University of Pennsylvania, U.S.A. He teaches courses in public policy analysis, economics of public policy, and program planning and evaluation. Also, he has developed program-planning methods for needs valuation and implemented impact analyses and benefit-cost evaluation in the human services.

Zoran Stiperski

Zoran Stiperski received his M.A. and Ph.D. degrees in geography from the University of Zagreb, Croatia, where he is a Docent in the Department of Geography and teaches courses in industrial geography and the regional geography of Asia. He is also an associate of the Faculty of Transportation Sciences and the

Zagreb School of Economy and Management, where he teaches transportation and economic geographies. His research topics include border regions, globalization, regionalization and current socio-economic trends.

Mónika M. Váradi

Mónika M. Váradi has been a senior research fellow at the Regional Research Centre of the Hungarian Academy of Sciences since 1989. Her research interests include the demographical and socio-economic processes in the transformation of Hungarian rural society, such as suburbanization, transformation of agrarian society and the local politics. She heads research on the position of national and ethnic minorities in Hungary.

Doris Wastl-Walter

Doris Wastl-Walter is a Professor of Human Geography at the University of Berne, Switzerland. She is a recipient of several prestigious awards and scholarships. She is presently the Chair of the IGU Commission on Geography and Public Policy, and the Director of the Interdisciplinary Centre for Women and Gender Studies at the University of Berne. Her main research interests include the development of theory and qualitative methods, political geography (especially border regions studies) and gender studies.

Richard Welch

Richard Welch is a teacher and a researcher in political and economic geography at the University of Otago, Dunedin, New Zealand. Dr. Welch has served as Head of the Department of Geography and Dean of the School of Social Science at Otago University. He has been an executive member of the IGU Commission on Geography and Public Administration (now Public Policy) since 1993.

Pablo Wong González

Pablo Wong-González, an economist, is the Director of the Regional Development Division at the Centro de Investigación en Alimentación y Desarrollo, A.C. (CIAD), in Hermosillo, Sonora, Mexico. He holds a M.Sc. degree in regional and urban planning studies at the London School of Economics and Political Science. He has carried out several international missions as a consultant for the United Nations Organization in the area of regional development planning. His main research interests are globalization and territory and regional development, as well as transborder regional development.

Bruce A. Wright

Bruce A. Wright is the Associate Vice President for Economic Development at the University of Arizona, U.S.A. He is also the chief operating officer of the University of Arizona Science and Technology Park, a research and development facility and he has served in several different capacities at the University of Arizona, including director of the Office of Community and Public Service, Assistant to the President, and Senior Officer for Community Affairs and Economic Development. A political scientist, Wright's research interests are regional development, transborder economic development, issues of science and technology, and community development and leadership.

Preface

The original idea for the book was born several years ago during a special session at the annual meeting of the Association of American Geographers that brought together a diverse group of researchers interested in transformations occurring in North American and European borderlands. Fascination with the rapid changes occurring in border areas, which until recently were deeply divided by ideological, economic and cultural differences, provided an initial impetus for discussion and exchange of ideas. Despite profound differences in regional geographies between the United States-Mexico borderlands and border areas along southeast edges of the European Union, it was immediately apparent that the two regions shared a number of common issues. Curiosity about the nature and importance of the commonalities and differences we had found prompted a desire to investigate these overarching themes within a more structured framework. The result was an international conference organized jointly by the University of Klagenfurt, Austria, the University of Ljubljana, Slovenia and the University of Arizona, the United States. Twenty researchers from different disciplines – geographers, economists, historians, sociologists, political scientists – gathered in Krumpendorf near Klagenfurt, Austria, in late September of 1997 for an intensive three-day conference. A follow-up field trip guided the participants into and across the Austrian-Italian, Italian-Slovenian, Slovenian-Austrian and Slovenian-Croatian borderlands.

The conference turned into a remarkable event. A relatively small but energetic group engaged in rousing debates about borders, boundaries and border spaces, which stretched far beyond official presentations. In one particularly memorable setting, intense discussion resulted in the profound, and boisterous, conclusion that, no matter what the topic, generalization about borderlands inevitably resulted only in agreement that "it depends". On a more serious note, the ambiance of a Carinthian resort with its post-season quietness provided an ideal place for continuous construction, deconstruction and reconstruction of perspectives on geographical scales, historical contexts, economic forces, cultural heritage, and political power.

The outstanding hospitality and organizational skills of the hosts, the University of Klagenfurt and the University of Ljubljana, contributed to an atmosphere in which bridging differences between disciplines and diverse personal backgrounds could occur almost effortlessly. After the conference, none of us was able to think about borders and boundaries in the same way we had before we met.

Borderlands, as we are well aware, are not a new phenomenon, but are constantly changing, and thus being perpetually rediscovered. Inevitably, the narratives assembled here can only reflect conditions as of the date the last sentence was crafted. More durable are the recurring and persistent patterns of relationships and processes that tend to shape and to characterize border areas. The acts of terrorism that occurred on September 11, 2001 and the new strategies that emerged to cope with global terrorism, demonstrate that, even as things change, so too do they reflect the underlying social constructions and relations that depend on boundaries. By offering perspectives on the influence of global, national, regional and local processes and structures on our borderland study areas, we also provide a context for pondering on current efforts, which are occurring everywhere, to reassess boundary functions from the perspective of heightened security concerns.

More broadly, the perspectives represented in this collection offer a useful matrix for understanding the complex, multi-layered implications embedded in border/boundary redefinition processes. We illuminate these implications through examination, in a multidisciplinary context, of key concepts regarding globalization, borders, and identities. We then unpack these concepts by introducing a series of empirical studies at local and regional levels. The chapters represented in this edited volume were purposefully selected to allow us to make links between and among scales ranging from the global to the national, regional and local, and to join concepts with applications in empirical research. This, we believe, constitutes a unique contribution to the existing literature on borderlands.

In our many discussions as we proceeded with our project, it became ever more apparent that our insights would be best articulated through emphasizing several compelling factors that underpin borderland dynamics today. The first of these is the importance of geographical factors such as location and region-specific combinations of cultural identities and politics that encourage or hinder cross border interactions. The second is the increasing impact of global change and interconnectedness on events occurring at the local level. Third is the growing complexity of decision making in borderlands as an increasing number of levels of political decision-making comes to be involved, and fourth is the role of the actual players within institutional and informal frameworks.

We designed this book to be useful to scholars and practitioners who deal with border issues. We hope that college students and concerned readers, whomever and wherever they may be, will also find it enlightening and thought provoking.

Tucson, the United States and Berne, Switzerland, 2004

Vera Pavlakovich-Kochi, Barbara J. Morehouse and Doris Wastl-Walter

Acknowledgements

This book would not have been possible without the time, energy and enthusiasm of many people. First of all, we thank the participants of the Krumpfendorf, Austria, international conference, who prepared the initial drafts and helped mold the content of the book. We also thank the University of Klagenfurt Department of Geography and Regional Studies, and in particular, Professor Martin Seger and Andrea Ch. Kofler, for hosting the conference and co-organizing a memorable field trip through the borderlands of Austria, Italy, Slovenia and Croatia in cooperation with the University of Ljubljana and the University of Zagreb's Department of Geography. Professor Ana Barbič and Angelca Rus of Ljubljana and professors Zlatko Pepeonik, Andrija Bognar and Dane Pejnović of Zagreb, helped the participants with practical matters in crossing the newly redefined borders and provided local and regional interpretations of the new political landscapes.

The Fulbright Association deserves a particular mention. It was the fellowships awarded to Doris Wastl-Walter (USA 1996) and Vera Pavlakovich-Kochi (Austria 1997-98) that fostered the original idea that led to the conference and further developed into the book project. We also thank the University of Arizona's Office of Economic Development and especially the Associate Vice President for Economic Development, Bruce A. Wright, and the University of Berne's Department of Geography for partial financial and in-kind support for the project.

We thank Bettina Fredrich and Rita Echarte Fuentes-Kieffer of the University of Berne, Department of Geography for their diligent work on preparation of this document. Our special thanks go to Andrea Ch. Kofler, Research and Teaching Assistant and Ph.D. candidate, and Markus Schär in the same department, for their crucial role in preparation of graphic materials, coordination with the Ashgate Publishing Group and for finalizing the document for publishing.

And last, but not least, we thank Ashgate for including this book in their respectful list of publications, and in particular Val Rose and Gemma Lowle.

PART I
INTRODUCTION:
PERSPECTIVES ON BORDERLANDS

Introduction: Perspectives on Borderlands

Barbara J. Morehouse, Vera Pavlakovich-Kochi and Doris Wastl-Walter

> We are in the epoch of simultaneity; we are in the epoch of juxtaposition, the epoch of near and far, of the side-by-side, of the dispersed. We are at the moment, I believe, when our experience of the world is less than that of a long life developing through time than that of a network that connects points and intersects with its own skein.
>
> (Foucault, 1986, p. 22; in Soja, 1989, p. 10)

The early 1990s saw a surge of anticipation and hope as borders within Eastern Europe and between East and West began to open. After almost 50 years, people saw opportunities for renewed political, economic, and cultural ties. The increasing flow of goods, capital, ideas, and people across political boundaries in Europe promised to reduce physical and cognitive distances. Increased permeability of European borders, stimulated by globalization processes, offered a bright hope for constructing and reaffirming national and cultural identity. At the same time, in the course of this process of (re)construction, challenges to identity have arisen within and between the European nation-states themselves, driven not only by internal cultural and political dynamics but also by processes of globalization.

Concurrently, the US-Mexico border emerged in public consciousness as a location of new opportunity, largely due to public perception of the benefits of the 1994 North American Free Trade Agreement (NAFTA). The US-Mexico border historically has been quite porous; NAFTA served primarily to officially sanction existing economic ties associated with the movement of goods and capital. In sharp contrast, the movement of people from Mexico to the United States, and from the less developed to more developed parts of Europe has become a growing point of contention along the border. Thus, Foucault's (1986) 'epoch of simultaneity, the epoch of juxtaposition, the epoch of near and far, of the side-by-side' not only extended deep into the 1990s, but was intensified particularly in parts of Europe and North America.

This book explores some of the contradictory yet simultaneous processes affecting border regions between the European Union and the newly independent countries of southeastern Europe, and between the United States and Mexico. The overarching goal of the book is to explore linkages among different spatio-temporal scales and to present alternative perspectives on the interactions among economic, political, and cultural forces in the two regions. The two regions, although apparently quite different and geographically distant, present provocative opportunities for comparative study. Both regions are characterized by profound differences in political systems, languages and cultures. At the same time, both regions enjoy a high degree of interconnectedness based on shared histories, cultural interaction, and complementarity. Introduction of initiatives such as PHARE-CBC (program supports cross-border cooperation at the external borders of the European Union), INTERREG (initiatives promoting cross-border cooperation in the European Union's internal and external border regions), and NAFTA (North American Free Trade Agreement) (along with the Border XXI side agreement), provide important institutional structures for advancing border-region economic development. Yet, despite ongoing economic integration in both regions, new barriers associated with pronounced inequalities in economic development and different political agendas continue to stymie effective integration.

The processes of globalization and related economic inequalities are extremely important influences on the economic, political, social, and cultural dynamics of border communities as well as of their parent states. However, these processes, while providing opportunities, also restrict the latitude of communities and of entire countries to influence the course of events occurring at larger transnational and global scales.

Especially within the supra-structure of the European Union, the power to make decisions shifted in many aspects from the nation-state to the European community. The European Union has been attempting to define guidelines for a common immigration policy. At the same time, the Treaty of Schengen has highlighted the importance of borders in redefining the flow of people across the external EU boundary. Thus, inside 'Schengen-Europe', borders are open for people to cross; by contrast, the crossing boundary between the Schengen and non-Schengen states has become much more difficult due to decisions being made at the broader intra-European level.

Achieving a comprehensive understanding of contemporary borderland dynamics requires a combination of top-down and bottom-up approaches. While the processes of globalization and status of international political relations provide the overarching framework, local practices, structures, and processes influence how the larger-scale processes affect everyday life. Thus, arriving at satisfactory explanations of border dynamics requires analysis of how the recursive interactions between the global, national, and local processes produce similarities and differences from one border area to another. It is here that the role of 'place' comes strongly to the fore as a specific geographic-historical context for borderland transformation. Situated knowledge (Massey, 1999), as it exists among local residents, provides a useful construct for understanding how the juxtaposition of distinctive yet interrelated borderland places comes to be articulated in terms of the power geometries. Place-based (i.e., situated) knowledge and experiences of border dwellers (see e.g. Martinez, 1988; Herzog, 1990; Meinhof, 2002) are rich in local insight and reflect what are often highly pragmatic ways of negotiating contradictions posed by the processes of globalization and incompatible political and bureaucratic institutions peculiar to each of the bordering nation-states. These larger forces establish important political and economic parameters that set the terms of cross-border relations, but do not wholly control local interactions and practices of bricolage (i.e. 'making do'; see DeCerteau, 1984). Such modified responses to distant policies and decisions to fit local values, needs, and practices constitute a form of tactical response, one that may be more or less effective or successful depending on many factors, including local capacity and larger-scale concerns about enforcing strategic perspectives. For example, local borderland residents may find considerable profit in taking advantage of lower land or commodity prices on the other side of the international boundary, even though national policy may emphasize a 'spend at home' strategy. On the other side of that same boundary, national policy may promote transborder commerce in some areas while discouraging or banning it in others, such as land sales, which it may see as a form of neocolonialism. Such strategic-tactical conflicts may be found in both borderland areas, particularly with regard to land ownership: Mexico has long resisted allowing sale of land to foreigners; more recently, strategic actions have been contemplated, for example, on the Austro-Hungarian border to curtail sale of Hungarian land to foreign entities.

The case studies presented in this book provide incisive examples of how local action and larger structural forces interact to produce particular sorts of relations and action spaces in the borderlands. Wong González and Llera Pacheco reflect on how forces of globalization, and NAFTA more specifically, influence contemporary US-Mexico borderland dynamics, while Pavlakovich-Kochi, Wastl-Walter and Váradi, Janschitz and Kofler, Barbič, and Pavlakovich-Kochi and Stiperski examine the dynamics along the eastern and southeastern EU borders. Taken together, these studies illustrate not only the similarities in experiences among borderlanders with regard to opportunities and challenges, but also how the same global and transnational structures and processes are playing out differently in each of the borderlands.

Here, the production of scale (see e.g. Marston, 2000) is a crucial component. According to critical theory, scale (e.g. national. global, local, etc.) is not something that is universal and can be taken for granted, as assumed by most physical scientists, but is the product of social process. Reflecting this perspective, we acknowledge that those processes that we identify here as global, national, or local are products of social process and as such are not immutable. Nowhere is this more apparent than in the study of borderland dynamics, for it is in the borderlands that contests over the definitions of these socio-spatial scales is most readily apparent. For example, the drawing of a new international boundary between Slovenia and Croatia redefined the scale of the 'national', the 'international', the 'regional' and the 'local' for people on both sides of the border. As both

Pavlakovich-Kochi and Barbič note, the process of scale production and reproduction through both policies and practices has had significant implications for the border region. These implications range from the local (e.g. transboundary interactions and transactions), to binational (e.g. transboundary flows of people and goods), international (e.g. accession to the European Union) and global (e.g. financial transactions, membership in the World Trade Association and the United Nations, etc.). Changes in international political relations discussed by Welch and in US economic relations with Mexico discussed by Clement and Wong González provide other examples of how society produces scale to fit its needs and aspirations in particular times and at particular places.

Differences in living standards and profound lack of opportunities to earn a living, in part the outgrowth of national political and economic decisions and in part the result of intensified globalization of production and financial transactions, constitute key drivers pulling and pushing migrants across the border into the United States and into the countries of the European Union. Added to these influxes is the in-migration of individuals escaping adverse political conditions and persecution.

The political economy of globalization, characterized by capital's restless search for ever cheaper sources of labor and other inputs to production, may at some times benefit border communities through the introduction of new employment-generating production operations and opportunities for businesses providing supporting materials and services. These opportunities may, however, just as easily disappear if opportunities emerge to earn better profits elsewhere. Further, introduction of significant numbers of new jobs into border communities may result in large population influxes that strain the ability of those communities to provide adequate infrastructure and social services. Examples of these processes are readily found in Mexican border cities across the entire length of the US-Mexico border.

The influx of new migrants – both from within the country and from foreign origins – can place significant social and cultural pressures on both the border community and on the nation-state. The sedimented cultures of local border societies are typically characterized by values, language, traditions, and practices of the home country, but mixed to a greater or lesser extent with cultural elements of the neighboring country. Thus, on the US-Mexico border, for example, a Chicano dialect has emerged that freely mixes English and Spanish vocabulary and grammar. At the same time, patriotism, and pride in being Mexican or American, respectively, is readily apparent. At the local-state and nation-state scales, core nationalistic and cultural values are more pronounced. Fear of dilution of core cultural values and economic opportunities, brought on by large influxes of foreign migrants, have prompted strong reactions ranging from movements to ban bilingual education to efforts to strangle migration at the border in the name of protecting jobs. In the countries of the European Union, transboundary inflows of migrants have been denounced by right-wing political groups, and have resulted in periodic outbreaks of violence.

The economic institutions of the European Union and those of the North American Free Trade Agreement are examples of suprastructures having international scope and implications. A related process of increasingly complex regional transformation in the borderland areas is currently underway. Economic explanations of this process tend to focus on rationality as the major underlying motive for abolition of borders. These explanations, however, ignore the power of politics and culture in shaping region-specific responses to global challenges. Political analysis, on the other hand, tends to overemphasize the role of institutions and individual players while ignoring economic realities and the power of market forces. Understanding what happens at the intersection of these converging forces is essential to developing a richer explanation of contemporary borderland dynamics. The case studies presented in this book represent an effort to integrate political, economic, and cultural perspectives in a manner that more fully illuminates key processes that are occurring in various parts of the world today, and the influences of these processes on local borderlands.

The idea that internationalization and globalization would eventually bring people, cultures, and places closer together through expansion of trade and formation of economic alliances is reflected in contemporary discourses that focus on concepts such as borderless economies, global villages, cross-boundary cooperation, bi-nationalism, multiculturalism, and transboundary regional planning. These discourses reflect the unprecedented changes sweeping the globe. Yet, in parallel with this 'de-bordering' process, political forces of nationalism, economic forces associated with regionalism, and cultural forces embedded in identity and everyday life continue to reinforce existing borders and build new boundaries. The tensions and interactions between globalization and nationalism redefine borderlands as condensation points, where changes in economic organization and power relations meet cultural identities, thus creating new complexities and contradictions. This combination of dualism and simultaneity poses challenges for the social construction of border geographies and for the everyday life of border people.

The US-Mexico and European contexts examined in this book share striking commonalities with regard to governing the movement of people. NAFTA, primarily a trade agreement, grew out of a previous border industrialization program intended to divert migration of Mexican citizens to the United States into assembly operations established in the border zone of northern Mexico. NAFTA, like its predecessor, retains barriers to the free movement of people northward into the United States. Similarly, European border policy provides a strong institutional framework for governing the movement of people from non-EU to EU member states. These institutions have significant implications not only at the national level, but also at the local scale where national-level border policies affect everyday border life and transboundary flows.

Southeastern Europe is characterized by fundamental political and economic changes that began in the late 1980s and culminated in the disintegration of the East European Block and the collapse of Yugoslavia. Geopolitical and economic reorientation among the newly independent countries back toward 'Europe' is producing ongoing changes that are being manifested at the more abstract national political level, as well as at scales ranging from the regional to the individual. Individuals and communities are faced with the advantages and the drawbacks of the opening to free-market forces. Greater freedom among the former Eastern Bloc countries with regard to entrepreneurial endeavors has unleashed talents and skills, as well as opportunities for higher returns to individuals are now more readily available than was the case under the former centrally managed economies. At the same time, dependency of places, communities and individuals upon global trends has increased, as has vulnerability to developments outside regional or national control.

A similar mix of increased opportunities, interdependencies and vulnerabilities can be found in the US-Mexico borderlands. Globalization processes, and more specifically NAFTA, encourage a stronger orientation of the Mexican border states toward the United States. In the US-Mexico borderlands, NAFTA initially elevated expectations about benefits of complementary use of resources on both sides of the border. However, by expressly limiting coverage only to the free flow of goods and capital, while excluding freer south-north transboundary movement of people, NAFTA actually presents a mixed bag of benefits and burdens to border communities and border residents.

In both Southeastern Europe and the US-Mexico borderlands, residents' hopes for new political and economic arrangements that would allow freer movement of not only goods and capital, but people and ideas as well, remain largely unfulfilled. Both border areas have seen a significant increase in border-area militarization. Along the most heavily crossed portions of the US-Mexico border, physical walls and electronic walls based on advanced surveillance technologies have been built to halt illegal flows of people and contraband. At the edges of the European Union, surveillance formerly sustained by Communist Bloc countries has transferred to EU members themselves. So, today, the armies of the Schengen states control the borders of the European Union to prevent illegal immigration and, like the US-Mexico border, are becoming increasingly militarized. For the inhabitants of the border regions this means that, in contrast to the past when for example the Hungarian army guarded the border on the eastern side, today the Austrian army protects the border from the western side. Heavy control, carried out with military personnel and equipment, continues to predominate in the region. Further, new international boundaries (for example, between Croatia and Slovenia) have been drawn where formerly differentiation was at best symbolic. This has significantly changed prior patterns of flows and cross-border interactions. In some cases formal and informal rules for who can or cannot cross a border are now refined to the level of evaluating whether the person arrived by automobile (easier crossing) or bus (much more difficult passage, for buses are seen to be more likely to contain workers trying to enter the country illegally). Further, enforcement of border crossing rules in both the European and US-Mexico contexts may be highly asymmetrical, with crossing *into* the United States or an EU country being much more difficult than crossing *from* these areas into the neighboring country. Thus, for many Eastern Europeans as well as Mexicans, political boundaries remain as difficult to bridge today as they were before; in some instances, even more difficult. In the process, the two opposing processes of integration and exclusion continue to shape the daily lives and economies of border places in both regions.

The coexistence of opposing yet related processes is only one of several overarching themes addressed in the book. The growing interconnectedness between global, national and local scales has caught the attention of borderlands students and practitioners alike. Traditionally, the destiny of border areas was determined largely through the local relationships with national centers of political and economic power. Today, decisions affecting border people are made, more often than in the past, at supranational and global levels. Increasingly, the centers of political and economic powers are not only more distant, but more complex as well. At the same time, the shift in power relations opens new spaces for action, not all of it in the national interest. For example, smuggling is big business in the borderlands. Likewise, borderlands provide a congenial context for resistance activities of all kinds. Although these factors are not directly addressed in this book, they constitute an undercurrent of activity that in turn influences the dynamics explored by the authors of the individual chapters.

The chapters in Part II, Borders, Boundaries, and Border Spaces, take a top-down look at some of the forces that are currently influencing cross-border interactions at all scales from the global to the local. Morehouse explores the ways in which boundaries are constructed through social discourse, and examines some of the ways in which boundaries serve as crucial markers for relations of power between those on either side of the line. She emphasizes the fact that, because they are social constructs, boundaries are very protean, changing in terms of their location, configuration, and legitimacy based on the relative capacity of different interests at any given time to assert their authority. Her analysis provides a framework for understanding the transboundary processes and interactions discussed in subsequent chapters of the book. Clement focuses on the U.S-Mexico border, highlighting the role of economic factors in structuring cross-border relations. Demand for ever-freer movement of goods and capital across international boundaries continues to influence the structuring and restructuring of those boundaries. His examination of how economic interactions continue to exert a strong influence on cross-border relations all along the US-Mexico border illuminates important commonalities, and differences, between the European and North American case studies examined later in the book. By contrast, Klemenčić and Schofield examine boundaries from a political point of view. Their chapter, which focuses on the reasons behind why boundaries come to be contested, highlights the importance of boundaries as loci of power relations. They provide a useful typology of borderlands experiencing territorial disputes, one that provides insight into actual and potential tensions on the borderlines examined in subsequent chapters.

Part III, International and National Forces Redefining 'We' and 'Others' addresses questions associated with inclusion and exclusion in borderland regions and among border populations, as a result of major efforts to redefine boundaries at the macro-regional scale. Welch discusses the implications associated with expansion of the European Union. His analysis, which examines this question within the context of the dissolution of the former Soviet Union and the emergence of the former 'Iron Curtain' states as leading candidates for inclusion in the EU, provides valuable context for understanding some of the forces that influence decision making and action at both the state and local level. Pavlakovich-Kochi provides an example of these processes in her analysis of how the interplay of internal and external forces is driving a redefinition of what constitutes the Zagreb 'region', within the context of the recently independent states of Slovenia and Croatia. Hajdú examines the challenges that arise as the international boundary between Hungary and Croatia comes to be redefined in the wake of international war. The fourth case study returns to the US-Mexico border. Wong González discusses an advanced cooperative process to improve cross-border economic relations between two very uneven partners, the US state of Arizona and the Mexican state of Sonora. This process, which receives strong support from the two state governments, is occurring largely outside the traditional realm of nation-to-nation diplomacy. Silvers takes a look at how maquiladora activity on the US-Mexico border has affected poverty rates in the borderland. His mathematically based analysis provides a valuable contribution to methodological approaches to such questions, and encourages researchers to exercise caution with regard to assumptions about cause and effect relationships between economic processes and society.

Part IV, Living With Changing Borders, brings the scale of analysis to the local level and shows how border people cope with the consequences of global, national and regional forces in their everyday life. The five studies examine, respectively, the Austria-Hungary border, the Austria-Slovenia border, the Slovenia-Croatia border, and the US-Mexico border. In the first case study, Wastl-Walter and Váradi illustrate the challenges of building new relationships and infrastructure in a border region that had been virtually bereft of cross-border interactions for half a century. In the second study, Janschitz and Kofler examine how local communities along the Austria-Slovenia border have been attempting to develop new forms of cross-border cooperation by using traditional historical and cultural ties. These activities have emerged in response to the new opening of the international boundary, following the breakup of Yugoslavia and the rise of Slovenia as a new independent state. Barbič's case study of the Slovenia-Croatia borderlands highlights the consequences for the everyday lives of border residents who now find themselves living on an external border, one that was formerly a porous internal line of division between the Slovenian and Croatian cultures. Pavlakovich-Kochi and Stiperski examine the same border from the other side, and illuminate how local perceptions are being affected by changing national agendas towards the new international boundary. The last two case studies turn to the US-Mexico borderlands. Llera Pacheco discusses how the construction of a transboundary regime in the US-Mexico border region encompassing Ciudad Juarez, Chihuahua and El Paso, Texas has come to constitute a new factor in land utilization on the border. Morehouse and Salido examine how transboundary spaces of health care are produced and played out in the everyday lives of border residents, reflecting the contradictions between international boundary politics and production of local, transboundary geographies of shared culture, values, and knowledge.

In Part V, Wright and Pavlakovich-Kochi outline important implications of changing borderlands for policy- and decision-makers. While some are not new, it is the changing perspectives that have reiterated their importance. An overarching message is that a comprehensive policy requires incorporating local knowledge, recognizing historical experience, understanding complexities of borderland geographies, and a context-specific, regionalized approach. Changing nature of interactions vertically (between local, regional and global scales) and horizontally (between nearby and far away places) continues to redefine borders and boundaries, and requires an increasing flexibility at all levels.

References

DeCerteau, M. (1984), *The Practice of Everyday Life*, University of Carolina Press, Berkeley.

Foucault, M. (1986), 'Of other spaces', *Diacritics*, 16, pp. 22-27, cited in E.W. Soja (1989), *Postmodern Geographies. The Reassertion of Space in Critical Social Theory*, Verso, London.

Herzog, L.A. (1990), *Where North Meets South: Cities, Space and Politics on the US-Mexico Border*, University of Texas, Center for Mexican American Studies, Austin.

Marston, S.A. (2000), 'The Social Construction of Scale', *Progress in Human Geography*, 24(2), pp. 219-242.

Martinez, O.J. (1988), *Troublesome Border*, University of Arizona Press, Tucson.

Massey, D. (1999), 'Power-geometries and the politics of space-time', Hettner-Lecture, 1988, pp. 27-46, in H. Gebhardt and P. Meusburger (eds.), *Hettner-Lectures*, 2, Department of Geography, University of Heidelberg, Heidelberg.

Meinhof, U. (ed.) (2002), *Living (With) Borders. Identity Discourses on East-West Borders in Europe*. Border Regions 1, Ashgate, Aldershot.

PART II
BORDERS, BOUNDARIES AND
BORDER SPACES

Borders, Boundaries and Border Spaces

Barbara J. Morehouse and Vera Pavlakovich-Kochi

> When we speak of the space of the subject in terms of geography, it is clear that we are not strictly referring to transparent, identifiable, self-evident physical space. We are referring to cultural coordinates, national and regional commitments, which, though they may refer to a place, are not confined to it and can be (and often must be) preserved outside its bounds or shaped to fit different parameters.
>
> (Kirby, 1996, p. 17)

Advertisers and futurists alike expound on the virtues and imminent emergence of a borderless world, yet a quick perusal from the news media on any given day is likely to uncover yet another story of border conflict or progress in 'transboundary cooperation'. The political, economic, and cultural forces behind continual drawing and redrawing of territorial boundaries are multiplicitous and complex. The particular mix of these forces changes, depending on the particular time, place and mix of social factors. Achieving a broad understanding of the interactions among global processes, national agendas, and local experience in borderland contexts requires mobilizing multiple conceptual approaches in a manner that allows generalization without losing sight of the particularities of individual border regions.

This section is comprised of three chapters, each of which examines broad conceptual questions about boundaries and border spaces in the contemporary world. In the first chapter Morehouse takes a social theoretical approach to understanding how society discursively constructs, deconstructs, and reconstructs boundaries and borderlands. She argues that boundaries are deeply embedded in our contemporary regime of knowledge where they operate as a key organizing concept. No matter what their functions are – as barriers, expressions of natural law, filters, expressions of nationalism, points of conflict, or points of contact and cooperation – boundaries are embedded in daily discourse and action. Boundaries, however, do not exist by themselves. They are socially constructed and thus constantly produced and reproduced. She also points out that borderlands acquire their basic identity from interaction with the boundary and its rules, and from transactions across boundaries. Yet borderlands are not passive spaces. Rather, they have dynamism of their own. They function, according to Morehouse, like a limen, a space 'in-between', where society can 'deconstruct, examine, change and reconstruct policies and actions at the larger scale'.

Clement focuses on economic forces that influence the changing nature of boundaries and borderlands. Recent impressive increases in international trade provide a clear indication of some of the forces that are erasing boundaries as barriers to the movement of internationally marketed goods and services. He draws attention to four major trends where globalization has become a major engine propelling growth in international trade. These trends include technological changes in transportation and communication, new principles of industrial and commercial location, changes in firm organization and strategies, and the changing role of government in economic development and international trade. The ease with which capital, goods, and services move internationally between different and distant locations is one of the most common descriptors of globalization. This has prompted some observers to refer to the phenomenon as the 'borderless' economy. Yet the very processes that are transforming international boundaries from external to internal boundaries within trading blocks or custom unions tend to draw new boundaries aimed at excluding those who operate outside the trading blocs or unions. This process is clearly illustrated by the recently created North American Free Trade Agreement, which brought Canada, United States, and Mexico closer together but at the same time raised protective barriers against imports from non-NAFTA countries. In a similar way, the recently enlarged European Union has reinforced its external boundaries with non-members.

Shifting to a consideration of border conflicts, Klemenčić and Schofield draw attention to the persistent and worldwide problem of boundary disputes. In early 1990s a large number of disputes occurred; ironically, these disputes were occurring at the time the world was celebrating an unprecedented opening of borders and increase in transboundary cooperation. What are the underlying forces that create and nourish border disputes? Although no region is completely immune from boundary disputes, some regions are more prone to discord that others. Regions such as the Middle East have a long history of disputes. Other regions, such as the Albania-Macedonia area, have only recently emerged as overtly contested areas. Although the authors provide no specific unifying theory to explain the phenomenon of border disputes, Klemenčić and Schofield's chapter suggests the importance of several factors: the role of historical context and collective memories, past political decisions imposing boundaries that disrupted existing local and regional flows, shifts in political power and associated redefinition of existing boundaries, and imposition of new boundaries.

Taken together, these three chapters provide a foundation for thinking about how politics, economics, and social process intersect, and collide, to produce new geographies of inclusion and exclusion, cooperation and contestation. Likewise, the three perspectives represented in these chapters lay a provocative foundation for incorporating consideration of boundaries and borders spaces into theories of globalization. The primary message the authors convey is that there is no borderless world, even from an economic perspective. Boundaries have not disappeared; rather, they continue to be defined and redefined, shifted, expanded, contracted. They persist for many reasons, and serve many functions. The sections that follow (in Parts III and IV), through providing regional and local perspectives on these points, offer rich perspectives on how political, economic, and social factors at scales from the global to the local interact in the production and reproduction of boundaries, border spaces, and border lives.

References

Kirby, K.M. (1996), *Indifferent Boundaries: Spatial Concepts of Human Subjectivity*, Guilford Press, New York.

Chapter 1

Theoretical Approaches to Border Spaces and Identities

Barbara J. Morehouse

There seem to be few things in the world today that are as ubiquitous as boundaries and borders. A referee steps in when the soccer ball goes out of bounds. A space shuttle approaches the boundary of the atmosphere. A refugee huddles in a border camp. A two-year old child learns about limits, while a ten-year-old sibling dreams of exploring the frontiers of space.

Michel Foucault suggested that knowledge regimes become so completely hegemonic that it is impossible to think in alternative terms (1982). I would argue that borders and boundaries are deeply embedded in our contemporary regime of knowledge, and that they remain vibrant concepts by virtue of their highly protean character. As many borderlands scholars have observed, borders and boundaries both divide and connect, attract and repel, shelter and watch. Boundaries are indispensable to membership in the nation-state system, and yet have been blamed for some of the most intractable conflicts in history.

Borderlands are spaces where the everyday realities of boundaries are played out. They are the proximate spaces of flows across the dividing line. They are spaces where cultural identity, sheltered by the boundary, becomes blurred, mixed, creolized. The practice of connecting ideas of difference with notions of spatial location and positioning has permeated our language and our discourse such that today it is not uncommon to find references to boundary cells in plant roots, borderline personality disorder, boundary conditions in mathematics, boundary layers in the atmosphere and the ocean, and borderlands art and music. These and a host of other examples illustrate the very great extent to which contemporary society operates within a spatialized ontology, although in many cases without being aware how geographical their worldview really is (Soja, 1989). Even from an epistemological perspective, our understanding of and knowledge about boundaries and borders remains incomplete, even in the face of a large and growing literature featuring boundaries and borders as key organizing concepts, if not specifically directed at border/boundary studies.

Boundaries

Simply stated, boundaries are material and metaphorical spatializations of difference. In their most basic forms, boundaries locate difference through establishing identity and mediating flows—according to Kirby, in fact, without spatialized difference, neither identity nor movement is possible (Kirby, 1996). These functions in turn imply the existence of rules. Thus, boundaries are necessarily made up of sets of rules for what forms of difference and when and where difference may or may not be invoked; of rules for deciding who will add to, delete from, or change the rules of differentiation and for determining why those particular rules will be invoked. In some cases, such as the boundary walls of living cells or the shoreline of a sea, observation of reality precedes the rules; in others, such as the drawing of boundaries to distinguish jurisdictional spaces, the rules often precede the reality. But in either case, mapping the edges is motivated by a desire to articulate, and most importantly, spatialize, rules of differentiation, is/is not, inside/outside, membrane/barrier, he/she/it.

Within contemporary regimes of power, difference is negotiated, inscribed on the material and/or metaphorical landscape, and reinforced through both action and signification. These processes are carried out by individuals who, using spatializing strategies, have the power to institutionalize difference. Yet this power is far from hegemonic, for, again according to Foucault, power requires resistance (Foucault, 1982). Because power is relational, it constitutes a condition which cannot exist without the active participation of its opposite. Combining Foucault's perspective with Lukes's argument (Lukes, 1974) that power can exist when there exists even a remote possibility of resistance, it may be argued that power emerges whenever some actual or even potential manifestation of resistance is perceived to exist. Thus, understanding and explaining boundaries requires recognition of their dual role as markers of the power make, define, legitimate, and symbolize rules and as focal points for resistance to those rules.

No explanation of the social construction of boundaries is complete without analysis of the historical, geographical, and socioeconomic contexts within which they exist. And understanding of context requires contemplation of the concept of scale. The spatial scales of locality, local state, nation-state, and supra-national (up to global) regions are a part of common parlance, even though the concept of scale itself remains insufficiently theorized (Smith, 1992). Less commonly used, but very helpful, are three temporal scales developed by Braudel and applied to border studies by Paasi (1996): short term (taking place within an individual life span), mid-term (taking place in cycles), and long-term (taking place within larger time frames where structural factors promote equilibrium or slow change). The spatial scales noted above cannot always be specifically linked these individual temporal scales, but the two concepts of scale, taken together, present a useful means for understanding continuity and change in the location, configuration, functionality, and importance of individual boundaries and portions of boundaries.

Much of the power of 'boundary' as a concept lies in a certain kind of faith, faith that, through drawing lines, one will cease to be lost (Kirby, 1996); that one will have form, substance, identity, protection, and shelter. Equally powerful is belief in boundaries as limits to be exceeded, lines to be crossed, barriers to be crashed. Science fiction is full of adventurous explorers reaching warp speed, breaking the light barrier, and discovering new worlds. In its extreme, this quest aspires to reach the Aleph of Jorge Luis Borges, for the Aleph signifies the point of ultimate oneness, that point where no boundaries are necessary because their is no other than the One. At the opposite extreme is the black hole, the borderless point of ultimate nothingness, the danger most feared. In both cases, Is and Is Not are finally reconciled. In neither case is there room for a borderland of transition, nor is there a space of play where different possibilities might be tried out.

Evolution of Boundaries and Boundary Studies

We have come a long way with regard to how we spatialize our differences and divide our territories. Boundaries were defined by walls, for example, in China and in the Roman Empire; however, it was not until the beginnings of European state formation, arising out of the changes in political structure during the Enlightenment, that modern territorial boundaries came to predominate (Prescott, 1978). Whereas the walls of China and Rome appear to have represented the edge of the frontier (Jones, 1959), the edge of civilization where a wall was built to keep out the uncivilized, modern boundaries encompass territory incorporated within adjoining units of political jurisdiction and sovereignty. The frontiers are closed now, and only adjustments are possible on Earth's land base.

Recent economic discourse has focused on a geographical transformation from a space of places to a space of flows (Castells, 1989). However, economic globalization has not rendered traditional boundaries at all obsolete, even though certain boundary functions, notably control over the international trade in goods and the global flow of ideas and knowledge, have been rendered increasingly problematical. As integral elements in the particular combination of politics (including law), economics, and social process that makes up our contemporary regime of knowledge, boundaries, in fact, remain very alive and well.

The historical evolution of boundaries has preoccupied scholars such as Jones (1959), Pounds (1963, in Tagil, 1983), and Prescott; Pounds is among those who have proposed typologies of boundaries. According to Pounds, boundaries may be classified into four groups: antecedent boundaries (drawn before human settlement occurred); subsequent boundaries (delineated after the area was populated, and in agreement with the population pattern); superimposed boundaries (drawn after the cultural area developed but without regard for the spatial development of the territorial patterns of that culture group); and relict boundaries (no longer functioning as political lines of division, but still evident on the landscape). Most importantly, Pounds stressed that there is no such thing as a 'natural' boundary nor is the classification of 'artificial' boundaries useful; rather, he emphasized that all boundaries are social constructs. This is the predominant perspective of borderlands scholars today, although attempts to use natural features for boundaries, in an effort to render them more recognizable and more stable, continues in the geopolitical world.

Tagil extended Pounds's approach when he argued that the definitions and functions of boundaries change over time, and that attempts to understand these boundaries must be framed by the types of questions being asked. He emphasized the need to incorporate relativity into projects to understand and explain boundaries, a need that remains salient today, not only in the many studies that look at particular boundaries within their own contexts, but also in the ongoing debate over how, when and even whether, individual empirical work on boundaries should be homogenized into general theories or other overarching constructs. He suggested that theories associated with center/periphery relations, economic integration, power politics, or group/individual social behavior might prove useful, depending on the boundary being studied and the questions being asked. Tagil also emphasized the need to incorporate history into boundary studies. It is important, he argued, to know when and how the boundary came into being, what historical relationships exist between patterns of settlement and the process of drawing the boundary, and what policies have been associated with that boundary. In addition, he noted that it is important to assess the degree to which the interests of the border population have been harmonized with those of the 'official' border policies (Tagil, 1983, p. 21).

Tagil lamented that there was a notable lack of a broad perspective (Tagil, 1983, p. 21) in the research being done on the history of borders. This shortcoming was particularly evident with regard to a lack of comparative studies framed around general research questions. Certainly Tagil's concern is being addressed today, not only in the contributions to this book, but also in many other publications. Nugent and Asiwaju's edited volume on African boundaries (1996), and Anderson's treatment of European boundaries, African and Asian frontier disputes, internal boundaries, and boundary drawing in uninhabited zones (1996) are but two examples of the array of works that have appeared in recent years.

Newman and Paasi (1998), in an important review of contemporary boundary studies, include in their discussion the convergence of political geography and social theory. Their review recognizes the work being done from postmodernist perspectives and includes studies focused on the construction of socio-spatial identities, on discourse analysis, and on narratives constructed around the role of boundaries in the construction of 'self' and 'other'. They advocate greater awareness of the multidimensional nature of boundaries, the importance of geographical scale, and more incorporation of environmental perspectives and multicultural approaches into boundary studies.

The history of particular boundary areas has also been a subject of considerable interest for writers such as Burghart (1962), Reyner (1964), Sahlins (1989), and Klemencic (1991), and Paasi (1996). Nineteenth-century improvements in the technologies of mapping, combined with more precise knowledge of the physical terrain, made it possible for cartographers to produce relatively accurate maps. With the ability to inscribe boundaries on maps, in indelible ink, came new capabilities to defend those boundaries and to give them a material history. In turn, the tangible documentation of territorial boundaries made it easier both to defend the legitimacy of those boundaries and to challenge them. The ability to delineate boundaries, and thus to control the identity and nature of the nation-state, came to represent the orderliness, and thus the superiority, of the nation-state vis-à-vis less well-organized societies (Herzog, 1990), as well as the superiority of certain state formations over others. Other innovations in the technologies of transportation and communication facilitated control of areas farther from the heart of the state. With the new technologies, central administrations could learn more quickly of border problems and could respond more rapidly. Further, by facilitating flows between the center and the margins of the state, the central government could more tightly integrate border populations into the processes, structures, ideologies, and everyday life of the nation-state.[1]

Reconstruction of the history of particular boundaries and the use of this history to justify the size, configuration, and location of nation-states, as well as to defend or contest existing (state and internal) boundaries, continues today.[2] A good example of these processes may be found in the formation of new nation-states out of the fragments of the former Yugoslavia. 'Croatia, A New European State' (1994), is one of many publications that delves deep into the history of territoriality in southern Europe to find support for the particular state boundaries that have appeared on maps of the region in the past few years. Here, a detailed historical and contemporary geography of the location and concentrations of Croatians relative to the other ethnic groups inhabiting the area, and historical analysis of spatial interactions among Croatians and between Croatians and the other ethnic groups of the area, provide powerful rhetorical devices for justifying the delineation of the crescent-shaped country that appears today on the world political map. In this instance, the drawers of Croatia's boundaries have superimposed a wide variety of cultural attributes (language, religion, historical experience), over economic and political patterns of location and interaction in an effort to claim a place among the world's nation-state system and to use geography to achieve peaceful resolution to the incendiary tensions that wracked the region in the late 1980s and early 1990s.

As may be seen in the Croatian example, when viewed as spatializations of difference and sets of rules for how the process of differentiation is to be operationalized, boundaries may be understood in terms of the functions they perform in particular contexts. Embedded in discourse and action, these functions range widely. Some of the more easily identifiable functions are described below.

Boundaries as Barriers

The function of boundaries as barrier continues to be very important today, just as it was during the height of the state-building era, which lasted from around 1800 to 1945. During this era, boundaries were identified as the place where danger would be stopped, thus sheltering those inside. Boundaries have traditionally been invoked to bar entry of goods, people, resources, and communications deemed to be illegal or undesirable. Closely connected with this function is the idea of the cordon sanitaire, which uses boundary drawing as a material and metaphorical mechanism for defining and barring 'disease'. For example, there is a long history in Uganda of attempting to use the threat of the spread of disease (variously sleeping sickness, tuberculosis, sexually transmitted diseases, and AIDS) to bar the entry of the Banyaruanda, a people originating in neighboring Rwanda. The Ugandans have repeatedly and unfairly blamed the Banyaruanda, migrant laborers who over the years have crossed into Uganda seeking refuge from famine or war, or seeking employment, for their public health problems. To protect themselves, the Ugandans have at various times attempted to turn back these people at the international boundary or, because in reality the labor of these migrants was sorely needed, detained at the border until they were 'cured'. Though repeated efforts to erect a cordon sanitaire were unsuccessful (Lyons, 1996), the attempt provides an excellent example of the importance of the barrier function of boundaries within social discourse.

Boundaries and Natural Law

These boundary drawing activities tended to reflect the general Enlightenment concern with discovering, articulating, and applying universal laws based on the laws of nature. Proponents of this viewpoint believed that, by appealing to the higher authority of nature, disputes over where boundaries, and thus difference, should be physically located would be eliminated. This doctrine, largely developed in France, resulted in much attention being paid to the use of natural landscape features as boundary markers and delimiters. Because they were easily recognizable and, at least in theory, were permanently inscribed and provided barriers to incursion, rivers were a favorite dividing line, followed closely by mountain ridges. Historical studies of boundaries reveal, however, that quite frequently social process has overruled boundaries based on natural features (Jones, 1959; Sahlins, 1989).

Firmly delineated boundary lines continue to dominate world affairs, even in the face of technological innovations in transportation, communications, and control technologies.[3]

Boundaries as Filters

When invoked as a filter, the boundary, in its capacity as a screen or membrane, allows some flows to cross the line but not others. In an early version of this concept, Ratzel developed a law, an organismic analogy, of the boundary line as an outer layer, within which the state itself exists as the heart of the organism (Jones, 1959; Prescott, 1978; Herzog, 1990). While more flexible than mechanistic views of boundaries as barriers, regarding the state as a unitary organism invokes many of the same problems. Most critically, viewing the state as a unitary organism assumes that policies, processes, and events associated with boundaries and border areas exclusively emanate from and are controlled from the center of the state. Such a viewpoint fails to acknowledge the effects, much less the importance, of processes occurring at the local level. In an attempt to redress the imbalances inherent in Ratzel's type of organismic analogy, other borderlands scholars have developed a modified framework in which the boundary is viewed as a membrane (Ingram et al., 1990). From this perspective, there is no body; rather, there is a filter that may operate at various scales from the individual or local (perhaps analogous to the individual cell) to more complex forms of organization, such as institutions, states, regions, and nations. Although not articulated, there is an implication in this viewpoint that the higher forms of organization might be analogous to organs, living organisms, and families of organisms.

In yet another variation on the theme of boundary as filter, some borderlands scholars have suggested that boundaries be studied as systems (Strassoldo and Gubert, 1973; Strassoldo, 1980; Ricq, 1983; Herzog, 1990). In this view, the components of the system are not associated with life forms, but rather are elements comprising subsystems of larger, more integrated systems that in turn encompass social, economic, cultural, environmental, legal, and other processes. Within the system, the boundary allows or deters flows, depending on the content of the flows and on the context within which the process occurs. The border as a functional planning zone is a good example of the way in which systems concepts have been incorporated into border studies (Herzog, 1990).

Boundaries as Expressions of Nationalism

A very common function of boundaries is to define national identity and to affirm the territorial extent of a nationality group. Jones has attributed the development of this concept to German reactions to the largely French concept of natural boundaries (Jones, 1959, p. 248). Linguistic and cultural boundaries, as points where nationality finds its other, were seen to reflect the realities of a higher law than the natural laws of rivers and other landscape features in nature. Efforts to create nation-states based on concepts of self-determination (i.e. nationalism) were especially strong after the breakup of the Habsburg and Ottoman empires in the wake of World War I. Wilsonian ideology drove these efforts, although in the end power politics played a strong role in the actual location and function of the final boundaries (Jones, 1959). More recently, and within the old Austro-Hungarian empire, the ethnic groups encompassed by Yugoslavia have been attempting by military and peaceful means, to use ethnicity, and associated qualities of nationalism to assert themselves as individual nation-state participants on the world stage. The relatively short history of nationalism as a focus of identity in some parts of the Balkans, notably Macedonia, and the problems of lack of contiguity between the imagined communities of the various ethnic groups and the territory they claim, have rendered the process excruciatingly difficult for all concerned (Danta and Hall, 1996; White, 1996; Pusich, 1996; Oberreit, 1996; Papadopoulos,

1996). Likewise, nationalism continues to underlie intractable territorial, and boundary, disputes in many other places (see for example DeMarchi and Boileau, 1982), including Northern Ireland and the Basque country.

Boundaries as Points of Conflict

One of the most frequently recurring themes in boundary studies, particularly among political geographers, has been that of boundaries as focal points of conflict. Considering that many battles and two world wars have been fought over how territory should be divided (and thus difference spatialized), it is not surprising that this has been a source of considerable interest and activity. Based on notions of geopolitics, borders and boundaries are seen as locations where threats to security have occurred. The aggressive nationalism's of the nineteenth century, for example, generated serious border confrontations in Europe (House, 1964). In Latin America, the positioning of boundaries has continued to be a source of actual and potential conflict (Calvert, 1983). Starr and Most (1983) examined African boundaries in light of their role in generating conflicts; general treatments of boundary disputes may be found in Prescott (1978) and Day (1982). Martinez (1988) also looked at boundaries as agents of conflict in his examination of the US-Mexico border. According to Martinez, 'by nature, border zones, especially those that are far removed from the core, spawn independence, rebellion, cultural deviation, disorder, and even lawlessness' (Martinez, 1988, p. 2).

The role of boundaries as generators of conflict has been challenged, however. In a critique of Starr and Most (1983), Kirby and Ward (1987) suggested that, rather than being the sources of conflict, boundaries were the outcomes of—and reflections of—those conflicts. This more recent view places much greater emphasis on the roles of context and social process in the social production and reproduction of boundaries.

Boundaries as Points of Contact and Cooperation

In recent years, contact and cooperation have been a key theme with regard to the functions of boundaries, at all levels from the local to the supranational. As industrial, commercial, and financial transactions and processes have come to assume global proportions, for example, cooperation has become a byword in relations between states. Within the context of global economic restructuring, the role European boundaries as barriers to the movement of goods and people within the European Union have diminished, to be replaced by cooperation among the member states. It is important to observe, however, that the opening of borders within the EU has also generated the phenomenon of Fortress Europe, in which the barrier function of the boundaries between the EU and other countries has come to take on ever greater significance. Internally, the contact and cooperation functions of the states' boundaries have stimulated transboundary political and administrative cooperation at all scales of resolution from the nation-state to the individual.

Justification for transboundary cooperation has generally been expressed in terms of either human rights (couched in concepts of natural equality among humans) or utilitarianism (political cooperation and administrative coordination would facilitate more efficient allocation of resources, avert unnecessary duplication of effort, and generally improve human welfare) (Anderson, 1983). Barbič's work on the socioeconomic implications of the new Slovenian-Croatian border, for example, grapples with the challenges posed by a new international boundary imposed where previously none had existed (Barbič, 1995).

Modern technology, which has resulted in a monumental increase in the number, intensity, and kinds of communications that flow freely across boundaries, has rendered boundaries obsolete in some ways. However, these technologies and their implications for the nation-state system, have prompted nation-states to intensify their search for ways to preserve their sovereignty, and thus their boundaries; but their efforts are ones to establish points of contact and cooperation rather than to engage in conflict. Increases in scientific knowledge, as exemplified by current debates about global climate change, have likewise generated concern for the preservation of boundaries. International pressure to address these concerns has prompted explicit interest in finding solutions to differences in needs and perspectives through cooperative interactions.

In some cases, relations of power and resistance swirl strongly around the contradictions posed by an unwavering belief in the indispensability of sovereignty and the growing recognition that the existing system, and especially existing boundary rules, create as many or more problems than they resolve. Among the many studies that have explicitly looked at boundaries in terms of contact and cooperation are Gibbons (1989) and McKinsey and Konrad (1989) who have written about these issues from the Canadian perspective and Anderson (1983) who has written on cooperation in Europe. Cooperation has also been key to studies of natural resource management in borderlands. The sharing of natural resources in the US-Mexico boundary context provided the focus for publications by Mumme (1988) and Szekely (1987), among others. Issues surrounding transboundary environmental and pollution issues have been covered by many observers, including Ingram and Fiederlein (1988), Teclaff and Teclaff (1987), and Bath (1986). I myself have looked at a variety of boundary functions in the context of natural resource management along both international and internal boundaries (Morehouse, 1993; 1995; 1996a; 1996b). Among those who have discussed the role of governmental activities in the context of transboundary resource issues are Igram (1988); Hayton and Utton (1989), Goldie (1987), Dupuy (1983), and Varady et al. (1996).

Transborder labor issues (Ricq, 1983) and the effect of border commerce and industry on women (Ruiz and Tiano, 1987) are other examples of the many studies that take issues of contact and cooperation into account. Economic cooperation across boundaries are themes that have been explored by Weintraub (1990), Hansen (1988), and many others. The science and politics of natural resource boundaries have been the subject of inquiries by Newmark (1985), Schonewald-Cox and Bayless (1986), and Yahner (1988). It is in these areas of study that the conflicts between using natural law to define boundaries versus using politics to accomplish the task of assigning spatial differentiation stand out. Today, recognizing that both ecological and jurisdictional boundaries exist but that they seldom coincide, natural resource managers have begun searching for ways, based on models of cooperation, to reconcile the contradictions and conflicts in drawing these types of boundaries.

Boundaries as Contexts

One of the more interesting approaches to understanding boundaries has arisen from contemporary interest in pluralistic approaches, the importance of context, and the need to place greater emphasis on localities and on their linkages to other scales of resolution. These studies are representative of a movement away from reliance on global, generalizable laws and toward a focus on material conditions in the real world. While context has been recognized for many years as an important element in boundary and borderlands studies (House, 1964; Prescott, 1978), only recently have social, political, economic, and ecological contexts been recognized as significant factors in any explanation of the processes of spatializing difference.

Good examples of this approach may be found in Sahlins's study of the Cerdagne-Catalonia region of the Pyrenees mountains between France and Spain (1989) and Paasi's examination of Finnish boundaries (1996), especially in the Karelia area between Finland and Russia. In both of these examples, the authors stress the need to take into account local experience, as well as recognizing the influence interactions between the local, regional, and national/international scales, in theorizing boundaries and understanding borderlands processes. Sahlins finds that, while a unitary cultural group was divided into two parts when the formal boundary was drawn between France and Spain, the individuals on both sides of the border were soon reinforcing or challenging the boundary, depending on what material advantages they sought to gain. Thus, while continuing to self-identify as a unitary ethnic group in some instances, the residents on either side of the French-Spanish boundary were not adverse to identifying themselves as citizens of France or Spain when opportunities, such as access to state-sponsored services or benefits, intruded on local life and transboundary interactions.

In the case of Paasi's work on the Finnish-Russian boundary (1996), common language, culture, landscape, and historical experience form a backdrop to twentieth century efforts by the Finns to assert their sovereignty in the face of an overpowering Soviet presence. In Karelia, a boundary that had been heavily militarized and that severely impeded interactions between Karelians on the two sides of the line became, in the context of the breakup of the Soviet Union and the rise of the European Union, both a locus of tentative interactions and a site where Finnish identity, and its difference from Russian identity, could at long last be firmly asserted.

Other reflections of the importance of contextuality to understanding boundaries and borderlands may be found in arts and culture. Lipset (1990) and Blaise (1990), for example, have examined the importance of culture, including production of Canadian films, television programs, and publications, in maintaining Canadian identity in a context of strong US domination. Likewise, a large body of works exists that reflects culture on the US-Mexico border. On the US side, for example, Weisman (1986), Miller (1981), and Williams (1962), are among the many who have tried to capture borderlands contexts from an 'Anglo' point of view. Alternative views of the US-Mexico border may be found in works such as those of Anzaldúa (1987), one of a number of artists and writers working from Chicano experience.

Borders and Borderlands

Related to the continued vitality of boundaries in the contemporary world, and in part due to the spatial reorganization that is accompanying contemporary globalization, borderlands continue to attract considerable attention. The discourse that has grown up around the nature, function, culture, politics, and economics of borders and borderlands reflects concern about their history, their present-day condition, and their future viability.

Where boundaries slice and glue, borderlands airbrush differences, mix things up. Fundamentally, a borderland is an area through which a boundary line runs, but the most important key to understanding borders and borderlands, i.e. the territorial spaces along the boundary, lies in recognizing their transactional nature. Borderlands acquire their basic identity from interactions with the boundary and its rules, and from transactions that take across the boundary, between inhabitants of the borderland territory.

During the first and second world wars, when geopolitical theories were exerting strong influence on world events, terms such as shatterbelt, buffer zone, and demilitarized zone came to have popular currency. All of these terms were attempts to deal with those areas, located between two stronger powers, where, because of long histories of overlapping claims, entrenched hostilities, and other conflicts, difference could not be easily explained or resolved through the drawing of simple boundary lines. Shatterbelt came to be used to describe areas, such as Hungary, where conflicts repeatedly occurred and where local populations and states were politically and militarily dominated again and again by neighboring powers.

The buffer zone concept, on the other hand, refers to areas that lack status as distinctive political units. Buffer zones were designed to absorb the stresses of otherwise-adjacent states, and thus to prevent conflicts from spilling over into the states themselves (Kristof, 1959, p. 280, footnote 59). While not often used at the nation-state scale, buffer zones became popular in the 1970s as territorialized strategies for mitigating the effects of encroaching civilization on natural areas. The development of the biosphere reserve concept, for example, is based on having one or more core areas where nature is strongly protected. These areas are surrounded by a buffer zone where activities and resource uses that do not threaten the natural processes or the aesthetic value of the core(s) are allowed. Surrounding the buffer zone is the rest of the territory, where restrictions are minimal or nonexistent (Morehouse, 1996a; 1996b).

The idea of a demilitarized zone is similar to that of the buffer zone, but has particular salience in areas wracked by long-term conflict. These zones, such as the infamous DMZ between North and South Korea, are intended to separate rival armed camps and, thus, increase the prospects for maintaining peace.

A related concept, that of free trade zones, is designed to allow buyers and sellers to interact within specially designated areas near border crossings and other points of entry and exit (such as the duty-free shops in airports). Free trade *regions*, such as the European Community and the North American trade area created under NAFTA, have begun to eliminate the need for specific free trade zones, but, given the vicissitudes of the world economy, it is too early to eliminate the latter term from our lexicon of border concepts.

Even with concepts such as the ones discussed above, borderlands remain difficult to map, for, in most cases, distance decay seems to be more operational than the more directly difference-laden process of differentiation that accompanies the drawing of a boundary. A border may be quite narrow, huddling close to the boundary, or it may extend for many miles in one or both directions from the dividing line.[4] The territorial size of the borderland then, depends on the geographical reach of locally based transboundary transactions. These transactions may range from visits to family members, or to the graves of family members, located across the boundary to intensive flows of workers, goods, information, and technology.

Borderlands are sometimes seen to constitute the best of human aspirations for reconciling differences while allowing for individual or group identity. More often, they are seen to reflect the most 'dangerous' of human conditions: indeterminacy. Amorphous shapes and beings unsettle us, and ambiguous situations promise not only excitement but danger; they are situations in which one tries to maintain control over the ability to exit. Contradictions abound which open opportunities for resistance, subversion, new beginnings, escape from the strictures of a customary milieu. Anzaldúa (1987), for example, finds possibilities for Chicana empowerment in the US-Mexico borderlands, while bell hooks (1990) identifies the marginality of African Americans, particularly that of African-American women, as holding potential for effective resistance to white power and for construction of empowered identities.

Borders provide spaces of transition, thresholds of entry and exit. Sometimes borderlands may constitute liminal spaces of becoming, spaces for redefining 'what is', and thinking about 'what might be'. As elaborated by Victor Turner (1967; 1974), the limen (Latin for threshold) may be a physical or a metaphorical space; in either case, it is a place betwixt and between other spaces of life. Liminal spaces are where rites of passage may occur, pollution removed, purity reasserted (Douglas, 1966; 1970; Babcock, 1975). It is here that existing understanding and knowledge of the world can be deconstructed, examined, perhaps changed, then reconstructed (Morehouse, 1997).

Even though borderlands are located between different socially constructed spaces (both material and metaphorical), the borderland and liminal spaces are not synonymous. Borderlands become liminal only when individuals or groups actively take advantage of the in-between space to remove themselves from conflictual or contradictory situations for the purpose of reconciling or removing those conflicts or contradictions. Likewise, liminal figures may be instrumental in negotiating otherwise intractable situations. In folk tales and cultures around the world, liminal figures such as shape changers, shamans, frogs, and coyotes populate this in-between space, this borderland of what may—or may not—be. They are important for they mediate differences, absorb contradictions into themselves, draw away the dangers of in-betweenness.

As this discussion suggests, liminality has a temporal as well as a spatial dimension. In fact, we might think in terms of liminal moments which, like Bhabha's caesuras (1994), allow for a certain time of stillness within which an individual may be reconstituted, a social group remolded, a space reaffirmed or reshaped outside the strictures of customary structural barriers. It is a time-space of tactical maneuvering where agency and structure meet in creative ferment. As DeCerteau (1984) observed, tactics (often in the form of bricolage, making do with what is at hand) can support opposition to state-authored grand strategies. It is important to keep in mind, however, that tactics have their own spatial logic of fragmentation and, in the long run, disregard for boundaries, whereas state-authored strategies may often be designed to reinforce and reassert those very same boundaries (DeCerteau, 1984; Kirby, 1996).

Border communities and borderlands inhabitants, due to their location on or near a boundary, are ideally located to invoke liminality, especially in situations where policies and actions at larger scales of resolution, particularly the international level, transgress the politics and culture of the locality, its spaces of representation, and its representational spaces (Lefebvre, 1991; Keith and Pile, 1993). It may be that a series of liminal moments occurred at the local scale, for example, in 1991, when the environmental side agreement to NAFTA was being negotiated. At the time, environmentalists concerned about the US-Mexico border made a strong bid to have a separate and distinct border environmental policy and administrative structure established. As negotiations progressed and the border environmental structure began to acquire material form, it became increasingly apparent that decisions were going to be made and structures (including rules) established, without input from the local border communities. The communities reacted by forcing the negotiators to hold, and attend, meetings in their local localities. In essence they attempted to create a series of liminal situations where the attendees, especially the representatives of the federal government, could participate in the deconstruction, examination, and reformulation of the border environmental structure so that it more effectively reflected local needs and viewpoints.

Although in the end, as in most relations of power between unequal players, the localities got less than they wanted, they were at least able to force some concessions in rules and procedures allowing for more local input to decision-making and access to funding for environmental infrastructure projects. Thus, these quasi-liminal moments allowed local participants to reaffirm their local experience and values and to instruct outsiders about the local contexts. Whether they succeeded in reforming the viewpoints of the outsiders is arguable, given the lack of progress that has been made in addressing existing problems such as water and pollution, hazardous waste disposal issues, and so on. They did succeed, however, in translating their very specific and highly contentious issues between the local and national scales of resolution and the contradictions between the material world of their everyday lives, and their cultural worlds of identity, tradition and expectation.

Perhaps the most striking example of widespread borderlands experience is found in Canada. For Canadians, and I am sure others as well, being a border society (approximately 80 percent of the country's population lives within 100 miles of the US-Canadian border) often means maintaining a state of alertness against excessive Americanization (Gibbons, 1989). Understanding the unmilitarized, but defended, border entails seeing the borderland on the Canadian side of the line 'more as a state of mind than as a simple physical or geographic fact' (Gibbons, 1989, p. 2). Because Canadians live so close to the edge, as it were, Canadian identity requires persistent reinforcement in literature, film, politics, and other venues that offer opportunities for reaffirmation of both their national identity and their differences from their neighbors across the line. Carrying the analysis further, many Canadians believe that identity must, therefore, be defended at the national as well as at the local scale. This is particularly the case with regard to the strong northward current that carries American products across the line and into the very heart of Canada. Here economics and cultural identity collide, and the borderland becomes contested terrain.

Drawing the Threads Together

As this exploration of boundaries and borderlands has emphasized, the concept of socially produced space is one of the most powerful theories at the disposal of borderlands scholars, for the process of producing space, as played out in the regimes of knowledge that structure our world, frequently entails the drawing of boundaries. Drawing upon Foucault's idea of regimes of power, the persistent use of boundaries to produce space—and spatializing difference—suggests that the existing, spatially informed structures of power and knowledge are alive and well. Entire systems of law, in fact, use boundaries as a foundation for enforcement of public and private will. It is not so much the drawing of boundaries, however, that embeds formally delineated spaces in the political, economic, and social structures of society; rather it is the reproduction of the boundaries, and the spaces enclosed within, through institutionalized processes, regimes of power (Keeley, 1990) and the everyday actions of individuals.

To carry the argument further, and assuming an active role for individual agents, it may then be observed that boundaries, as (re)produced through discrete discourses and actions, are plastic. They change in location, length, function, and value depending on who is exerting greatest influence at that moment. Every decision and action that accepts the rules and functions of a given boundary reproduces that boundary. Every decision and action that challenges the boundary rules and functions also challenges the legitimacy of the boundary, *for that purpose*. An accretion of challenges, as happened in former East Germany, can result in the erasure of the contested boundary.

Boundaries, then, are perhaps best understood as rules and practices, material demarcators of edges, and barriers to flows; they are also abstract metaphors that are useful for articulating, and spatializing, concepts and perceptions of difference. Boundaries provide the edges needed to contain space and its contents, and to protect that space from outside penetration. They sever what was formerly a unitary space, regulate and filter flows, and, of great importance, they provide legitimation and a material location for engaging in surveillance and enforcement.

Borderlands typically exist because they have been produced and repeatedly reproduced by individuals and institutional forces, rather than by legal action. Like boundaries, borderlands cease to exist when the rules and practices, discourses and actions that give them meaning and value are no longer reproduced. Unlike boundaries, borderlands tend to be somewhat amorphous in size, shape, and configuration, and to change considerably over time and space, depending on what natural, political, economic, social, and cultural processes are involved in their integration and definition. Indeed, borderlands shrink and expand in response to both local and non-local influences. Furthermore, multiple borderland spaces typically exist, which operate either simultaneously or at different times and places. The borderland may or may not overlap the boundary it adjoins (in Berlin, a discernible borderland existed on each side of the wall, though every effort was made to ensure that there was essentially no interaction between them).

Typically defined as spaces of politics, commerce, and culture, borderlands have both physical and abstract presence and feature both material and metaphorical characteristics. In Braudelian terms, they have an everyday, short-term existence, experience the effects of mid-term cyclic events, and exist within longer-term structural contexts. Understanding borderlands dynamics from any perspective requires taking into account all of these factors, as well as the recursive relationship that the borderland has with its boundary. In other words, each influences and affects the other. The subversive spaces created by illegal migrants and smugglers in the borderlands, for example, redefine boundary rules. Conversely, boundaries functioning as focal points for cooperating on shared public health issues (Morehouse et al., 1997), serve to integrate borderland communities on each side of the boundary as well as across it.

In conclusion, the abundant literature on borders and boundaries demonstrates that we know how to reproduce their stories (Anzaldúa, 1987; Velez-Ibañez, 1996;

Paasi, 1996) and that we can understand something about their landscapes and processes (Rumley and Minghi, 1991; Weisman, 1986; Arreola and Curtis, 1993). However, we still lack a sufficient fund of knowledge regarding how we produce and reproduce boundaries and borderlands, and what these social constructions mean to various societies in different times and places, and at different scales. There is considerable room for research into the significance space, borderlands, and boundaries for the production of liminal moments, and for understanding the roles of liminal figures in our lives.

As Clapham has observed about concepts of boundaries held by people in the Horn of Africa, 'boundaries ... mean different things to different people and in different contexts' (Clapham, 1996, p. 237). Nugent made the same point when he noted that, when European began colonizing Africa, 'whereas Europeans thought of political space as a kind of chequer-board in which every state shared borders with others of its kind, the West African map looked more like a raisin bun with centers of political power interspersed between no man's lands and the scatterings of decentralized polities' (Clapham, 1996, p. 39).

We need to continue grappling with the question of whether life without boundaries and borders as we know them today is thinkable. At least some Native American groups lack adequate terms for boundaries in their native languages (Morehouse, 1993; 1996b). Can we reach a condition where no language is needed because difference is no longer spatialized either physically or metaphorically? And would we want to experience this state? Would it be a matter of reaching the Aleph or perhaps of falling into a black hole?

Notes

1   An excellent example of the incorporation of borderland populations into the state, in this case, the Catalonians in borderlands between France and Spain, may be found in Sahlins, 1989. See also Schneider (1991) and Halland Danta (1996).
2   For an example of these processes with regard to internal boundaries, see Morehouse, 1996.
3   See Kern, 1983, for an excellent discussion of the evolution of concepts of time and space that emerged between 1880 and 1918.
4   Historian Oscar Martinez, in *Border People*, University of Arizona Press, 1994, developed a typology of borderlands in which the width and symmetry of the border zone varies from virtually non-existent in alienated (tension-filled) borderlands, to the narrow strips of coexistent borderlands (featuring on-and-off stability), and the wider zones characteristic of interdependent borderlands (more interactive, cooperative), and integrated borderlands (featuring permanent stability, free flows across the boundary, and the functional merging of economies).

References

Anderson, M. (1983), 'The political problems of frontier regions', in M. Anderson (ed.), *Frontier Regions in Western Europe*, Frank Cass and Co. Ltd., London.

Anderson, M. (1996), *Frontiers: Territory and State Formation in the Modern World*, Polity Press, Cambridge, UK.

Anzaldúa, G. (1987), *Borderlands-La Frontera: The New Mestiza*, Spinsters/Aunt Lute Press, San Francisco.

Arreola, D.D. and Curtis, J.R. (1993), *The Mexican Border Cities: Landscape Anatomy and Place Personality*, University of Arizona Press, Tucson.

Babcock-Abrahams, B. (1975), 'Why frogs are good to think and dirt is good to reflect on', *Soundings*, 58, pp. 167-181.

Barbič, A. (1995), 'The socioeconomic effects of the new Slovenian-Croatian border', *Resource Reports, Biotechnical Faculty of the University of Ljubljana*, 65, pp. 111-128.

Bath, C.R. (1986), 'Environmental issues in the United States-Mexico borderlands', *Journal of Borderlands Studies*, 1(1), pp. 49-72.

Bhabha, H. (1994), *The Location of Culture*, Routledge, New York.

Blaise, C. (1990), 'The Border as Fiction', *Borderlands Monograph Series*, No.4, Canadian-American Center, University of Maine, Orono, Maine.

Bufon, M. (1994), 'Theory and Practice in Central European Border Areas. The Slovenian Example. Croatia: A New European State', *Proceedings of a symposium held in Zagreb and Cakovec, Zagreb, September 22-25*.

Burghardt, A.F. (1962), *A Historical and Geographical Study of Burgenland, Austria*, University of Wisconsin Press, Madison.

Calvert, P. (1983), *Boundary disputes in Latin America*, Conflict Studies No. 146, Institute for the Study of Conflict, London.

Castells, M. (1989), *The Informational City: Information Technology, Economic Restructuring, and the Urban-Regional Process*, Basil Blackwell, Oxford.

Clapham, C. (1996), 'Boundary and territory in the Horn of Africa', in P. Nugent and A.I. Asiwaju (eds.), *African Boundaries: Barriers, Conduits, and Opportunities*, Pinter, London, pp. 237-250.

Danta, D. and Hall, D. (1996), 'Contemporary Balkan questions: The geographic and historic context', in D. Hall and D. Danta (eds.), *Reconstructing the Balkans: A Geography of the New Southeast Europe*, John Wiley and Sons, Chichester and New York, pp. 15-32.

Day, A.J. (ed.) (1982), *Border and Territorial Disputes*, Longman, Essex, UK.

DeCerteau, M. (1984), *The Practice of Everyday Life*, University of California Press, Berkeley.

DeMarchi, B. and Boileau, A.M. (1982), *Boundaries and Minorities in Western Europe*, Franco Angeli, Milan.

Douglas, M. (1966), *Purity and Danger: An Analysis of Concepts of Pollution and Taboo*, Penguin Books, Middlesex, UK.

Douglas, M. (1970), *Natural Symbols: Explorations in Cosmology*, Pantheon Books, New York.

Dupuy, P.-M. (1983), 'Legal aspects of transfrontier regional cooperation', in M. Anderson (ed.), *Frontier Regions in Western Europe*, Frank Cass and Co. Ltd., London.

Foucault, M. (1982), 'The subject and power', *Critical Inquiry*, 8, pp. 777-795.

Gibbons, R. (1989), 'Canada as a Borderlands Society', *Borderlands Monograph Series*, No.2, Canadian-American Center, University of Maine, Orono, Maine.

Goldie, L.F.E. (1987), 'Equity and the international management of transboundary resources', in A.E. Utton and L.K. Teclaff (eds.), *Transboundary Resource Law*, Westview Press, Boulder.

Hall, D. and Danta, D. (1996), *Reconstructing the Balkans: A Geography of the New Southest Europe*, Wiley, Chichester and New York.

Hansen, N. (1988), 'The nature and significance of transborder cooperation in the Mexico-US borderlands: some empirical evidence', *Journal of Borderlands Studies*, 1(2), pp. 57-65.

Hayton, R.D. and Utton, A.E. (1989), *Transboundary Groundwaters: The Bellagio Draft Treaty*, University of New Mexico, International Transboundary Resources Center, Albuquerque.

Herzog, L.A. (1990), *Where North Meets South: Cities, Space and Politics on the US-Mexico Border*, University of Texas, Center for Mexican American Studies, Austin.

Hooks, b. (1990), 'Choosing the margin as a space of radical openness', in bell hooks, *Yearning: Race, Gender, and Cultural Politics*, South End Press.

House, J.W. (1964), 'A local perspective on boundaries and the frontier zone: two examples from the European Economic Community', in C.A. Fisher (ed.), *Essays in Political Geography*, Methuen and Co., Ltd., London.

Ingram, H. (1988), 'State government officials role in US-Mexico transboundary resource issues', *Natural Resources Journal*, 28, pp. 431-449.

Ingram, H. and Feiderlein, S.L. (1988), 'Traversing boundaries: a public policy approach to the analysis of foreign policy', *Western Political Quarterly*, 41(4), pp. 725-745.

Ingram, H.; Kirby, A.; Laituri, M. and Morehouse, B. (1990), 'On the edge of all possibilities: political-economic change where core meets semi-periphery', paper prepared for Urban Planning and Government Reorganization in Poland: Polish Needs, US Lessons conference, University of Arizona, Tucson, Arizona, November 1990.

Jones, S.B. (1959), 'Boundary concepts in the setting of place and time', *Annals of the Association of American Geographers*, 49(3), pp. 241-255.

Keeley, J.F. (1990), Toward a Foucauldian analysis of international regimes, *International Organization*, 44(1), pp. 83-105.

Keith, M. and Pile, S. (1993), 'Introduction, Parts 1 and 2', in M. Keith and S. Pile (eds.), *Place and the Politics of Identity*, Routledge, London.

Kern, S. (1983), *The Culture of Time and Space 1880-1918*, Harvard University Press, Cambridge, Massachusetts.

Kirby, A.M. and Ward, M.D. (1987), 'The spatial analysis of peace and war', *Comparative Political Studies*, 20(3), pp. 293-313.

Kirby, K.M. (1996), *Indifferent Boundaries: Spatial Concepts of Human Subjectivity*, Guilford, New York and London.

Klemencic, M. (1991), 'A recent historico-geographical basis of the Yugoslav outer and inner borders with special reference to Croatian borders', *Geographical Papers*, 8, pp. 325-341.

Kristof, Ladis K. (1959), 'The nature of frontiers and boundaries', *Annals of the Association of American Geographers*, 49(3), pp. 269-282.

Lefebvre, H. (1991), *The Production of Space*, translated by Donald Nicholson-Smith, Basil Blackwell, Oxford.

Lipset, S.M. (1990), 'North American Cultures: Values and Institutions in Canada and the United States', *Borderlands Monograph Series*, No. 3, Canadian-American Center, University of Maine, Orono Maine.

Lukes, S. (1974), *Power: A Radical View*, British Sociological Association, London.

Lyons, M. (1996), 'Foreign bodies: the history of labour migration as a threat to public health in Uganda', in P. Nugent and A.I. Asiwaju (eds.), *African Boundaries: Barriers, Conduits and Opportunities*, Pinter, London, pp. 131-144.

Martinez, O.J. (1988), *Troublesome Border*, University of Arizona Press, Tucson.

McKinsey, L. and Konrad, V. (1989), 'Borderlands Reflections: The United States and Canada', *Borderlands Monograph Series*, No. 1, Canadian-American Center, University of Maine, Orono Maine.

Miller, T. (1981), *On the Border*, University of Arizona Press, Tucson.

Morehouse, B.J. (1993), 'Power relationships in the spatial partitioning and natural resource management of the Grand Canyon', Ph.D. Dissertation, Department of Geography and Regional Development, University of Arizona, Tucson, Arizona.

Morehouse, B.J. (1995), 'A functional approach to boundaries in the context of environmental issues', *Journal of Borderlands Studies*, X(2) pp. 53-73.

Morehouse, B.J. (1996a), *A Place Called Grand Canyon: Contested Geographies*, University of Arizona Press, Tucson.

Morehouse, B.J. (1996b), 'Conflict, space, and resource management at Grand Canyon', *The Professional Geographer*, 48(1), pp. 46-57.

Morehouse, B.J. (1997a), 'Defining boundaries, constructing borderlands: A case study from the Arizona-Sonora border', paper presented at the First International Conference on Critical Geographies, Vancouver, British Columbia, August 10-13 1997.

Morehouse, B.J. (1997b), 'Difference, liminality, and geographies of power', paper presented at the Annual Meeting of the Association of American Geographers, Fort Worth, Texas, April 1-5 1997.

Morehouse, B.J.; Driesen, K.; Kunz, S.; Salido, P.L.; Taddei Bringas, C.; Taddei Bringas, A. and Santillana Macedo, M. (1997c), *Health Services in Arizona and Sonora: Opportunities for Transboundary Integration*, Report published for the Arizona-Mexico Commission, Phoenix, Arizona.

Mumme, S. (1988), *Apportioning groundwater beneath the US-Mexico border*, Research Report Series, No. 45, University of California, San Diego, Center for US-Mexican Studies, San Diego.

Newman, D. and Paasi, A. (1998), 'Fences and neighbours in the postmodern world: boundary narratives in political geography', *Progress in Human Geography*, 22(2), pp.186-207.

Newmark, W.D. (1985), 'Legal and biotic boundaries of western North American national parks: a problem of congruence', *Biological Conservation*, 33, pp. 197-208.

Nugent, P. (1996), 'Arbitrary lines and the peoples minds: a dissenting view on colonial boundaries in West Africa', in P. Nugent and A.I. Asiwaju (eds.), *African Boundaries: Barriers, Conduits, and Opportunities*, Pinter, London, pp. 35-67.

Nugent, P. and Asiwaju, A.I. (eds.) (1996), *African Boundaries: Barriers, Conduits, and Opportunities*, Pinter, London.

Oberreit, J. (1996), 'Destruction and reconstruction: the case of Dubrovnik', in D. Hall and D. Danta (eds.), *Reconstructing the Balkans: A Geography of the New Southeast Europe*, John Wiley and Sons, Chichester and New York, pp. 67-77.

Paasi, A. (1996), *Territories, Boundaries and Consciousness: The Changing Geographies of the Finnish-Russian Border*, John Wiley and Sons, Chichester and New York.

Papadopoulos, A.G. (1996), 'Single human geography, multiple Macedonian histories', in D. Hall and D. Danta (eds.), *Reconstructing the Balkans: A Geography of the New Southeast Europe*, John Wiley and Sons, Chichester and New York, pp. 79-88.

Prescott, J.V.R. (1978), *Boundaries and Frontiers*, Croom Helm, London.

Pusich, S.S. (1996), 'The case for regionalism in Croatia', in D. Hall and D. Danta (eds.), *Reconstructing the Balkans: A Geography of the New Southeast Europe*, John Wiley and Sons, Chichester and New York, pp. 53-65.

Reyner, A.S. (1964), 'The case of an indeterminate boundary: Algeria-Morocco', in C.A. Fisher (ed.), *Essays in Political Geography*, Methuen and Co., Ltd., London.

Ricq, C. (1983), 'Frontier workers in Europe', in M. Anderson (ed.), *Frontier Regions in Western Europe*, Frank Cass and Co. Ltd., London.

Ruiz, V.L. and Tiano, S. (eds.) (1997), *Women on the US-Mexico Border: Responses to Change*, Allen and Unwin, Boston.

Rumley, D. and Minghi, J.V. (eds.) (1991), *The Geographies of Border Landscapes*, Routledge, London.

Sahlins, P. (1989), *Boundaries: The Making of France and Spain in the Pyrenees*, University of California Press, Berkeley.

Schneider, P. (1991), *The German Comedy: Scenes of Life after the Wall*, Farrar, Straus, and Giroux, Inc., New York.

Schonewald-Cox, C.M. and Bayless, J.W. (1986), 'The boundary model: a geographical analysis of design and conservation of nature preserves', *Biological Conservation*, 38, pp. 305-322.

Smith, N. (1992), 'Geography, difference and the politics of scale', in J. Doherty, E. Graham and M. Makek (eds.), *Postmodernism and the Social Sciences*, MacMillan, Houndmills, Basingstoke, Hampshire, UK, pp. 57-79.

Soja, E.W. (1989), *Postmodern Geographies: The Reassertion of Space in Critical Social Theory*, Verso, London.

Starr, H. and Most, B.A. (1983), 'Contagion and border effects in contemporary African conflict', *Comparative Political Studies*, 16, pp. 92-117.

Strassoldo, R. (1980), 'Centre-periphery and system-boundary: culturological perspectives', in J. Gottman (ed.), *Centre and Periphery: Spatial Variation in Politics*, Sage Publications, Beverly Hills, CA.

Strassoldo, R. and Gubert, R. (1973), 'The boundary: an overview of its current theoretical status', in R. Strassoldo (ed.), *Boundaries and Regions: Explorations in the Growth and Peace Potential of the Peripheries*, Edizioni LINT, Trieste.

Szekely, A. (1987), 'Transboundary resources: the view from Mexico', in A.E. Utton and L.K. Teclaff (eds.), *Transboundary Resource Law*, Westview Press, Boulder.

Tagil, S. (1983), 'The question of border regions in Western Europe: an historical background', in M. Anderson (ed.), *Frontier Regions of Western Europe*, Frank Cass, Ltd., London.

Teclaff, L.K. and Teclaff, E. (1987), 'International control of cross-media pollution: an ecosystem approach', in A.E. Utton and L.K. Teclaff (eds.), *Transboundary Resource Law*, Westview Press, Boulder.

Turner, V. (1967), *The Forest of Symbols: Aspects of Ndembu Ritual*, Cornell University Press, Ithaca.

Turner, V. (1974), *Dramas, Fields, and Metaphors: Symbolic Action in Human Society*, Cornell University Press, Ithaca.

Varady, R.G.; Colnic, D.; Merideth, R. and Sprouse, T. (1996), 'The US-Mexican Border Environment Cooperation Commission: collected perspectives on the first two years', *Journal of Borderlands Studies*, XI(2), pp. 89-119.

Velez-Ibanez, C.G. (1996), *Border Visions: Mexican Cultures of the Southwest United States*, University of Arizona Press, Tucson.

Weintraub, S. (1990), *A Marriage of Convenience: Relations Between Mexico and the United States*, Harcourt Brace Jovanovich, San Diego.

Weisman, A. (1986), *La Frontera: The United States Border with Mexico*, Harcourt Brace Jovanovich, San Diego.

White, G.W. (1996), 'Place and its role in Serbian identity', in D. Hall and D. Danta (eds.), *Reconstructing the Balkans: A Geography of the New Southeast Europe*, John Wiley and Sons, Chichester and New York, pp. 39-52.

Williams, W.C. (1962), 'The desert music', in *Pictures from Breughel and Other Poems*, New Directions Books, Norfolk, Connecticut.

Yahner, R.H. (1988), 'Changes in wildlife communities near edges', *Conservation Biology*, 2(4), pp. 333-339.

Chapter 2

Economic Forces
Shaping the Borderlands

Norris C. Clement

Introduction

Historically, the economic functions of borders were derived from the political, economic and strategic policies of the nation state and were largely determined in national capitals. Thus, borders were utilized to regulate the entry (and sometimes the exit) of goods and services (things and people) in accordance with the policies of the nation state, independent of the specific needs of border-regions.[1] Consequently, economists tended to treat borders primarily as barriers to commerce, frequently depriving the adjacent regions of their natural hinterland, thereby limiting their development.

Recently, however, a new political-economic environment has emerged out of the growing acceptance of free market policies, which include global 'free trade', the formation of regional trade blocs and the end of the Cold War. This new 'borderless' global economic environment has significantly eroded the historic functions of international borders, which are now being viewed more as 'contact zones' between neighboring countries while opening up new options for the development of transborder regions throughout the world. In fact, the very process of globalization seems to be giving rise to a generalized process of regionalization whereby regions are forced to take more responsibility for their own economic development through policies of regional planning explicitly cast in the setting of an increasingly competitive, globalized economy. In this process of 'glocalization'[2] many regions have come to regard the nation state as increasingly irrelevant to many of the tasks that they believe are essential to achieving higher levels of prosperity and quality of life.

Thus, subnational (government) actors at the state and city level as well non governmental organizations (NGOs) have assumed a more active role in international affairs and are seen as a significant and growing challenge to the authority of the nation state (Mathews, 1997; Newhouse, 1997). Transborder collaboration can be regarded as a special subset of this new arena of 'regionalization' which, especially in the European case, has stimulated alliances of cities in relatively close proximity, such as the Rhone-Alps region of France which includes Lyon, St. Etienne and Grenoble, in order to develop common infrastructure, technology and marketing strategies, thereby improving the competitiveness, and hopefully the prosperity, of the entire region.

Perhaps the most important economic factor contributing to the new borderlands reality is globalization. Therefore, in the first section, we examine this concept in some detail: what it is; what has stimulated it; how economic enterprises are responding to it; how it affects the location of economic activity; and how governments at all levels are being forced to change in this new economic environment. In the second section we explore the changing economic functions of borders in the context of the increasingly 'open' internationalized economic environment and the implications for the development of border-regions specifically.

In the third section we briefly discuss the economic forces underlying the concept of transborder collaboration, which is increasingly viewed as a necessary but not sufficient condition for border-region development. This section develops some of the implications of the analysis for public policy in border regions and briefly touches on some of the responses that have been implemented in response to these changing global economic conditions.

While the analysis is based on the literature and experiences of Europe and North America, the author believes that it has some relevance to other regions as well.

The Dynamics of Globalization

In this section we identify and discuss four main dimensions of change associated with globalization: (1) technological innovation as the 'driver' of globalization; (2) how firms are being forced to restructure in light of rapid technological innovation and increased global competition; (3) the changing locational requirements of industry in this new, globalized economy; and (4) the effects on government structures and functions of these far-reaching technological, economic and locational changes.

The term 'globalization' has no one widely accepted definition and is used in many ways depending on the perspective. For example, it is frequently noted that multinational corporations are involved in the 'globalization of production' because they buy (source) component parts from and/or construct factories in many countries of the world. Similarly, the concept of the 'globalization of capital markets' usually refers to the heightened integration of the world's major stock markets so that what happens in one spills over into the others, as happened in October, 1997 when the crisis of Asian stock markets reverberated throughout the world. In the present context, however, we have adopted the United Nations' description of the concept which captures its multi-dimensional nature: '... the widening and deepening of international flows of trade, finance and information in a single, integrated global market' (United Nations Development Program, 1997, p. 82).[3]

A common question about globalization is, what stimulated its development? While there are many causes, it is generally acknowledged that the General Agreement on Trade and Tariffs (GATT), created in 1948, has performed a catalytic role in expanding international trade. GATT was designed to reduce trade barriers in the belief that free markets would increase economic efficiency, which in turn would increase economic growth and human welfare.[4] Of course, reducing trade barriers reduces the protection that certain industries previously enjoyed. Therefore, while consumers usually benefit from the increased competition and the lower prices that can result, jobs and profits in certain industries can be seriously affected. Thus, free trade produces both winners and losers and opens up national (and regional) economies to the sharply fluctuating forces of the international economy.

Nevertheless, it is generally acknowledged that the GATT has been relatively successful in reducing artificial trade barriers (tariffs, quotas and qualitative restrictions) and exchange controls. In 1947 the average tariff on manufactured imports was 47 percent; by 1980 it was only 6 percent and with full implementation of the (GATT) Uruguay Round in the 1990s, it falls to 3 percent.

Other artificial barriers to international economic transactions were eased with the resolution of political conflicts that divided the world for decades, such as the Cold War and the apartheid system in South Africa.

Another stimulus to globalization has been and continues to be technological innovation. Most important have been the huge reductions in transport and communication costs:

- Between 1920 and 1990 maritime transport costs fell by more than two-thirds;
- Between 1960 and 1990 operating costs per mile for the world's airlines fell by 60 percent;
- Between 1940 and 1970 the cost of an international telephone call fell by more than 80 percent and between 1970 and 1990 by 90 percent.

So what have been the measurable results of these liberalizing influences? First, global trade grew 12-fold in the postwar period. Now more than $4 trillion a year, it is expected to grow 6 percent per year for the next 10 years. Second, in the 1980s telecommunication traffic was expanding by 20 percent per year. Finally, the expansion of capital flows has been even more dramatic:

- Flows of foreign direct investment in 1995 reached $315 billion, nearly a sixfold increase over the level for 1981-85;
- Between the mid-1970s and 1996 the daily turnover in the world's foreign exchange markets increased from around $1 billion to $1.2 trillion.

While there are other dimensions to globalization (e.g. the development of a global culture) the main point from an economic perspective is that technological and institutional changes have made it possible for multinational corporations to do business (i.e. export, import, invest, speculate) anywhere in the world where adequate infrastructure exists, quickly and cheaply. Consequently, international economic transactions have increased dramatically, changing virtually all aspects of economic life.

Technological Change

In Figure 2.1 the major stimulus to globalization is identified as technological change, primarily in the transportation, communications and information/computer sectors. As noted above, not only have these key services become cheaper, they also have become faster and more widely available throughout the world. Thus, many firms are now freer to 'go international', to geographically (re)locate any or all phases of production wherever costs are lowest or conditions most appropriate to the firm's overall strategy.

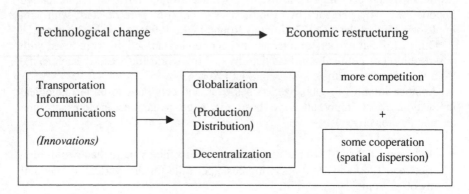

Figure 2.1   Technological change and economic restructuring

'Smart firms' are now able to devise global strategies and decentralize and/or disperse their operations and manage them from afar through fax, voice and data transmission while shipping components and products via transportation systems which each day become cheaper and offer more options (Grunwald and Flamm, 1985; Wilson, 1992). The resulting spatial (geographic) redeployment of production, along with the tendency toward trade liberalization carried out under the auspices of multilateral institutions such as GATT and the newly formed World Trade Organization (WTO) and the creation of regional integration schemes such as the EU and the NAFTA as well as the emergence of many Third World Newly Industrializing Countries (NICs) as major manufacturing centers, have dramatically increased global competition in certain sectors such as apparel, automobiles, toys, footwear and automobiles. At the same time, as we will see below, the accelerated pace and higher cost of technological innovation has compelled firms to enter into cooperative relationships with other firms, governments and universities in order to spread the enormous costs of developing new products and new production techniques while sharing technology.

Changes in the Organization of Production and Firm Strategies

Table 2.1 outlines recent changes in how firms organize and do business in response to the increasingly open international economy and rapid technological change. In the post World War II period the structure of production in developed economies has changed dramatically. Previously, employment tended to be concentrated in the 'real goods' sectors (agriculture and basic manufacturing). In today's 'post industrial' countries' employment has become more concentrated in the service and technology-based sectors. There has also been a shift from large to small and medium-sized firms as an important source of new jobs and technological innovation (National Council for Urban Economic Development, 1993), while many firms have moved from a regional or national perspective to an international one (i.e. sourcing inputs, both component parts and human services, 'offshore' and marketing outputs globally). This process began many decades ago with the rise of multinational firms (Barnet and Muller, 1974) and is now trickling down to most small and medium-sized enterprises.

Enormous changes are also taking place within firms, especially high tech companies, changes which are characterized by the emergence of computer-aided technologies which permit manufacturing firms to efficiently design and produce small quantities of 'custom made' products. Such flexible production systems are based on 'economies of scope' instead of the 'economies of scale' associated with the rigid assembly lines of traditional manufacturing firms.[5]

Frequently referred to as the Japanese model of production (Kawano, 1993), this approach involves a shift from the traditional (Fordist) 'mass production' assembly line and hierarchical organizational structures to a (post-Fordist) model incorporating the just-in-time (JIT) system of inventory control, quality control (QC) circles and job rotation (Lipietz, 1987; Kawano, 1993). These changes, in turn, require more horizontal organization structures and new roles for workers who, frequently, through training and 'learning by doing', must combine mental and manual work, higher skill levels. Another aspect of the Japanese model, lifetime employment, unfortunately, has not been transplanted to the US nor European firms and may even be losing its hold in many Japanese firms as a consequence of the depressed conditions there since the 1990s. Instead, the numbers of temporary and part-time workers are increasing, usually receiving lower pay and, frequently, few or no vacation, health, or retirement benefits.

While these new practices often result in lower costs and an enhanced ability to respond to new market opportunities, employees' work roles and traditional notions of job security are changing considerably, increasing the need for worker retraining, counseling and relocation, services usually provided by government (see Table 2.3).

Table 2.1   Economic structures: How firms organize and do business

Old/traditional		New/emerging
Agriculture and basic manufacturing	→	More service and high tech activities *Information/ finances/ tourism and* *advanced manufacturing*
Large firms: 'economies of scale'	→	Smaller firms: 'economies of scope' *Flexible production system*
Hierarchical organizations *Fordist assembly lines*	→	Work rules more flexible *Post-Fordist Japanese, model*
Separation of mental and manual work *Taylorism*	→	'Learning by doing' *Upgrading worker's skills*
Stable work force *Hi-pay with full benefits*	→	More temporary, part-time workers *Lower pay, fewer benefits*
Centralization of functions *Everything 'in house'*	→	Decentralization of functions 'Bluring' of manufacturing and service sectors results in: • increased 'out-sourcing' • growth of industrial 'clusters'
National market perspective *Inputs and outputs*	→	International perspective (+) • 'off shore' sourcing *inputs* • production phases *dispersed* • global marketing *outputs*
Competitive activities *Exclusively*	→	Strategies require cooperation *Complex alliances and networks* *Firm-governments-universities*

Today's firms utilize more outside technical and business services, as well as sub-contractors to produce component parts ('outsourcing'), as firms focus more on their 'core competencies' (e.g. concentrating on developing new computers instead of manufacturing the entire line of products offered). Outsourcing tends to blur the traditional distinction between manufacturing and services while creating complex 'industrial clusters'.[6] The presence of such clusters is increasingly viewed as essential to the modern firm's competitiveness.

Finally, note that relations between firms are no longer exclusively competitive. The need to innovate rapidly and the enormous costs of developing new products and techniques have pushed firms into cooperative networks and alliances with competing firms, governments and university research centers (Reich, 1992). Such pooling of resources, together with increased international competition, accelerates the pace of technological innovation that is widely regarded as the key factor in achieving competitiveness in today's dynamic markets. This process in turn heightens competition between firms, compelling all firms to work harder (and smarter) just to keep up in this supercharged environment.[7]

The Changing Criteria for Locating Economic Activity

Table 2.2 summarizes the effects of the changes noted above (in Figure 2.1 and Table 2.1) with respect to the criteria firms use to determine the optimum location (geographically) for their plants, headquarters and warehouses. Such decisions are, of course, very important for the regions selected, including border regions, in terms of creating new jobs and bringing new business for those firms already located there. Consequently, the competition for attracting new firms is enormously sharp and regions frequently vie against each other by offering attractive incentive packages to prospective firms.[8]

Table 2.2   Changing criteria for locating economic activity

Old/traditional		New/emerging
Core-periphery: Dynamic industries in core	→	'Old core' *restructured, diverse* 'New core' *small, niche markets* 'Periphery' most other regions
Location factors *Costs: proximity to resources, markets and suppliers*	→	Congestion costs in 'core' rise mature industries Low wage areas new industries Climate, QOL, labor force, research facilities
Border regions in periphery	→	New opportunities available

Traditionally, regional structures were viewed in a dichotomous framework of 'core – periphery'. Traditional core areas, formed on the basis of proximity to resources, suppliers, and markets, were characterized by the dominance of large scale manufacturing firms involved in the production of producer goods and consumer durables. Large financial firms usually were located in or near to these industrial heartlands. Meanwhile, activities like agriculture, forestry, fishing, mining and small-scale manufacturing activities tended to be located in the periphery.

Now, however, it is clear that since industrial restructuring began in both the United States and Europe in the 1970s, traditional core areas have been transformed in terms of both production techniques and product types (i.e. most mature products have either been automated or moved to lower cost regions, either domestically or 'off shore') and a 'new core' has emerged, mainly in southern states. Simplistically, it can be said that new core areas are populated mainly by businesses possessing the characteristics of the modern firm, as portrayed in Table 2.1.[9]

What is important here is that these firms seek different location characteristics which, within some limits, tend to emphasize qualitative aspects (e.g. a well-trained labor force, quality education and research institutions, and a high quality of life) over quantitative cost factors. This changing perspective on location criteria presents new opportunities for cities/regions in the old periphery, including border regions.

Effects on Government Structures and Functions

Over the last several decades technological innovations and the tendency toward freer trade and market-oriented policies have resulted in greater international competition and forced dramatic changes in the organizational structures of manufacturing and service firms as well as how and where they conduct business. These changes have also led to important shifts in the spatial (geographic) distribution of economic activity and employment which, in turn, have stimulated governments at all levels to reassess their organizational structures and the functions they provide. The major changes in governmental structures and functions are outlined in Table 2.3. Here several trends are worth exploring.

First, at the national level traditional macroeconomic stabilization measures (Keynesian monetary and fiscal policies), traditionally used to reduce the extremes of business cycles (i.e. alleviate deep recessions and high inflation), have become less effective in the 1990s due primarily to: a) increased global integration of financial markets, resulting in fewer degrees of freedom for national governments,[10] b) consistently large budget deficits creating large national debts that have made stimulatory policies politically unacceptable, and c) a growing consensus that economic problems such as low productivity growth are not 'cyclical' in nature and therefore must be resolved by deep structural reforms at the microeconomic level (e.g. tax reform).

Second, growing dissatisfaction and frustration with the perceived consequences of a growing state sector (e.g. high unemployment and rising welfare costs) has resulted in a shift to a more market-oriented, conservative philosophy involving less reliance on and more selective uses of government.[11] During the 1980s and early 1990s a strong debate raged in the United States regarding the effectiveness of national industrial policies as a means for regaining competitiveness in the new, globalized economy (Thurow, 1985; Krugman, 1994) while in Europe national industrial policies were subordinated to EU policies designed to help lagging regions. On both continents, however, there has been a shift of emphasis away from national governments with local governments assuming more responsibility for their own economic development by formulating what in effect are regional industrial policies.

Third, restructuring of private sector firms frequently has been 'good for the economy, but bad for the people', at least in the short run, resulting in a growing demand for government services (e.g. retraining) and increased transfer payments such as welfare payments and unemployment compensation.[12] At the same most Western democracies – beginning with Prime Minister Thatcher in England and President Reagan in the United States, have been attempting to 'downsize' government programs, especially in the areas of business regulation and social programs. However, the 'size' of government, as measured in relation to GDP, continues to grow. Programs in which citizens are 'vested' (i.e. social security and medical care) continue to expand while devolution of development-infrastructure programs to subnational governments also continue to 'grow' government (Cook, 1997).

Table 2.3   Changes in governmental structures and functions

Old/traditional		New/emerging
Stabilization policies: monetary/fiscal	→	Less national autonomy due to globalization, budget deficits
National industrial policies	→	(In US) now expanding at regional/local level (In EU) subordinated to regional policies shaped in Brussels
Social welfare systems	→	Under attack everywhere as unemployment and welfare costs grow *Immigrant role here important*
Large, centralized *National level*	→	Decentralization to regions *'Reinvent government' with emphasis on local economic development* • International borders disappear EU • Strategic urban networks form
Universities: national governments support education and basic research	→	R & D training functions at regional level increase as do alliances with firms/governments *Private-public-academic partnerships*

In this context it should also be noted that conservatives and racist groups on both continents have led a widespread revolt against the many alleged evils of national welfare systems while immigrants (both 'legal' and 'illegal') have become the scapegoats for the frustrations of groups facing higher unemployment rates, declining real wages and rising taxation.

Fourth, as national governments attempt to 'reinvent government' (Osborne and Gaebler, 1992), new organizational structures and policies have been implemented, especially by state and local governments in the United States (Gore and National Performance Review, 1993). These efforts frequently begin with decentralization (or 'devolution') of responsibilities and finances from central governments to state, regional and local governments, which then are obliged to formulate regional economic development planning efforts. In the European Union regional development policies have stressed the formation of 'strategic urban networks' (Martinos and Caspara, 1990), which can be used to disseminate 'best practice' solutions for solving common problems as well as developing key infrastructure projects benefiting neighboring regions.

Finally, in response to the increased competition between regions, many local and regional governments have devised comprehensive competitiveness strategies designed to raise the productivity of the region's firms while enhancing the general quality of life. These include: streamlining government functions; increasing investment in physical and social infrastructure; the creation of mechanisms to increase the region's exports; developing new collaborative relations between private, public, and academic institutions in order to accelerate technological innovation and dissemination and workforce preparation as well as efforts to raise cultural levels and clean up the environment (National Council for Urban Economic Development, 1993).

Thus most city and regional governments, recognizing the increased competition between regions, are striving to develop economic development programs appropriate to the requirements of the new economy in partnerships/alliances with local firms and academic institutions. It is in this context that we now turn to the changing functions of international borders.

The Changing Economic Functions of International Borders

The Traditional View of Borders

In economics, borders are usually associated with 'barriers to trade', including tariffs and quotas as well as qualitative restrictions.[13] Such barriers tend to reduce the volume and value of trade and its associated benefits (i.e. production efficiencies and higher living standards). Additionally, to the extent that they are temporary or politically unstable, borders are associated with higher levels of risk and therefore tend to discourage investment and (legal) economic activity in adjacent regions.[14]

Of course, borders are not absolute barriers to trade but serve mainly as 'screening agents' ('permeable membranes') regarding what can legally flow from one political jurisdiction (country) to another and under what conditions. Commodities (and persons) that cannot legally pass through the ports of exit/entry are either excluded from international trade (or passage) or are compelled to utilize illegal means if they are to get to 'the other side'. Thus, informal/illegal markets develop for smuggling items of high value and low volume (e.g. drugs, exotic animals, persons), while 'crossing costs' vary according to the degree of risk and the severity of penalties, which in turn, depend mainly on the strength and effectiveness of the two countries' law enforcement capabilities. Nevertheless, there are usually many opportunities for realizing profits in border regions given the many differences in price, quality and availability of goods and services on each side of the border.

Historically the quantity and quality of restrictions imposed on the flows of commodities and persons at their borders varied significantly between countries in accordance with national political, economic and cultural norms and policies. In many cases there were (and still are) these differences between national norms and policies that create(d) many of the opportunities for international trade and investment flows. For example, foreign multinational corporations (mostly from the United States) dramatically expanded their (direct) investments in Mexico because of protectionist policies associated with the period of import substitution industrialization (from the 1940s through the 1980s). Similarly, informal border transactions[15] expanded rapidly as a result of Prohibition Laws (prohibiting the sale of liquor) in the United States and played an important role in the development of Mexican border cities during the 1920-33 period.

In summary, the traditional view of borders in market-based economies was that goods and services, technology and people flow across international borders in response to a constellation of market and non-market (i.e. social/cultural) conditions.[16] However, in order for international transactions (i.e. sales/purchases) to be realized all commodities (and persons) must somehow pass 'the border' (i.e. through ports of exit/entry). At that stage they are scrutinized according to the regimens of the two countries. That is, importing countries allow goods, services and people to enter only upon payment of required fees, presentation of necessary documentation and compliance with elaborate sets of regulations, all of which are usually formulated at the national level in accordance with the accepted perception of 'national interests'.

Borders in the New Economy

In the last decade, due to the changing economic, political and strategic factors (noted above in the section on the 'dynamics of globalization'), Western European and North American borders have become less significant, as economic barriers, than at any time since the Great Depression of the 1930s, when tariffs were at their highest during this century. Tariff rates have been reduced significantly while quotas and qualitative restrictions are being phased out, largely due to negotiations carried out in the context of the GATT/WTO and the formation of regional integration schemes (i.e. the European Union and the North American Free Trade Agreement).[17]

In Western Europe, where the process of regional economic integration has advanced the most, restrictions on the mobility of goods/services, capital and labor have been dramatically reduced within the EU creating two significantly different types of borders: 'internal' (between EU member states) and 'external' (between EU member and non-member states). In this context borders, especially internal borders, have begun to take on the character of 'contact zones' between neighboring countries as opposed to the traditional view of borders as 'barriers' that separate them (Ratti, 1994). And, with the expectation of expansion of the EU to new members in Central Europe, even some external borders are taking on this new character.

Looking at Europe as a whole, the disintegration of the Soviet Union and the reduction of Cold War hostilities resulted in dramatic changes in relations between nations that were previously on different sides of the 'Iron Curtain'. Paradoxically, however, this has not resulted in a uniform easing of restrictions. In many places, as old regimes suddenly disintegrated, more 'openness' on borders prompted an urgent need for new mechanisms to facilitate flows of persons and products across international borders,[18] but in others (most notably between the states of the former Soviet Union) the establishment of new boundaries has resulted in less openness.

In North America, where the process of regional integration is still rather limited in comparison with Europe, it is likely to be many years (or decades) before the concept of internal and external borders becomes operational.[19]

Nevertheless, for 'internal' borders the traditional economic functions are changing significantly while for 'external' borders they are still relevant, but decreasingly so, due to the expanding influence and coverage of the GATT/WTO in the entire world economy. Thus, except where borders are still being contested (e.g. between some of the Republics of the former Soviet Union) or are still relatively 'closed' for national security reasons (e.g. between Estonia and Russia) the volume of (trans)border crossings both goods (i.e. exports, imports and border transactions) and people seems to be increasing. Similarly, interaction between people and governments formerly separated by international borders is increasing as they attempt to improve living standards and manage the many local transborder problems that inevitably 'spill over' international borders.

In the traditional (neo-classical) economics literature the 'gains from trade', which incidentally are not necessarily evenly distributed geographically or between industries, emanate from 'comparative advantage, economies of scale, and more competitive, and hence more efficient, domestic markets' (Wonnacott, 1991, p. 10). However, economics does not systematically treat the 'costs of trade', (i.e. the increases in unemployment and bankruptcies that can lead to the demise of entire communities as a result of decreased protectionism), since the models indicate that gains from freer trade will outweigh the losses. What is important here is that opening a border is likely to incur costs as well as benefits and that those individuals and firms suffering the losses are not likely to be compensated by the winners as the theoretical literature suggests.[20]

The traditional economic functions of borders, as barriers to international commerce, are rapidly eroding as a consequence of a constellation of technological, economic, institutional and political-strategic factors. This erosion of the traditional functions of border will likely, ceteris paribus, stimulate the following changes, in varying magnitudes and over time, in the affected countries and their border regions:

- increased (transborder) flows of trade[21] including both traditional exports/imports and informal border transactions as well as investment and labor (if permitted under the new regime);

- changes in the 'structure' of trade, investment, output, consumption and employment;[22]
- changes in the 'location' of many economic activities.[23]

These changes are likely to occur in response to the changing structure of prices that now confronts producers and resource owners, both within and outside of the area, who will respond to new profit and income maximizing opportunities.

Implications for Border Regional Development

The chief implication of our analysis of the globalization process is that many border regions previously relegated to the periphery of economic activity may now be able to attract new industries and/or stimulate the expansion of existing ones which, in turn, could lead to new forms of economic development in the region.[24] Similarly, the main implication of our analysis of the changing economic functions of international borders is that making them more 'open' is likely to increase the volume of cross border economic flows while changing the structure (composition) of economic activity in those regions adjacent to the border.

Thus, the economic development prospects of border-regions are changing in the new/emerging economic and institutional environment. For example, local governments in regions adjacent to borders that formerly were relatively closed, isolated, underpopulated and usually poor (e.g. located on a remote European 'external border') are now freer to actively explore development policies that will include collaboration with localities on the other side. However, such localities often differ greatly in 'geographical size, population density, their economic characteristics and problems and degree of development as well as cultural-linguistic characteristics' (Martinos and Caspari, 1990, p. 3) and therefore they frequently have difficulty in achieving an effective level of collaboration.

In quite a different situation are those localities which formerly benefited from 'the development of trading activity at the border, the storage of goods and earnings derived from the collection of duties ...' (Hansen, 1981, p. 25). Such communities might be located on what is now an EU 'internal border' which previously benefited from a high volume of dutiable trading; however, with the virtual disappearance of barriers to goods and people between EU member nations the economic activities associated with the border (perhaps a large part of the region's economic base) have also dwindled or, in some cases, disappeared.

Another example might be the border of a country that only recently joined the EU, but borders a non-EU country (i.e. is now on an external border). Previously, this border was relatively open, but now due to the requirements of Schengen Treaty of 1992 the country is obliged to carry out extensive border inspections to control the passage of illegal products/substances and/or persons. Residents of this border are now concerned that the delays caused by the longer inspections will interrupt the cross border integration that previously existed.

In all of these cases, the economic fortunes of 'border regions' have changed due to the changing economic functions of their particular border, factors outside the control of the regions themselves.

Therefore, the effects of this new 'openness' are dependent on the specific conditions of each border region and cannot be determined a priori. In some cases border regions will see economic activity increase while in others it will decrease. Additionally, it should be noted that development in the new economy may be even more difficult to achieve than before, precisely because of the new, more competitive environment that now exists. Thus, the development potential of some border regions will improve while others are likely to remain in the periphery, both geographically and economically.

What then differentiates those regions that will prosper in the new economy from those that will stagnate or deteriorate? There is no one factor that can be identified; clearly, a region's location is important as is a diverse economic base, a well-trained work force, links with research institutions, modern tele-communications and transport facilities, a high quality of life and 'the institutional capacity to develop and implement future-oriented development strategies' (Commission of the European Communities, 1992, p. 22). However, in the case of border regions there is yet another factor that is important: a well-developed system of transborder cooperation (TC).

Border regions vary a great deal with respect to population density and the level of economic development but most tend to suffer from certain handicaps including: lower incomes and higher unemployment rates in their own national context, a peripheral position with respect to national economic and political decision-making, a multitude of problems imposed by the propinquity of different legal and administrative systems, poor cross-border communications and a lack of coordination in public services as well as differences in culture and language.

The challenge then is to economically, administratively and culturally consolidate the regions that were previously divided by the international border. Alternatively, it can be said that not only must border regions do everything that every other region must do in terms of increasing their 'competitiveness', but they must also do it in collaboration with the region(s) on 'the other side'. This not only increases the number of decision makers but also increases the heterogeneity of the decision-making body – if one can be created, and complexity of the decision-making process, especially when these processes become complicated by questions of national sovereignty.

The Economic Forces Underlying Transboundary Collaboration

From an economic perspective there are three basic concepts that militate for the concept of transborder cooperation: economies of scale, externalities and transaction costs.

The concept of 'economies of scale' in this context is usually associated with the creation of the physical infrastructure facilities needed to facilitate the development process. That is, the construction of bridges, highways and port facilities frequently are only feasible if financed by all parties deriving the benefits (i.e. the positive externalities) they generate. And even if only one side were able to finance the construction of, say, a regional airport, some of the benefits would accrue automatically to 'the other side' in the form of increased access and lower travel costs. The same can be said for the provision of social infrastructure (i.e. educational and health services as well as police and fire protection). Similarly, regional marketing efforts to promote the region's exports and transborder tourism as well extol the region's virtues as a retirement haven or 'good place to invest and do business' can frequently be done cheaper and more effectively in concert. Lobbying efforts in the two nations' capitals or before transnational governmental bodies (e.g. the EU in Brussels) can frequently be much more effective if done collaboratively.

There are also 'negative externalities' that must be taken into account and managed in the border context. Thus, for example, transmittable diseases as well as air and water pollution present on one side of the border can 'spill over' to the other side in many ways, raising health costs and lowering the quality of life. Transborder collaboration can result in better management of such problems, increasing the quality of life on both sides of the border.

Finally, 'transaction costs' (i.e. the costs associated with buying/selling including gathering information on market conditions, negotiating and enforcing agreements) in cross border situations are likely to be high in comparison with expected profits, thus discouraging economic activity. That is, faced with a lack of information regarding market conditions, legal constraints, common business practices, language and culture 'on the other side', entrepreneurs are reluctant to do business there, even though it would otherwise be regarded as part of the local (regional) market area. High transaction costs can also inhibit the realization of economies of scale in the production of private goods by limiting the size of the market.[25]

It follows therefore that transborder consultation-coordination mechanisms must be formed in order to realize potential economies of scale, manage spillover effects and lower transaction costs. In other words, decision-making must be 'regionalized' even in regions divided by an international boundary.

Transborder collaborative mechanisms can be informal and/or formal and the nature of the transborder relationship can range from 'peaceful coexistence' to 'partners in development'. The precise forms vary greatly according to local conditions and conditions in the border-regions' respective nation states.

It should also be acknowledged even when a strong element of transborder collaboration exists there will still be competition between the two subregions in such areas as attracting tourism and new investment. Nevertheless, it can be argued that virtually anything that increases economic activity on one side of the border can result in some increased activity on the other through a variety of cross-border flows that arise because of the many asymmetries and complementaries between the subregions.

While the over riding goals of TC are to increase prosperity, enhance the quality of life and reduce transborder conflict, the main objective of TC in this context is to create a management framework built on (evolving) informal or formal relationships that can economically, administratively and culturally integrate the border subregions that are divided by an international boundary. This implies that such a framework be able to manage the many opportunities and challenges inherent in all border-regions.

Given the widespread and growing interest in transborder collaboration throughout the world it is not surprising that economists, regional scientists and others are now beginning to formulate theories in this area (see Guo, 1996; Ratti and Reichman, 1993). Nevertheless, theory alone cannot tell us how to form successful transborder collaborative relationships. Recognizing this the EU created a project, 'Linkage Assistance and Cooperation for the European Border Regions', (LACE) to facilitate learning on the basis of other border-regions' experience. This project attempts to disseminate 'know how' on a wide variety of border issues among European border communities (Association of European Border Regions, 1991).[26]

Along the US-Mexico border no such network exists, at least in any formal sense. Each 'twin city' seems to struggle to 'make do' with an ad hoc blend of informal and formal mechanisms while the annual meeting of the ten border governors (four from the United States and six from Mexico) provides a slim thread of coordination between the otherwise disparate state governmental efforts to coordinate transborder collaboration along the 3,200-kilometer (2,000-mile) boundary. Additionally, a private lobbying group, the Border Trade Alliance, focuses on border issues of special interest to private firms (e.g. border crossings, bridges and toxic waste disposal sites).

While much more can and should be said regarding the theory of borders, border-regional development and transborder collaboration, serious treatment of this topic lies outside of the scope of this paper (see Clement, 1997). Nevertheless, some sort of theoretical framework is needed as both academics and decision makers wrestle with the intricacies of border-related policies.

The absence of a theoretical framework and appropriate policies is especially evident along the US-Mexican border. For example, it is well known that rapid demographic and economic growth in recent decades have wreaked major havoc on the region's environment. In response, the two institutions created by the NAFTA Environmental Supplemental Agreement, the Border Environmental Cooperation Commission (BECC) and the North American Development Bank (NADBank), show some promise of stimulating systematic thinking and institutionalizing formal transborder collaboration, at least in this one area. Additionally, the 'US-Mexico Border XXI Program' (United States Environmental Protection Agency, 1996), designed to bring together the efforts of diverse US and Mexican agencies to protect the environment, human health and natural resources of the region, also promises to take formal transborder collaboration to higher levels.

Nevertheless, more systematic efforts to implement comprehensive 'sustainable development' policies into the border-regional context are clearly needed.[27] The concept of sustainable development, while still relatively undefined at the regional level, has received much more attention in recent years and, in this author's view, represents the most fruitful vehicle for guiding the development of border-regional theories and policies in the immediate future.

Notes

1 Throughout this chapter the terms region and border-region will be used. It is understood that in each 'region', however defined, there can be a leading city and a 'hinterland' as well as smaller cities, towns or settlements. The term border-region will be used in reference to those regions that are divided by an international boundary into two or more subregions adjacent to that boundary. The methodological question of what constitutes a region will not be addressed here. Suffice to say that this question frequently is answered simply by defining the 'border region' in terms of administrative units (i.e. those municipalities/counties adjacent to the international boundary). Other approaches define border regions in more conceptual terms, utilizing the concepts of 'internationality' and/or the concepts of 'intensity' and 'extension' of border relations (Hansen, 1981; Bustamante, 1989).

2 'Glocalization' is a term that refers to the growing tendency of the globalization process to push local entities, public and private, to become more active in the economic development arena.

3 Widening refers to extending new elements to the global level (e.g. adding global marketing to global production and capital markets) while deepening refers to intensifying those global efforts (i.e. more and more international transactions). The time period in which this more integrated, global market developed is generally taken to be the Post World War II period; however, its origins go back much further and there is evidence that elementary forms of globalization were present in the earlier centuries. For 17 industrial countries for which there are data, exports as a share of GDP in 1913 were 12.9 percent, not much below the 1993 level of 14.5 percent. And capital transfers as a share of industrial country GDP are still smaller than in the 1890s. Earlier eras of globalization also saw far greater movement of people around the world. Today immigration is more restricted (UN Development Program, 1997, p. 83). Much of the data in this section come from this same publication.

4 It is worth noting here that the principles of free trade have been applied largely to the international movement of goods and capital while labor movements, particularly those of unskilled labor, are restricted. Commonly, the increased flows of goods and certain types of services are praised while the massive movements of 'illegal aliens' are condemned.

5 'Economies of scope' usually refers to controlling costs while producing many variants of a product at the same time while 'economies of scale' refers to reducing per unit costs by producing large quantities of a uniform product. See Wilson 1993, Chapter 2, for an in-depth overview of this process and how it has revolutionized manufacturing in recent decades.

6 Economic or industrial clusters can be defined as geographical 'concentrations of competing, complementary and interdependent firms across several industries, including suppliers, service providers and final product manufacturers' (Morfessis, 1994, p. 33).

7 In order to maintain competitiveness firms must either automate their operations and/or export the (mainly) labor-intensive phases of production to off-shore, export processing zones where labor costs are a small fraction labor costs in developed countries.

8   One study estimates the cost of incentive packages provided by local governments vying
     for new automobile plants in Midwestern US cities in the period 1978-90 at $3,900 to
     $108,000 per job (Glickman and Woodward, 1989).
9   In this context the Rust Belt of the US Northeast probably best represents the 'old core'
     while the Sunbelt of the Southeast and Southwest best represents the 'new core'. For
     more on this and how it relates to the US-Mexican border region see Herzog, 1990, pp.
     43-44. In Europe the region stretching from Southern England through northern France
     down the Rhine Valley into Switzerland is regarded as the 'old core' while the 'new
     core' ranges from northern Italy across southern France into Northern Spain
     (Commission of the European Communities 1991).
10   With respect to monetary policy, changes in interest rates frequently result in unintended
     changes in exchange rates as short term capital moves to take advantage of the
     differences in yields.
11   The high (over 10 percent) rates of unemployment in most European countries are often
     blamed by conservatives on 'over generous' welfare benefits and excessive government
     regulation. Nevertheless, there has been considerable political opposition to dismantling
     the policies put into place decades ago by social democratic regimes. In the US
     conservative, anti-government sentiment has emerged in recent decades and
     conservatives were able to push through a comprehensive welfare reform that President
     Clinton accepted, much to the chagrin of many members of his own (Democratic) party.
12   In the US restructuring has meant the creation of new jobs, many of which are low-paid
     and do not provide health care and other benefits. In Europe restructuring has largely
     resulted in a rise in unemployment rates while benefits have generally been retained.
13   Chapter 2 of Niles Hansen's book on the US border region with Mexico (1981) provides
     an accessible summary of the relevant theoretical work in economics on borders and
     border regions. Guo (1996) provides a more comprehensive and more recent, but less
     accessible perspective on this literature. See also Herzog (1990).
14   In the orthodox economic literature 'barriers to trade' are generally regarded as 'barriers
     to economic development', however, economic history is replete with examples of how
     protectionism was used to stimulate national development. Indeed, it can be argued that
     'import substitution industrialization', which usually provides for high degrees of
     protection, has been an important phase in most countries' development, from Japan and
     the US to the 'NICs' (newly industrialized countries) of the post World War II era. See
     Chapter 2 of Wilson (1992) on this point.
15   Informal border transactions such as shopping and tourism expenditures by consumers
     and small purchases by businesses largely go unreported and therefore cannot be
     analyzed in the same way as formal exports and imports between countries.
16   A study of 'border crossers' at San Diego-Tijuana ports of entry (San Diego Dialogue,
     1994) resulted in the following classification of 'primary purpose' (listed in order of
     declining importance): shopping, social visits, work, tourism, and 'other' (including
     attendance at cultural and sporting events).
17   From the orthodox perspective regional integration efforts are regarded as 'second best'
     to multilateral (i.e. GATT/WTO) initiatives for at least two reasons:
     •   Lowering trade barriers only between member countries can result in costs (i.e.
          'trade diversion', switching import purchases from lower cost non-member
          countries to higher cost member countries) as well as benefits (i.e. 'trade creation'
          switching purchases from higher cost domestic producers to lower cost member
          countries);

- External barriers to trade from non-member countries can be raised to protect member countries from international competition thereby creating a 'fortress' with respect to the rest of the world.

18 Crossings on borders between Western European and Soviet bloc countries were strictly regulated during the Cold War. With the sudden disintegration of the old order came sudden and unanticipated waves of border traffic of people as well as goods. Anecdotal evidence suggests that most local governments were not prepared for such events and a great deal of chaos and improvisation occurred.

19 A 'free trade area' provides for the elimination (over a specified period of years) of trade barriers between member countries on a specified group of goods (or all goods) with each country determining its own level of external tariffs against nonmembers. The next higher level of integration, a 'customs union', provides for free trade and a common external tariff while a 'common market' adds free movement of labor and capital. Finally, an 'economic union' includes group-determined policies (e.g. macroeconomic stabilization policies), harmonization of standards and eventually a common currency.

20 The body of literature underlying what is usually referred to as 'the Heckscher-Ohlin theory' has created a concept know as 'the compensation principle' to deal with this situation. This principle maintains that because winners gain more income from free trade than the losers, the winners can fully compensate the losers and still have a positive benefit (Dunn and Ingraham, 1996, pp. 73-75).

21 This will occur for a variety of reasons including the decline of 'transactions costs' (see below) associated with the reduction of the 'barrier effects' of borders.

22 Changes in exchange rates can also affect these variables by changing the relative prices that border shoppers and ex/importing firms face on a daily basis. Additionally, exchange rate instability can influence the volume and type of investment in border regions.

23 Under most forms of regional economic integration incentives and/or subsidies for firms locating in border regions, which frequently are poorer than regions located in core areas, must be phased out over a specified period of time. The absence of subsidies then provides a 'level playing field' for firms in the border region and the interior of the country as well as from both sides of the international boundary. A good of example of this situation is the 'Zona Libre' of Baja California and neighboring states on the Mexican-US border which will be phased out under the NAFTA.

24 The phrase 'new forms of economic development' can be interpreted in two ways:
- In 'traditional' or 'mainstream' economics this would refer to changes in the structure of output of a region as it moved from reliance on the 'primary sector activities' (i.e. agriculture, forestry and mining, which traditionally has characterized resource-based, 'under-developed economies') to the 'secondary and tertiary sector activities' (i.e. manufacturing and construction as well as commerce and information-related services). These structural changes would, in the traditional theory, result in increases in efficiency that would, in turn, result in changes in certain economic indicators (e.g. GDP per capita and higher urban/rural ratios) that signal a higher stage of development;
- An alternative concept of development, 'sustainable development', holds that traditional structural changes and concomitant changes in economic indicators might lead to short term gains in output and consumption while reducing both the carrying capacity of the physical environment and the quality of life usually associated with stable human communities.

25 High transaction costs can also stimulate the growth of businesses on both sides of an international border, which specialize in being able to efficiently do business 'on the other side' and can therefore lower transaction costs for other firms doing business there.

26 Specifically, LACE provides the following services: technical assistance to border regions; the establishment of a data base; the promotion of networking between border regions; and dissemination and publicity (Association of European Border Regions, 1991). Note also that the Inter-American Development Bank has created an Institute for the Integration of Latin America (INTAL) has developed special programs in relation to 'the border as factor of integration' (Pérez Castillo, 1992).

27 A common definition of sustainability is 'ensuring that the use of resources and the environment today does not damage the prospect of their use by future generations'. (International Center For Sustainable Cities, 1994, p. 6). For a comprehensive documentation and analysis of the growing literature on the concept, see Pezzoli (1997).

References

Association of European Border Regions (1991), 'Information Brochure: Linkage Assistance and Cooperation for the European Border Regions', *EUREGIO*, Gronau, Germany.

Barnet, R. and Muller, R. (1974), *Global Reach: The Power of the MNC's*, Simon and Schuster, New York.

Bustamante, J.A. (1989), 'Frontera México-Estados Unidos: Reflexiones Para Un Marco Teórico', *Frontera Norte*, 1.

Clement, N. (1995), 'Local Responses to Globalization: New Opportunities for the San Diego-Tijuana Region', in E. Fry and P. Kresl, (eds.), *North American Cities and the Global Economy: Challenges and Opportunities*, Sage Publications, Thousand Oaks.

Clement, N. (1997), 'Economic Integragion on an Unequal Border: Concepts and Examples', paper presented at the conference, The Economy and Security of the Border Region, Joensuu, Finland, June 1997.

Commission of the European Communities: Directorate-General for Regional Policy (1991), *Europe 2000: Outlook for the Development of the Community's Territory*, Brussels.

Commission of the European Communities: Directorate-General for Regional Policy (1992), *Regional Development Studies: Urbanization and the functions of cities in the European Community*, Brussels.

Cook, C. (1997), 'Survey: The World Economy', *The Economist*, September 20.

Dunn, R. and Ingram, J. (1996), *International Economics*, John Wiley and Sons, Inc., New York.

Glickman, N. and Woodward, D. (1989), *The New Competitors*, Basic Books, New York.

Gore, A. and National Performance Review (1993), *From Red Tape to Results: Creating a Government that Works Better and Costs Less*, New York Times Books, New York.

Grunwal, J. and Flamm, K. (1985), *The Global Factory: Foreign Assembly in International Trade*, The Brookings Institution, Washington, D.C.

Guo, R. (1996), *Border-Regional Economics*, Physica-Verlag, Heidelberg.

Hansen, N. (1981), *The Border Economy: Regional Development in the Southwest*, University of Texas Press, Austin.

Herzog, L. (1990), *Where North Meets South: Cities, Space, and Politics on the US-Mexico Border*, University of Texas Press, Austin.

International Center for Sustainable Cities (1994), *Opportunities for Achieving Sustainability in Cascadia*, The Cascadia Institute, Vancouver, B.C. and Discovery Institute, Seattle, WA.

Johnson, C. (ed.) (1984), *The Industrial Policy Debate*, ICS Press, San Francisco.

Kawano, E. (1993), 'The Japanese Model of Production: Cooperation or Coercion?' in G. Epstein, J. Graham, and J. Nembhard (eds.), *Creating a New World Economy: Forces of Change and Plans for Action*, Temple University Press, Philadelphia.

Kresl, P. (1992), *The Urban Economy And Regional Trade Liberalization*, Praeger, New York.

Krugman, P. (1994), 'Competitiveness: A Dangerous Obsession', *Foreign Affairs*, 73(2).

Lipietz, A. (1987), *Mirages and Miracles: The Crises of Global Fordism*, Verso, London.

Martinos, H. and Caspara, A. (1990), *Cooperation Between Border Regions For Local And Regional Development*, Commission of the European Communities, Directorate-General XVI, Brussels.

Mathews, J. (1997), 'Power Shift', *Foreign Affairs*, 76(1).

Morfessis, I. (1994), 'Cluster Analytic Approach to Identifying and Developing State Target Industries: The Case of Arizona', *Economic Development Review*, Spring 1994.

National Council for Urban Economic Development (1993), *Forces in the New Economy: Implications for Local Economic Development*, Washington.

Newhouse, J. (1997), 'Europe's Rising Regionalism', *Foreign Affairs*, 76(1).

Osborne, D. and Gaebler, T. (1992), *Reinventing Government: How the Entrepreneurial Spirit is Transforming the Public Sector*, Addison-Wesley Publishing Company, Inc., Menlo Park.

Pérez Castillo, J.P. (1992), 'Free Trade, the Border, and Integration', in P. Ganster and E. Valenciano (eds.), *The Mexican-US Border Region and the Free Trade Agreement*, Institute for Regional Studies of the Californias, San Diego State University.

Ratti, R. (1994), 'Spatial Effects of Frontiers: Overview of Different Approaches and theories of Border Region Development', in P. Nijkamp (ed.), *New Borders and Old Barriers in Spatial Development*, Avebury, Brookfield USA.

Ratti, R. and Reichman, S. (eds.) (1993), *The Theory and Practice of Transborder Cooperation*, Verlag Helning Lichenhahn, Basel and Frankfurt.

Reich, R. (1990), *The Work of Nations: Preparing Ourselves for the 21st-Century Capitalism*, A.A. Knopf, New York.

Scott, A. and Storper, M. (eds.) (1986), *Production, Work and Territory*, Allen and Unwin, Boston.

Stoddard, E.R. (1986), 'Border Studies as an Emergent Field of Scientific Inquiry: Scholarly Contributions of US-Mexico Borderland Studies', *Journal of Borderlands Studies*, 1(1).

Thurow, L. (1985), *World Class: America in a Competitive World*, Simon Schuster, New York.

United Nations Development Program (1997), *Human Development Report*, Oxford University Press, New York/Oxford.

University of California (1994), 'Who Crosses the Border: A View of the San Diego/Tijuana Metropolitan Region', *San Diego Dialogue*, San Diego.

Wilson, P.A. (1992), *Exports and Local Development: Mexico's Maquiladoras*, University of Texas Press, Austin.

Wonnacott, R. (1991), *The Economics of Overlapping Free Trade Areas and the Mexican Challenge*. Canadian-American Committee, C.D. Howe Institute (Toronto) and National Planning Institute, Washington, D.C.

Chapter 3

Contested Boundaries and Troubled Borderlands

Mladen Klemenčić and Clive Schofield

Introduction

The demise of the nation-state and the emergence of a borderless world have in recent time been predicted by a number of writers, particularly economic theorists. Such bold predictions of vanishing boundaries have emerged in response to the undeniably powerful forces working towards internationalization and globalization in the world today.

Advancing global economic integration and resulting interdependence from transfers of capital and technology across borders have led to arguments that nation-states have lost the ability to function without reference to the global economy and powerful, placeless, transnational corporations over which states lack tangible influence. This 'borderless world' argument appears superficially persuasive given the fact that the communications revolution has led to a time-space compression of the world and an access to information outside of state's control, while the proliferation of regional and international regimes have increased joint management of transboundary security and environmental problems.

While it is recognized that these global trends may have profound influence on the nature of the nation state, borders and borderlands, convincing evidence of the death of the nation state, the emergence of a borderless world and an end to the importance of space and geography is sorely lacking. It is certainly true that in many cases we can witness a change in the notion of borderlands from a traditional association with division, conflict, instability, restricted movement and limited development, peripherality and alienation, to a new paradigm of internationalization, cooperation and interaction, treating the border as an opportunity and the borderland itself as an integrated entity. However, this is by no means always the case.

Similarly, although many international boundaries may no longer be the obstacles that they once were to the international exchange of people, goods, capital and information, they retain great significance politically. The nation state too has proven resilient, a fact not least demonstrated by the proliferation of 'new' states in SE Europe and former Soviet Union that have gained international recognition in recent years. In this context it is often precisely those global trends, which are serving to undermine the nation state which are in fact promoting the emergence of new states, regional groupings and thus, boundaries, as well as smaller entities seem able to survive in this changing global political and economic environment. Certainly, nationalism and territoriality seem to be alive and active and it seems likely that the nation state will remain the key building block of the world political system (Blake, 1998).

The continuing significance of territory and boundaries is also amply illustrated by the actions of existing states. In general, it may be observed that states are continuing a process of more precisely defining the limits of their jurisdiction on land and at sea. This may be concluded from the steady growth in the number of agreements providing for the precise delimitation of boundaries in remote areas (for example Oman's conclusion of boundary agreements with Saudi Arabia and Yemen in the early 1990s) or for the physical demarcation of troublesome borders (the demarcation of the Iraq-Kuwait boundary in the aftermath of the Gulf War being a case in point) and the submission of certain intractable boundary and territorial disputes to international adjudication or arbitration in order to achieve a clear decision as to the extent of each state's jurisdiction (for example the International Court of Justice cases involving El Salvador and Honduras and Egypt and Israel and the arbitration between Argentina and Chile over certain sections of their Andean boundary). States therefore clearly remain fiercely defensive of territory.

The process is even more clearly evident in relation to maritime jurisdiction. The rapid post-Second World War development of the international law of the sea and consequent extension of national maritime claims from areas in close proximity to a particular state's coastline to up to 200 nautical miles offshore (and in some cases even further) has resulted in a dramatic increase in the number and scope of potential maritime boundaries worldwide and, inevitably, resulted in numerous overlapping claims to maritime jurisdiction. Nevertheless, many states have sought to conclude maritime boundary agreements with their neighbors, often driven by the desire to acquire and manage ocean resources, with the result that in a limited space of time over one third of the potential maritime boundaries of the world have been agreed. The 1993 Charney and Alexander survey of international maritime boundary agreements covered 134 such agreements. According to the International Boundaries Research Unit, specialized center for boundary's studies at the Durham University, there are 427 potential maritime boundaries worldwide. Thus in 1993 some 31 percent of potential maritime boundaries had been wholly or partially delimited.

In light of the importance of control over territory, be it on land or in terms of maritime space, it is therefore not surprising that, even if many borders and borderlands have provided opportunities for interaction, cooperation and convergence, on the other hand, there exist many troubled borderlands where boundaries remain a source of considerable stress between states.

It should also be recognized that these globalizing influences have led to fresh challenges for states in the form of increased refugee flows, illegal immigration and escalating cross-border crime (Galeotti, 1995).

The aim of this section is to identify contested and disputed boundaries at the global and continental levels and discuss a relationship between disputes worldwide and cooperation in borderlands.

Types of Boundary Disputes

Maps we are used to seeing merely represent a 'snapshot' view frozen in time. The bold red boundary lines on the map hide variety and complexity of types of boundary in terms of their political status, permeability and a host of other factors including disputes.

Boundary disputes are generally divided into three main groups (Prescott, 1987). *Territorial disputes* are usually the most serious. They occur when large portions of land or entire regions are contested. Some of them are long-lasting. At certain stages they can be dormant, but later they may be renewed or intensified. *Positional disputes* usually emerge following delimitation of the boundary line. The boundary alignment may not be in question, but precise location usually is not known or certain. *Functional disputes* occur about everyday management and the operation of the boundary, most often with reference to the allocation of resources like water or hydrocarbons, or because of regime of boundary crossing.

It is also to be emphasized that boundaries are not equally mature. Traditionally, a boundary can be thought of as evolving through four stages: allocation, when sovereignty over territory is determined in broad sense; delimitation, when a precise division of territory is achieved; demarcation, when the boundary is accurately surveyed and marked on the ground; and, management relating to the administration of the boundary thereafter (Prescott, 1985; Rushworth, 1997).

Territorial disputes may occur when there is a dispute over the allocation of territory, positional disputes in the delimitation phase and functional disputes at the management stage.

It may be also interesting to point out that the broad outlines of the international political division of the world that we see on our wall maps and in atlases today is largely the product of European imperial activity in the nineteenth and early twentieth centuries. France and the United Kingdom alone were responsible for the alignment of 39 percent of the land boundaries of the developing world and those two countries together with the other main European imperial powers – Germany, the Netherlands, Portugal and Spain – established fully 52 percent of them (Blake, 1998).

Current Situation

The proposed classification is a general one, and some disputes may be difficult to assign in one of the groups. However, we find the classification to be convenient for the cross-section of the current situation of the boundary disputes world wide.

As a basis for a survey we used recently published boundary encyclopaedia (Biger, 1995), which contains information on each existing land boundary in the world. Each boundary forms an entry, each entry describes boundary with its geographical setting, historical background and present situation. That unique source includes information on all 'new' boundaries (those which became international boundaries in the 1990s) and all small boundaries, like the boundary between the Republic of Cyprus and the Turkish Cypriot area referred to as the Turkish Republic of Northern Cyprus or the China-Hong-Kong boundary, which in the meantime ceased to exist. Maritime boundaries were not systematically covered by the encyclopaedia. We assumed that each dispute worth mentioning was registered in the encyclopaedia and that criteria applied were balanced for all continents and regions. In our analysis all disputes registered by the encyclopaedia were distinguished according to available information into mentioned three groups: territorial, positional and functional disputes.

Findings of the analysis are highly interesting. Differences between the continents are clear.

The largest number of the most serious, i.e. territorial, disputes are to be found in Asia. They include long-lasting, seemingly hopeless, almost 'chronic', disputes like those between India and Pakistan over Kashmir, between India and China, or the one between Iran and Iraq. The most dangerous flashpoints are within that group, for example boundaries of Israel, especially in relation to Syria and Lebanon. Saudi Arabia-Yemen boundary dispute, possibly the dispute encompassing the largest area in the world today, is also in that group. We found 30 boundaries which can be considered to be contested in a way which can be described as a territorial dispute. A significant number of territorial disputes is to be found on boundaries between former Central-Asian republics of the Soviet Union. Former outer boundaries of the Soviet Union are not contested but boundaries between ex-republics are far from agreed and settled. Usually there are conflicting claims on both sides. Positional and functional disputes were also registered but they were overshadowed by territorial disputes. All together more than a half of the total number of boundaries appeared to be disputed in such a way. Asia was found as the only continent having that big ratio of disputed and contested boundaries (see Table 3.1).

Why should this be the case? One explanation that may be advanced relates to the fact that in this context the term 'Asia' encompasses an area stretching from the Red Sea to the Bering Strait. This represents huge area with an extremely complex historical and ethnic inheritance. Significantly, although there are fewer boundaries in Asia than, for example, Africa in the former there is a lack of consensus among states in relation to dealing with the region's colonial legacy. Unlike in Africa or America no regional grouping exists in Asia that has regulated the region's approach to inherited boundaries and thus there has been little to prevent the occurrence of disputes.

The situation found in Africa was very much different. The most frequent type of dispute in Africa is positional. Only 9 boundaries can be considered internationally disputed because of real territorial claims. Among the best-known disputes in this category are those between Ethiopia and Somalia and Egypt and Sudan. The majority of the positional disputes observed are related to the riverine sectors of the boundaries and problems concerning the allocation of islands or disputes over navigational rights. Those boundaries were demarcated in the colonial era but it appeared later they lack clear definitions for some localities. Most of them do not cause real international conflicts.

Table 3.1   Boundary disputes in the world (as of 1995)

Type of dispute	Africa	Asia	Americas	Europe
Territorial	9	30	6	24
Positional	27	6	2	2
Functional	4	7	2	1
No dispute	58	37	28	55
Total	98	80	38	82

Source: Biger, G. (ed.) (1995), The Encyclopaedia of International Boundaries. Jerusalem Publishing House, Jerusalem.

Basically, the consequences are minor uncertainties, sometimes only on the local level. However, the majority of African boundaries were allocated in the group 'no disputes'.

A key reason for the limited number of major territorial disputes evident in Africa is the influence of the Organization for African Unity (OAU) Cairo Declaration of 1963, which provided a framework whereby African states undertook not to challenge existing boundaries. In general this principle has retained its validity and continues to form the basis of relations among African states with disputes more frequently caused by lack of precision in colonial-era boundary making rather than through overt challenges to major territories. Although the OAU Declaration has not proved a panacea, insulating Africa from major territorial disputes and boundary changes – as Eritrea's successful bid for independence from Ethiopia illustrates – it may be viewed as having, and continuing to exert, a significant influence on the management of boundary and territorial issues on the continent.

Since there is only one Anglo-American boundary (United States-Canada), all other international boundaries in both Americas are in fact between so called Latino-American states. The main finding of the analysis is that American boundaries are settled to a very high degree. We registered 6 territorial disputes. The largest disputed territory is Essequibo between Venezuela and Guyana, while the most long-lasting is between Bolivia and Chile. It refers to an old Bolivian claim for a direct access to the coast over territory that is part of Chile. Another traditionally contested American boundary was Argentina-Chile. That old dispute was resolved in the 1990s and therefore we considered that boundary as being without disputes. In the light of the conflict they had in the late 1990s the Ecuador-Peru dispute might be the most serious dispute in South America at the moment.

Functional and positional disputes are not characteristics of the American international boundaries. Of course, it does not mean that functional disputes do not occur, especially considering the amount of cross-border crime activity associated with drugs, among others.

One of the main reasons why the boundaries of the American states are not subject to many significant territorial disputes lies in the region's historical inheritance. The majority of the area under consideration was for centuries under the control of just two colonial powers – Spain and Portugal. To an extent therefore there is a shared colonial inheritance among the American states. Through the Organization of American States (OAS) the countries concerned have accepted the principle of *uti possidetis*, that is, acceptance of colonial boundaries as the basis for modern delimitations. In a similar manner to that experienced in Africa, this has to a large extent served to moderate the number of territorial disputes. What disputes there are tend to arise from uncertainties in the definition of certain colonial boundaries, particularly in remote areas. One additional problem associated with American boundaries, in contrast to those of Africa, is that because large areas of the region fell within the jurisdiction of a particular colonial state, be it Spain or Portugal, several modern boundaries between American states are based on the limits of internal colonial administrative areas and these were not always defined with the same degree of precision as the boundaries between areas controlled by different colonial powers (e.g. Ecuador-Peru and Argentina-Chile).

Findings for Europe are also interesting. The analysis ended with a few positional and functional disputes, but an unexpectedly large number of territorial disputes. Most of them are dormant, typical examples being boundaries like the Hungary-Romania. They may never be reactivated but as long as there are no legal arrangements for the problems, we decided to treat them as existing disputes. The majority of open European disputes refer to boundaries between the former Yugoslav and Soviet republics. Serbian territorial claims caused bloodshed and wars in the first half of 1990s. In spite of peace accords reached meanwhile (Dayton package), we decided to keep such a disputes on the list. For the time being we do not see clearly settled either the Croatia-Yugoslavia boundary or the boundaries of Bosnia-Herzegovina. Territorial claims between former Soviet republics are less well known. However, they should be registered in spite of the current reluctance of political officials to acknowledge them. They are advocated by informal, non-governmental groups. Sometimes those groups are nothing else but spokesmen of the officials. A dispute between Russia and Ukraine over sovereignty over Crimea is certainly not as threatening and dangerous as three or four years ago, but has not been completely settled either. There is still a potential it can cause serious problems again. Disputes between Russia and the Baltic states, especially Estonia and Latvia, are not likely to develop into a serious conflicts simply because of the obvious imbalance in the size and power among states. Nevertheless, we decided to count them as still existing territorial disputes. In spite of the relatively high number of territorial disputes, Europe also offers many examples of once seriously contested borders which are today completely settled. Transboundary cooperation along, for example, France-Germany or Germany-

Denmark boundary today entirely substituted conflicts over Alsace or Schleswig. In that context we'd like to mention Italy-Slovenia boundary. During WWI the valley of the Soča (Isonzo) River was the site of the heavy fights. The frontline followed the valley of the river during 1915-17 period. The traces of the war landscape are still to be found. Many military cemeteries of the both sides are still visible features of the landscape but today, instead of guns, they are surrounded by a flourishing tourist industry, involving not only Italians and Slovenians, but visitors from other regions as well.

Summing up European experience it can be noticed that territorial disputes are more common between former Eastern countries than between Western or between Eastern and Western countries.

Since our main source of information generally did not treat maritime boundaries we have to add few words on that issue.

In recent years boundary and territorial disputes involving frequently small, remote and obscure islands and over jurisdiction over maritime space have commanded news headlines around the world. One of the reasons is that the world map of maritime boundaries is far less settled and less mature than the one showing political division of land areas.

The United Nations Convention on the Law of the Sea allows states to claim jurisdiction offshore out to 200 nautical miles and, in certain cases, continental shelf rights beyond that limit. However, although signed in 1982, it only came into force on 16 November 1994 one year after the deposition of the 60th instrument of ratification or accession with the United Nations. By December 1997 the number of states that have ratified or accepted UNCLOS have increased to 122.

As far as their maritime boundaries are concerned many states have not arrived further than at the 'allocation' stage of making their claims to extended offshore jurisdiction, while others proceeded to the 'delimitation' stage and concluded boundary agreements with their neighbors. Differing interpretations of the provisions of the UN Convention have led to numerous areas of overlapping maritime claims that require delimitation agreements to resolve.

The entry into force and increasing acceptance of the UN Convention has highlighted the fact that small islands, hitherto regarded as insignificant, might be able to generate extensive maritime claims. Coupled to this is the perception on the part of governments that valuable resources and thus the state's vital interests may be at stake. In an era where near-shore (as well as on-shore) resources such as fisheries and hydrocarbons are reaching their limits, where improved technology allows the economically viable exploitation of offshore oil and gas resources in deeper waters, further and further offshore and where economic and population growth impose increasing demands for food and energy the significance attached to recent islands and maritime boundary disputes becomes clear.

In this context a distinction may be made between disputes over maritime space exclusive of islands, disputes over role of the islands in constructing a maritime boundary, and disputes over the ownership of a particular island or islands. That said, it is probably fair to observe that any dispute over ownership of an island will inevitably have a maritime space and marine resource jurisdiction dimension.

As noted, in recent years a rash of these island-based disputes have commanded widespread attention. This has led some commentators to blame the UN Convention for causing such contention. In every case, however, disputes over island sovereignty predate the Convention, often (if the claimant countries themselves are to be credited) by hundreds of years. An overview of disputes over island disputes also indicates a particular concentration in South East and east Asia.

Types of Borderlands

American scholar O. Martinez (1994) distinguished four types of borderlands according to degree of transboundary cooperation. These are: alienated, coexistent, interdependent and integrated borderlands. Alienated borderlands are characterized by warfare, political disputes, conflicting claims, ethnic or/and religious rivalry and the absence of cross-boundary interaction. Borderlands on both sides of the boundary are total strangers to each other. Currently alienated borderlands are found mostly along the boundaries that are in previous analysis identified as contested. There is a high degree of correlation between two phenomena.

A resolution of a serious dispute is a main precondition for evolution from a state of alienation to the state of co-existence. Usually, two nations would withdraw maximal claims and reach general agreement, but a lot of details are to be resolved. Co-existence is very often a transitional phase leading towards two more advanced modes of interaction between borderlands. Very often this type of borderlands coincide with boundaries that are characterized by positional disputes.

Interdependent borderlands are those that are often economically and socially complementary. Relations between countries are friendly and stable. Borderlands usually promote closer cooperation and are interested to develop more ambitious projects in future. Interdependence may be asymmetrical, if economic conditions in two adjoining countries are significantly different. The US-Mexico boundary and borderlands provides an illustrative example of asymmetrical interdependence (Martinez, 1994).

When economies of neighboring countries are functionally merged, and when cross-boundary movement is unrestricted, we deal with integrated borderlands. All political and other differences are eliminated as well as the most of existing barriers to movement of goods and people across boundary. Borderlands are fully connected and they take advantage of their position along the international boundary.

Concluding Remarks

On the basis of the survey of boundary disputes we may assume that world boundary network has proved to be a changing system, but changes do not occur so frequently and they are increasingly a subject of international control and conduct. Unilateral claims for redefinition have not been accepted. The events of the post-

Yugoslav period in Southeastern Europe proved that military supremacy was a factor of limited importance in the remaking of the political map. Generally, territorial expansion was not granted and international mediators proposed a solution which was based on the widely proclaimed principle that existing boundaries must be respected.

Globalization trends have had an impact, indeed a profound influence in some borderlands but the experience is uneven and contradictory. Again, there is a post-Yugoslav situation that provides an interesting case. Reintegration of the Eastern Slavonia-Croatian borderland situated next to the Croatia-Serbia (Yugoslavia) international boundary was a process conducted and supervised by the UN mission. After the 1992-1995 period, in which UN presence was a total disaster (Cohen and Stamkoski, 1995), the mission was redefined and reorganized. After an additional two years, the mission in Croatia, always somehow overshadowed by massive, US-led mission in neighboring Bosnia, successfully finished and fulfilled its mandate. In the region, which was occupied and ethnically cleansed in 1991, Croatian authority was introduced and in January 1998 the mission officially ended. However, final results will be known only years after the UN mandate ended. Although a legal and political framework exist, and once disputed boundary should be considered stable accordingly, it is still not clear what type of borderland will develop in the area (Klemenčić and Schofield, 2002). Moreover, it is also hard to predict how different social groups in the area will act in the post-UN period: to what extent former refugees will return, and whether newcomers will stay or leave.

Nevertheless, we believe that there are grounds for optimism. Number of disputes is generally decreasing, especially if only serious, territorial disputes are concerned. On the other hand, a number of interdependent and integrated borderlands is and will be increasing. More and more neighboring states are adopting peaceful resolution of disputes and promote cooperation in their relation with neighboring states. Therefore, what is expected in borderlands worldwide is coexistence in spite of and across borders, rather than separation and alienation along borderlines.

References

Biger, G. (ed.) (1995), *The Encyclopaedia of International Boundaries*, Jerusalem Publishing House, Jerusalem.

Blake, G.H. (1994), 'The Mapping of International Boundaries', *The Bulletin of the Society of Cartographers*, 28(2), pp. 1-7.

Blake, G.H. (1998), 'Globalization and paradox of enduring boundaries', in L. Boon Thong and T. Shamsul Bahrin (eds.), *Vanishing Borders: The New International Order of the 21st Century*, proceedings of the Commonwealth Geographical Bureau Conference, Kuala Lumpur, 19-23 August 1996, Ashgate, Aldershot.

Charney, J.I. and Alexander, L.M. (1993), *International Maritime Boundaries*, I-II. Martinus Nijhoff, Dordrecht.

Cohen, B. and Stamkoski, G. (eds.) (1995), *With no Peace to Keep ... United Nations peacekeeping and the war in the former Yugoslavia*, Grainpress, London.

Galeotti, M. (1995), 'Cross Border Crime in the Former Soviet Union', *Boundary and Territory Briefing*, 1, International Boundaries Research Unit, Durham.

Klemenčić, M. and Schofield, C. (2002), 'An Emerging Borderland in Eastern Slavonia?', in D.H. Kaplan and J. Häkli (eds.), *European Borderlands in Geographical Context*, Rowman & Littlefield, Lanham, Boulder, New York and Oxford, pp. 200-216.

Martinez, O. (1994), 'The Dynamics of Border Interaction', in C. Schofield (ed.), *Global Boundaries*, World Boundaries, 1, Routledge, London and New York, pp.1-15.

Newman, D. and Paasi, A. (1998), 'Fences and Neighbours in the Postmodern World: Boundary Narratives in Political Geography', *Progress in Human Geography*, 22(2), pp. 186-207.

Prescott, J.R.V. (1987), *Political Frontiers and Boundaries*, Allen and Unwin, London.

Rushworth, D. (1997), 'Mapping in Support of Frontier Arbitration: Delimitation and Demarcation', *Boundary and Security Bulletin*, 5(1), International Boundaries Research Unit, Durham, pp. 61-64.

PART III
INTERNATIONAL AND NATIONAL
FORCES REDEFINING
'WE' AND 'OTHERS'

International and National Forces Redefining 'We' and 'Others'

Barbara J. Morehouse, Vera Pavlakovich-Kochi and Doris Wastl-Walter

> Borders play an important role in distinguishing between 'us' and 'them'. However, the lines are not fixed and closed, but flexible and fluid. The information and identification of who we are is grounded in space and time.
>
> (Grimes, 1998, p. 26)

The dual nature of boundaries, to include that which belongs, and to exclude that which doesn't belong, has been a critical factor in and a predisposition for borderland development. Recently, in both Europe and America, boundaries have been redefined in conjunction with formation and augmentation of regional alliances; the result has been new definitions of political boundaries based on decisions regarding what spaces and people are being included or excluded. European Union expansion has resulted in a shift of external boundaries eastward and southward, providing an opportunity for some of the countries bordering the former Iron Curtain to be reunited with the European core. At the same time, these same boundaries have excluded others, in the process creating conditions for marginalization.

Welch suggests that the concept of an exclusionary 'Fortress Europe' made up of the EU states, could never succeed. Indeed, the very concept of a single boundary distinguishing East from West does not hold up under contemporary theorizing that simultaneously takes political, economic, and social-cultural drivers into account. He suggests that, while EU enlargement to include the Central and Eastern European (CEE) states is inevitable, how the process will unfold and the form that membership will take remains to be determined. Indeed, notions of 'Fortress Europe', envisioned in the context of the former Iron Curtain boundary, remain very much alive.

The Fortress Europe-Iron Curtain boundary, Welch notes, was defined by global superpower relations, and reflected the consequences of ideological conflict. He goes on to suggest that the current 'uncertainty of purpose' being felt in the EU may be traced at least in part to the demise of bureaucratic socialism in Eastern

Europe, and to the removal of the Iron Curtain. Individual activities, such as those undertaken by Germany to increase trade across the EU boundary, raise questions regarding the viability of Fortress Europe as an idea. Indeed, Welsh notes that the peripheral regions of the EU have the most concern with regard to closer economic and political ties with the CEE states; and with good reason: these are the areas that are most vulnerable to competition. Such concerns, Welch emphasizes, highlight the tensions that exist at local, regional and national levels with regard to EU identity.

Using examples from the Alps-Adria and Polish Euroregion areas to reflect on cross-border cooperation, Welch finds two key lessons. First, even where there is a history of mistrust and enmity, contemporary economic imperatives drive movement toward cooperation. Second, even given a world where economic imperatives are dominant, interactions among territorial units do not behave in a strictly hierarchical fashion (local-regional-state-suprastate), but in fact open doors for new forms of territorial-economic cooperation. In sum, ethnic and nationalistic conflict fly in the face of market-driven futures. Welsh calls this 'a fundamental disjuncture between the economic and ethno-nationalist perspectives'. If 'Fortress Europe' is no longer an option, what are the implications for a wider Europe? What will it take for successfully achieving a 'politics of inclusion'? Foreshadowed is a complex, multi-layered Europe comprised of political checks and balances, regional economic arrangements that bypass and challenge state governments, and increased sensitivity with regard to ethno-national identity. But for this to happen, the existing 'politics of exclusion' will have to be modified, and the EU boundary moved progressively eastward.

Pavlakovich-Kochi views Zagreb, the capital of the recently emergent state of Croatia, as operating at the interface between two driving forces: two doorsteps, one giving entry to now independent state of Slovenia and the other opening the way toward European Union. The drawing of international boundaries delineating individual nation states brought with it the need to establish new regulations and processes (e.g., border controls, customs processes and tariffs). It also generated interruptions in flows on the boundary, where previously no such interruptions had existed. Territorial disputes arose, requiring active solution.

After Croatia achieved independence, Zagreb became the focal point for political and economic organization of the nation's territory. It exists as the heart of Croatian nationality and economic activity, but must be evaluated in the context of its own peripheral position (and Croatia's more generally) in the context of larger-scale relations and processes occurring in Europe and beyond.

Pavlakovich-Kochi examines the dynamic relationship that exists in this context between the new international boundaries and regional transformation. The redefined boundaries, in combination with geopolitical changes occurring in larger contexts, have altered the geographical location of Zagreb's 'region'. At the same time, she suggests, key characteristics and functions of the Croatia-Slovenia boundary have proven to be explicit factors influencing Zagreb's regional economic development. Connections via transportation lines, and related accessibility of more distant markets, are among the factors that exert a particularly strong influence on Zagreb's options. Pavlakovich-Kochi finds that the Croatian government's narrowly defined national agenda has contributed strongly to reinforcement of the border with Slovenia, thus further blocking trade flows and transboundary human movement. Croatia's desire to be a member of the EU has been delayed, she notes. Yet even without this stumbling block, Croatia faces the challenge of having no direct land access to the European Union. Comparing Croatia with Slovenia, Pavlakovich-Kochi finds that Croatia has faced a difficult uphill struggle to consolidate its nation state and to position itself for EU membership. Indeed, Croatia was doubly cursed: war weakened its ability to adjust to increased traffic demands to/from Central and Eastern European markets; at the same time, Slovenia was in a position to offer alternative routes and direct traffic links to its territory. Increased trade competition between Croatia and Slovenia is evident. Even more notable, however, the current exclusion of Croatia from European organizations is likely to deter much-needed investment, thus undermining its long-term economic and ultimately political stability.

Hajdú trains his analysis on the possibility of renewing cross-border cooperation along the boundary between Hungary and Croatia, an area not often considered in international geopolitics. He begins by tracing the 800-year history of cross-border relations in this area, noting that the region has been characterized by repeated contests as far back as the 11th century. Until 1918, he observes, cross-border relations were occurring not only at the national level, but also at the macro regional scale, along an axis running from Budapest through Zagreb to Rijeka on the Adriatic Sea. However, in the period between the two World Wars, relations deteriorated, even though citizens of both countries were allowed to retain their rights to use and sell property they owned on the other side of the boundary. Recent political transformation in Hungary has again opened possibilities for transboundary interaction, particularly with regard to environmental management.

The establishment of an independent Croatia, Hajdú notes, changed the context. Several waves of migration, generated by refugees from former Yugoslavia attempting to enter Hungary, posed new challenges in terms of definition of the role of the border in supranational and local affairs. Not the least of these was the strain on welfare and charity entities to provide for the basic needs of the refugees. In some areas refugees came to represent more than five percent of the population. The residence of Yugoslav refugees in Hungary resulted in various relationships with local Hungarian residents, leading to a reshaping of life in the settlements to which they had been relocated. Some of these settlements became as a result notably more 'eastern' or 'Balkan' in their characteristics.

While the refugees' residence in Hungarian communities was originally viewed as short-term, lengthening residence times ensued, leading to tensions between local Hungarians and the refugees, and among the refugees themselves. Reviewing the history of interstate relations between the two countries since 1945, Hajdú notes that unifying developments, such as increases in transboundary flows, and agreement on the joint use of the Mura and Drava Rivers, present reason for optimism about the future. Concurrently, however, cross-border economic relations have deteriorated, leading to reorganization and continuation of significant difficulties. Other problems persist as well. Serbian emplacement of mines in the Baranya triangle of the border area rendered this area the most unusable border in Europe. Some border-crossing points are open only for a limited number of hours. In sum, Hadjú observes, given the Croatian need to secure sovereignty throughout its territory and complete the job of establishing its state structure, cross-border relations remain a secondary issue. Thus, even in the absence of significant interstate problems today, he does not expect any reshaping or deepening of border relations to occur in the near future.

Turning to the US-Mexico border, signing of the North American Free Trade Agreement by Canada, the United States, and Mexico has stimulated transboundary efforts to establish integrated economic regions. Wong González uses the emergence of a new regionalism to examine the emergent phenomenon of 'virtual regions' (those that result from contractual agreements between regions even if these regions are not geographically contiguous). He also reviews efforts to create regional-scale dynamism in Mexico, particularly with regard to enhanced transboundary interaction. Wong González focuses particularly on one such effort underway between the US state of Arizona and the Mexican state of Sonora. Based on recent thought regarding the nature of competition and international competitiveness at the regional scale, he investigates the nature of regional integration in this context, from the perspectives of functional integration and formal integration.

The Strategic Economic Development Vision for the Arizona-Sonora Region, which lays out the guideposts for transboundary regional development in the two states, reflects recognition on both sides of the border of the impacts of globalization and technological change. NAFTA is but one expression of these global trends. The goal to create a single economic region with competitive advantage on global markets is paramount, followed by a drive to facilitate complementary economic development in the two states, create new markets for the region's products, and to facilitate transboundary flows of goods, services, people and information. Wong González observes that the initiative poses both opportunities and challenges. In many cases these opportunities and challenges reflect the long history in the region of negotiating between the smooth ground of a shared 'we' and the rocky ground of 'other'. The area shares many historical and cultural ties, and has a long history of good transboundary relations. At the same time, strong economic and political disparities exist.

Wong González notes that a substantial degree of economic integration exists between Arizona and Sonora. However, this integration is primarily related to trade rather than to technical manufacturing or capital investment forms of integration. To achieve its goals, the region needs, among other things, to develop a dynamic trade corridor with other productive areas, extending from Canada to central Mexico. Current back-yard strategies, such as the current assembly plant operations ('maquiladoras') and static trade corridor arrangements, and neo-taylorist arrangements must be discarded, according to Wong González. Achieving a form of integration that is more fair to both sides, and that better reflects integration of the entire region, rather than just the functional areas that link the two states today, is required, as is greater participation at the local community level. Whether the processes of convergence or divergence will gain priority in the end remains to be seen. Wong González suggests that, given the likelihood that existing asymmetries will persist into the indefinite future, perhaps much of any ultimate success will depend on intelligent use of the existing asymmetries and enhancement of complementarities.

From a broader perspective, Wong González notes that, based on formal aspects of integration in North America, the success of transboundary economic regions in meeting stated objectives would depend largely on the extent of cross-border cooperation links and wider participation of local actors. Also critical is the region's organizational structure and capacity to negotiate with governmental entities at other scales with regard to territorial, financial and political decisions. These requirements in turn hinge on regional and local-scale achievement of greater autonomy and decentralization of power.

Silvers examines the relationships between profitability of maquiladoras located in Mexican border states and the industry's economic impacts on employment and personal income on both sides of the US-Mexico border. His findings indicate that the maquiladora industry has had a positive impact on the Mexican side of the border in terms of reductions in poverty and underemployment. In the US border states Silvers found that maquiladora activity has contributed to an increase in average personal income, but has not influenced poverty levels. Thus while the maquiladoras have benefited individuals on both sides of the border, the economic impacts in the Mexican border states differ notably from those of the US border states.

The collection of chapters included here highlight important implications for policy and decision making in borderland contexts. Macro-regional alliances, such as the EU and NAFTA, have added another layer in decision-making, one that directly and indirectly affects borderland communities and residents. In the past, when decisions affecting borderlands were made at the national level, the destiny of the borderlands was affected primarily by the relationship between their respective national centers of political and economic power. Today decisions are often made at the supranational or global scale. Thus, the centers of political power are even farther removed from the local level, a situation that encourages the emergence of regionalism as a response to feelings of marginalization. Regionalism can, on the other hand, generate new boundaries that operate in contradiction to trends occurring at supranational scales demanding abolition of boundaries. In the process, definitions of 'we' and 'other' change in ways that generate both abstract and material consequences in borderland areas, in transboundary regions, in national centers, and at supranational scales.

References

Grimes, K.M. (1998), *Crossing Borders: Changing Social Identities in Southern Mexico*, University of Arizona Press, Tucson.

Chapter 4

From Iron Curtain
to Fortress Europe and Beyond

Richard Welch

Introduction

The Iron Curtain constituted an effective barrier between Western Europe and the 'East', limiting both political and economic interaction. But it was not a boundary defined by intra-European relations so much as by global super-power relations; a geopolitical consequence of a conflict of ideologies. Among the many ramifications of the imposition of this artificial, often impermeable, boundary was that for more than a generation the definition of the eastern edge of Europe was little more than an academic issue, so permanent did the Iron Curtain appear to be.

The speed with which bureaucratic socialist systems collapsed in Central and Eastern Europe (CEE) was surprising and, following initial euphoria, the daunting task ahead for states both east and west soon became evident. The high costs of transformation, inevitably, emerged as a major consideration, particularly for the constituent states of the EU which initially at least were expected to shoulder much of the financial burden (Van Ham, 1995). But of greater longer term significance have been issues relating to identity and position within Eastern Europe, questions frozen for more than four decades.

Three interrelated themes stand out. First, as Jessop (1995, p. 678) observes, the introduction of market reforms has not necessarily been compatible with attempts to (re)establish democratic government and, as a result, postsocialist societies have experienced 'acute structural crises, fiscal and financial crises, and social disintegration'. Second, ethnic and nationalist expression has reemerged seemingly undiminished after four decades of bureaucratic socialism. Third, there are fundamental, long-standing differences between the eastern and western parts of Europe in approach to ethnicity, nationalism and minorities which, according to Liebich (1995, p. 313) result from different relationships between state and society, a divergent character of urbanization, and weaker ethnic identity in the East. We will return to these issues later. Quite simply, despite emotional calls for a united Europe (an 'imagined space' according to Wallace, 1990), East and West Europe have different histories and are different places.

These themes emphasize some complexities inherent in the process of re-weaving the fabric of Europe, of defining the new European order, but they represent only part of the picture. While the depth of ethnonationalist feeling in parts of Eastern Europe is undeniable, its expression may be seen as anachronistic, given moves to minimize the impacts of such differentiation within the EU and the bypassing of such issues with economic globalization (Welch, 1996). While, for some, images of Europe may be defined in historic ethnonationalist terms, in practice there can be no return to pre-World War II conceptions of Europe because the capitalist economic world (and the EU in particular) moved on during the bureaucratic socialist interval; increasingly, identity will be defined by position in a supranational economic order. This point notwithstanding, the states of Europe are now required to define the boundaries of (and within) Europe for the first time in a political generation AND they must do so in a context of economic and ethnonationalist disjuncture. It is the purpose of this chapter to examine the parameters of this process.

Differences between East and West

According to Liebich (1995) the particular ethnic character of Central and Eastern Europe represents an essential difference between Eastern and Western Europe. Liebich argues that whereas nationalism and national groups within Western Europe have reinforced the process of state building, in Eastern Europe states emerged from the fragmentation of the Ottoman, Habsburg and Russian Empires with scant acknowledgement of constituent nationalities. Furthermore, as cities were centers of colonial administration and not nationalist sentiment, a non-urban character to CEE nationalism evolved that further isolated ethnonationalist movements from the process of state building.

The years of bureaucratic socialism subsequently disguised the discontinuity between state boundary and ethnonationalist identity but did not reduce the intensity of nationalist feeling. Indeed, Verdery (1996, p. 81) argues that Communist Party rule institutionalized the ethnonational principle in the region's three federations – the Soviet Union, Czechoslovakia and Yugoslavia. As a consequence, the reexpression of ethnonational differences that has followed the demise of bureaucratic socialism has at times been forceful. Liebich proposes another difference between East and West; that because linguistic boundaries within Central and Eastern Europe have been historically unstable, individual identities have also been difficult to define and minor differentiating characteristics have assumed unwarranted significance. He observes that 'instead of the demarcation lines of Western Europe one encounters transitional "shatter zones" of acute diversity where religion and linguistic borders are blurred' (Liebich, 1995, p. 316). Such conditions add to the complexity and confusion inherent in the process of economic restructuring and are an important constituent of the economic and ethnonationalist disjuncture evident in some CEE states.

Accordingly, the baggage brought by CEE states to the process of structural adjustment was quite different from the norm in Western Europe for two reasons. The first, a bureaucratic socialist overlay, was expected. The second, an East European perspective on state and nation, alluded to earlier and of much longer standing, was less well understood. But this was not the only complication. Economic restructuring in the CEE postsocialist states was never likely to be a straightforward process. There was no blueprint to follow, no single political-economic model to emulate because, as soon became clear to the CEE states, capitalism itself does not have a single form but varies significantly between different national and ethnic cultures (Hamilton, 1995, p. 70). Insights proffered that conceptualized the transition as 'a unilinear process by which one coherent system based upon the Plan is replaced by a successive system based on the market and private property relations' (Smith, 1995, p. 761) have proved quite inadequate. The CEE states have struggled to establish the institutional and organizational structures necessary for the development of consensual regulatory frameworks. As a result, the extent of economic restructuring has been uneven (Jessop, 1995; Myant, 1995).

The EU and Enlargement

Confusion and uncertainty about contemporary change do not apply only to the CEE states. Within the EU the picture is equally complex. In his article Smith (1996, p. 23) comments that 'the EU and its members have had to learn a new politics of inclusion which focuses less on difference than on variety, and less on the maintenance of boundaries than on their continual redrawing. Boundaries in this conception are for crossing rather than defending'. Smith goes on to argue that the defining of boundaries in the late 1990s results from three discourses: a legacy of earlier Community policy making, in which the qualities that define insiders/outsiders are affirmed; contemporary Union policy making, which allows constituent states to evaluate the costs of inclusion and exclusion; and negotiated order, by which the process of determining boundaries in the EU is itself negotiated by member states. That few certainties have resulted from these parallel discourses should not be surprising for they reflect coincidental upheaval within the EU and in the EU's relationship with the European order.

The issue is not a new one for the EU (EC). As Fraser noted in the early 1990s, the shape of relations within an integrated Europe would depend upon the structure of the EC and whether the EC would seek to deepen relations between member states or widen the spatial extent of what was then the Community. We are now aware that it has sought to do both, but within a context of growing disenchantment with the principle of full integration (Hama, 1996). While Europe Agreements with the Visegrad-4 states, Romania and Bulgaria came into force in 1994 or 1995, this first step in eastern enlargement through the designation of associate nation status has been undertaken without a consensus as to the appropriate ultimate form of the Union. While the Maastricht Treaty was supposed to lead to a single European (i.e. EU) identity through the creation of a single market and monetary union, progress has been halting. Indeed, there is both uncertainty about whether a single market and monetary reform will provide greater wealth and generate more employment, and pessimism about whether the combination of market forces and a regional policy will lead to a convergence of fortunes of regional economies.

Paradoxically, the demise of bureaucratic socialism in Eastern Europe and the removal of the Iron Curtain have contributed to this uncertainty of purpose within the EU. When the eastern boundary was both an impenetrable barrier and the symbol of threat to West European capitalism, constituent states provided military security, with the EU functioning largely as a symbol of capitalist economic progress in the West. But EU member states are no longer seen to be important as sources of military security (Newhouse, 1997). Contemporary security issues, such as threats of mass migration and environmental disaster, are similarly European in scale but, with the superiority of capitalism affirmed, it is the EU that seeks to assume a more strategic role in their management. One reason for this is the inability of constituent states to manage the supranational and local level problems which confront Europe in the beginning of the new millennium. Another is that the security of the EU is now at least partly dependent on the success of the transformation process in the states of Central and Eastern Europe, and this lies beyond the powers of individual states to determine.

This is not to say that member states of the EU no longer pursue individual interests. Germany, in particular, has both encouraged the eastwards expansion of the EU to include the states of Central Europe and resurrected the dream of an integrated Middle Europe (Van Ham, 1995). German trade and investment in CEE states has exceeded that of any other member state. Hama (1996, p. 27) suggests that Germany's interest in Central Europe is not simply a rekindling of old fires but also represents a pragmatic acknowledgement that macroeconomic equilibrium may not be achievable within the united Germany nor within the highly competitive EU framework. He argues that encouragement to extend the EU eastwards, initially through the accrediting of association status, is a mechanism for raising per capita wealth in the Länder of the former GDR without further reducing living standards in the western parts of Germany.

While such pursuance of individual objectives may seem to fly in the face of the integration principle and challenge the authority of the EU, in practice it also demonstrates that the security of member states depends upon the success of economic transformation and the solving of environmental problems in the CEE states (Welch, 1997). Such unilateral moves also indicate that while the concept of 'fortress Europe', an EU which retains its current identity and does not concern itself with CEE transformation, may represent deep seated sentiments within some, perhaps all, member states it does not constitute a viable strategy for the EU. We will return to this issue later in this chapter.

It is in the peripheral regions of the EU that concern about closer economic and political relations with CEE states is most anxiously expressed. Concern has focused on several issues: possible competition between CEE states and peripheral regions of the EU for inward investment; the prospect of increased competition in manufactured goods disadvantaging EU peripheral regions; and the diversion of structural funds to new Central or East European member states (Hudson, 1994). Peripheral EU regions have good reason for anxiety. As Jessop (1995, p. 679) observes, the postsocialist economies have shown themselves to be 'significant competitors' with peripheral economies of the EU and, as Newhouse (1997, p. 75) notes, Munich investors are more interested in the Czech Republic, Hungary and other Central and East European countries than they are in the new Länder of Eastern Germany.

On the other hand, Brocker and Jager-Roschko (1996) suggest that for less developed regions of the EU the challenge of Union enlargement may not be as serious as first envisaged. This is because a diversification of export commodities from the Czech Republic and Hungary, at least, could lead to a reduction in direct competition with the EU's peripheral regional economies. Also, the establishment of Europe Agreements, the objective of which is to establish a free trade area by the turn of the Century under conditions imposed by EU Competition Policy, should mean that the probable nature of competition within an enlarged EU can be assessed before full membership is achieved by CEE states. Whichever, the expression of concern serves to emphasize the continuing struggle at local, regional and member state levels with the question of EU identity.

The Post-Iron Curtain Border as a Boundary between People

We have suggested that EU enlargement to include CEE states is inevitable, whether this enlargement will be by way of adding more full members or by the creation of a range of permanent membership categories. The political, economic and environmental arguments for closer association are largely understood, although not necessarily welcomed by all member states. With respect to economy and environment there is a growing acceptance that with the removal of the Iron Curtain both principle and problem transcend political boundaries, even that the concept of boundary requires radical revision. But the perspective of difference based on ethnicity, nationality and history has proved more resistant to modification, and especially so following ethnonationalist strife in parts of Eastern Europe.

Despite the cases of the Basques, the Catalans, the Scots and the Welsh, for example, there is little understanding in Western Europe of the depth of feeling of ethnonational minorities. Such terms as cultural revivalism, political autonomism, territorial self-determinism, separatism and irredentism (Bugajski, 1995) are assumed to relate to upheaval and to be foreign to the West. Indeed, there is concern that such tensions may be imported to Western Europe through immigration. As a result, while the concepts of economic and environmental 'boundaries' may be undergoing radical reformulation and assuming greater flexibility, this flexibility is not extended to the mobility of people.

Jacobson (1996) argues that the EU was not designed to deal with transnational migrations either within or from outside the Union, and it was not until 1987, and the Single European Act, that a common approach to migration was adopted. But the principal objective of this legislation was to create a macroregional market unobstructed by internal frontiers rather than to establish a basis for immigration from outside. Only following the Maastricht Treaty was the EC's mandate extended to include political integration and the policing of external borders (O'Dowd et al., 1995). Yet migration to Western Europe since 1945 has been extensive by any standards. Castles and Miller (1993) estimate that from the end of World War II to the early 1970s some 30 million people entered Western Europe as workers or dependents. In the 1970s and early 1980s this number was augmented by the migration of dependents, and for the last fifteen years by refugees, asylum seekers and illegal alien workers (Messina, 1996). While immigration from CEE states was quite limited between 1961 and 1989, since the beginning of the 1990s there has been concern in the EU that eastwards enlargement in whatever form might 'open the floodgates' to migration from the East. Of particular concern is the possibility of extensive illegal immigration from CIS countries, an issue now confronting CEE states. While transnational migration is reducing the factor of difference within the existing EU, the potential social, as well as economic, costs of such migrations within an enlarged EU appear too great to contemplate in the short term.

The Post-Iron Curtain Border as a Region of Opportunity

The Iron Curtain was the archetypal border; a physical impediment to the free flow of people, goods and information. As we have already noted, the symbolic and physical dismantling of the Iron Curtain has generated much debate as to what should take its place. Earlier Polish concerns that it might be replaced by a 'silver curtain', an economic wall dividing Western from Eastern Europe, have been largely dispelled with the establishment of Europe Agreements and the prospect of full EU membership by 2004. But, as yet, there is no coherent pattern of transformation emerging in the regions once adjacent to the Iron Curtain, in part because in an enlarged EU the notions of what is the 'border' and 'peripheral' will inevitably change.

The regional response to this geopolitical uncertainty varies according to local conditions, but three emphases are evident: to enhance contact where ethnic groups straddle the border; to facilitate cross-border commuting to work; and to establish cross-border economic alliances. The first two seek to introduce a measure of permeability to the boundary but do not challenge its existence. On the other hand, the establishment of cross-border alliances undermines the efficacy of the East-West boundary, mirroring intra-Union cross-border initiatives and illustrating the potential advantages of EU enlargement.

Brief reference to two cases, the Alpe-Adria Working Community and the Polish Euroregions (see Figure 4.1) will illustrate the evolving approach to cross-border cooperation. Nearly twenty years ago the two Italian regions of Friuli-Venezia Giulia and Veneto, the Austrian provinces of Carinthia, Styria, Upper Austria and Salzburg, together with Bavaria, Slovenia and Croatia formed an action association to promote dialogue about common development issues and approaches to jointly experienced problems such as environmental conservation.

The Working Community has since been extended to include more Austrian and Italian, together with Hungarian and Swiss territorial administrative areas (see Figure 4.1). The wide range of issues considered and the timing of its establishment have limited its potential as an agent for economic change, although Horvath earlier asserted (1993, p. 159) that the 'association could become the integrator of the EC, the European Free Trade Association ... and the regions of Eastern Europe'.

The Euroregions straddling the border between Poland and Germany, and the Czech Republic in the case of the Nysa Euroregion (see Figure 4.1), are more recent in origin, dating from the early 1990s. They have resulted from groups of local authorities on both sides of the border agreeing to work together to generate economic development in the border region. As with much of the former Iron Curtain border, the divide between Poland and Germany remains relatively thinly populated and underdeveloped, with an infrastructural disjuncture, inadequate inward investment and a limited regional market. The Euroregions, still lacking legal status, have been set up to address these common problems.

Despite the focus on economic development and achieving a measure of economic independence of Berlin, Warsaw and Prague, there remain significant misgivings about possible costs of that independence. We have already referred to the concerns of industrial and agricultural producers in peripheral border regions of the EU that the integration of CEE states will lead to competition from lower priced products. But in the case of the Euroregions, to date, the misgivings are greater from the Polish side. Bojar (1996) notes the continuing emotional resistance to close links with groups of German local authorities. Also noted are Polish concerns that the more economically powerful German parts of the Euroregions will benefit unfairly by gaining access to raw materials and cheap labor without generating increased economic activity in the Polish parts. This last argument is further developed by Gorzelak (1996) who observes that while there has been considerable, particularly German, investment in the border regions of Poland and the Czech Republic, this has tended to be focused in key centers such as Szczecin rather than spread across the border regions. Thus while the definition of peripheral may be changing for some communities in the Polish-German border region, for others it is not (see Figure 4.1).

Nonetheless, investment is taking place in the Polish Euroregions, potential advantages of cross-border alliances are perceived to outweigh the costs and uncertainties, and the proximity to Berlin and the prospect of enhanced access to the wider German market cannot be resisted. From a German perspective, a Pareto optimal outcome suggests itself with an expected enhancement of German economic influence in Middle Europe. Both the Alpe-Adria and Polish Euroregion examples of cross-border cooperation, despite their tentative nature and still limited scope for action, have important implications for the redrawing of the boundary between East and West Europe. Two realities are emphasized. First, even between states whose histories have been ones of mistrust, even enmity, the prevailing economic imperative of the late 20th century requires cooperation rather than separation. Second, in a world where economic values predominate, relationships between territorial units do not operate strictly hierarchically, i.e. local-regional-state-suprastate, and this allows for new forms of territorial-economic association. In turn, this challenges the concept of borders as concrete phenomena.

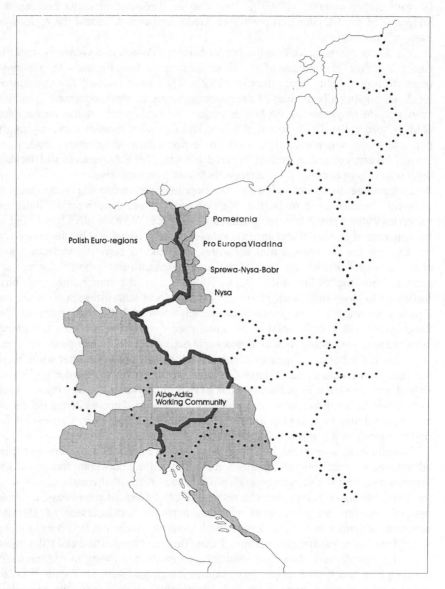

Figure 4.1 Examples of cross-border cooperation: Polish Euroregions and Alpe-Adria working community

A Europe beyond the Iron Curtain and the Fortress Economy

We have not asserted that cultural difference is no longer of relevance. Indeed, if anything the opposite case has been made. Jacobson (1996, p. 133) argues, that in the emerging order boundaries can be culturally meaningful, differentiating imagined communities on the basis of such characteristics as ethnicity and religion. But such communities may be transterritorial, only coincidentally reflecting the political spaces of states. Furthermore, rather than defining economic spaces as in earlier decades, such cultural differentiation may be better conceptualized as constituting but one layer in a multilayered Europe.

We have suggested that in contemporary Eastern Europe the existence of ethnic differences, and the unleashing of their (self)destructive energies, does not sit comfortably with the idea of market driven futures. Indeed, we have referred to this as a fundamental disjuncture between economy and ethnonationalist perspective. What, then, are the implications for the wider Europe at the end of the millennium, given that a 'fortress EU' is not a realistic political option? Put another way, what are the requirements of the EU, as the prime player in Europe, if the 'politics of inclusion' is to be successful? In response to a similar question, Smith (1996) suggests that it is important to reject the notion of linear development and to stress variety and lateral thinking when it comes to defining 'insiders' and 'outsiders' in Europe. He concludes that if this path is followed, the requirement for fixed boundaries can be relaxed and an environment created in which 'the geopolitical, the institutional, the transactional and the cultural can mingle very closely' (Smith, 1996, p. 23). Foreshadowed is a complex, multi-layered Europe. As we have argued, such complexity was inevitable once the Iron Curtain came down. Constituent aspects of this new Europe include the following: an EU enlarged by the inclusion of the Visegrad-4 states as full members early in the next century, and with more East European and Baltic states as associate members; a Germany with strong interests in Middle Europe ensuring that the EU's 'politics of exclusion' and conceptions of economic fortress are kept in check; regional economic arrangements, cross-border and otherwise, which bypass and challenge state governments; localities operating in a Europe-wide quasi-market; and awareness and sensitivity to cultural differences, to ethnonational identity. To ensure that these layers remain in some coherent relation to each other some modification to the 'politics of exclusion' will be necessary, with the boundary between East and West moving progressively eastwards, as will a common approach to the management of environmental externalities. The earlier conceptualization of a single step from Iron Curtain to Fortress Europe failed to recognize the significance of capitalist economic relations to the definition of Europe in the 1990s. What we have sought to show in this Chapter is that Fortress Europe could only ever be a fleeting image, and that the very concept of a single boundary, let alone fortress ramparts, distinguishing East from West is challenged by contemporary theorizing.

References

Bojar, E. (1996), 'Euroregions in Poland', *Tijdschrift voor Economische en Sociale Geografie*, 87(5), pp. 442-447.

Brocker, J. and Jager-Roschko, O. (1996), 'Eastern reforms, trade, and spatial change in the EU', *Papers in Regional Science*, 75(1), pp. 23-40.

Bugajski, J. (1995), *Ethnic Politics in Eastern Europe*, M. E. Sharpe, Armonk, New York.

Castles, S. and Miller, M. (1993), *The Age of Migration: International Population Movements in the Modern World*, Guilford Press, New York.

Gorzelak, G. (1996), *The Regional Dimension of Transformation in Central Europe*, Jessica Kingsley Publishers, London.

Hama, N. (1996), *Disintegrating Europe*, Praeger, Westport, Connecticut.

Hamilton, F.E.I. (1995), 'Re-evaluating space: locational change and adjustment in Central and Eastern Europe', *Geographische Zeitschrift*, 83(2), pp. 67-86.

Horvath, G. (1993), 'Restructuring and international cooperation in Central Europe: the case of Hungary' in R. Cappellin and P. Batey (eds.), *Regional Networks, Border Regions and European Integration*, Pion, London.

Hudson, R. (1994), 'East meets west: the regional implications within the European Union of political and economic change in Eastern Europe', *European Urban and Regional Studies*, 1(1), pp. 79-83.

Jacobson, D. (1996), *Rights Across Borders*, Johns Hopkins University Press, Baltimore.

Jessop, B. (1995), 'Regional economic blocs, cross-border cooperation, and local economic strategies in postsocialism', *American Behavioral Scientist*, 38(5) pp. 674-715.

Liebich, A. (1995), 'Nations, states, minorities: why is eastern Europe different?', *Dissent*, 42, pp. 313-317.

Messina, A. (1996), 'The not so silent revolution: postwar migration to Western Europe', *World Politics*, 49, pp. 130-154.

Myant, M. (1995), 'Transforming the Czech and Slovak economies: evidence at the district level', *Regional Studies*, 2(88), pp.753-760.

Newhouse, J. (1997), 'Europe's rising regionalism', *Foreign Affairs*, 79(1), pp. 67-84.

O'Dowd, L.; Corrigan, J. and Moore, T. (1995), 'Borders, national sovereignty and European integration: the British-Irish case', *International Journal of Urban and Regional Research*, 19, pp. 272-285.

Smith, A. (1995), 'Regulation theory, strategies of enterprise integration and the political economy of regional economic restructuring in Central and Eastern Europe: the case of Slovakia', *Regional Studies*, 29(8), pp.761-772.

Smith, M. (1996), 'The European Union and a changing Europe: establishing the boundaries of order', *Journal of Common Market Studies*, 34(1), pp. 5-28.

Van Ham, P. (1995), *The EC, Eastern Europe and European Unity*, Pinter, London.

Verdery, K. (1996), 'Nationalism, postsocialism, and space in Eastern Europe', *Social Research*, 63(1), pp. 77-95.

Wallace, W. (1990), *The Transformation of Western Europe*, Pinter, London.

Welch, R. (1996), 'Redefining the frontier: regional development in the post-welfare era', in Y. Gradus and H. Lithwic (eds.), *Frontiers in Regional Development*, Rowman and Littlefield, Lanham, Maryland.

Welch, R. (1997), 'Local government and sustainable environment: European perspectives', *European Environment*, 7, pp. 16-24.

Chapter 5

The Zagreb Region at Double Doorsteps: Implications of a Redefined Boundary for Regional Development

Vera Pavlakovich-Kochi

Introduction

The territorial system of nations, states, regions and the boundaries between them has seen a continual transformation reflecting economic, political, military and administrative changes, decisions made by state organs, rulers, various classes, social groupings and enterprises (Paasi, 1996). Recent transformation in the territorial organization and ideological landscape of the former Yugoslavia has rendered the perpetual regional transformation process particularly visible. All boundaries were redefined, as were the contents of social spaces, which were endowed with new cultural and political terms. This process of territorial reorganization coincided with the transformation of the economy of the advanced capitalist societies and a new articulation of global, national and local scales associated with the increasing transnationalization of capital accumulation (Robins and Morley, 1993, cited in Paasi, 1996).

While the functional space of the organization of economic activities, supported by rapid increase in communications and international trade, has partly exceeded the absolute space of nation-state, the questions of nation, state and territory, have returned to the top of political agenda. The struggle over the redefinition of space within new boundaries can be seen as an expression of restructuring of economic, political and administrative practices, as well as the restructuring of the contests of social consciousness (Barth, 1969, cited in Paasi, 1996). Furthermore, the process of restructuring is not a pure mechanism of adjustment, but 'a politically contested and determined process enacted by governments and organizations' (Paasi, 1996). Equally important to note, these practices are never abstract processes, but 'unfailingly manifest themselves on local, regional or national scales and are in fact produced, contested and reproduced in the local, everyday life of human beings' (Passi, 1996).

Specific territorial ideologies and discourses, such as nationalism, can play a significant role in spatial socialization, a process through which individuals and collectives are socialized as members of specific territorially bounded spatial entities (Paasi, 1996). Particularly, the role of various forms of persuasive argument (rhetoric) put forward by individuals (politicians, editorials, and advertisers) or organizations (professional, scientific, social movements, non-governmental organizations) can become a powerful factor in boundary reproduction and redefinition of space.

The elevation of the Croatian-Slovenian boundary from an internal boundary between two republics of former Yugoslavia to the status of an international boundary between two sovereign states in 1991 did not at first cause much attention on either side. This was partly due to the fact that this boundary represented one of the oldest, least contested and most persistent boundaries in Europe. This particularly pertains to the segment of the boundary between eastern Slovenia and northwestern Croatia, in the influence zone of the Croatia's capital, Zagreb. As the new regulations (customs, border patrol) were implemented, the new boundary interrupted daily economic ties and traffic flows. However, as these changes coincided with the restructuring of the economy from socialist to capitalist mode, coupled with the devastating effects of the war on Croatia's territory, the implications of the changing Croatian-Slovenian border were at first overshadowed by the nation's other priorities.

Historically peaceful relations between Croats and Slovenes and shared challenges in the post-independence era at first gave rise to a consideration of a customs union between two countries (Pak, 1993). The idea, however, was soon abandoned, and, contrarily, the boundary between Croatia and Slovenia was reinforced. Several territorial disputes soon emerged and, although miniscule in comparison with other Balkan conflicts, the boundary issue became a major problem in the bilateral relationship of two countries. According to Slovenian geographer Gosar (1996) 'areas along the Slovene-Croatian border have become a major problem for Slovenia'.

The implications of the redefined Croatian-Slovenian boundary for regional economic development of the Zagreb region did not, at first, attract much attention among regional planners and practitioners. Discussions with academic geographers[1] revealed a widely held perception that the redefined boundary with Slovenia had little impact on Zagreb's economy. Lost economic ties with a portion of Zagreb's gravitational zone on the Slovenian side did not seem to raise concern, since, as many believed, those ties were insignificant for the Zagreb economy anyway. Yet even a cursory glance at a map of the area reveals potentially critical implications of the new boundary for regional transformation. These implications exist not only because of its physical proximity – Zagreb's CBD is about 25 kilometers (15.5 miles) from the Slovenian border – but also because all roads and railroads (existing and planned) connecting Croatia with Central and Atlantic Europe pass through Slovenia's territory. Of the seven industrial regions in Croatia (Feletar and Stiperski, 1994), six are border regions, and of these, the Zagreb region and three others are adjacent to Croatian-Slovenian boundary. With the exception of Hungary, where direct land routes are available, land connections with other future members of an extended European Union, i.e., Poland, Czech Republic and Slovakia all pass through Slovenia. Thus, physical proximity and linkages with

Slovenia are critical for Croatia's integration with Europe. The Croatian Academy of Science (HAZU, 1996) was among the first to publicly acknowledge this fact.

Examination of this case study demonstrates a dynamic relationship between boundaries and regional transformation. It shows how a redefined boundary, in combination with geopolitical changes in the larger, macro-regional context, alters the geographical location of a region. It further demonstrates the powerful role of historical accident in determining the shape of a region's economy. If economic development were independent of politics, historical baggage, culture, and the ever-changing meaning of geographical location, a region's economy would be basically determined by factors of production, such as land, natural resources, infrastructure, labor and capital (Berry, Conkling and Ray, 1993; Porter, 1990). In the real world, however, actions by governments and other actors can profoundly influence the path of development. National governments, in particular, can set some developments in motion, or by ignoring other developments, can miss opportunities; the results of such decisions can have long-lasting implications for regional economic development (Krugman, 1994).

Under the influence of Croatia's national agenda and changing relationships in the new European periphery, the Croatian-Slovenian boundary acquired new and multifaceted meanings. Today, its peripheral location within the larger European context and its central location within the national territory constitute primary characteristics defining the Zagreb region. The centrality hypothesis – the Zagreb region as a central Croatian region in the newly defined national territory – explains the initial perception that the boundary was an insignificant factor in region's economic development. The periphery hypothesis – the Zagreb region as a peripheral European region – explains how increasing competition in new European periphery added a new meaning to the boundary with Slovenia and profoundly altered Zagreb's geographical location on a supranational European scale.

The Croatian-Slovenian Boundary as a Factor of Zagreb's Regional Development

The Croatian-Slovenian border was rarely recognized as an explicit factor of Zagreb's regional economic development. Croatia's geographers commonly associate Zagreb's development with its favorable location on the intersection of two principal transportation axes: the northeast-southwest axis and the northwest-southeast axis. The former, known as the Adriatic transit corridor (Malić and Božičević, 1996) connects the Danube basin with the north Adriatic region. The latter, referred to as the Sava transit corridor (Malić and Božičević, 1996) connects western and central Europe with Southwest Asia (Figure 5.1). The importance of these historical routes shifted in accordance with social changes occurring at larger scales and in conjunction with new means of communication. Thus, as noted by Žuljić (1965), Zagreb's geographic location did not change by adding new communication routes, but was influenced primarily by shifts in the importance of existing routes.

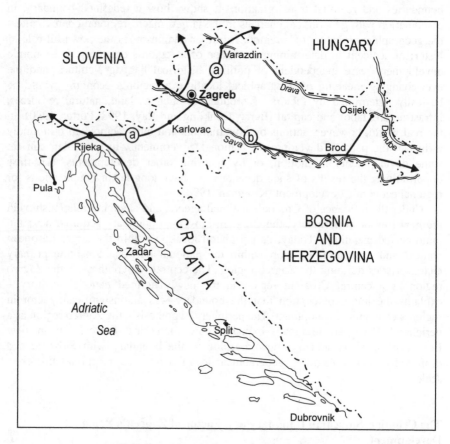

Figure 5.1   Geographical location of Zagreb on the juxtaposition of two principal transit corridors in Croatia: (a) the Adriatic, (b) the Sava corridor
(Adapted from Malić and Božičević 1996; redrawn by Gabi Eigenmann and Andrea Ch. Kofler, University of Berne, Department of Geography)

The Croatian-Slovenian border along river Sutla and the Žumberak Mountains (called the Gorjanci Mountains in Slovenia) intersects the northwest-southeast communication route, making its role immediately apparent. Over the course of history, the border was redefined several times. Depending upon its function as an internal or external border, it influenced flows of goods and people, affected infrastructure investments, and influenced overall development dependent upon interaction with the larger area. One of the most profound impacts of the Croatian-

Slovenian border is still visible in the railroad layout. When, in the second half of the 19th century, Slovenia and Croatia became integrated into the Austro-Hungarian Monarchy, the Sutla River-Žumberak (Gorjanci) boundary was redefined as an internal border, dividing the Vienna-controlled portion of the monarchy (i.e. Slovenia) from the Budapest-controlled portion of the monarchy (i.e. Croatia). This period, which has been referred as the 'first modernization' in Zagreb's development (Rogić-Nehajev, 1997), left a long lasting impact on the whole region. The Slovenian-Croatian boundary delineated spaces between two major economic centers, Vienna and Budapest, each of which built its own railroad connection with the northern Adriatic ports: Vienna-Trieste through Slovenia, and Budapest-Rijeka through Croatia (Rogić, 1982; Žuljić, 1965).

The railroad connecting Vienna with Trieste, completed in 1857, was built exclusively on the territory of old Austrian provinces (Lower Austria, Styria, Krain, Gorizia and Trieste), although the terrain was much less favorable than an alternative route on the eastern edge of the Alps. The main rationale for the Austrian route, according to Rogić (1982), was to purposely stay away from the territory controlled by Hungary, even at the expense of having to solve difficult technical problems of building railroad tracts in hostile karst topography. Hungary's railroad connection between Budapest and Rijeka was built on Croatia's territory, passing through Zagreb in 1872.

The disintegration of the Austro-Hungarian Monarchy after World War I and the formation of Yugoslavia[2] in 1918 provided a basis for a new spatial organization that included Croatia and Slovenia. A new power center, established in the eastern part of the new political-administrative entity, profoundly altered the existing exchange routes. For Croatia and Slovenia this meant shifting the emphasis from predominantly north-south connections (with Vienna and Budapest) to west-east connections (with Belgrade). The subsequent ideological divide between Western and Eastern Europe after World War II, in combination with Yugoslavia's disalignment from the Soviet block, further emphasized the west-east routes. Particularly during 1960s, Yugoslavia became a major transit route between Western Europe and the Southeast Europe/Middle East area (Rogić and Žuljić, 1972; Pelc, 1996). The volume of goods transported by rail in the early 1970s demonstrated the dominance of the west-east axis connecting Ljubljana, Zagreb and Belgrade – Yugoslavia's main economic centers and transportation nodes (Rogić and Žuljić, 1972).

During the Yugoslav era the integrated lines of communication along rivers the Sava, Morava and Vardar emphasized Zagreb's position on the northwest-southeast (the Sava corridor) axis (see Figure 5.2) and its status as the second-largest city in Yugoslavia, after Belgrade. In combination with a strong manufacturing base, geographic location helped Zagreb established itself as a center within the western part of Yugoslavia, particularly relative to Ljubljana, the capital of neighboring Slovenia (Žuljić, 1965; Rogić and Žuljić, 1972). Despite continuous political struggle against the centralizing tendencies of Yugoslav government in Belgrade, Zagreb benefited from its geographical position within Yugoslavian State. Zagreb succeeded in expanding its economic influence zone beyond the territory of Croatia, into Slovenia, and shared the functions of a leading urban center with Belgrade, Yugoslavia's capital and the center of the eastern part of the state (Sić, 1968; Žuljić, 1965; Žuljić, 1974/75).

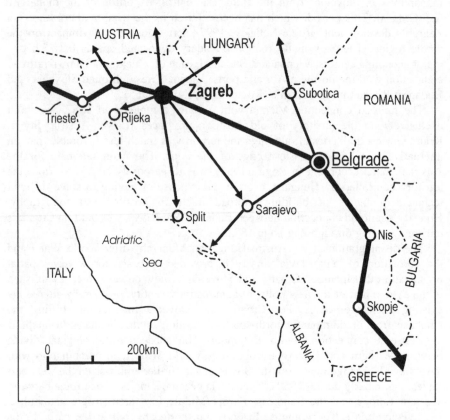

Figure 5.2   Zagreb's position on the main NW-SE transit corridor during the Yugoslav era (1918-1991)
(Adapted from Žuljić, 1965; redrawn by Gabi Eigenmann and Andrea Ch. Kofler, University of Berne, Department of Geography)

Despite a unified economic system and a common market, economic practices were bound within internal administrative boundaries and each republic tended to favor and protect the establishments on its own territory. If one considers only physical proximity, Zagreb's zone of influence potentially exceeded its administrative boundary with Slovenia. However, in a study of the dispersion process of Zagreb-based manufacturing industries, Feletar and Stiperski (1990) found that almost all branch plants of the Zagreb-based manufacturing industries were located within Croatia, reflecting 'the overwhelming role of the political boundaries'. Despite the same economic system, a common market and a strong centralist government, economic decisions and practices in Yugoslavia were extensively influenced by existing political-administrative boundaries.

Evidence of Zagreb's zone of influence notwithstanding, the internal division of (former) Yugoslavia's territory into separate, distinct republics was reinforced in professional (geographic) and educational literature in both Croatia and Slovenia. For example, in the official textbook of Geography of Yugoslavia for the senior high school class, which was written by two leading geographers Rogić and Žuljić (1972), the geographic region of Northwest Croatia was clearly delimited by the boundary with Slovenia. Although the authors pointed out that an important dimension of the Northwest's location on the transportation crossroads derived from its favorable location in relation to industrially developed Slovenia, the accompanying map clearly limited the region within the administrative boundaries of the Republic of Croatia. The visual presentation of the geographic location of Zagreb and its influence on the surrounding network of cities and towns implicitly suggests the impact of the boundary with Slovenia. The 50-km radius around Zagreb, within which the major economic foci have developed in northwestern Croatia, theoretically transcends the border with Slovenia, but in practice has commonly been represented by an empty space. A rare reference to Zagreb's hypothetical influence zone, which transcends Croatian-Slovenian boundary, is found in Žuljić (1965) and Jelen (1970). Based on one- and two-hour distance by train, Zagreb's hypothetical influence zone encompassed a large portion of east Slovenia, stretching to and overlapping (hypothetically) with Ljubljana's influence zone.

The fact that Zagreb's west gate sector (adjacent to Slovenia) lacks urban centers of comparable size to the urban centers in Zagreb's northern (Varaždin), eastern (Sisak) and southern (Karlovac) sectors support the argument about the boundary impact. Although the presence of the Slovenian border was obvious, it was rarely or never explicitly mentioned. This practice has been found to dominate professional works of Croatian geographers throughout 1980s.

For instance, Vresk (1984a) studied daily commuting to Zagreb as one of the best indicators of the functional relationship between a city and its surroundings. Daily migrations from Slovenian border communities, although probably significant in numbers, were neither included nor alluded to. Consequently, Vresk's map of daily commuter flows depicted only Croatia's territory, ending abruptly at the Croatian-Slovenian border. If it were not for the border, and assuming that physical proximity had the same effect in all directions, one could expect that Zagreb would have attracted up to 50 percent of all employed persons in the Slovenian border communities. In a related work, Vresk (1984b) defined Zagreb metropolitan region as encompassing the city of Zagreb and that portion of its surroundings that 'is being transformed through daily migration of the labor force'. Based on this definition, the Zagreb metropolitan region was defined in 1981 to include ten urban municipalities (encompassing the administrative area of the City of Zagreb) and an additional 138 settlements in the surrounding area. The area of the metropolitan region had a star-like shape in accordance with the major traffic routes stretching from the city center toward the satellite nodes. The western extension was considerably shorter than the north, east and south extensions, obviously due to the proximity of the Slovenian-Croatian border. This fact, however, was neither explicitly mentioned nor alluded to.

Similarly, the spatial pattern of the public transportation system in the Zagreb region, studied by Sić (1984), suggested the presence of a boundary. The city public transportation system was basically organized within a 30-km radius from the city center. In its western part, this 30-km line theoretically included parts of the Slovenian territory; in practice; however, city's public transportation system did not cross the border. Again, the Slovenian-Croatian border and its impact on the configuration of the public transportation system were not mentioned, either explicitly or implicitly.

Evidently, the prevailing practice among geographers during the Yugoslav era was reflected in regional studies, the scope of which was determined by existing politico-territorial units. Rogić (1982) complained that nobody seemed to be inspired by the pioneer work of the Slovenian geographer Anton Melik, who was the first one to address Yugoslavia's territory as a geographical unit regardless of internal boundaries. With exception of a few geographic textbooks covering the physical (and occasionally economic) geography of the Yugoslav territory, professional geographic work continued to be limited within the politico-territorial boundaries. Today it seems rather strange that the boundary with Slovenia and its possible impacts were never explicitly mentioned, although it was continuously reproduced in professional geographic writings. Paraphrasing Rogić (1982), one can argue that the implicit reproduction of the Croatian-Slovenian boundary reflects the fact that, in reality, interactions among social actors and professional actors, as well as patterns of every day life, were limited by existing political-territorial boundaries.

There was common knowledge, however, that Zagreb's functional region transcended the administrative – political boundary with Slovenia. The nearby spa in Čatež and several other resorts in Slovenia depended heavily on visitors from Zagreb. On the other side of the boundary, Zagreb was major center of higher education for residents of southeastern and eastern Slovenia. The Krško nuclear plant, built in late 1970s, is another example of cross-border economic ties during the Yugoslav era. Built in the Slovenian town of Krško barely 17 kilometers (10 miles) from the Croatian border, the plant was meant to become the major supplier of electric power for the Zagreb region as well as for all of northwestern Croatia. During its construction and afterward, through 1991, the majority of employees were commuters from Zagreb. These functional relationships, however, remained largely outside Croatia's professional geographic interest. One reason might be that the boundary was never perceived an issue; however why there was no interest in exploring real extent of Zagreb's spatial influence remains unexplained.

The evidence so far suggests that during the whole Yugoslav era the internal boundary between Croatia and Slovenia had been continuously reproduced despite a 'common' market and unifying tendencies on the part of the central government. Indeed, the very stability and uncontested nature of the boundary with Slovenia made it possible to neglect the boundary, but with the consequence of ignoring Zagreb's functional relationships with an area stretching beyond the political boundary. Geographic writings demonstrate that professionals contributed to the process of boundary reproduction, either through description of existing functional regions or through intellectual creation of potential functional regions. In either case, the functional relationship between Zagreb and its hinterland was actually and artificially contained within the political-territorial boundaries.

The International Boundary and the National Agenda

The stability of the Croatian-Slovenian boundary, in combination with more urgent issues stemming from war-devastated regions bordering Serbia (rump Yugoslavia) and war-infested Bosnia and Herzegovina in the early 1990s, resulted initially in neglect of the Croatian-Slovenian boundary by the independent Croatia. A perception was created that there was nothing to worry about. Compared with threats along Croatia's eastern, southern, and southwestern borders, this was largely true. The focus of national attention on these other areas obscured the larger picture and impeded preparations for developments that were taking place in the larger area.

Since independence, Croatian leadership has focused on establishing Zagreb's central role in the new political and economic organization of national territory. The national priority (outside of the liberation of occupied territory) has been the linking of the Zagreb region with the Republic's southern (Adriatic coast) and eastern regions. Partly, these needs were an outgrowth of the redefined territorial organization. First, links with other adjacent areas, now within new (and still hostile) political-territorial entities (rump Yugoslavia, Bosnia, and Herzegovina), were cut off or significantly reduced. Secondly, it was politically important to link peripheral regions in the process of consolidating the redefined national territory.

During the first few years after proclamation of independence integration with Central and Western Europe was of secondary importance for Croatia's political leadership. Serbia's aggression on Croatian territory and its relationships with Bosnia and Herzegovina, together with ethnic issues arising from these new relationships, dominated the professional literature as well. In the proceedings of a 1993 symposium organized by Croatian geographers (Crkvenčić, Klemenčić and Feletar, 1994), the majority of papers dealt with issues of ethic structure, aggression, and relationships with neighboring countries. Only two papers (Foucher, 1994; Haberl, 1994), out of a total of 18, explicitly discussed Croatia's position within the new geography of Europe.

Croatia's initial lack of focus on the boundary with Slovenia was matched by Slovenia's neglect of its east and southeast boundary. Several reasons can be cited for this neglect. First, except for a short conflict with the Yugoslav army during the first week after breaking away from Yugoslavia, Slovenia's transition to independence was peaceful. Second, Slovenia continues to enjoy the most favorable geographic location of all former Yugoslav republics in relation to

Western and Central Europe. This has allowed Slovenia's leaders to focus on building trade relations with Europe as fast as possible, while detaching themselves from the rest of Yugoslavia. Third, traffic and trade with Croatia and the rest of former Yugoslavia were severely disrupted by war on Croatia's territory, further contributing to the detachment of Slovenia from the other former Yugoslav republics. This coincided with an overall cultural shift in orientation toward 'Europe' and away from 'the Balkans'. The Croatian-Slovenian boundary, as perceived by leading actors in Slovenia, came increasingly to coincide with the boundary separating Slovenia from the 'rest of Yugoslav republics' (Klemenčič, 1993; Kukar, 1993). The border was further reinforced as a hard boundary when large numbers of refugees from war-torn Bosnia and Herzegovina tried to enter West Europe through Slovenia.

The overwhelming focus of Croatia's leadership on internal restructuring in part explains why it was not immediately clear what the implications might be of a dispute over boundary definition in Piran Bay, the location of Slovenia's main port of Koper, for the economic development of Zagreb and the whole Republic. Soon, however, it became clear that the outcome would be costly. The land boundary between Croatia and Slovenia reaches the sea in the small Bay of Piran. According to Blake (1994) of the International Boundaries Research Unit, the maritime extension of this boundary should have been technically easy to delimit. Slovenian geographer Gosar (1996) argued that the problem stemmed from different views on the principles of boundaries, and differences between judicial definition and geographical demarcation. To the contrary, Klemenčić and Schofield (1996) argued that the bay was of minimal significance to Croatia and that the whole issue was tied to other unresolved boundary issues in a larger context. A resolution to this dispute might well have been achieved were it not for the existence of a much more sensitive maritime and territorial dispute with Montenegro (part of the Yugoslav federation), bordering on southern Croatia. And so, partly because of a fear of being forced to grant Montenegro the same privileges as Slovenia, Croatia's government prolonged resolving the dispute in Piran Bay. It is hard to decipher exactly whether Croatia's refusal to accommodate Slovenia's demand for free access in the Piran bay was a consequence of or a reaction to Slovenia's downgrading of highway system priorities in the Maribor area, which is a crucial link in Croatia's central European connection (see Figure 5.3). It is clear, however, that the two are closely related (Klemenčić and Schofield, 1996).[3] Two other minor disputes soon also emerged along the Croatia-Slovenia boundary. One involves a small military post on the mountain ridge (Sv. Gera); the other one concerns several small villages in Istria along a meandering river.

Although the prevailing perception in Croatia is that the Croatian-Slovenian boundary disputes are a temporary thing (*Croatia Weekly*, 1998-99), a solution has not yet been found, as of this writing.[4] In the end, the narrowly defined national agenda of the Croatian government has greatly contributed to reinforcement of the boundary with Slovenia. Not only has the boundary been redefined, but it may also be that some long-lasting 'intrusions' into development paths have been made. It is difficult to gauge what the real effects on trade would have been had the boundary dispute been avoided. Without the disputes, would Slovenia reprioritize its northeastern (Maribor) segment, and thus support Croatia's physical link with Central Europe? Would the development path have then been different? As for the Zagreb region, it is clear that the national agenda-driven policy toward the boundary with Slovenia increased Zagreb's 'borderness' by reinforcing the boundary with Slovenia. A narrow national interest has prevented reevaluation of the boundary in the context of increasing need to link Croatia with Europe.

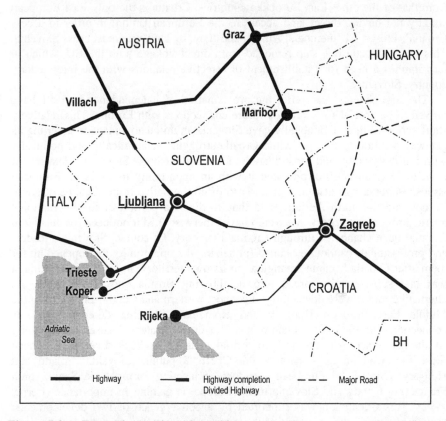

Figure 5.3   Zagreb's position after 1991
(Adapted from *Atlas Europe*, 1997; redrawn by Gabi Eigenmann and Andrea Ch. Kofler, University of Berne, Department of Geography)

Competition for a Gateway Position in the New Europe

With accession of Austria to the EU in 1995 as the last of the 'Western democracies', the outer border of the EU became superimposed on the recently abolished Iron Curtain. Mere physical proximity placed Slovenia and other former East Block countries – Hungary, Slovakia, the Czech Republic and Poland – not only in the first tier of potential new members in an expanding EU, but put each of these countries in a position of being a gateway to Europe's economic core. The decision by the EU to postpone Croatia's membership was largely based on issues associated with the war against Serbia's aggression (1991-95) followed by complex political efforts to address problems associated with international pressures to reabsorb persons displaced by the war.[5] The international EU community gave particularly heavy scrutiny to this latter issue. Regardless of these special conditions, Croatia's physical position in relation to the EU is different from that of the other East European countries. Croatia is the only East European country not having direct land access to the European Union; in order to access Croatia's closest EU members, Austria and Italy, by land, one must cross Slovenia. This keeps Croatia one step removed from direct linkage with the EU, which in turn implies a need for establishment of effective relations with the intermediary country, Slovenia.

The first several years after the proclamation of independence in 1991 have proved to be crucial for Croatia's future connections with Europe. This relatively short period of time undoubtedly gave Slovenia an initial advantage in asserting its gateway position to Europe, while Croatia struggled economically and politically with war devastation and consolidation of national territory. Slovenia's detachment from the Balkan conflict provided it with an opportunity to focus on European issues. Slovenia was also in a position to offer alternative routes between Central Europe and the north Adriatic, and thus to divert a portion of the international traffic through its territory that would have otherwise (had it not been for the war in Croatia) been channeled through Croatia's territory. Of course, Slovenia's leaders and professionals cannot be blamed for seizing the opportunity that opened up for them after Croatia became entangled, on its own territory, in a war with Serbia, a war that subsequently spread into neighboring Bosnia and Herzegovina. As alternative routes were developing to connect western and Central Europe with the Middle East (through Hungary and Romania), Slovenia de-emphasized its connection with the trans-Balkan routes. Slovenia's strategy focused on providing an alternative access to the northern Adriatic for the landlocked central European /East European states – namely the Czech Republic, Slovakia, Poland and Hungary. One of the European corridors, connecting Portugal via Spain, south France, north Italy and Slovenia to SE Europe, is gaining in importance (Černe, 1993). This orientation was supported by a convergence of two developments: transformation of the economy of these states under a free market ideology (and increased foreign investment), and general instability of the Croatian territory, which had historically served as the Adriatic connection.

Thus, Croatia was double 'cursed'; first, by mere fact that the war weakened its ability to adjust to the demands of increased traffic from and to Central and Eastern European markets; and second, by the ability of Slovenia to offer alternative routes and direct traffic and trade to its territory. Of course, aside from the (questionable) benefits of transit traffic, the question here is associated with the importance of routes in a larger, European and international context, and associated with this, the potential to attract international capital to fund infrastructure improvements. The completion of Europe's southeast-northwest axis (Istanbul-Athens-Belgrade-Zagreb-Hamburg) on Slovenia's territory was postponed until 2010 (Gosar, 1996), thus weakening Zagreb's second major transportation axis. The current changes in traffic flows have already influenced long-term construction plans important for participation in the economic flows in Europe. For example, Slovenia's priorities are focused on the southwest-northeast direction (with completion expected in 2003) and connection between the Austrian border (Šentilj), Italian border, and Koper in the southwest. By contrast, the connection between Maribor and the Croatian border (so vital for Croatia) was postponed until 2005 (see Figure 5.3). Slovenia also plans to construct a direct railroad link with Hungary, leaving Croatia out (Pelc, 1996). All this has a negative impact on Croatia, since it slows her integration with Europe.

Slovenia's initial detachment from its former 'brotherly' republics has been systematically reproduced in the Slovenian professional geographic literature. The Croatian-Slovenian boundary has been reinforced not only as the administrative–territorial divide, but as a cultural divide as well. Gams (1994) for example, used 'geographical constants' to justify Slovenia's separation from Yugoslavia. By implicitly reinforcing the boundary with Croatia as a line where Europe ends and Balkans begins, the politico-geographical concept of 'the Balkans' was stretched to its maximum extent. In a recently published *Geography of Europe* (Brintovec, Drobnjak, Pak and Senegačnik, 1994), Slovenia's geographers have excluded Croatia from Central Europe, which they have defined as encompassing Germany, Poland, the Czech Republic, Slovakia, Switzerland, Austria, Hungary, and Slovenia. Croatia, according to these Slovenian geographers, is defined as a part of southeastern Europe together with Bosnia and Herzegovina, Romania, Albania, Macedonia, and Bulgaria. The authors grouped these countries together and identified them as 'the Balkans' based on 'geographical location, accessibility for transport, national tension, continuous border disputes, and economic underdevelopment'. Consequently, by definition, the Zagreb region was included in politico-cultural designation 'Balkans' and thus excluded from politico-cultural 'Europe'. Despite the fact that the last statement looks most ridiculous, one should not forget the power of professional rhetoric. As noted by Paasi (1996), scientists in particular have the power to make people believe in their accounts, and thus signifying and legitimizing various practices and distinctions.

While Croatia's national political agenda was still very much focused on the consolidation of the national territory, the professional interest of leading geographers shifted to Croatia's new geographical position. An opportunity to showcase Croatia internationally and present it as a gateway to Europe came with a special issue of GeoJournal (Crkvenčić, 1996). Out of 12 papers, five focused on Croatia's position within restructured Europe. The selection of papers reflected Croatia's need to justify its victory in achieving independence from Yugoslavia. It was also obvious that Croatia had to fight for its status within Europe. After succeeding in politically detaching itself from Yugoslavia and the Balkans, Croatia's new struggle began against exclusionary tendencies in the new Europe. Besides tremendous material damage and lost economic benefits due to the war against Serbia, the real war would soon begin for Croatia's position in Europe. This is viewed as particularly important in Croatia, where there is 'a deeply held desire on the part of both government and most Croats to be seen as a central rather than south-eastern European country' (Klemenčić and Schofield, 1996).

Increased competition between Zagreb and Ljubljana for the most favorable link between Central and Eastern Europe and the north Adriatic ports has been documented in several studies by Slovenian geographers. For instance, Jurič (1996) presented data that suggested that Slovenian port of Koper was developing into the 'first Austrian port' by accounting for 35 percent of Austria's maritime cargo in 1995. His data also show that Koper increasingly attracted cargo from and to Hungary, even though the Croatian port of Rijeka has a better railroad connection with Budapest via Zagreb. However, this may change as Slovenia improves its highway and railroad connections with Hungary.

Another study (Pelc, 1996), which gathered evidence on highway traffic patterns, suggests profound changes in the importance of main routes relevant for the Zagreb region. First, Pelc's data indicate increased traffic flows between Slovenia and Hungary. Border crossing at Dolga Vas on the Slovenian-Hungarian border experienced the highest increase in total traffic, and particularly in cargo traffic, to and from Hungary. The share in total cross-border traffic increased from less than 2 percent in 1985 to almost 9 percent in 1996. By contrast, the border crossing at the Croatian-Slovenian border near Zagreb experienced a drop of almost 50 percent in 1995 compared to 1985. Furthermore, Pelc's (1996a) data suggest that the importance of the Zagreb-Vienna route through Maribor (Slovenia) decreased from about 25 percent in 1985 to about 14 percent of all traffic through Slovenian border crossings in 1996. In another article Pelc (1996b) shows that non-commercial traffic through Maribor is largely related to Zagreb's connection with Austria. This is one of the routes commonly used by thousands of temporary workers in Austria and Germany, and by Croatian citizens outshopping in Graz.

While new and more systematic data are needed to more objectively assess changing traffic flows, these figures clearly reflect changes in geographical and transportation utilization of the Slovenian and Croatian territory in relation to Central Europe.

Conclusions

In combination with macroregional geopolitical changes, the upgrading of an internal boundary to an international border changed the relative meaning of the geographical location of the Zagreb region. First, the mere physical proximity of the new international boundary with Slovenia made Croatia's capital Zagreb and its surrounding area implicitly a border region. While this fact was obvious, its implications were less clear. The new borderness was overshadowed by Zagreb's role as Croatia's central region based on its historical role and contemporary emphasis on consolidation of national territory in the aftermath of the 1991-95 war.

Meanwhile, the restructuring process in the larger European context continued to redefine spaces within the new national boundaries.

The rise of 'Fortress Europe' (see Welch, Chapter 4 in this book) and prospects of Slovenia's acceptance into the European Union further reinforced the Croatian-Slovenia boundary. Increased competition for gateway positions on the edge of the European Union continued to redefine all boundaries and spaces. The implications of the current exclusion of Croatia from European organizations, as noted by Klemenčić and Schofield (1996), is likely to deter badly needed investment and thus undermine long-term (economic and ultimately political) stability.

In summarizing the implications of the Croatian-Slovenian boundary one cannot avoid a comparison with a historical 'accident' of the 19th century, when the basis for today's railroad network was built under the Austrian and Hungarian models. As noted by Rogić-Nehajev (1997) the formation of the Croatian transportation network during the first modernization phase was primarily a reflection of strategies outside Croatia's space. It was because of the 19th century Hungarian interests in the northern Adriatic that Zagreb was included in the railroad network. It is as true today as then that Zagreb's position needs to be evaluated in a larger context, i.e. in the context of a periphery. Zagreb, and Croatia as a whole, was then and is today, part of a periphery. From a regional economic development perspective, Croatia will benefit more whenever its interests are aligned with those of the European center. Because of intensified competition, today's Croatia competes with a number of other contenders for a favorable position on the periphery, most notably with Slovenia.

To change the country's status, several initiatives must be taken. First, Croatian intellectuals need to rethink globalization and determine how to make the best use of foreign investment. Second, while the current focus on nationalism is understandable, the country needs to explicitly recognize its peripheral location and to act on this recognition. This includes consideration of the current and potential roles played by the nation's boundaries in impeding or facilitating Croatia's development and integration into both European and world contexts. Third, national, regional, and local policy needs to reflect recognition of the fact that international and global forces will inevitably continue to affect Croatian interests. It is in the best interest of Croatia to define ways to develop international and global alignments that benefit the country and its citizens. Finally, a degree of flexibility should be built into the nation's structures, in reflection of the fact that geographies are constantly being redefined by changing constellations of power relationships, economic processes, and cultural imperatives. Responding to such changes effectively requires a will to balance national identity with larger structural realities.

Acknowledgments

This article would not have been possible without the Fulbright Research Award (Austria, 1997-98) that allowed the author to experience firsthand the new winds in the region and learn from numerous exchanges with European colleagues and their works. Special thanks to the University of Klagenfurt Department of Geography for being a wonderful host.

Notes

1 Discussions with leading geographers at the University of Zagreb, Croatia, during 1997.
2 1918-29: The Kingdom of Serbs, Croats and Slovenes; 1929-41: Yugoslavia (monarchy); 1941-45: disintegrated, with large parts occupied by Italians and Germans; 1945-91: federative republic of Yugoslavia.
3 In Slovenia's plan, construction of the stretch of highway between Maribor and Croatia's border was postponed.
4 As of December 2001, an agreement on boundary delineation in the Piran Bay was proposed and signed by the presidents of Croatia and Slovenia. However, neither parliament was ready to ratify it. See: 'Problem granice ne smije utjecati na Krško', *Zajedničar*, December 19, 2001. For a more detailed discussion of the proposed solution see A. Gosar and M. Klemenčić (2000). 'Les problèmes de la délimitation de la frontière Italie-Slovénie-Croatie en Adriatique septentrionale', p 123-134 in *Mare Nostrum. Dynamiques et mutations géopolotiques de la Méditerranée*. Série 'Culture et politique', Paris and Montéal: L'Harmattan, Inc.
5 The Yugoslavian conflicts resulted in multiple episodes of 'ethnic cleansing' (i.e., relocation of ethnic groups outside the boundaries of the state). Recently, international pressure has mounted on the former Yugoslav republics, including Croatia, to reabsorb these displaced persons, including Serbs and Bosnians. However, there are no simple answers. In Croatia, for example, the homes of these individuals largely now are occupied by Croats expelled from the other republics.

References

Barth, F. (1969), 'Introduction', in F. Barth (ed.), *Ethnic Groups and Boundaries: The social Organization of Culture Differences*, Allen and Unwin, London, (Cited in Paasi, 1996).
Berry, B.J.L.; Conkling, E.C. and Ray, D.M. (1993), *The Global Economy, Resource Use, Locational Choice and International Trade*, Prentice Hall, Englewood Cliffs, NJ.
Blake, G.H. (1994), 'Croatia's Maritime Boundaries. Croatia – A New European State, Hrvatska – nova europska država', *Proceedings of a symposium held in Zagreb and Čakovec, Zagreb, September 22-25*.
Brintovec, S.B.; Drobnjak, B.; Pak, M. and Senegačnik, J. (eds.) (1994), *Geografija Europe*, Mladinska knjiga, Ljubljana.
Crkvenčić, I. (ed.) (1996), 'The Republic of Croatia: Mediterranean and Central European State', *GeoJournal*, 38(4).
Crkvenčić, I.; Feletar, D. and Klemenčić, M. (eds.) (1994), 'Croatia – A New European State, Hrvatska – nova europska država', *Proceedings of a symposium held in Zagreb and Čakovec, Zagreb, September 22-25*.

Černe, A. (1994), 'The Transport System of Slovenia', *GeoJournal*, 33(4), pp. 335-338 (Reprint).

Croatia Weekly: Politics, Economy, Culture and Sports, Croatia's weekly newspaper, Published by Croatian Institute for Culture and Information, Various issues 1998-99.

Feletar, D. and Stiperski, Z. (1990), 'Razvojne faze I procesi disperzije industrije Zagreba', *Acta historico-oeconomica Iugoslavae*, 17(1), pp. 175-198.

Feletar, D. and Stiperski, Z. (1994), 'Die Umstrukturierung der Industrie Kroatiens in den neuen Bedingungen. Croatia – A New European State, Hrvatska – nova europska država', *Proceedings of a symposium held in Zagreb and Čakovec, Zagreb, September 22-25*.

Foucher, M. (1994), 'Croatia, a New geography of the European Continent. Croatia – A New European State, Hrvatska – nova europska država', *Proceedings of a symposium held in Zagreb and Čakovec, Zagreb, September 22-25*.

Gams, I. (1994), 'The Republic of Slovenia – Geographical Constants of the New Central European State', *GeoJournal*, 33(4), pp. 331-340 (Reprint).

Gosar, A. (1996), 'Selected Topics in Political Geography', in *Slovenia. A gateway to Central Europe*, The Association of the Geographical Societies of Slovenia, Ljubljana, pp. 7-16.

Haberl, O.N. (1994), 'Croatia and Germany in Europe. Croatia – A New European State, Hrvatska – nova europska država', *Proceedings of a symposium held in Zagreb and Čakovec, Zagreb, September 22-25*.

Hrvatska akademija znanosti i umjetnosti (HAZU) (1996), Hrvatska. Prilozi za strategiju razvoja.

Jelen, I. (1970), 'Stanje zagrebačke industrije 1967 godine i neka gledanja na dalji razvoj njene strukture i prostorni razmještaj', *Geografski glasnik*, 32, pp.123-135.

Jurič, I. (1996), 'Koper - Maritime Gateway to Central Europe', in *Slovenia. A Gateway to Central Europe*. The Association of the Geographical Societies of Slovenia, Ljubljana, pp. 33-41.

Klemenčič, M. (1993), 'Slovenia - Between the East and the West, Between the North and the South', paper presented at the European Summer Institute in Regional Science, Joensuu, Finland, June 1993.

Klemenčić, M. (ed.) (1997), *Atlas Europe*, Leksikografski zavod Miroslav Krleža, Zagreb, Croatia.

Klemenčić, M. and Schofield, C. (1996), 'Croatia's territorial consolidation and prospects for the future', *GeoJournal*, 38, pp. 393-398.

Krugman, P. (1994), *Peddling Prosperity. Economic Sense and Nonsence in the Age of Diminished Expectations*, WW Norton & Co, New York.

Kukar, S. (1993), 'Regional Challenges of a Small Open Economy. The Case of Slovenia', paper presented at the European Summer Institute in Regional Science, Joensuu, Finland, June 1993.

Malić, A. and Božičević, D. (1996), 'Croatia in the Continental Traffic Network of Europe', *GeoJournal*, 38, pp. 463-468.

Paasi, A. (1996), *Territories, Boundaries and Consiousness: The Changing Geographies of the Finish-Russian Border*, John Wiley & Sons, New York.

Pak, M. (1993), 'Slovenia and its neighboring countries', paper presented at the European Summer Institute in Regional Science, Joensuu, Finland, June 1996.

Pelc, S. (1996), 'European Significance of the Slovene Traffic Network', in *Slovenia: A Gateway to Europe*, Association of Geographical Societies of Slovenia, Ljubljana, p. 25-31.

Porter, M.E. (1990), *Competitive Advantage of Nations*, The Free Press, New York.

Robins, K. and Morley, D. (1993), 'Euroculture: Communications, community and identity in Europe', *Cardozo Arts and Entertainment Law Journal*, 11, pp. 387-410. (cited in Paasi 1996).

Rogić-Nehajev, I. (1997), *Tko je Zagreb? Prinos sociološkoj analizi identiteta grada Zagreba*, Hrvatska sveučilišna naklada, Zagreb.

Rogić, V. (1982), *Regionalna geografija Jugoslavije, Knjiga 1. Prirodna osnova I historijska geografija*, Školska knjiga, Zagreb.

Rogić, V. and Žuljić, S. (1972), *Geografija Jugoslavije za IV razred gimnazije*, Školska knjiga, Zagreb.

Sić, M. (1968), 'O pojavi prostorne decentralizacije industrije Zagreba', *Geografski glasnik*, 30, pp. 127-142.

Sić, M. (1984), 'Razvoj mreže gradskog autobusnog prometa kao pokazatelja urbanizacije Zagreba', *Radovi Geografskog odjela*, 19, pp. 51-58.

Vresk, M. (1984a), 'Dnevni urbani sistem Zagreba', *Geografski glasnik*, 46, pp. 109-118.

Vresk, M. (1984b), 'Metropolitanska regija Zagreba 1981. Godine', *Radovi Geografskog odjela*, 19, pp. 59-66.

Žuljić, S. (1965), 'Zagreb i okolica. Utjecaj gradskog organizma na regiju', *Geografsi glasnik*, 25, pp. 65-82.

Žuljić, S. (1974/75), 'Razvoj Zagreba i urbanizacija Središnje Hrvatske', *Geografsi glasnik*, 36/37, pp. 43-57.

Chapter 6

Renewal of Cross-Border Cooperation along the Hungarian-Croatian Border

Zoltán Hajdú

Introduction

The 355-kilometer stretch of border between Hungary and Croatia is the most unique and complex portion of the Hungarian national boundary, and is the only section of the nation's boundaries that has a long historical tradition. For 800 years, in fact, the borderlands in this region were interlinked, rather than segregated, by a boundary line.

The outcomes of political and administrative changes related to the formation and dissolution of Yugoslavia (1918, 1941, 1945, 1991),[1] affected the outcomes in the Yugoslav space influenced by Hungary differently. The characteristics of the present Hungary-Croatia state boundary, its functions of linking or separating the two countries, are significantly influenced by the situation in the neighboring border regions, by the legal status of Croatia and by changes in contacts between Hungary and its southern neighbors.

The admission and provision of Croatian, Serbian, Hungarian and Bosnian refugees who crossed the border out of Croatia (referred to in the text as 'Yugoslav' refugees, because they came from the territory of former Yugoslavia) without doubt contributed to a growth in trust and respect between the two countries. This is especially true with regard to the populations living in the border regions. Historically strained relations across the border also lessened, though new types of tensions also evolved.

During their stay in Hungary, Yugoslav refugees created diverse relationships, which in some cases even reshaped life in the border communities. In some communities of South-Transdanubia, the proportion of refugees was greater than five percent of the total population; in refugee literature this is considered to be a critical threshold. Both the picture and the lifestyle of some settlements in Baranya County, for example, developed an 'eastern' or 'Balkan' character.

For the new, independent Croatia the priority was, and partly still is, achieving sovereignty over its entire internationally accepted state territory,[2] and carrying out the tasks of state establishment. In comparison with these priorities, problems of cross-border cooperation are, of course, treated as a secondary issue. Notwithstanding that Hungary-Croatia interstate relations are free of problems, the reshaping and deepening of border-region relations cannot yet be expected.

Historic Landmarks and Characteristics of Cross-Border Cooperation

The history of the 800-year Hungarian-Croatian commonwealth reflects a series of contests that arose, beginning in the 11th century, from internal and external developments. Yet, despite frequent disputes, the border retained its peaceful character. Indeed, during these years, the boundary between Hungary and Croatia retained a largely administrative function. This boundary function persisted even though the actual boundary location changed several times, reflecting a gradual drawing back into Hungarian territory to the Drava-Danube Rivers following the intrusion of the Ottoman Empire into southeastern Europe. The drawing back of the boundary, in turn, was accompanied by Croatia's territorial expansion; thus, the living space of the Hungarians shrank while that of the Croatians and Serbs expanded.

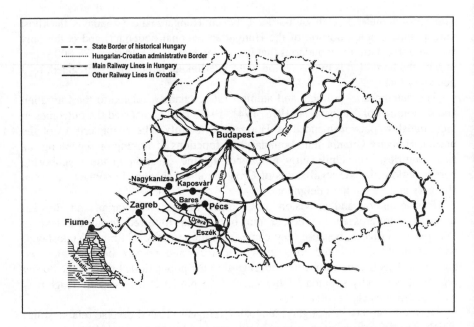

Figure 6.1   The transport-geographical position of Croatia in the historical Hungary before 1918

A compromise reached in 1868 between Hungary and Croatia, both within the Austro-Hungarian monarchy, allowed for separate legal regulation of the districts on each side of the shared boundary. The outcome of the compromise was that Croatia-Slavonia was accorded co-dominion status with Hungary, and was given considerable autonomy with regard to internal governance. This autonomy did nothing, however, to disrupt existing spatial patterns of economic relations, transportation, finance, and citizenship.

During this same time period, at all scales from micro- to macro-level, railway infrastructure was developed to connect the lands on either side of the Drava River and thus create a single integrated social structure. Linkages with the Croatian port of Rijeka were strengthened as well, in recognition of the strategic importance to Hungary of having access to a modern seaport. These linkages prompted development of the only macro-regional level connection between Croatia and Hungary: that running between Budapest, Zagreb, and Rijeka (Fiume). A supplementary transportation axis evolved from this spatial relationship, as illustrated in Figure 6.1.

The Drava River was the most important navigation corridor in the region, and the ferry that connected the two sides of the river played an important role in micro-regional relations. Of particular significance, the ferry allowed the mixed-nationality population living on either side of the river to establish a range of economic and social relations. Further, the community of Barcs, on the Hungarian side of the river, became a very important shipping center on the Drava River.[3]

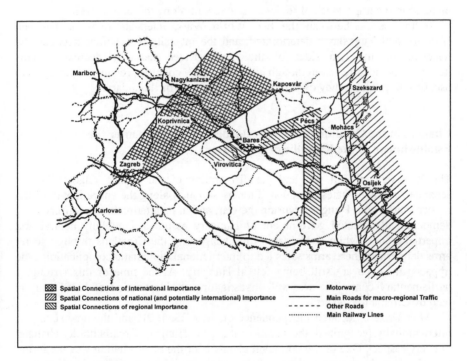

Figure 6.2   Spatial connections and structures across the Hungarian - Yugoslavian border before 1990

In 1910, 194,000 Croatians lived in 'mother Hungary', most of whom (174,346) were concentrated in the South-Transdanubia area. By contrast, in that same year, only 105,000 Hungarians lived in Croatian territory, with the largest populations concentrated in Osijek (3,729), Zagreb (4,028) and Rijeka (6,493).

After 1918 in the wake of World War I, state formation, development and dissolution processes within the former Austro-Hungarian empire changed the nature of the Croatia-Hungary borderlands and the role of the boundary itself. One of the most important events was the signing of the Trianon Peace Treaty. The Treaty, far from accepting the former administrative border as the formal national boundary in this southern frontier of Hungary, actually de-annexed territories in the Mura region and in the Baranya triangle. These lands were absorbed into the new Serbo-Croatian-Slovene Kingdom. The new boundary severed former spatial, economic, transportation, and social connections between the two borderland regions, as well as between individual communities.

By the end of the epoch, interactions between Hungary and Croatia were operating at the national and macro-regional level (see Figure 6.2). These interactions preserved the Budapest-Zagreb-Rijeka axis. At the same time, the importance of the Danube as a primary transportation route increased, leading to an increase in the importance of regional interactions along this axis as well.

In the period between the two World Wars, interstate relations between Hungary and Yugoslavia deteriorated, and the intensity of relations between the residents on the two sides of the Drava River markedly decreased. This deterioration occurred even though citizens of both countries retained their rights to use, or sell, property they owned on the other side of the boundary.[4]

Changes in the Conditions of Cross-Border Cooperation after the Establishment of the Republic of Croatia

The Yugoslavian civil war and the dismantling of the former Yugoslavia into separate sovereign states has created a new situation along the entire length of the border shared with Hungary. During the war, and in its aftermath, the conservative, democratically elected government of Hungary assumed a publicly neutral and impartial stance, while at the same time supporting the Croatians through secret arms deliveries. These arms sales led to international diplomatic complications, the impacts of which are still being felt in Hungary. At the time of this writing, a parliamentary committee was still investigating the destination of US$1 million paid by Croatia for the arms.

After Croatia declared independence on June 25, 1991, and the new state was internationally recognized, the situation along the Hungary-Croatia border changed in every respect. One of the dominant elements of the new situation was the influx into Hungary, beginning in 1991, of several waves of refugees from various parts of former Yugoslavia. This change was superimposed on existing transboundary relations and on the social structure of the border region.

The refugee crisis in South-Transdanubia began in 1991, with the declaration of independence by Croatia and the beginning of the war between Croatia and 'rump Yugoslavia'. Open acts of war occurred on the Hungary-Croatia border in August, 1991, followed by Serb occupation of the Croatian territories in the Baranya triangle, eastern Slavonia, and western Syrmia, all of which have substantial portions of population of Hungarian descent. The occupation prompted large numbers of these individuals to flee their homes for the South-Transdanubia region.

Background information on the South-Transdanubia region provides a context for understanding the unfolding of the refugee situation. The four counties of South-Transdanubia, Baranya, Somogy, Tolna, and Zala, occupy a combined area of 18,010 square kilometers, 19.4 percent of the total territory of Hungary. The total population of the four counties is 1.3 million, constituting 12.7 percent of Hungary's total population. The region has a short border, located along the Danube River, with Serbia; a 133-kilometer common border with Croatia; and a 102-kilometer shared border with Slovenia.

The first refugee stations to accommodate the migrants were established in the South-Transdanubia border communities of Mohács, Nagyharsány, Siklós, and Harkány. The ethnic composition of the refugees arriving in these areas varied considerably, though in most periods Hungarians constituted the relative – and in some periods, absolute – majority. This fact is important for, prior to 1993, these refugees were able to acquire Hungarian citizenship relatively easily and quickly, and to integrate easily into Hungarian society.

The Hungarian communities, as well as the state institutions and religious and secular charity organizations, were hard pressed to establish a system for adequately sheltering and supplying the refugees. Temporary shelters were set up in the cities of Máriagyüd, Mohács, Nagyatád, Pécs, and Szigetvár immediately upon arrival of the refugees. In Nagy Harsány an ecumenical charity organization opened a refugee camp. These border communities made efforts that were often beyond their means to take care of the refugees. For example, the convalescent holiday settlement of Harkány, home to 3,500 inhabitants, sheltered and supplied more than 8,000 refugees. The communities of Kásád and Beremend, both located directly on the border and settled in part by Croatian minorities, also sheltered populations of refugees that exceeded the total resident population of the towns.

In January 1992, a cease-fire was introduced and a United Nations peace-keeping force (UNPROFOR) marched into the Croatian territories that had been under Serb occupation. The 'frozen situation', and the introduction of UN public administration (under UNTAES) brought some relief to the local population; however, the refugees did not return to their homes. Rather, they dispersed into the settlements and cities of South-Transdanubia. Depending on their financial resources, they either sustained themselves or registered officially as refugees. Most of the registered refugees became inhabitants of the existing refugee stations and camps.[5] Some of the refugees, however, primarily those arriving with financial reserves, could step away from the refugee situation and operate independently through running their own businesses. These individuals were able to stabilize their status as other than that of a refugee. The enterprises established by the Yugoslavs were either ones the Yugoslavs owned themselves or involved mixed ownership arrangements. Most were operated as partnerships. Some of the enterprises did not require substantial capital resources, while others involved less capital-intensive, limited-liability companies. Most of these businesses were trade or service companies, and therefore could be liquidated quickly and easily. Indeed, only a small number of these enterprises became productive businesses. Some of the firms engaged in illegal activities as well as legitimate business.

During their stay in Hungary, Yugoslav refugees developed a variety of relationships with local Hungarian residents, and even reshaped the life of the settlements to which they had relocated. In some settlements of the South-Transdanubia area, refugees came to account for more than five percent of the population.[6] Throughout the period, basic food supplies for refugees were maintained. However, the increasing length of the refugees' stay, originally expected to be no more than the equivalent of a short-term visit, gradually began to cause difficulties among the refugees themselves, and between the refugees and local residents. By January 1, 1997, the number of refugees had decreased to less than 4,000. Most were living in small towns such as Mohács, Siklós, and Nagyatád, and in Pécs. Those living in villages experienced, in some respects, the most difficulties. Even given the stresses associated with the border-area changes, however, trust and respect between Hungary and Croatia have grown in recent years. This trust is particularly evident among the local border populations, and has led to an easing of otherwise strained relations.

Beginning with the Croatian local government elections of April 13, 1997, reintegration of the border region gradually unfolded and returning home became a realistic possibility for the refugees living in Hungary. For these refugees, return was conditioned upon being registered by the Croatian Authority for Refugees and upon being a Croatian citizen. In the process, the boundary between Croatia and Hungary, established after the 1991 disintegration of Yugoslavia, became reaffirmed as the recognized international boundary between the two states.

Recently, new tensions have arisen. Uncertainty deriving from these tensions has not favored further development of amicable cross-border relations. As a result, relations in the borderlands, that is, between 'Greater Croatia' and 'Extended Hungary', remain somewhat clouded.

The return of the remaining refugees is not likely to occur quickly. According to the UN High Commissioner, within the span of only one month, the month of May 1997, more than 6,000 refugees[7] in Baranya County, all former residents of Croatia, were informed of the possibilities, conditions, and consequences if they chose to return to their former homes. By the end of August 1997, only 30 of the refugees had decided to return to Croatia.

Some of the ethnic Hungarian refugees, mostly those who had emigrated with their entire family and all of their property, will not ever return to their original place of residence. These individuals have already obtained Hungarian citizenship, or their requests for citizenship are in process. On the other hand, most of the others claiming Hungarian backgrounds will probably return eventually, especially if they have close ties with others who stayed 'home' to maintain the legal continuity of their family.

Most of the Croatian refugees will probably return to their original places of residence as well. For these individuals, it is important that, upon return, they will be members of a state-creating nation. Thus, in terms of history and in consideration of the fact that they will be living in the same state with their compatriots, significant advantage exists for returning home.

A Brief History of Interstate Relations

After 1945, the system of interstate relations between the two countries changed several times, and in contradictory ways, in no small part due to the nature of the socialist centralized state systems of the two countries. Beginning in 1948/1949, the Hungary-Yugoslavia border became one of the most critical border sectors within the political, ideological, and military oppositions existing in Europe. A landmined zone was created along the entire border and military entrenchment was initiated on the Hungarian side. The actions were unprecedented in this border region.

Beginning in the early 1960s, interstate relations gradually returned to normal. This process had a positive impact on the relationships between counties, cities, and economic entities on both sides of the border. In the 1970s, this positive impact extended to the transboundary movements of people as well. The city of Pécs and Baranya County were in the vanguard with respect to development of transboundary contacts between administrative units. In addition to the establishment of partnerships between cities and counties, development of the border region was identified as a requirement.

Initially, along the Hungary-Croatia border only one road crossing point existed, at Letenye, and only three railway crossings existed, located at Gyékényes, Magyarbóly, and Murakeresztúr to support macro-regional traffic. Later, the number of border crossings gradually increased with the addition of crossings at Udvar, Drávaszbolcs, Barcs, and Berzence. This pattern of traffic flows at the crossing points reflects the evolution and intensity of cross-border relationships at the macro- and micro-regional scale, as well as at the municipal scale.

In terms of cross-border economic relationships, through contracting out production of sugar beets, soybeans, etc., Yugoslav food-processing companies predominated in Hungary during the 1970s. Economic cooperation emerged in other areas as well.

Beginning in the 1970s, a new factor arose, which increased transboundary flows: cross-border shopping, in which the mix of products changes constantly. At the end of the 1970s, social and family relations came to be shaped, to a large extent, by these large volumes of transboundary movements, and intermediate trade became the defining characteristic of the lifestyles of ever-larger numbers of people.

Other unifying events occurring in recent years include the agreement reached in 1988, facilitating joint use of the common reaches of the Mura and Drava Rivers. This agreement stresses energetic use and cooperation. Other new opportunities to facilitate development on the Hungary-Croatia border also arose as a result of Baranya (in 1990) and Somogy (in 1989) joining the Alpe-Adria Working Committee. In conjunction with these arrangements efforts to stimulate development were undertaken, although they could not be completed due to lack of time. Nonetheless, the Alpe-Adria working Committee established a very important framework for interregional cooperation. Besides, European Union funded projects are initiated.

The Decline and Reorganization of Cross-Border Economic Relations

As a result of the Yugoslav war of 1991, political instability, and the cumulative impacts of the transformations that followed internal changes in the Hungarian social, economic, and political systems, most cross-border economic relations froze or ceased to exist. Already in 1990, border crossings had begun to radically decline.

Due to economic, social, and especially military events, portions of the Croatian market became uncertain and highly risky for Hungarian entrepreneurs. Cross-border trading relations grew with regard to the proportion of individual trade in areas such as gasoline and gun running. Counter trade and cash orders also grew. Unfortunately, however, there was no opportunity, in this context, to plan for the medium to long term.

Table 6.1   Croatian arrivals and Hungarian travelers crossing the
             Croatian-Hungarian boundary 1992-June 1997 (in thousands)

Period	Croatian Arrivals	Hungarian Travelers
1992	416.5	220
1993	2.198.8	583
1994	5.148.7	575
1995	5.573.3	283
1996	5.429.6	340
January 1997	310.5	18
February 1997	369.7	22
March 1997	559.4	15
April 1997	494.6	27
May 1997	544.1	31
June 1997	418.8	48

Source: Statisztikai Hav Kozlemények (Monthly Bulletin of Statistics) 1997/6, Budapest, Központi Statisztikai Hivatal, pp. 128-130; Idegenforgalmi Évkönyv (International Tourist Yearbook) 1994, Budapest, Központi Statisztikai Hivatal, pp. 30-32.

Following privatization in Hungary, the Hungarian economy, including the South-Transdanubia area, turned westward. Parallel to this change, the once-substantial agricultural production and trade with the former Yugoslavia declined. Ties with southern and southeastern Europe declined, and relationships among enterprises were restructured. This, in turn, hindered the reorganization of relationships between the two countries. New elements in cross-border relations included foreign trade companies established by refugees. These enterprises specialized to some extent in acquiring various export subsidies to sustain their activities.

In 1992, a growing number of Croatians began crossing into Hungary in search of consumer goods. Turnover in retail trade in the small cities along the border increased significantly, with statistics showing that 50 to 70 percent of all purchases of some goods were being made by Croatians. By contrast, the frequency of travel by Hungarians to Croatia decreased (see Table 6.1).

As the Croatian situation began to return to normal, during the period when the state of Croatia was under reconstruction, the Chamber of Industry and Commerce of Pécs and Baranya began organizing cross-border economic relations through opening a coordination and representation agency in Osijek. Even here, however, cross-border relations have continued to be plagued by significant difficulties.

Development in the Borderlands

Conditions along some sectors of the Hungary-Croatia border and the traffic at the different border crossings have developed in a variety of ways. The most problematic border sector was, and still is the Baranya triangle. The Serbs closed and mined the Hungarian-Croatian border in this area, rendering it for many years the most militarily closed and, in terms of cross-border cooperation, the most completely dead border in Europe. There was no legal way to cross the border; the road crossings at Udvar and Beremend, and the railway crossing at Magyarbóly were eliminated. Notably, some of the mines that exploded at this border affected Hungary.

The road crossing at Udvar was opened in October 1996, although with limited hours of operation and initially only for international peace-keeping traffic. Later, on January 6, 1997, it was opened for Hungarian citizens. However, it has only been since July 21, 1997, that the crossing point has been open 24 hours a day. The railway border crossing at Magyarbóly was first opened for cross-border traffic on September 3, 1997. At first, most of this traffic involved UN peace-keeping (SFOR) vehicles destined for Bosnia-Herzegovina; now, civilian traffic is growing at the crossing.

By contrast, the border crossing at Drávasszabolcs has operated continuously, with few exceptions. Notably, at the ridge where the Croatian-Serbian battle lines were located, maintenance of traffic flows required significant effort on the part of the Croatians. Professional traffic continued to show the most significant increase at this border crossing, even after the intervention of the international community into the conflict in Bosnia. There have been significantly fewer problems at the Barcs border crossing, although accidental bombardment of the outskirts of the town by the Yugoslavs posed the threat of more serious conflicts. Barcs has gradually become the most important center for Croatian transboundary shopping. About half, and in some cases 80 to 90 percent, of the entire retail turnover of this small town of 13,000 is generated by Croatian guest shoppers.

Along the historic and strategic axis extending between Budapest and Zagreb, with regard to cross-border relations, only temporary disturbances have occurred. Since this route has been viewed as more secure, part of the traffic has shifted here from other border crossings.

For the newly independent Croatia, the priorities were, and to some extent still are, securing sovereignty throughout its entire internationally accepted state territory, and carrying out the tasks associated with state-building. Not surprisingly, in this context, cross-border relations with Hungary have become a secondary issue. Thus, despite the fact that Hungarian-Croatian relations are today free of problems, no reshaping nor deepening of border relations can yet be expected to occur.

Prospects for Cross-Border Cooperation

The conscious development of Hungarian-Croatian relations, based on mutual interests, could provide a good opportunity to reshape and redevelop cross-border relations. Peripheral and underdeveloped border areas in the region are especially interested in such development. But to achieve development, the issues and needs of the two states, at the national, macro-regional, county, micro-scale, and inter-community levels, must be considered. Among the issues important at the national level are transportation infrastructure, utilization of the Adria oil pipeline, and management/usage of the Drava River.

Establishment of high-capacity road connections is currently underway, based on national and international interests. The M7 motorway in Croatia has reached the Hungarian border, and planning is underway in Hungary for constructing the Hungarian portion of the motorway. Completion of the M7 will significantly shorten the distance to Rijeka and will increase that city's role in shaping contacts between sectors of the Hungarian economy and the outside world.

In the new European transportation system, sanctioned by the Helsinki Conference of the European Ministers of Transport in July 1997, the Budapest-Osijek-Sarajevo-Ploče axis, as a branch circuit, would serve security interests first, but it could also come to have a growing economic role. Unfortunately, the construction of the southern (Hungarian) sector of the system cannot be financed because of limited national resources, making establishment of the linkage, the need for which has so often been cited, questionable.

The Danube River plays, at present, a less important role in cross-border relations between Hungary and Croatia, but it could become a significant space of cooperation. The 'rediscovery' of the Danube after the Yugoslavian war and the related UN embargo offers significant opportunities for Hungarian entrepreneurs to join in Croatian reconstruction along the river. This activity has, to date, only partially been initiated, due to lack of capital among Hungarian companies and even more due to hindrances posed by Croatian protectionism.

The idea of a 'Danube region', though today still only an illusion, could become the locus of Hungary-Serbia (Yugoslavia)-Croatia trilateral cooperation. If this were to occur, Hungary could play a key role in the establishment and maintenance of cross-boundary contacts. Plans call for establishment of the first entrepreneurial zone in the South-Transdanubia area, which is of national importance to Hungary, in the town of Mohács. This economic region has potential to become the long-term motor of development for the tripartite border area.

The only issues concerning differences in border philosophy between the two countries are those associated with differences in approaches and interests with regard to the stretch of the Drava River. Croatia insists on sustaining the utilization formula for the river embedded in a 1988 agreement achieved by Hungary and Croatia; the Hungarian government has denounced the agreement. Similarly, regional parties have concerns regarding the need to give priority to environmental protection considerations. By establishing the Danube-Drava National Park, Hungary has clearly articulated its long-term interests with regard to development in this area.

Demands for development of the border region are embedded in Hungary's regional development policy, as well as in the regional and county-level development policy for South-Transdanubia. This goal can, over the long term, be implemented only in collaboration with Croatia. This in turn requires at least a minimal set of common interests.

At the local level, the counties (Croatian Baranya, and Hungarian Baranya, Somoby and Virovitica), cities, and communities (including Pécs, Szigetvár, Barcs, Zalaegerszeg, and others) have, without exception, reestablished contacts with their former Croatian counterparts (Croatian Baranya, and the Croatian communities of Osijek, Prodrovska Slatina, Virovitica, and Varaždin). This is especially true with regard to the Hungarian communities.[8] Further extension and deepening of transboundary relationships is uncertain, however, due to the existence of a wide range of opportunities available to local Hungarian governments to establish contacts with other international entities located elsewhere in the world.

The existence of other opportunities elsewhere notwithstanding, numerous initiatives aimed at linking the two states across their common boundary are currently underway. Territories in the southern portion of the Hungarian county of Baranya, for example have an opportunity to develop an extended gas supply via Croatia's delivery system. This is due to the fact that the Croatian pipelines, which are located about 10 kilometers from the border, currently have significant surplus capacity. Negotiations have been initiated to construct the extension, though issues remain with regard to estimating supply risks.

Renewed cooperation is also evident in the array of agreements that have been reached between the two states. These agreements address the demands for development in the economic, cultural, sports, and institutional arenas and support a renewed emphasis on exchange programs and cooperation between schools. Settlements in the Baranya triangle located close to the boundary have initiated cross-border, inter-community interactions. Eighteen local governments in Croatia and 19 local governments in Hungary have expressed common interest in establishing economic, social, and environmental cooperation. At the same time, local Hungarian governments have significantly assisted reorganization of life in the communities within the Baranya triangle.

Barcs, already a center for cross-border shopping, has been a focus of both local and national initiatives aimed at transforming the community into a (broadly defined) economically strategic border town. In addition to modernization of the vehicular bridge, enhancement of road system capacity, and transformation of the community into an entrepreneurial zone, demand has also arisen to reconstruct cross-border railway connections.

Development of micro-regional relations more generally requires establishment of new border crossings. Isolation of peripheral areas in the border region could be reduced through development of more local border crossing points. The opening of border crossings at Beremend, Vajszló-Sellye and Vizvár appear, at present, most likely. The opening of the Beremend border crossing, for example. would improve the ability of the Beremend Cement and Lime Works to participate in Croatian reconstruction activities.

In terms of the movement of people across the boundary, previous traffic volumes have not yet been restored, in no small part because the border was so heavily mined by the Yugoslav Army during the 1991 war. The number of entries into Hungary by Croatian citizens is gradually growing, while the crossing of Hungarians into Croatia, especially at border crossings east of Barcs, lags far behind levels experienced before the 1991 war. In this case, travel and contacts by Hungarians remain problematic.

Conclusions

The history of Hungary-Croatia cross-border relations has been quite varied, and in some periods, such as the 1990s, even tragic. The conditions and framework of cross-border relations have always been determined in the first instance by the relationship between the two countries, and sometimes even by larger international interests. At the same time, the lives of the populations of the border region have been characterized by adjustments to given conditions and circumstances. Their lives have been influenced primarily by the disadvantages, though also sometimes by the advantages, of being located in a border location.

Croatia's achievement of independence, followed by internal stabilization, has created favorable preconditions for development of cordial relations with Hungary, ones founded on a balancing of interests. Due to the historical experiences of the two countries, the reshaping of various micro-regional cross-border relations can only be expected to occur over the long term; however, it is in the best interests of the populations of both countries, and of the border regions, to pursue these goals.

Notes

1   The years 1918-1941 a constituted the period of the first Yugoslav state (the Kingdom of Serbs, Croats and Slovenes, later the Kingdom of Yugoslavia); the period from 1941 to1945 was characterized by the formation of an independent Croatian state; the period from 1945 to 1991 constituted the Federated Republic of Yugoslavia. In 1991, the disintegration of Yugoslavia occurred, followed by the formation of the Republic of Croatia as an independent state, as well as the independent state of Slovenia.
2   At the time of this writing, the Baranya triangle bordering Hungary was still under the control of Serbian forces.
3   Unfortunately, although the city was planned to be another Chicago in terms of its expected role as a transshipment point, it remained simply 'Barcs'.
4   In recent years, in the wake of political transformation associated with the demise of the former Soviet Union, Hungary has refocused its management of its border rivers to address environmental problems.
5   The largest refugee camp occupied the former army post of Natyatád. The camp housed as many as 2,800 refugees. The entire population of Kórógy, a Hungarian community in Slavonia, was housed at the camp in Vésy.
6   This is considered to be a critical threshold.
7   This figure indicates a need to remain skeptical with regard to data produced by various sources.
8   As of 1997, Croatian communities were rather constrained in their latitude to establish such contacts because of unresolved questions, associated with military unrest, about consolidation of territory in the region.

References

Hajdú, Z. (1996), 'A magyar-horvát határmenti együttmuködés delemmái', in Pál, Á. and Szónokyné Ancsin, G. (eds.), *Határon innen – Határon túl*, JGYTF, Szeged, Jate, pp. 306-312.
Hajdú, Z. (1997), 'Emerging conflict or deepening cooperation? The case of Hungarian border regions', in P. Ganster, A. Sweedler, J. Scott and W.D. Eberwein (eds.), *Borders and Border Regions in Europe and North America*, State University Press, San Diego, pp. 193-211.
Idegenforgalmi Évkönyv (International Tourist Yearbook) 1994, Budapest, Központi Statisztikai Hivatal.
Juhász, J. (1997), *A dészláv háborúk*, Napvilág Kiadó, Budapest.
Kocsis, K. (1993), *Jugoszlávia. Egy felrobbant etnikai mosaik esete*, Teleki László Alapítvány, Budapest.
Litauszki, I. and Todorovic, B. (eds.) (1975), *A magyar-jugoszláv vízgazdálkodási együttmuködés 20 éve*, Vizdok, Budapest.
Pavlicevic, D. (1996), 'A review of the historical development of the Republic of Croatia', *GeoJournal*, 38(4), pp. 381-391.
Pribicevic, D. (1996), 'Croatian approach of regional cooperation in Central Europe', in P. Bajtay (ed.), *Regional Cooperation and the European Integration Process: Nordic and Central European Experiences*, Hungarian Institute of International Affairs, Budapest, pp. 153-156.
Sokcsevits, D.; Szilágyi, I. and Szilágyi, K. (1994), *Déli szomszédaink története*, Bereményi Könyvkiadó, Budapest, Népek Hazája, No. 4.

Statisztikai Hav Kozlemények (Monthly Bulletin of Statistics) 1997/6, Budapest, Központi Statisztikai Hivatal.

Toldi, F. (1995), *A Jugoszláv állam kialakulása és felbomlása*, MTA Állam- és Jogtudományi Intézete, Budapest.

Zsilincsar, W. (1996), 'Az 1991-es jugoszláv válság: egy regionális földrajzi vizsgálat kísérlete', in *Tér, Gazdaság, társadalom*, Huszonkét tanulmány Berényi Istvánnak, MTA Földrajztudományi Kutató Intézete, Budapest, pp. 191-204.

Chapter 7

Conflict and Accommodation in the Arizona-Sonora Region

Pablo Wong González

Introduction

Paradoxically, megatrends in international integration and globalization are being accompanied by the emergence of new regionalisms seeking to achieve greater territorial, economic, and political autonomy. Europe represents perhaps the best example of these tendencies. Some analysts have pointed out that European integration has led to the rise of *super-regions*, which Delamaide (1995) describes as territories spanning national borders and reflecting historical patterns of migration and trade, ethnic and linguistic heritage, and social customs.

Although different in nature and extent, similar processes are taking place in North America, particularly in the border regions. Apparently, in contradiction to notions of the 'disappearance' of national borders and increasing loss of control over national economies by nation-states, regions are becoming active players in forms of regional economic development that transcend international boundaries.

Although the development of *functional* regions in North America preceded the North American Free Trade Agreement (Swanson, 1994; Pavlakovich and Walker, 1996a), the signing of the agreement (NAFTA) encouraged the formation of *formal* transborder regions. Today, formal transboundary regions in North America exist in the Pacific Northwest Economic Region and the Red River Trade Corridor on the US-Canada border, and in the Camino Real Economic Alliance and the Arizona-Sonora Region on the Mexico-US border. These new developments, based on joint transborder actions, support Kenichi Ohmae's (1993) concept of 'region-state', and Boisier's (1993) notion of 'virtual regions'.

It has been recognized, however, that in the process of international integration and the rise of 'borderless' economies, former border regions are likely to manifest differences depending upon their economic potential or locational characteristics (Nijkamp, 1993). For example, differentiated sectoral and regional impacts in Mexico, generated by NAFTA, have been identified (Wong-González, 1991; Gutiérrez, 1994). But, unlike provisions embedded in the institutions of the European Union, NAFTA does not provide for any compensatory policies or funds aimed at reducing wide socio-economic differences among the different border regions. This renders the process of transborder regional integration between uneven partners more complex. As noted by Nijkamp (1993) these kinds of cases warrant some sort of regional policy or strategy aimed at avoiding unacceptable regional disparities that erode the benefits that might otherwise be gained from emerging integration.

Further complicating transboundary regional development, recent *development strategy visions* developed by the emerging transnational border regions do not explicitly set out goals for regional conversion. On the contrary, development strategies are strongly influenced by issues associated with the need to increase economic efficiency and regional competitiveness. Economic integration has become a common concept in the literature, but is still rather abstract when applied at regional levels. Faced with this problem, achieving a wider positive impact from transborder regional development programs requires the inclusion of, at a minimum, consideration of the following issues related to integration between uneven partners: (a) the nature/modality of integration; (b) the intra-regional spatial impacts of integration; (c) regional convergence/divergence; (d) sectoral impacts (complementarity versus intra-regional competition); (e) local community participation, and (f) decentralization and regional autonomy.

In this chapter, the case of the Arizona-Sonora Region will be used to discuss the major points and dilemmas faced in complex integration processes occurring among transnational border economic regions emerging in North America. The discussion will begin with consideration of concepts of the nation-state and emerging regionalism; this will be followed by a review of emerging formal transborder regions in North America.

The Decline of the Nation-State and the Emergence of a New Regionalism

One of the most notable consequences of globalization and international integration processes has been nation-states' gradual loss of control over their economies. As Nigel Harris (1986, p. 200) points out, 'the conception of an interdependent, interacting, global manufacturing system cuts across the old view of a world consisting of nations-states ...'. According to Harris, in the process of economic restructuring, the state's role tends to be reduced to that of mediator between external markets and local populations. This leads to erosion of the social foundation of the exercise of state power and the loyalty of the country's citizens (Harris, 1996). Further, the nation-state's diminishing monopoly over power is closely associated with megatrends that impose decentralization and a consequent redistribution of roles and decision-making among different levels of government (Boisier, 1992).

This phenomenon has been approached by different disciplines and from differing viewpoints. For instance, Kenichi Ohmae (1993) forecasts the end of the nation-state and, as a result, the rise of the 'region-state'. He argues that in a 'borderless world', the nation-state has become an artificial unit, one that is dysfunctional for the organization of human activities and the management of economic duties. Ohmae defines region-states as natural economic zones, as 'functional regions' that go beyond the limits of national borders (examples include

Tijuana-San Diego on the Mexico-US border and Hong Kong-Guandong in southern China). Similarly, Robert Reich (1993) suggests that this phase of profound transformation is leading to the end of what is 'national', there will no longer be any 'national' products, technologies, or industries. With regard to the nation-state, Reich goes even further, pointing out that 'the nations can no longer promote the welfare of the citizens through subsidies, protection, or increasing the profitability of its companies' (1993, p. 153).

From the perspective of technological innovation, it has been suggested that the nation-state is about to become a casualty of the information science revolution (Angell, 1995). There are those who even argue that, at present time, the principal obstacle to economic globalization (mundialización) is the survival of national states, expressed in different legislation and national economic conditions, as well as in the persistence of 'state' interest (Vidal Villa, 1996). According to Vidal Villa, a phenomenon accompanying nation-state crises is the appearance of 'country' nationalisms. Manifestations of this type of nationalism, which is manifested as 'regionalism' inside the country, may be found in the contexts of the former Soviet Union and the former Yugoslavia. Though displaying different characteristics and levels of conflict, the Basque Country in Spain and Northern Ireland, constitute other examples of this process.

As mentioned above, within the European trend of 'regionalisms', the founding of the European Economic Community (EEC), which later evolved into the European Union, prompted creation of 'super-regions' (Delamaide, 1995). For Delamaide, these super-regions give shape to territories that transcend national borders. According to Delamaide, the European super-regions show a paradoxical double trend wherein economic and political integration occur simultaneously with a trend toward greater autonomy of the smallest regional levels, where social and cultural unity is greater. In terms of this redefinition of what is 'regional' in post-capitalist society, Peter Drucker (1994) argues that globalization has induced a return to tribalism, producing vindication at local levels.

New Forms of Competition and International Competitiveness of Regions

Regionalisms that have arisen in North America differ in tone, context, and causal elements from the ones in Europe. Some analysts, for example, see Quebec's most recent attempt to obtain independence from Canada as resulting from economic opening and free trade.[1] Others say that Quebec's actions should not be seen as an isolated event, but as a manifestation of more general trends present in other parts of the world, including Mexico – specifically the state of Chiapas.[2] These events have prompted the press to begin talking about possible 'Balkanization of the continent'.[3]

Without going to those extremes, it is possible to argue that, in Mexico, the conjunction of structural and circumstantial conditions that have pierced the country's economic, social, and political foundations have resulted in the rise of 'emergent regionalisms' (Wong-González, 1997a). Some of the expressions of regionalism are related to endemic socio-economic slowdown at the regional level, and patterns of domination (for example, challenges to national-level domination posed by the Chiapas Zapatista Army of National Liberation [EZLN]). In other cases, the rise of regionalisms reflects the negative impact of industrial restructuring, combined with regional inadequacy and social exclusion embedded in the prevailing policy framework (for example, depressed regions characterized by a traditional industrial base). Regionalisms related to the recent economic crisis and inconsistencies in economic policy have also emerged (as, for example, in agricultural valleys in Sonora and Zacatecas). Finally some expressions of regionalism are related to the ongoing process of international integration and globalization of the economy, notably in the new industrial regions of Northern Mexico.

Substantial differences exist among these 'regionalisms'. For instance, the objectives of the regional movements in Chiapas are to improve the quality of life of the people, to overcome social exclusion, to eliminate political-ethnic domination, and to achieve higher levels of local autonomy, democracy, and community management of resources. The new industrial regions in Northern Mexico, on the other hand, are demanding greater decentralization in all forms, whether at the level of the state or municipal government, or in terms of the activities of social and private promotion groups (such as the communally owned lands known as ejidos). Here the aim is to broaden negotiating power and economic promotion capabilities, through taking advantage of the development possibilities offered by globalization of national and regional economies. This expression of regionalism gives rise to a fifth type of emergent regionalism, one that has produced new forms of transborder regional planning and negotiation.

These regional actions, being taken at the international level, have generated intense competition among Mexican states, counties, and cities with regard to expanding exports and attracting investments. Similarly, competition among US states has increased with regard to participating in technology-transfer activities and signing trade agreements in Mexican territory.

During the last decade, most of Mexico's states have undertaken a variety of actions, including promotion efforts, abroad. This strategy has been carried out by northern states (Baja California, Sonora, Chihuahua, Nuevo León, etc.), as well as by the mid-western states (Aguascalientes, Jalisco and Colima), the southeastern states and the states in the Yucatán Peninsula (Oaxaca, Yucatán and Quintana Roo). Recognition of the importance of foreign trade for the development of regional economies, combined with recurrent unemployment, high costs, lack of national capital, and growing fiscal indebtedness have prompted a search for new forms of promotion and competitiveness.

A wide variety of strategies and actions have been developed to address these concerns, including the opening of promotion offices abroad and trade missions, development of special infrastructure, donations of land, creation of centers for special technical training, arrangement of favorable credits and fiscal incentives. Other strategies and actions include payment of relocation expenses, deregulation, programs for simplification of procedures, and establishment of organizations or offices specializing in economic development and foreign trade (see Table 7.1). Another recent action, induced by NAFTA and the globalization trend, has been the creation of 'Strategic Plans' or 'Great Vision Projects'. Among the most important are 'Chihuahua: the First XXI Century Economy in Mexico' (1994); 'Jalisco 2000: Facing New Realities' (1994); 'Veracruz in Front of the New Century' (1995); and 'Strategic Economic Development Vision for the Arizona-Sonora Region' (1995-1997). Paradoxically, as national states continue to neglect planning-oriented structures, the states and regions are subsuming such structures within their 'strategic models'.

Table 7.1   Activities for promotion of economic development and foreign investment attraction in selected states of Mexico

State	Types of Activities, Incentives, or Strategies
Aguas-calientes	Creation of the 'Development and Foreign Trade State Commission'; design of a promotion program abroad; granting of fiscal incentives to manufacturing enterprises; reduction of predial and real estate acquisition tax payments; granting of building permits; issuance of certificates, authorizations, etc., for amounts up to 50%; creation of a multi-modal loading terminal, the first of its kind for reception and shipment of containers carried via railroad and commercial transport.
Campeche	Supports the payment of the relocation expenses of any *maquiladora* with means from the Campeche fund, a group with private and public resources, whose headquarters are in San Diego, California.
Chihuahua	As part of development under the long-term plan 'Chihuahua XXI Century', 'Chihuahua Now' was created (this is a mixed organization that concentrates on overseas promotion efforts); advertising campaigns, opening of representation offices in key cities of Mexico, US and Canada, in order to carry out tasks more directly; and shipment of promotional materials to cities and strategic regions.
Estado de México	Support for 3 months' technical training, when required by the company.
Guanajuato	Founding of a public-private society called COFOCE to promote foreign investment.
Hidalgo	Elimination of lien duplication through reduction in procedures of state and local governments.
Jalisco	Temporary fee reduction and tax exemption; donation, rent or sale of properties at competitive prices; personnel training program; foreign trade and exports promotion program; deregulation and bureaucratic procedures-simplification program; legal and fiscal consulting; state of Jalisco economic promotion law; strategic development plan, 'Jalisco 2000: Frente a las Nuevas Realidades' ('Jalisco 2000: Facing New

State	Types of Activities, Incentives, or Strategies
	Realities').
Queretaro	Payment of three months' technical training, when requested by a company that will be starting operations in the state.
Sonora	New employees training program; support in the negotiation of procedures required by federal state and local authorities; measures for deregulation of economic activities; negotiation for the creation of the Sonora Competitiveness Center; promulgation of an economic development promotion law for the State of Sonora; carrying out of fairs and overseas promotion tours; opening of a trade-promotion office in Arizona; binational project 'Strategic Economic Development Vision for the Sonora-Arizona Region'.
Tlaxcala	Building of plants for companies wishing to establish themselves – these are later rented/sold to these companies; state support in negotiations to facilitate the installation of utilities, such as electric power and telephone lines.
Veracruz	The promotional activities that this state has carried out are from a project called 'Veracruz Facing the New Century', which is based on research done by state entrepreneurs, and where potential development sectors have been identified. With this project, Veracruz is developing a common strategy with states in southeastern Mexico and thus is creating new commercial relations among the Mexican states on the Gulf of Mexico seaboard and with states in the southern United States.
Yucatan	An industrial park has been designed to attract large and medium companies, especially high technology ones; once the company chooses a location, the state government procures for it a fifteen-year credit, with reduced interests that can be paid by on a leasing program; later on, the government pays for two-month training expenses for all the new company employees. This area has also developed promotion campaigns in the United States in order to attract investment, especially in the maquiladora sector, as well as partners in agribusiness, raw materials, and manufactured goods.

Source: Based on promotional official information from various state governments; complemented with information from the magazine Expansion, May 24, 1995, and the newspaper Excelsior, October 13, 1994.

Competition in promoting economic development, and the opening of markets for exports or attracting investments, not only occurs among the states, but also among sub-state regions, counties, and specific cities. For example, promotional activities in the State of Sonora have defined the area as a 'land of diversity'. These activities have been centered in Ciudad Obregon and in Hermosillo (the capital of the State of Sonora), where a promotion council was created. Notably, Hermosillo is now advertised as the 'capital of the Northwest' and the Municipal Economic Development Council was formed in Tijuana (capital of the State of Baja California). The council features both public and private participation in a bid to strengthen the city's diverse economic sectors; the council also provides the framework for promotion and strategic planning of Tijuana's development. On a national scale, local agents involved in economic promotion have declared that strong competition for the attraction of companies with foreign investments exists, especially in the maquiladora manufacturing sector, among three dynamic cities: Monterrey (Nuevo León), Ciudad Juárez (Chihuahua), and Tijuana.[4]

Although European and Asian capital has consistently been increasing its share in the Mexican market, American investments continue to be dominant in Mexico, due to geographical proximity and historical economic ties. Although trade promotion has been intensified in European and Asian markets, a large portion of business activity remains concentrated in the United States. Similarly, in the United States, competition is growing among business groups and states with regard to investing in and trading with Mexico. The trend has manifested itself in many ways. One has been the increasing presence of state representation offices in Mexican territory. The main purpose of these offices is to promote and facilitate trade, investments, and tourism. By the end of 1994 there were 21 offices, an increase from the 13 that existed in 1993.

One motivation for such activity is rooted in the idea that the state plays a vital coordinating role for business people in the NAFTA member countries, and that personal relations are the foundation of long-term business (Case, 1994). Among the states that now have offices in Mexico are Arizona, Arkansas, California, North Carolina, Idaho, Illinois, Oregon, Puerto Rico, Rhode Island, Texas, and Wisconsin. Though some of these offices were opened many years ago (the Texas office was opened in 1971), most are more recent and are an outcome of the opening of the Mexican economy in the second half of the 1980s and the expectations of NAFTA in the 1990s. Due to the increasing presence of these type of activities, and in order to support the activities of the state offices located in Mexico, the American Chamber of Commerce in Mexico created a new committee called the 'Am Cham-US State Offices Liaison' (Geyer, 1990).

Similar activities have been carried out in the United States. Such is the case of the so-called Capital Region Economic Development Corporation (CREDC), whose main objective is to support and promote the region's economic growth. CREDC is made up of the Pennsylvania counties of Dauphin, Cumberland, and Perry; it covers a territory of 1,625 square miles and encompasses a population of almost half a million. In order to achieve its goals, the group created a regional umbrella organization that coordinates the efforts of the various business associations, and works to enhance the efficiency of the economic development programs in the region. This association, known as the Susquehanna Alliance, has the objective of increasing quality of life in the Capital Region, fostering economic vitality, and encouraging cultural and education opportunities. The CREDC carries out trade missions abroad, including in some Mexican cities.

Another type of competition that has arisen between states and local business groups involves missions and visits from state governors to their counterparts across the border and to the neighboring nation's president. Such visits include, for example, visits to Mexico in 1993 by governors Fife Symington of Arizona and Zell Miller of Georgia. More recently, Guy Chevrette, Minister of National Resources of Quebec, made a visit to Mexico, together with businessmen and government officials, in order to initiate several agreements on cooperation and technological exchange. In the past, acts of negotiation between particular states and foreign governments were uncommon. However, now it is a very common occurrence. The competition between those levels of government (or organized territories – i.e. regions) is expected to grow as a result of trade patterns and trends. According to international reports, it is estimated that total trilateral trade among NAFTA partners will double by the year 2000, to $646.2 billion (Jean, 1996). Undoubtedly, this represents a very attractive incentive to those states and regions looking to keep a larger slice of the trade pie.

The Emergence of 'Virtual' Regions: the Formalization of Transborder Regions

In region-states, characterized by Ohmae as natural economic zones, the boundaries are not defined by political administrative criteria, but by global market forces. The main links tend to develop within the global economy rather than within the regions' respective national economies. Among these kinds of transboundary regions are those formed by Hong Kong and the Province of Guangdong in the South of China, the 'growth triangle' between Singapore and Indonesia, and the Tijuana-San Diego region on the US-Mexico border (Ohmae, 1993).

In the context of the North American borderlands, which includes the neighboring zones between Canada and the United States and between the United States and Mexico, at least eleven regions have been identified as fitting into, or containing some of the elements defined as 'state-regions'. Larry Swanson (1994) has drawn attention to the emergence of transnational economic regions in North America. These are regions spurred by agreements for commercial opening, such as NAFTA.

Among the multinational regions or commercial corridors, according to Swanson (1994) there are, along the Canada-United States border (see Figure 7.1) Cascadia, Rocky Mountain West, Northern Great Plains, Great Lakes Frontier, New York-Quebec, New England-Atlantic Provinces, and Alaska-Costa Yukon. Along the US- Mexico border, the regions are San Diego (California)-Tijuana (Baja California), Sonora-Arizona, New Mexico-West Texas-Chihuahua, and Texas-Gulf of Mexico (Nuevo Leon).

These transnational economic regions, which are functional in nature, are comprised of entrepreneurial boards and groups, community associations, and local government actions. In the latter instance initiatives are developed to, for example, increase trade flows, attract industries, plan transportation, and improve border ports of entry.

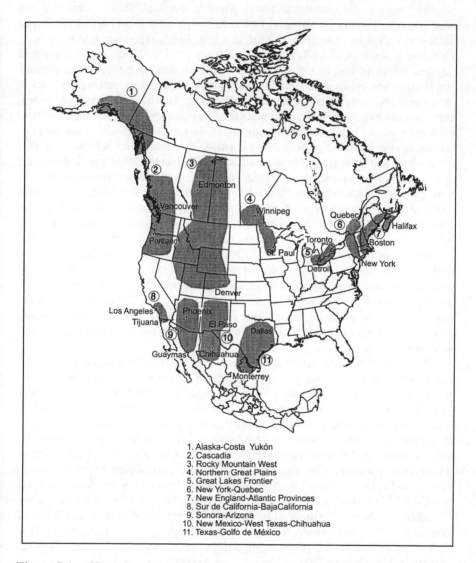

1. Alaska-Costa Yukón
2. Cascadia
3. Rocky Mountain West
4. Northern Great Plains
5. Great Lakes Frontier
6. New York-Quebec
7. New England-Atlantic Provinces
8. Sur de California-BajaCalifornia
9. Sonora-Arizona
10. New Mexico-West Texas-Chihuahua
11. Texas-Golfo de México

Figure 7.1   Transborder regions or economic corridors in North America
(Source: Adapted from Swanson (1994))

An additional strategy, designed to seize the opportunities resulting from the commercial liberalization among North American countries, has been the design of transnational 'superhighways' or trade 'corridors'. In recent years, trade corridors have come to be seen as new planning regions, complementing the more traditional planning units of sub-national administrative areas or river basins. These new planning regions cut across traditional physical, political, social, economic and administrative boundaries (Bender, 1997). Although there is no clear definition of what constitutes an international trade corridor, key components that have been identified include (Arizona Trade Corridor Study 1993, p. 2): (a) a well developed physical infrastructure, including highways, rail, air and sea linkages, and ports of entry; (b) an established commercial infrastructure and appropriate trade incentives, including distribution and warehousing facilities, foreign trade zones, and a harmonized regulatory environment; (c) a regionally integrated technological infrastructure, including corridor-wide trade data bases and electronic bulletin boards; (d) business and professional expertise, including customs brokers, freight forwarders, and internationally sophisticated accountants, attorneys, consultants, and academicians; and (e) well-developed social, political, and business linkages throughout the trade corridor. Similarly, it has been noted that international trade corridors must contain at least four components: (a) commercial and financial standards and norms; (b) governmental requirements or demands; (c) infrastructure, vehicles, equipment and facilities; and (d) actors (services and inspection and regulatory agencies) (CEPAL, 1992). According to Bender (1997), trade routes for intra- and inter-regional commerce that are built around international trade agreements support already-existing urban connections as well as forging new links between dominant and growing cities. In this view, corridors use new ways to group together cities characterized by changing dependencies, economic and social physical infrastructure, labor markets, service areas, and welfare demands.

Within the North American area, the main idea of such projects is to foster North-South growth, besides strengthening the position of the involved states, regions or localities, on the east-west routes. Among the most important corridors being developed are: (a) Interstate 69, an Eastern highway; this corridor would join Quebec, Montreal, and Toronto, in Canada, along with Indianapolis and Houston, in the United States, to Monterrey and Mexico City, in Mexico; (b) Interstate 35, also known as the 'International NAFTA Superhighway'; this mid-eastern corridor would unite Winnipeg, Canada, along with Kansas City, Dallas/Forth Worth and Laredo, in the United States, with Monterrey and Mexico City, in Mexico, and (c) the CANAMEX Corridor. The latter, being in the West, would connect the Canadian Provinces of British Columbia and Alberta, together with the States of Washington, Oregon, Nevada, Idaho, Montana, Wyoming, Utah, and Arizona (The United States), with a corridor from Sonora to Mexico City, running through Guadalajara (see Figure 7.2).

In the face of the emergence of functional transnational economic regions, a formalization process has recently emerged. This trend has spurred the creation of organized territorial forms for regional development management, which Boisier (1993) has conceptualized as 'virtual regions'. Boisier sees a 'virtual region' as being the result of a contractual agreement between two or more pivotal and associative regions, although it is not necessary for the entities to be geographically adjacent, in order to achieve certain short- and medium-term goals.

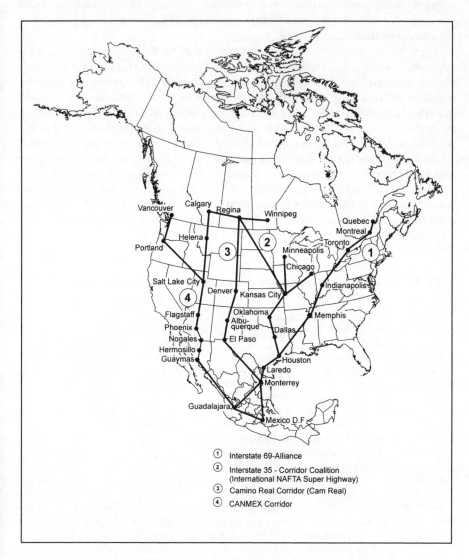

Figure 7.2 Trade corridors – 'superhighways' in North America
(Source: Based on various sources, including newspaper articles and trade magazines)

Formalization of the integration processes associated with these transnational border economic regions does not imply loss of their political-administrative status or place within their own countries. Rather, it represents a non-orthodox form of regional development management involving schemes of binational regional planning. In the process, new forms of international competitiveness among regions are established.

Regional integration processes assume a variety of forms, such as 'binational economic regions', 'commercial corridors' or 'great vision cross-border projects'. However, regardless of their specific form or structure, all have in common the objective of improving their competitive stance in North America and in world markets. Following Boisier's (1992) conceptualisation, some schemes try to invest the regions with a '*quasi*-state' and '*quasi*-enterprise' character with regard to the political-administrative or economic/technical-manufacturing arenas, respectively.

In North America, among the most notable initiatives that have reached an important degree of maturity with regard to their formalization are the Pacific Northwestern Economic Region (PNWER) and the Red River Trade Corridor on the US-Canada border, and Camino Real Economic Alliance (CREA) and the Arizona-Sonora Region on the US-Mexico border.[5] The main characteristics of these initiatives are summarized in Table 7.2 and Figure 7.3.

Table 7.2   Characteristics of selected transborder economic regions in North America

Region	Geographic location	Objectives	Principal Agents	Basic Characteristics
1. Pacific Northwestern Economic Region (PNWER)	Provinces of Alberta and British Columbia (Canada); states of Alaska, Idaho, Oregon, Montana and Washington (US).	Vision of the region as a world economic power; highlight regional competitiveness in national and international markets.	State and Province governments as well as private and social agents.	Joint GDP of $350 billion. Created by legislative agreement in 1991.
2. Red River Trade Corridor	Province of Manitoba (Canada); states of North Dakota and Minnesota (US).	To turn the region into a key entity in North America and the global marketplace; to facilitate discussion of problems and regional economic strategies.	Local, state and provincial governments, business and community groups.	Regional population of 1.5 million; $7 billion in exports in 1992; $20 billion in annual sales; more than 50 private and public research and development centers.

Region	Geographic location	Objectives	Principal Agents	Basic Characteristics
3. Camino Real Economic Alliance (CREA)	Cities of Las Vegas, Santa Fe, Albuquerque, Las Cruces (New Mexico) and El Paso (Texas) in the US; Ciudad Juárez and Chihuahua (Chihuahua) in Mexico.	To promote international trade and regional tourism.	Chambers of commerce, universities, local governments and private groups.	Area of Ciudad Juárez and Chihuahua has one of largest complexes of maquiladora industries in Mexico (17% of the plants, 30% of the employment on a national scale); the 'Camino Real' region has eight universities and several technology centers.
4. Arizona-Sonora Region	States of Sonora (Mexico) and Arizona (US)	To conceive the States of Sonora and Arizona as a joint economic region in order to rise complement-tarity levels and international competitiveness. Carrying out the 'Strategic Economic Development Vision for the Sonora-Arizona region' project.	State governments, private and social development agencies, Arizona-Mexico and Sonora-Arizona bi-national commissions, university groups from both states.	Regional population of 6 million; $12 billion dollars in exports; region was officially created in 1993.

Source: Based on regional promotional information, and Pavlakovich and Walker (1996a).

Besides these ambitious macro-regional projects, some more specific, but no less important, examples of transborder collaboration between regions or cities have gained strength during the last years. Some of these cases are shown in Table 7.3.

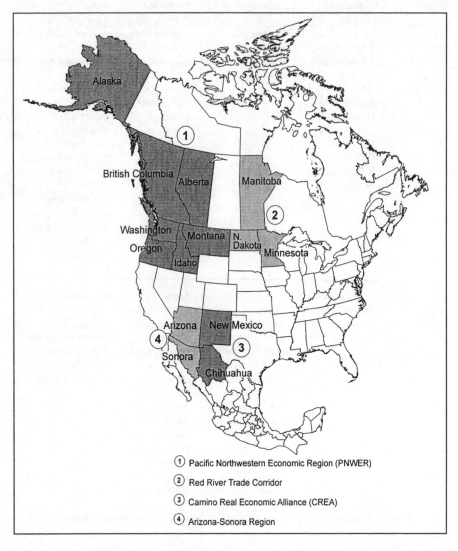

Figure 7.3   Formalized transborder economic regions in North America
(Source: Based on regional promotional information, and Pavlakovich and
Walker (1996a))

Table 7.3   Transborder collaboration agreements between local, state, and provincial governments, and other economic agents

City, County, State or Province	Type of Collaboration
1. States of Baja California (Mexico) and California (US)	Joint promotion of investment and economic development: 'Discover the Californias: Two Countries, One Region'.
2. Tijuana (Mexico) and San Diego (US)	Collaboration agreement between both Chambers of Commerce
3. Tijuana (Mexico) and San Diego (US)	Project to jointly build an efficient high-level international airport, in order to promote the region as one of the world's strategic centers for international trade.
4. States of Chihuahua (Mexico) and New Mexico (US)	Cooperation agreement to promote border development, build a large maquiladora city and to take advantage of NAFTA related opportunities.
5. States of Durango (Mexico) and the Province of Saskatchewan (Canada)	Alliances for co-investment and exchanges of information, technologies and strategic markets.
6. State of Yucatan (Mexico) and the Province of Quebec (Canada)	Agreement for the creation of a trade and entrepreneurial services corridor.
7. State of Yucatan (Mexico) and State of Louisiana (US)	Actions for the improvement of commercial exchange.
8. Border counties from northern Mexico and south-western United States	Mayors' initiative for the creation of a bi-national city council bloc that would jointly try to solve common problems, as well as promote regional development.
9. Counties and States of Yucatan, Quintana Roo and Chiapas (Mexico) and Central American counterparts.	Development of a collaboration program among tourism associations and business groups, along with state and municipal administrations, with the idea of jointly promoting the 'Mayan World' in international tourism markets.

Source: Based on a variety of documentary sources.

The Process of Integration in the Arizona-Sonora Region

For decades, the states of Sonora and Arizona have maintained economic and social linkages, and have shared natural resources, environment and history. Both states belong to the 'culture of the desert' and in the past, were united: under Nueva Vizcaya (prior to 1732); Sonora and Sinaloa, between 1732 and 1786;

Intendencia de Arizpe, 1786-1821; Estado de Occidente, 1824-1830; and the Estados de Sonora y Sinaloa, from 1831 to 1854.[6]

The common origins of the local ethnic groups, which dates back to the pre-colonial era, the development of Catholic missions in the 17th and 18th centuries, activities associated with livestock trading and mining in the 19th century, and contemporary (and increasing) international relationships generated by new trade flows and industrial and agricultural integration, all, in one way or another, have helped account for the extensive interrelationship that exists between the two states.

The interdependence and linkages between Sonora and Arizona are manifested in several ways. Based on geographical-physical, historical, cultural, social and economic factors, Sonora and Arizona has been defined as a binational region (Lozano, 1993; Gomezcésar, 1995). According these authors, despite enormous national differences and the existence of an international political boundary, a regional identity persists. Indeed, many people from Sonora and Arizona do not feel they are entering a different country when they cross the border. Rather, they feel they are moving within a binational region.

The Nature of Regional Integration

The evolution of the integration process between Arizona and Sonora must be approached from two perspectives: functional (de facto) integration and formal integration. The two types of integration are complementary. The former, the oldest one, derives from the operation of the market, the performance of social actors, and the opening of the economies. The latter is a product of deliberate agreements between the respective governments.

Although accurate delimitation of the Arizona-Sonora regional configuration is a complex task,[7] two geographical spheres can be identified. These spheres are directly related to the type of integration. The first sphere includes the whole territory of both states, following the process of formal integration. The second sphere includes a smaller geographical area including the border fringe and the area extending from the southern tip of Sonora to the Phoenix metropolitan area; here flows and exchanges are much more intense, reflecting functional integration (see Figure 7.4).

Functional integration During the last ten years, cross-border trade has increased at significant rates, mainly driven by the in-bond (i.e. *maquiladora*) operations,[8] the automotive industry, and agricultural produce exports. Within this period, exports from Arizona to Mexico and from Sonora to the Unites States increased more than four-fold, with Mexico exporting approximately $2.5 billion dollars in goods and the United States about $5.3 billion by the mid-1990s. Similarly, from 1987 to 1992, commercial vehicle traffic crossing from Mexico through Arizona-Sonora border ports of entry grew by some 60 percent (Arizona Trade Corridor Study, 1993). At present Arizona is the third most important exporting state to Mexico, just after Texas and California. With regard to the growing linkages within the Arizona-Sonora Region, several studies estimated that more than 24,000 jobs in Arizona were supported by exports to Mexico (Pavlakovich, 1995a).

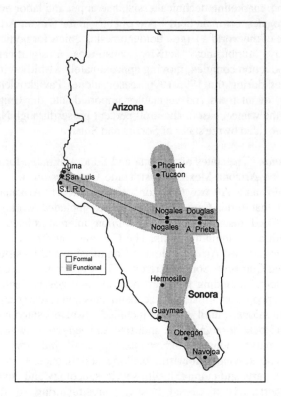

Figure 7.4   The spaces of formal and functional integration in the Arizona-Sonora region
(Source: Own Elaboration)

The importance of the maquiladora activity is demonstrated by the fact that, at national level, 24 percent of US exports to Mexico and 45 percent of Mexico's exports to the United States are related to the maquiladora program (Pavlakovich and Lara, 1994). According to Mexican sources (SECOFI), some 35 to 40 percent of in-bond plants located in Sonora have their maquila contracts in Arizona. In fact, the increasing integration of Arizona and Sonora maquiladora operations has produced a configuration of cross-border maquiladora corridors, as reflected in transport and input flows, technical assistance linkages, the existence of a regional labor market and flows, and in an intra-firm technical division of labor. Geographical proximity allows the exchange of managerial and technical staff on a daily basis.

Agribusiness activity represents one of the most dynamic sectors in terms of interactions among the regional actors, mainly private producers. Agribusiness functions as a kind of regional cluster. The sector is well integrated in terms of capital-financing, marketing, technical assistance, input and labor market (Tronstad et al., 1997). Nogales, the main border port of entry in the Sonora-Arizona Region, is emerging as one of the world's largest border crossing points for horticultural and fruit products. Today, agribusiness activity constitutes a significant transborder agricultural production complex, moving approximately $1 billion in fresh produce through Nogales during the 1995/1996 season alone (Pavlakovich et al., 1997). More generally, of all fruits and vegetables imported into the United States from Mexico during the winter season, about 60 percent passes through Nogales. Most of this volume is provided by the states of Sonora and Sinaloa.

Formal integration   The states of Arizona and Sonora initiated formal relations in 1959, through the Arizona-Mexico West Trade Commission, which was founded by Paul Fannin and Alvaro Obregon, Governors of Arizona and Sonora, respectively, at that time. Commission activities included working meetings to jointly analyze and discuss topics of common interest related to economics, education, health and communications. The Commission represents the origins of the current Arizona-based Arizona-Mexico Commission and its sister organization, the Sonora-based Comisión Sonora-Arizona. The Commissions are comprised of a variety of members, including governmental and non-governmental agencies and agents, business people, professionals, academicians and researchers.

The Commissions, until 1995 included twelve standing committees: agriculture, livestock, foreign trade, industry and *maquilas* (which included the subgroups of major industry and *maquilas*, small industry and franchises, infrastructure, and services), tourism, banking and finance, communication and media, education, arts and culture, health services, ecology and environment, legal affairs, and sports. As discussed below, a restructuring of the committees subsequently occurred. The stated general objectives of these Commissions are: (a) to promote and encourage a closer relationship between the citizens of the states of Sonora and Arizona, by fostering institutional and governmental relations, through closer and more direct contact between the different sectors of both states; and (b) to negotiate trade, scientific and technological interchanges; to improve the quality of education and health care services and to develop the productive activities of both states.

The Annual Plenary Meeting of the Arizona-Sonora and Arizona-Mexico Commissions held in Phoenix, Arizona in June, 1993, established a new stage in the relations of both states. During that meeting, the Governor of Arizona, Fife Symington, and the Governor of Sonora, Manlio Fabio Beltrones, agreed to carry out a *Strategic Economic Development Vision for the Arizona-Sonora Region* (SEDVASR). On December 1, 1993, at the Joint Legislative Protocol Session of the Arizona and Sonora legislative bodies, lawmakers endorsed this initiative for embarking upon a joint collaborative project based on a shared strategic economic development vision.

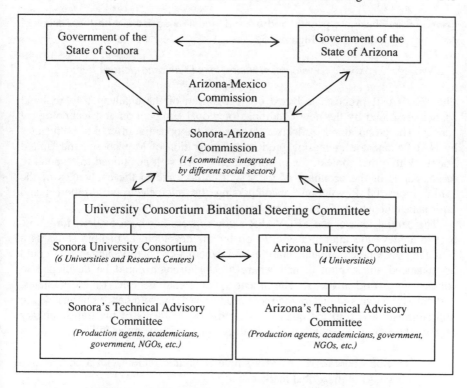

Figure 7.5   Main regional agents participating in SEDVASR
(Source: Own Elaboration)

The Commissions supported and oversaw the process of the Strategic Vision Project and provided a forum for coordinating activities. This move marked the beginning of the formalization of an ambitious process of a broader integration between the two states. Formalizing the integration process through the Strategic Vision Project also meant a strong change in emphasis and direction in the relationship between two states and the work of the Commissions. The new collaboration is intended to go far beyond cultural and social ties to strengthening economic, commercial and investment interactions.

With the change in emphasis, a restructuring of the Commissions' committees was suggested, in order to respond to the new emphasis on promoting business and to the new structure of the SEDVASR study components. Thus, the number of committees within the Commissions was increased to fourteen: agribusiness, education, environment, financial and business services, livestock, health services, legal matters, manufacturing, media and communications, mining, quality of life, small business, tourism, and, transportation and telecommunications. To conduct research and technical studies, the Arizona-Sonora University Consortium was formed, interacting vertically and horizontally with governmental agencies, the

Commissions, business people, and the individuals associated with the Technical
Advisory Committees (see Figure 7.5).

The Strategic Economic Development Vision for the Arizona-Sonora Region

The SEDVASR proposal is based on recognition of the challenges to regional
economies posed by the new conditions of global competition and technological
change. The proposal also reflects awareness of the potential offered to both states
by NAFTA and the increasing production integration of Mexico and the United
States. Within this context, the region expects to be well positioned to respond to
the demands of the economy of the 21st Century, and to the challenges of the
'Third Industrial Revolution' encompassing the microelectronics, robotics and
informatics industries (SRI International, 1992).

The central idea of the SEDVASR study process has been to determine how
best to achieve the joint strategic vision for the development of both states as a
single region, where complementarities and dynamic-competitive advantages could
be enhanced and exploited, and where greater strength could be developed to
compete in world markets. The intent is to create benefits for both states,
particularly in terms of generating more productive jobs, with better salaries, which
will stimulate a rise in the quality of life for the residents of the transboundary
region. The central objectives of the Strategic Vision Study are as follows:

- Develop Sonora-Arizona as a single economic region with a competitive
  advantage in the global market;
- Facilitate movement of goods, services, people and information through
  the region and promote the establishment of a trade corridor with Arizona
  and Sonora as the hub;
- Promote stronger linkages and eliminate barriers between both states, to
  facilitate economic development and to promote complementarity in trade
  and production;
- Encourage cross-border cluster development in the Sonora Arizona region
  to increase value-added economic activities;
- Create new external markets and new market opportunities for the
  Arizona-Sonora region;
- Identify and develop economic foundations, infrastructure and services
  needed to reach the desired level of competitiveness in the region.

The proposal represents an innovative approach with regard to regional
development strategies, particularly in light of current globalization and other
trends that have forced a search for non-orthodox forms of regional
complementarity and competitiveness. Thus, SEDVASR represents an innovative
process of binational regional planning, conforming to what Boisier (1993) calls a
'virtual region'.

Regional Economic Interaction: Conflict and Accommodation

The Arizona-Sonora initiative simultaneously possesses new development opportunities and new challenges. The process is not a smooth one, and the objectives are not easy to achieve. Sonora and Arizona are immersed in very different economic, social and technological contexts, including dissimilar human and financial capabilities. Further, their planning processes and traditions are quite different. Given this high degree of asymmetry, the following issues must be carefully analyzed and discussed in order to obtain wider positive impacts from implementation of SEDVASR. These issues are discussed next.

The Nature/Modality of Integration

Within the process of formalization of the Arizona-Sonora Region, and given the existing socio-economic and factor endowment unevenness, a question arises regarding what is the most suitable nature/modality of integration and intra-regional division of labor (sectoral specialization) that could offer positive results for both states. According to the Arizona's Strategic Plan for Economic Development (ASPED, 1992), the critical elements defining a successful economy of the future are high-quality jobs, competitive economic clusters, strong economic foundations, and economic diversity. Within this framework, and given the unique opportunity created by NAFTA, the complementarity between the economies of Arizona and Sonora based on the development of 'transborder industrial clusters' has been suggested as one of the more promising economic strategies. One way to address cluster development is to combine Arizona's capital, management and 'know-how' with Sonora's labor-force technical qualifications (SRI, 1992). By contrast, Sonora's Plan Estatal de Desarrollo, 1992-97 (1992) includes the strengthening of its industrial sector through increasing value added in primary products and transformation of the simple in-bond operations (*maquiladoras*), into a 'second generation' of *maquilas*. Through initiatives such as these, Sonora is attempting to improve use of its labor force through improving both labor force qualifications and technical innovations.

At this stage, a sensible and pragmatic strategy could be definition of forms of interaction and coordination for different time periods (short-, medium- and long-range), according to the resource endowments and competitive advantages both states possess. These forms of interactions can vary from simple complementarity to complex technical-manufacturing integration. The ultimate goal is to increase the general technical foundation of the industrial base as well as the standard of living and quality of life of both states' populations.

A substantial degree of economic integration between Sonora and Arizona already exists. Nevertheless, it also can be argued that this integration is mostly trade-related, as opposed to integration at the technical-manufacturing or capital-investment levels. This is particularly evident within the manufacturing sector (car and maquiladora industries). For instance, a recent survey of manufacturing companies in the region showed that only 13 percent of Sonoran firms export to

Arizona, and only 15 percent import from Arizona. A mere six percent of all their inputs came from Arizona. With regard to Arizona's firms, 17 percent export to, and 13 percent import from Sonora (Shunk et al., 1996). Likewise, Ford Motor Company, which is located in Hermosillo and accounts for about a third of Sonora's total exports, uses Arizona only as a crossing point for importing car parts from Detroit to Mexico and exporting assembled vehicles to the rest of North America.

The in-bond industry (*maquiladora*), which accounts for almost half of Sonora's exports, provides yet another example of the low level of effective transboundary integration. Although, as mentioned earlier, around 35 to 40 per cent of in-bond plants operating in Sonora have their headquarters or main offices in Arizona, these offices function mainly as a trading link to other American states or countries, rather than as a means for establishing technical-manufacturing integration on both sides of the border.

Thus, to some extent, in terms of the existing global trade patterns between Sonora and Arizona, the two states function most prominently as *static trade corridors* to other regions in North America. In this sense, given its important role in the North-South trade flows, the region should develop a trade policy linked to its production and potential capacity (trade creation) in contrast to its existing success in attracting trade flows through the region (trade deviation). In addition to the development of physical and commercial infrastructure, the intent here would be to establish a *dynamic trade corridor*, generating greater aggregate value. This would in turn serve as a source of propulsion for many of the region's industrial clusters.

As a strategic alternative, Arizona must evaluate whether it wants to remain primarily a trade corridor for goods imported from/exported to the Great Lakes or other regions in the United States or develop as a major manufacturing innovation center. In the case of Sonora's options, the strategic development scenarios developed by Nijkamp (1993) with reference to some Dutch border regions, might be useful. Under this framework, Sonora would need to evaluate its role as a backyard area, a corridor area, a 'green-tech' area, or a gatekeeper area.

Another framework of analysis for strategic regional scenarios may be found in the typology developed by Leborgne and Lipietz (1993), based on models of industrial organization. The framework suggests a choice between a neo-Taylorist region (i.e. simple assembly operations), a technology region or 'Californian' model (i.e. Silicon Valley), or a system-area region based on a 'Saturnian' model (i.e. high level of industrial clustering).

In evaluating these alternatives for achieving a wider development vision for Sonora, the strategies of 'backyard' area (which exemplifies a large part of the present maquila operations), static corridor area, and the neo-Taylorist region must be discarded. At present, or in the short or medium range, proper conditions do not exist in Sonora to warrant consideration of the 'green-tech' or 'Californian' paths, although this might be an option for Arizona. Rather, a combination of a 'gatekeeper' area (i.e. development of a dynamic trade corridor), and a 'system-area' region (high-level industrial clustering), might be the most desirable scenarios for the region's development. As pointed out earlier, perhaps by taking advantage of the positive complementarities between Arizona and Sonora, considered as a single transborder region, it might be possible to advance toward a more fair and equitable integration.

The Intra-Regional Spatial Impacts of Integration

Following the scheme of formal (de jure) integration, the entire territory of the region is included. Nevertheless, according to the geography of functional (de facto) integration, the impacts of economic growth are, rather, concentrated in certain border areas and principal localities of the region. In Sonora, for example, about 70 per cent of in-bond plants and employment are concentrated in three border towns (Nogales, Agua Prieta and San Luis Río Colorado). Hermosillo, the state capital, also provides important levels of dynamism, as does the Guaymas-Empalme area. Fully 35 percent of Sonora's total exports are made by Ford Motor Company, located at Hermosillo, and the primary manufacturing enterprises and exports (aside from in-bond activity) are concentrated in four municipalities (Hermosillo, Cajeme, Caborca, and San Luis Rio Colorado). Hermosillo alone accounts for half of all exporter-entrepreneurs. In the case of Arizona, a similar situation exists, with Phoenix and Tucson accounting for two-thirds of total exports to Mexico (Pavlakovich et. al., 1996b).

Another important trend is the changing role of border towns in the wake of the opening of the economy (liberalization) and the implementation of NAFTA. These processes have led to differentials in sectoral and spatial impacts. On the one hand, there appears to be a loss among border towns with regard to their comparative advantage as locations for some activities such as commerce. This is particularly the case on the Arizona side (e.g. Nogales). By contrast, Hermosillo has experienced a substantial growth in commerce and services linked to franchise operations and Phoenix has reinforced its position as a main distribution center.

Mexican peso devaluations have had negative impacts on the border economy as well. On the Sonoran side devaluations led to increases in the cost of living and the price of U. S. goods, causing a deep drop in sales revenues in Nogales, Arizona. An associated decrease in investments in shopping centers occurred, and low sales generated economic vulnerability both in Nogales, Arizona, and Nogales, Sonora. Some sources[9] estimated that by September 1995, due to the structural changes caused by the opening of the economy and the devaluation of the peso, more than 30 percent of retail and commerce establishments in Nogales, Arizona, had closed down, following a sales drop of around 60 percent. It is important to point out, however, that this negative impact on the retail sector of the border area was not generalized to other sectors or regions. A specific study of the sensitivity of Arizona's manufacturing industries to the recent peso devaluation found out that only 1 percent (13,400) of the total number of jobs in the state were peso-sensitive (Pavlakovich, 1995a). The number of peso-sensitive jobs in manufacturing industries (10,000) represents about five percent of total manufacturing employment.

An additional factor affecting border communities is increasing vehicle traffic, which causes negative externalities and urban congestion. This stress is an outgrowth of trade expansion associated with NAFTA: export and import activities have increased to the extent of making the present border port of entries' infrastructure insufficient.

Regional Convergence/Divergence

The issue of regional convergence and/or divergence has caused wide discussions in Europe, where recent studies have shown that regional inequalities have increased with international integration (Dunford, 1994; Cuadrado-Roura, 1994). As mentioned earlier in this chapter, in North America, unlike the case of the European Union, NAFTA does not provide for compensatory funding to support lagging or depressed regions. This situation constitutes a handicap in pursuing regional convergence. It also poses questions with regard to how to measure the process of convergence or divergence among uneven partners.

Although little empirical evidence exists, two general tendencies stand out with regard to the Arizona-Sonora region (Pavlakovich and Lara, 1994; Pavlakovich, 1995b). First, during the period 1980 to 1990, convergence occurred with regard to the geographical distribution of employment between Sonora and Arizona in the mining, manufacturing, construction, trade, transportation, communications and public utilities sectors. At the same time there was divergence in distribution of employment in the finance services sectors. Second, with regard to income levels, despite a slight decrease in inequality between particular border areas, the gap at regional level continued to widen, thus leading to divergence between the two states.

In general terms, analysis of the convergence/divergence process for transnational border regions must take into account three perspectives: (a) the evolution of the particular state, in relation to the rest of the states or regions of a country; (b) evolution relative to a country's own absolute base; and (c) evolution relative to the state(s) of the transnational region. In this last case, convergence should be a long-term objective.

Complementarity vs. Intraregional Competition?

Another important point of potential conflict involves the way in which the different actors of a region perceive their economic interactions. Actors in various economic activities or clusters have shown different attitudes towards interaction or association. For instance, in manufacturing there appears to be recognition of complementarities and interactions, and the forming of joint ventures and integration of trans-border activities. In-bond operations are perhaps the best example of this. Agribusiness is another sector that presents a substantial degree of transborder integration in several phases of the production chain. The same seems to be the case for tourism, where transboundary complementarities exist with regard to natural resources and investment (e.g. Grand Canyon in Arizona, the

Pinacate Mountains, beaches, and seaside resorts in Sonora). Yet another example of complementarity is found in health services, where transborder flows of consumers exist, based for example on searches for specialized services, cost savings, technical levels, and cultural approaches to medical care.

Nevertheless, in some clusters, actors see each other as competitors more than as potential partners. In particular, this is the case of transport and distribution services. The causes for this are varied and complex: unevenness in the size and capacity of enterprises, differences in rules and regulations, culture, and so on. In fact, transport associations in both Mexico and the United States rejected the opening of the border for transport services under NAFTA, a provision that was to be become operational in December 17, 1995, but as of now, has not yet been initiated. Even though problems exist in this sector with regard to developing binational associations and a transborder cluster, there are some areas where collaboration has already occurred and where potential for further interaction has been identified.

Local Community Participation

Up to the present, SEDVASR has functioned as a model of macro-regional plan, envisaged from the broader perspective of the Arizona-Sonora Region within North America and worldwide. Although the 'Vision Project' was not imposed from the federal level, it is, in a sense, a type of top-down development approach, promoted from the state government level with the participation of certain non-governmental actors. To obtain a wider consensus about SEDVAR as well as more generalized benefits, ways and means must be found to motivate greater participation by local community actors and development of local initiatives. Indeed, some analysts of this process (e.g. Pavlakovich, 1995b) conclude that a bottom-up approach is critical to the success and wider social impact of the project.

Decentralization and Regional Autonomy

In both the United States and Mexico, the federal governments see their border regions as zones of conflict and separation. This is particularly evident in issues related to illegal immigration, narcotics and national security. Thus, decisions about border areas are highly centralized. Differences exist between the two countries with regard to government regulations at the federal level. In areas such as transport and communications, border infrastructure, sanitary regulations, and others, differences exist at local levels. These differences require management based on greater regional or local autonomy. Therefore, in order to promote local and regional development a more decentralized border policy is needed. Also, new forms of coordination between the federal and state levels should be developed in order to allow more flexibility to the decision-making process at local level.

Concluding Remarks

The Arizona-Sonora Strategic Vision represents a great challenge from the perspective of regional development policy as well as from the perspective of the changing theoretical ground. The ultimate impact with regard to the question of convergence versus divergence remains to be evaluated at the macro and micro-regional levels, and in social and sectoral terms. Nevertheless, the state governments and social actors of the region expect that the opportunity and willingness to act on a common objective aimed at generating regional synergy can produce wider benefits to the population, rather than being a zero-sum game. A substantial part of the success of this endeavor will depend on the *intelligent* use of the existing asymmetries, in a manner that enhances complementarities. If this occurs, the project could generate, at least partially, positive results even under conditions of asymmetric interdependence.

In terms of building a comprehensive policy framework, a strategic binational project like this one should not be considered as a panacea for the development of the region. By themselves these types of strategic vision projects are seldom capable of solving a region's structural problems. Therefore, they must be seen only as particular and complementary policy actions.

On the other hand, based on formal aspects of the integration process in North America, the success of transnational border economic regions in achieving proposed objectives will largely depend on the extent of cross-border cooperation links and on wider participation and initiative-taking by local actors. Further, enhancing regional organization and capacity to negotiate with other governmental levels with regard to territorial, financing and political decision-making issues (e.g. moving toward greater autonomy and decentralization) will be critical. In the long run, these moves could diminish conflicts between the states and enhance accommodation between them.

Notes

1   See Financial Times, 'The opening caused a division in Canada', reproduced in *Excelsior* on October 28, 1995.
2   Comments of Juan Castaingts Teillery exposed in 'Quebec: is it the mirror of Mexico?' in *Excelsior*, October 28, 1995.
3   See Alfredo Jalife's article 'From Quebec to Chiapas: is it the balkanization of the continent?' in *El Financiero*, October 28, 1995.
4   Note published in *El Financiero*, 'Three states compete for the IE', August 30, 1996.
5   For more information see Pavlakovich and Walker (1996a).
6   Mexico lost more than two million square kilometers as a consequence of the war against the United States in the mid-1800s. With the Guadalupe-Hidalgo Treaty, Sonora lost legal domain over the land north of the Gila River. Furthermore, due to the Mesilla Treaty, Sonora lost around 27,000 square miles of the Pimería Alta in 1853, 24 per cent of Arizona's present territory.
7   It is complex in the sense that in the contemporary world, political borders, interregional linkages or regional 'hinterlands' are becoming blurred or difficult to identify and

measure. In the case of the Arizona-Sonora region, at least in functional terms, the state of Sinaloa plays an important role during the produce export season.

8 The maquiladora program allows temporary, duty-free entry of components and raw materials for assembly in Mexico and re-export as final product. Correspondingly, the US tariff regulations 9802.0060 and 9802.0080 permit return of the US component portion duty free, with taxes applied only the value added in Mexico.

9 See, for example, the news reported in El Independiente, 'La frontera mexicana: entre la devaluación y el dólar', April 18, 1995; El Independiente, 'El fantasma de la quiebra ... ronda por la calle Morley', June 18, 1995; El Imparcial, 'Aumenta desempleo en Arizona por cierre de establecimientos', July 3, 1995; El Independiente, En quiebra el comercio fronterizo', September 11, 1995; El Independiente, 'Ante la paridad peso-dólar, cerrarán comercios de Arizona', October 3, 1995; El Independiente, 'Vive Nogales, Arizona entre la espada y la pared', January 22, 1996; and, El Imparcial, 'Cierran por crisis', January 30, 1996.

References

Angell, I. (1995), 'Winners and Losers in the Information Age', *LSE Magazine, Economic and Political Sciences*, Centenary Issue, Summer, pp. 10-12.

Arizona Trade Corridor Study (1993), *Study Summary*, prepared for Governor Fife Symington and the Arizona Summit Six, Arizona Department of Transportation.

ASPED (1992), *Creating a 21st Century Economy: Arizona's Strategic Plan for Economic Development*, 1: Strategic Plan, Tempe, Arizona.

Bender, S. (1997), 'Trade Corridors: The Emerging Regional Development Planning Unit in Latin America', paper presented at the Regional Development Forum for Latin America and the Caribbean. Regional Development Planning in the 21st Century: Rethinking and Redefining Regional Development, United Nations Center for Regional Development (UNCRD), Santa Fe de Bogotá, December 1-3.

Boisier, S. (1992), *El Difícil Arte de Hacer Región: Las regiones como actores territoriales del nuevo orden internacional. Conceptos, problemas y método*, Centro de Estudios Regionales Andinos 'Bartolomé de las Casas', Cusco, Perú.

Boisier, S. (1993), *Postmodernismo territorial y globalización: regiones pivotales y regiones virtuales*, Doc. 93/19, Serie Ensayos, ILPES-ONU, Santiago de Chile.

Case, B. (1994), 'War. From Chihuahua to Chiapas, states fight for foreign investment', *Mexico Insight*, October 23, pp. 24-26.

CEPAL-ONU (1992), 'Canales, Cadenas, Corredores y Competitividad: un enfoque sistémico y su aplicación a seis productos latinoamericanos de exportación', *Cuadernos de la CEPAL*, No. 70, Santiago de Chile.

Cuadrado-Roura, J.R. (1994), 'Regional disparities and territorial competition in the EC', in J.R. Cuadrado, P. Nijkamp and P. Silva (eds.), *Moving Frontiers: Economic Restructuring, Regional Development and Emerging Networks*, Avebury, Aldershot, pp. 3-22.

Delamaide, D. (1995), *The New Superregions of Europe*, Plume, New York.

Drucker, P. (1994), *Post-Capitalist Society*, Harper Business, New York.

Dunford, M. (1994), 'Winners and Losers: The New Map of Economic Inequality in the European Union', *European Urban and Regional Studies*, 1(2), p. 95-114.

Geyer, A. (1990), 'Strengthening Trade Connections', *Business Mexico*, September, pp. 22-25.

Gobierno del Estado de Sonora (1992), *Plan Estatal de Desarrollo 1992-1997*, Secretaría de Planeación del Desarrollo y Gasto Público, Hermosillo, Sonora.

Gomezcésar, I. (1995), 'Sonora y Arizona: Apuntes para una historia', *Estudios Sociales, Revista de Investigación del Noroeste*, V(10), pp. 9-26.

Gutierrez, M. (1994), 'Las regiones de Mexico ante el TLC', *Comercio Exterior*, 44(11), pp. 1008-1014.

Harris, N. (1986), *The End of the Third World: Newly Industrializing Countries and the Decline of an Ideology*, Penguin Books, London.

Harris, N. (1996), 'Nations against the process of globalization. The end of nationalism?', paper presented at the Seminario La Globalización Económica y sus Impactos Socioterritoriales, Universidad de Guadalajara-Gobierno del Estado de Jalisco-SEMARNAP-RNICP, Guadalajara, Jalisco, September 23-27, 1996.

Jean, S. (1996), 'NAFTA makes the grade', *Business Mexico*, April.

Leborgne, D. and Lipietz, A. (1993), 'El Posfordismo y su Espacio', *Investigación Económica*, 205, Julio-Septiembre, pp. 173-204.

Lozano, F. (Coord.) (1993), *Sonorenses en Arizona: Proceso de Formación de una Región Binacional*, Gobierno del Estado de Sonora – Mexican-American Studies & Research Center, The University of Arizona, Tucson, Arizona.

Nijkamp, P. (1993), 'Border regions and infrastructure networks in the European integration', *Environment and Planning C*, 11(4), pp. 431-446.

Ohmae, K. (1993), 'The Rise of the Region State', *Foreign Affairs*, 72(2), Spring, pp. 78-87.

Pavlakovich-Kochi, V. (1995a), 'Sensitivity of Arizona's Manufacturing Industries to the Peso Devaluation', *Borderlands: Regional Economic Perspectives*, Research Paper Series 1995-I, Office of Economic Development, The University of Arizona, Tucson, Arizona.

Pavlakovich-Kochi, V. (1995b), 'Regional Inequalities, Infrastructure and Economic Integration: Policy Implications for the Arizona-Sonora Region', *Estudios Sociales, Revista de Investigación del Noroeste*, V(10), pp. 139-169.

Pavlakovich-Kochi, V.; Charney, A.H.; Vias, A. and Weister, A. (1997), *Fresh Produce Industry in Nogales, Arizona: Impacts of a Transborder Production Complex on the Economy of Arizona, an Economic and Revenue Analysis*, prepared for the City of Nogales, Arizona, Department of Community Affairs and Economic Development, The University of Arizona.

Pavlakovich-Kochi, V. and Lara, F. (1994), 'The Arizona-Sonora Region: Definition, Processes and Change', *Border Economy*, Inauguration Volume, The University of Arizona-El Colegio de la Frontera Norte, December, pp. 1-8.

Pavlakovich-Kochi, V.; Lara, F. and Wong-González, P. (1996b), *Trade Patterns in the Arizona-Sonora Region: Analysis and Recommendations for Development, Government of the State of Arizona*, Government of the State of Sonora, Arizona-Mexico and Sonora-Arizona Commissions.

Pavlakovich-Kochi, V. and Walker, M.P. (1996a), 'Transnational Regional Economic Development in North America: Problems, Challenges & Solutions in the 1990s', *Borderlands: Regional Economic Perspectives*, Research Paper Series 1996-1, Borderlands Economic Development Program, Department of Community Affairs and Economic Development, The University of Arizona.

Reich, R. (1993), *El Trabajo de las Naciones. Hacia el capitalismo del siglo XXI*, Javier Vergara Editor, S.A., Buenos Aires, Argentina.

SECOFI (Ministry of Commerce and Industrial Promotion), *Directorio de la Industria Maquiladora de Exportación*, México, D.F. (several issues).

Shunk, D.; Nystrom, H. and Lara, B. (1996), *The Arizona-Sonora Manufacturing Study: Analysis y Recommendations for Development*, Government of the State of Arizona, Government of the State of Sonora, Arizona-Mexico and Sonora-Arizona Commissions.

SRI International (1992), *Arizona-Sonora Complementarity: A Gateway between the United States and Mexico*, Center for Economic Competitiveness, Menlo Park, California.

Swanson, L. (1994), 'Emerging Transnational Economic Regions in North America under NAFTA', in M. Hodges (ed.) *Proceedings of the Symposium The Impact of NAFTA: Economies in Transition*, The London School of Economics and Political Science, London, pp. 64-93.

Tronstad, R.; Aradhyula, S. and Wong-González, P. (1997), *Arizona-Sonora Agribusiness Cluster: Analysis and Recommendations for Development*, Government of the State of Arizona, Government of the State of Sonora, Arizona-Mexico and Sonora-Arizona Commissions.

Vidal Villa, J.M. (1996), *Mundialización. Diez tesis y otros artículos*, Icaria Editorial S.A., Barcelona.

Wong-González, P. (1991), 'Impactos regionales del TLC', in J.L. Moreno and A. Covarrubiass (eds.), *Sonora ante el Tratado de Libre Comercio*, Fundación Friedrich Ebert-El Colegio de Sonora, Mexico, D.F., pp. 23-33.

Wong-González, P. (1997a), 'La Paradoja Regional y Regionalismos Emergentes en México: entre la globalización y el centralismo', *Serie Ensayos*, Documento 97/36, Dirección de Políticas y Planificación Regionales, ILPES-ONU, Santiago de Chile.

Wong-González, P. (1997b), 'Integración de América del Norte: Implicaciones para la Competencia y Competitividad Internacional de Regiones', *Serie Investigación*, Doc. 97/17, DPPR, ILPES-ONU, Santiago de Chile.

Chapter 8

Lower Income, Higher Income: Impacts of the *Maquiladoras* on Both Sides of the Border

Arthur L. Silvers

Introduction

When originated in 1965, the maquiladora program was intended to provide work for Mexicans in Mexican border regions. It replaced the Bracero program that provided seasonal farm work in the United States for Mexican migrant labor. But even by the early 1980s when the maquiladora sector was in its rapid expansion phase, it was clear that the *maquiladoras* had already become an important part of American competitive strategy. As branch assembly plants in Mexico, the *maquiladoras* provided cheap labor as a way for their parent US firms to remain profitable in the face of increasing global competition, particularly from a variety of manufacturers in the Pacific Rim nations and from apparel manufacturers in Turkey.

For the US economy, one study found that by the early 1980s, the profits of US parent firms were effectively impacted by their Mexican branch factories (Davila, 1990). The shift by US parent firms to maquiladora industry production was also impacting the geographic incidence of US intermediate and consumer goods employment (Silvers and Pavlakovich, 1994). Similarly, for Mexico, employment in *maquiladoras* exceeded one million by 1998, and while these jobs had earlier all been in factories located along the northern border, they were now spreading to the more inland states.

However, one issue that has not been well documented is the geographic pattern of impacts of maquiladora production on the incomes of poverty-level workers as well as the incomes of mid- and higher-level income populations.

For states in the United States, poverty rates may have worsened as local jobs in parent and supplier firms shifted to Mexico and the spending associated with these lost jobs decreased. But in US border states, these poverty rate impacts may have been offset as the *maquiladoras* and their Mexican workers made transboundary purchases of intermediate and consumer goods. At the same time, incomes of higher-skilled US employees and owners of capital may have risen with increased production of maquiladora-bound intermediate goods and with increased profitability of both parent and supplier firms.

For Mexico, state-wide poverty rates are particularly sensitive to peso devaluations that cheapen the dollar-denominated Mexican wage paid by US parent firms while concurrently increasing the peso-price of imports purchased by Mexican consumers. These effects lower Mexican real incomes even as the US parent firms use their increased profits to hire more Mexican labor for their *maquiladoras*. Further, Mexican state poverty rates would rise if the *maquiladoras* began to shift their labor demands away from lesser-skilled and toward higher-skilled workforce. Similarly, poverty rates could rise as border region maquiladora workers used their new earnings to shift their buying patterns away from Mexican border towns and toward shops in nearby American border towns.

Note that the hypotheses that could explain maquiladora income impacts in Mexico are linked with hypotheses that explain maquiladora income impacts in US states. For example, the same hypothesis that could explain rising profits for US parent firms at the same time could explain falling real incomes among Mexican maquiladora workers. Thus, while existing studies focus on state incomes either for Mexican states or for US states but not for states on both sides of the US-Mexican border, this study tests hypotheses concerning maquiladora impacts on poverty and income in states on both sides of the border.

To provide evidence in response to these questions, available data is obtained from US and Mexican census publications, and multiple regression analysis is used to test several maquiladora poverty and income impact hypotheses. This analysis is limited to state level data, including all Mexican states that had maquiladora firms at some time in the years 1980, 1990 and 1998, and the four US border states of California, Arizona, New Mexico and Texas with annual time series data over the period 1979 to 1997.

Earlier Research

Several previous studies of income and its distribution have been published that used sizeable databases to measure border region income and its distribution, but in few studies have statistical methods been used with these measures to test hypotheses concerning impacts of the *maquiladoras* on poverty and income. Peach (1985) used 1970 and 1980 US Census of Population data to measure income distribution in 25 US counties along the border with Mexico. He found a pattern of rising county-level income inequality going from the California counties in the western portion of the border to the Texas border counties along the easterly border regions, evidently correlated with the decrease in mean incomes moving from the western to the eastern counties. He subsequently found (1997) a trend of decreasing and then increasing county income inequality from 1970 to 1990. However, he does not analyze the causes of these trends, nor does he associate these patterns with the growth of the maquiladora sector.

Molina and Cobb (1989) have investigated the effects of several maquiladora variables on the size distribution of income in Texas border counties in 1980. They find that higher proportions of females employed in the *maquiladoras* and higher ratios of maquiladora profits to costs are both associated with reduced income inequality for Hispanic populations residing in the Texas border counties.

Pavlakovich (1995) has examined patterns of per capita income and its functional distribution (but not size distribution) in Arizona and its border counties over the period 1969 to 1991 using annual, quinquennial and decennial data. She compared these patterns with both minimum wage and earnings per employee in Nogales, Sonora using annual data over the period 1980-1989. The Pavlakovich research is the only study found that analyzes income and its distribution on both sides of the border. She finds a trend toward divergence between Arizona and its border counties in both real per capita income and in real earnings per worker, and traces basis for this trend to a declining trend in the border county employment-to-population ratio. She further finds a slight convergence in Arizona border county manufacturing wages relative to average maquiladora wages in Nogales, Sonora.

Several studies of the distribution of poverty in Sonora and in Mexico as a whole are available. Camberos, Genesta and Huesca (1994) have developed measures of poverty and extreme poverty for the state of Sonora and its distribution across its twelve economic regions for the 1980 and 1990 periods. They show data on sectoral composition of employment, employment rates, and productivity. They assert that the spatial patterns of poverty and its changes are the result of structural adjustments in response to the economic crisis, unemployment in the predominantly agricultural regions, low wages in regions that have a large maquiladora sector (implying without actually asserting causality) and declines in public sector expenditures.

Camberas Castro and Bracamontes Nevarez (1994) estimate indices of marginality for the municipios (communities) in the Sonoran regions of Yaqui-Mayo and Frontera Norte for 1970, 1980 and 1990, and project these indices to the years 2000 and 2020. They show the sources of marginality in terms of several measures of social welfare needs, including illiteracy, proportion of population not completing primary school, housing without bathrooms or plumbing, electricity or running water, housing with only one or two rooms and with dirt floors, percent of population living in small towns, and working population earning less than the minimum wage.

Kelly (1999) analyzed Mexican poverty at the national level, using data over the period 1980 to 1994. He used measures of the sectoral mean wages and poverty rates within sectors. Although sectors with higher mean wages were found to have lower poverty rates, the same negative correlation was not found for measures of change in mean wages and change in poverty rates. Particularly in the more capital-intensive manufacturing sectors, which also were the more export-oriented and more rapidly growing sectors, he found that growth in mean wages had no effect on sectoral poverty rates. This suggests that growth in the export-oriented maquiladora sector, although employing a high proportion of low wage assembly workers, also may not have reduced maquiladora sector poverty. Further, poverty rates in the agricultural sector rose with public policies involving reduced price subsidies, restricted public investment, credit and ejido investment (investment on communally owned lands), and a periodically overvalued peso.

In this study, poverty rates and mean income levels are measured at the aggregate state level; within-sector poverty rates are not considered. State-wide poverty rates and mean incomes are then related to state share of employment in the maquiladora sector, with other variables included to control for possible specification bias. This approach allows for the possibility that although within-sector poverty rates might not be impacted within the rapidly growing maquiladora sector, state-wide poverty rates may nevertheless have been impacted should rising maquiladora mean wages have increased the state-wide demand for labor.

A number of other studies have been published that are concerned with other social welfare effects of the *maquiladoras*. These have included maquiladora efforts to neutralize border-region unions (Williams, 1990; Carillo, 1991), their exploitation of Mexican workers, particularly female workers (Gambrill, 1981; Kelly, 1983) by paying wages only a fraction of what the US displaced workers had been paid (Silvers, 1991; Stoddard, 1987), and their reinforcement of Mexican dependency on US capitalism (Kopinak, 1993), among others.

In the next section, the relation between state maquiladora employment share and state-wide poverty rates, un- and underemployment rates, and mean income are analyzed for Mexican states. The subsequent section then analyzes the relation between several income-related measures in each of the four US border states with the level of maquiladora employment in the adjacent Mexican border state.

Maquiladora Sector Impacts on Mexican States

Data and Hypotheses

Multiple regression analysis (OLS) is used to test the effects of maquiladora employment on each of three dependent variables for states in Mexico: poverty rate, unemployment rate, underemployment rate, and income per worker. Several additional variables (described below) are included as controls for possible specification bias.

The poverty rate measure The Mexican census of population publications of the Instituto Nacional de Estadística, Geografía e Informática (INEGI) do not include poverty rates per se. However, they do provide data on the percentage distribution of employed population by income class. In 1990 and 1998, income class was defined in terms of multiples of the minimum wage. In 1980, income class was defined in pesos. Using a method developed by Sen (1976), Cambreros, Genesta and Huesca (1994) it is possible to obtain measures in pesos of extreme and moderate poverty for 1980 and 1990, and also show this measure in terms of multiples of the minimum wage. These measures were used to obtain estimates of the number and percentage of workers in each state with poverty-level incomes.[1] However, the minimum wage is not regularly adjusted by the Mexican government to keep pace over time with the peso value or the poverty level. To provide an implicit control for these changes, the year of the observations (1980, 1990, and 1998) was included as a variable in the regression analyses.

Other measures of economic welfare The state unemployment rate is measured as the percent of the state economically active population not employed; the state underemployment rate is obtained as the percentage of state employed workers that worked less than 34 hours per week.

State real income per worker is obtained by using published INEGI measures of gross state product, adjusted to 1980 pesos using a national consumer price index, and divided by state total employment. This measure serves as a proxy of state real income per worker, but as income by state of production rather than income by state of residence. For example, the state income measure includes all profits generated within the state even though a portion is paid to owners of capital residing in other states.

Data were obtained for thirteen Mexican states that had some employment in the maquiladora sector during at least one of the three time periods measured: 1980, 1990 and 1998. The following states were included: Baja California, Baja California Sur, Coahuila, Chihuahua, Distrito Federal, México, Durango, Jalisco, Nuevo Leon, Puebla, Sonora, Tamaulipas, and Yucatan (see Figure 8.1). Consequently, 39 observations were obtained.

Several variables are used as controls to obtain unbiased estimates of the impact of maquiladora employment share on state poverty rates, underemployment, and income per worker over the three time periods. Included are the proportion of the state's workers that are female, the illiteracy rate of the state's population age 15 and over, and the percentage of the state's total employment in each of four sectors: maquiladora manufacturing, non-maquiladora manufacturing, agriculture (including farming, cattle and fishing) and minerals (mining and petroleum). All measures, including maquiladora employment, are obtained from INEGI publications. Two alternative measures of time are included to control for changes in the minimum wage level relative to the poverty level. The first is the use of dummy (0,1) variables to indicate the years 1990 and 1998; the second is the year itself. Finally, a dummy variable is included that indicates whether a state is located at the US-Mexico border. This variable is used to control for the possibility of confounding effects on the maquiladora employment coefficient associated with a state's location at the border. The effects may be due to the enhanced demand for Mexican labor resulting from cross-border shopping by US tourists or to the impacts of out-shopping by maquiladora workers and the tendency of American maquiladora managers to reside on the US side of the border.

The direction of impact of a state's percentage employed in the maquiladora sector is unknown for all four independent variables. Arguments can be made either way. Concerning impacts on poverty rates, one possibility is that the maquiladora sector may pay relatively higher wages compared with other sectors, so that proportionally higher maquiladora employment increases the incomes of workers at all income levels and therefore lowers a state's poverty rate. A different possibility is that the maquiladora sector raises the demand for a higher skilled technical and managerial workforce, increasing their incomes, but shifting labor demand away from lower skilled workers. State poverty rates could then be unaffected or even become worse.

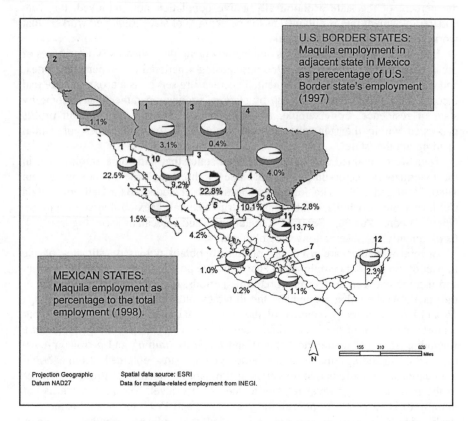

Figure 8.1   Maquiladora employment as percentage of total employment, by state

In sum, the impacts of the maquiladora sector on poverty, unemployment, and underemployment might be found to be either positive or negative.

A somewhat similar position is taken with respect to impacts on real income per worker. A larger maquiladora sector provides jobs for many low-wage laborers, but also for higher-wage technical and administrative workers and also for local entrepreneurs who, as recent data have shown (MacLachlan and Aguilar, 1998; Silvers, 2000), own a high proportion of the smaller *maquiladoras*. These will have multiplier effects on the state's economy, raising labor demand and, thereby, earnings per worker. But profits from US-owned *maquiladoras* are taken by the parent firms in the United States; also for *maquiladoras* located near the border, higher-paid American managers usually reside on the US side of the border. Further, employment and income multipliers for the maquiladora sector are small because, until North American Free Trade Agreement (NAFTA), linkages to other local sectors for intermediate goods purchases have been non-existent. Also, *maquiladoras* located near the border have even lower multipliers because a large portion of maquiladora worker wages is spent in the United States. Consequently, the direction of impact on real income per worker would either be positive or nil.

Estimated Maquiladora Impacts on State Poverty, Employment and Income

Table 8.1 shows coefficient estimates for Mexican state maquiladora employment share as an independent variable in regression equations for each of four dependent variables. The first is for state poverty rates, the second is for state unemployment rate, the third is for state percent underemployed, and the fourth is for state real income per worker. Results of the regression analysis of poverty rates in Mexican states are shown in Table 8.1. Regression coefficients are not shown for the regression constants, the year and the border location dummy variables, and for all other control variables: employment shares in non-maquiladora manufacturing, agriculture and mining, the female share of state employment, and the illiteracy rate.

Table 8.1   Regression results for Mexican state maquiladora employment share on each of four state-level dependent variables

Dependent Variable (n = 39)	No. Observations	Regression Coefficient	Prob. Value	Equation Adj. R-squared
Poverty rate	39	-89.37	0.01	0.60
Unemployment rate	39	-0.02	0.26	0.03
Percent underemployed*	26	-26.85	0.01	0.68
Real income per worker	39	63.98	0.78	0.48

*Observations for underemployment (hours worked < 34) were not available for 1980.

States with higher employment share in the maquiladora sector are found to have lower poverty rates. The coefficient for this variable is shown in column 2 as negative and shown in column 3 as highly significant (at the .01 level).

The regression analysis did not yield evidence that larger maquiladora employment shares had any significant effects on state unemployment rates in Mexico. The analysis for the underemployment rate yielded more interesting results. States that had higher employment shares in the *maquiladoras* were found to have significantly lower underemployment rates. Also estimated in this regression equation, but not shown here, is that all else held constant, state with higher proportions of females in the workforce tend to have higher underemployment rates (significant at the .01 level). This may imply that underemployment rates for females would decrease for states with higher maquiladora employment shares.

Finally, state real income per worker was not found to be significantly associated with state employment shares in the maquiladora manufacturing sectors.

In sum, as state employment share in the maquiladora sector rises, statewide poverty rates and underemployment rates significantly decline, but these maquiladora impacts do not extend either to statewide unemployment rates or to income per worker. These findings support the hypotheses that the effect of relatively larger maquiladora sectors has been to raise the demand for labor in state economies in Mexico, with the consequence that rates of both poverty-level employment and underemployment have been reduced.

The findings do not support the hypothesis that maquiladora wages are so low that they have increased state poverty rates. Nor do the findings support the hypothesis that the increased incomes generated by the *maquiladoras* are disproportionately incident to Mexico's higher income workforce or capitalists.

Maquiladora Sector Impacts on US Border States

The rapid growth of the maquiladora sector has had two types of impacts on US states. The first is that for the parent firms located all across the United States, especially the rust belt states, southeastern states, and the four states located along the US-Mexican border, jobs for production assembly workers were eliminated, replaced by the much lower wage jobs for Mexican maquiladora workers. Ensuing negative multiplier effects added to the loss of these jobs, impacting many local firms that had been providing intermediate goods both to the parent firms and to local consumer-oriented sectors. The consequent decline in local demand for labor would have raised poverty rates and lowered average state incomes. Offsetting these effects is that the resulting production cost savings enhanced profit incomes for the owners of the parent firms, and perhaps saved the preponderance of the jobs that had previously been eroding due to competition from firms located in lower cost Pacific Rim nations. These nation-wide effects have been analyzed elsewhere (Silvers and Pavlakovich, 1994) and will not be revisited here. Instead, this research will be limited to maquiladora-sector impacts on the four US border states: Arizona, California, New Mexico and Texas.

Hypotheses and Data

Three types of maquiladora impacts will be examined: impacts on US border state poverty rates, real median household income, and real per capita income.

Maquiladoras are located in Mexican, not US states. But the *maquiladoras* nonetheless have economic impacts on the US border states (Silvers and Pavlakovich, 1994). To measure the maquiladora variable for a given US border state, the maquiladora employment in the adjacent Mexican border state is divided by the total employment of the US border state (see Figure 8.1).

Maquiladora sector production in a Mexican border state can be expected to increase demand for intermediate goods produced by supplier firms in the adjacent US border state, increasing employment in that state. The Mexican border state's maquiladora workers also increase cross-border shopping, further increasing retail and service sector employment in the US border state. But the shift to maquiladora assembly would decrease employment in the US parent firms, some of which are located in the US border state. These several employment impacts would have offsetting poverty and income impacts in the US border states, so the net impacts of the *maquiladoras* could be either positive or negative.

In addition to the maquiladora variable, several independent variables are included in the regression analysis to control for possible specification bias. These are state farm employment, employment in the state's goods-producing sectors (manufacturing, construction and mining), and the real exchange rate in pesos per dollar. The latter two variables correct for possible confounding effects that could result from changes in the US economy. The year of each observation is included as a control because there has been a trend toward increasing state poverty rates since 1975 and real per capita incomes have been rising. Finally, since mean income in California is much higher than in the other three border states, a dummy variable indicating observations for California is needed to control for the effect of the income discontinuity.

Annual time series data for years 1979-1997 for sectoral full and part-time employment and per capita personal income by state, and national consumer price index series are obtained from databases of the Bureau of Economic Analysis (1990). Annual time series data for state median household income and population for the years 1984-1997, and for state poverty rates for years 1989-1997 are obtained for the four border states from publications of the US Bureau of the Census. The BEA consumer price index is used to deflate to 1998 dollars both per capita personal income and median household income. Data for maquiladora employment in the Mexican states adjacent to each of the four US border states are obtained from publications of INEGI cited earlier. This number is stated as relative to the total employment of the US border state. The real exchange rate in pesos per dollar is obtained from International Monetary Fond Statistic Department and adjusted by consumer prices indices for the United States (US Bureau of Labour Statistics) and for Mexico (INEGI and Banco de México).

Estimated Impacts on Poverty and Income

Table 8.2 shows coefficient estimates for maquiladora employment per US border state employee in regression equations for each of three dependent variables. The first is for state poverty rates, the second is for state real median income, and the third is for state real mean per capita income. Regression coefficients are not shown for the regression constants, the year and the California dummy variables, and for all other control variables.

Regression analysis findings are that poverty rates for the US border states are not significantly associated with the levels of maquiladora employment in their neighboring Mexican state. Instead, state poverty rates are found to rise with the proportion of workers in farming and to fall with the proportion in the durable goods producing sectors. The hypothesis that the *maquiladoras* have increased poverty rates, at least for US border states, is not supported in this analysis.

Table 8.2   Regression results for maquiladora employment per US border state worker on each of three dependent variables

Dependent Variable for US Border States	No. Observations	Regression Coefficient	Prob. Value	Equation Adj. R-squared
Poverty rate	36	0.136	0.71	0.66
Median real household income	56	913.4	0.02	0.88
Real per capita income	72	364.0	0.00	0.97

The regression equation for real median household income is positively and significantly associated with the maquiladora employment ratio. The regression equation for real per capita personal income shows a result that is roughly similar to that obtained for median household income. Real per capita income in US border states rises with the maquiladora employment ratio, and the coefficient is highly significant. But when adjusted for mean number of persons per household, the size of this coefficient is ten percent higher than that in the median household income equation. This suggests that maquiladora income impacts on incomes in US border states are skewed toward their high income populations,[2] e.g., their managerial and technical earners and owners of capital.

In sum, for US border states with greater maquiladora sector activity in the adjacent state are not shown to have worsened poverty rates, but neither are they shown to have reduced poverty rates. However, there is positive and significant association with the real per capita and median family incomes of the border states.

Conclusions and Caveats

The evidence obtained in this analysis of maquiladora sector income impacts supports several conclusions. First, Mexican states with relatively higher maquiladora sector activity are found to have improved, not worsened, incomes for low income workers. At the same time, they are found to have reduced underemployment. The increase in hours worked helps explain how the *maquiladoras* have had positive impacts on the incomes of lower income workers. But maquiladora activity is not significantly associated with state unemployment rates, nor with mean income levels in those states. The latter finding implies that the *maquiladoras* have not been found to substantially add to the higher technical and managerial labor and of owners of capital in those states.

Second, maquiladora sector activity is significantly associated with increased median household income and average personal income in US border states, but not significantly associated with the poverty rates of those states.

These findings suggest that the maquiladora sector, in absorbing some 1.3 million people into Mexico's workforce, has had a greater impact in distributing income at the lower rather than the higher end of the income scale. However, this conclusion can be considered along with evidence that the maquiladora sector is also distributing income to middle and upper income populations. The evidence, from findings published elsewhere, shows that the *maquiladoras* have been engaging a more technology-oriented workforce than had earlier been the case, and also involving Mexican capital to the extent that more of the smaller size *maquiladoras* are now under Mexican rather than American ownership.

At the same time, the finding that the *maquiladoras* have been not been impacting US border state poverty rates does not provide support for the hypothesis that increased maquiladora activity in Mexican border states substantially displaces factory workers in those states. The finding that increased maquiladora activity is positively associated with median and mean incomes of the US border states implies that the income impacts of the *maquiladora* are incident to the middle and upper income groups in those states. This supports the hypothesis that the major way that the maquiladoras impact income in the US border states is by raising the profits of parent firm capital and workforce earnings in the intermediate goods and consumer-serving sectors of those states.

These analyses are all based upon data at the state level. This spatial unit of analysis is quite large, and the possibility of aggregation bias cannot be ruled out. Additional analyses based upon data at the county and municipio level are essential.

Notes

1   In 1980, monthly income at the minimum wage level was 4,375 pesos. The extreme poverty income level for a family of 4.9 members was 3,456 pesos, so a worker earning the monthly minimum wage earned 26 percent above the family extreme poverty level. Workers earning the 1980 monthly minimum wage are shown in the 1980 Mexican census in the group that earned 3,611-4,890 pesos per month; the earnings of this group also exceed the extreme poverty income level, but are below the moderate poverty level. For this analysis, the 1980 poverty rate is measured as the proportion of all employed and paid workers with reported incomes of up to 4,890 pesos per month. In 1990, a worker earning the minimum wage earned 43 percent less than the family extreme poverty level; that is, a worker had to earn twice the minimum wage to exceed the family extreme poverty level. The poverty rate used for this study is the proportion of all employed and paid workers with reported incomes of up to twice the minimum wage, a measure that is reported in both 1990 and 1998 Mexican census publications. In the absence of the peso measure of family poverty for 1998, this is also the measure used as the 1998 poverty rate (source: Encuesta Nacional de la Dinamica Demografica, 1997. Metodologia y Tabulados).

2   Note that the coefficient for the maquila employment variable is substantially below the estimated coefficient this variable in the median income equation. But this reflects the fact that there are several people in a household that share their 'per capita' incomes. US Census data for 1990 shows that the mean number of persons per household for the four border states was 2.757. Multiplying the regression coefficient for the maquila employment ratio in the per capita income regression by 2.757 would raise the coefficient to 1,003.5. But this is 10 percent higher than the estimated median household income coefficient of 913.4. The finding that the *maquiladoras* have a greater impact on mean than on median incomes implies that the induced increase in US border state incomes is incident more to upper income than to the lower income classes of those states.

References

Camberos Castro, M.; Antonieta Genesta, M. and Huesca, L. (1994), 'La Pobreza en Sonora: Los Limites a la Modernización', *Estudios Sociales*, 5, Enero-Junio, pp. 167-197.

Camberos Castro, M. y Bracamontes Nevarez, J. (1994), *Evolución de la Marginación en los Municipios de las Regiones Yaqui-Mayo y Frontera Norte en Sonora: un Alalisis Comparativo*, Centro de Investicacion en Alimentacion y Desarrollo, Hermosillo, Sonora, pp. 1-24.

Carillo, J.V. (1991) 'The Evolution of the Maquiladora Industry: Labor Relations in a New Context', in K.J. Middlebrook (ed.), *Unions, Workers and the State in Mexico*, US-Mexico Contemporary Perspectives Series, 2; Center for US Mexican Studies, University of California, San Diego.

Fernandez, K. (1983), *For We are Sold, I and My People: Women and Industry in Mexico's Frontier*, State University of New York Press, Albany, N.Y.

Fujii, G.G. and Genaro Aguilar, G. (1995), 'La Distribucion del ingreso en Mexico, 1984-1992: un estudio por componentes', *Comercio Exterior*, August, pp. 609-614.

Gambrill, M.-C. (1981), 'La Fuerza de Trabajo en las Maquiladoras: Resultados de una Encuesta y Algunas Hipoteses Interpretativas', *Lecturas del SEESTEM:* Maquiladoras, Centro de Estudios Economicos y Sociales del Tercer Mundo, Mexico, D.F.

Kelly, T. (1999), *Structural Shifts and Changes in the Distribution of Poverty: the Case of Mexico*, Cuaderno de Trabajo, Departamento de Estudios Economicos, El Colegio de la Frontera Norte, Tijuana, Mexico, pp. 1-26.

Kopinak, K. (1993), 'The Maquiladorization of the Mexican Economy', in R. Grinspun and M.A. Camereon (eds.), *The Political Economy of North American Free Trade*, St. Martins Press, N.Y.

MacLachlan, I. and Aguilar, A.G. (1998), 'Maquiladora myths: locational and structural change in Mexico's export manufacturing industry', *Professional Geographer*, 50, pp. 315-331.

Molina, D.J. and Cobb, S.L. (1989), 'The Impact of Maquiladora Investment on the Size Distribution of Income Along the US-Mexico Border: The Case of Texas', *Journal of Borderlands Studies*, 4, pp. 100-118.

Pavlakovich-Kochi V. (1995), 'Regional Inequalities, Border Infrastructure and Economic Integration: Policy Implications for the Sonora-Arizona Border', *Estudios Sociales, Revista de Investigacion del Noroeste*, 5(10), julio-diciembre, pp. 139-170.

Peach, J. (1985), 'Income Distribution in the US-Mexico Borderlands', in L.J. Gibson and A. Corona Renteria (eds.), *The US and Mexico: Borderland Development and the National Economies*, Westview Press, Boulder, Colorado, pp. 57-80.

Peach, J. (1997), 'Income Distribution Along the United States Border with Mexico: 1970-1990', *Journal of Borderlands Studies*, 12, Spring and Fall, pp. 1-16.

Sen, A. (1976), 'Poverty: An Ordinal Measurement Approach', *Econometrica*, 44, March.

Silvers, A.L. (2000), 'Limited Linkage, Demand Shifts, and the Transboundary Transmission of Regional Growth', *Journal of Regional Studies*, May 2000.

Silvers, A.L. and Pavlakovich-Kochi, V. (1994), 'Maquila Industry Impacts on the Spatial Distribution of Employment in the US', *Journal of Borderlands Studies*, 9, pp. 47-64.

Stoddard, E.R. (1987), *Maquila: Assembly Plants in Northern Mexico*, Western Press, University of Texas at El Paso, El Paso,Texas.

Data Sources

Dirección de Evaluación Financiera y Estudios Económicos, con base en la información del Banco de México.

International Monetary Fund, International Financial Statistics, RF Series, prepared by IMF Statistics Department, various monthly issues.

Instituto Nacional de Estadística, Geografía e Informática (INEGI), Estadística de la Industria Maquiladora de Exportación, 1979-1989.

Instituto Nacional de Estadística, Geografía e Informática (INEGI), X Censo General de Población y Vivienda, 1980, Resumen General Abreviado, México, 1984.

Instituto Nacional de Estadística, Geografía e Informática (INEGI), 1990 Censo General de Población y Vivienda, Aguascalientes, México.

Instituto Nacional de Estadística, Geografía e Informática (INEGI), Estadística de la Industria Maquiladora de Exportación, 1991-1996.

Instituto Nacional de Estadística, Geografía e Informática (INEGI), Sistema Cuentas Nacionales de México, Producto Interno Bruto por Entidad Federativa, 1993-1998, México, 2000.

Instituto Nacional de Estadística, Geografía e Informática (INEGI), Sistema de Cuentas Nacionales de México (disco compacto), México, 1994.

Instituto Nacional de Estadística, Geografía e Informática (INEGI), Indicadores sobre características educativas de la población por entidad federativa, 1995, Conteo de Población y Vivienda, 1995. México.

Instituto Nacional de Estadística, Geografía e Informática (INEGI), Estadísticas Sociodemográficas: Estructura Porcentual de la población ocupada por grupos de ingreso según entidad federativa, 1997. Encuesta Nacional de la Dinámica Demográfica, 1997. Metodología y Tabulados.

Instituto Nacional de Estadística, Geografía e Informática (INEGI), Estadísticas Económicas, Industria Maquiladora de Exportación, Febrero, 1999.

US Department of Commerce, Bureau of Economic Analysis, Data Released June, 2000 from Table SA30, Per Capita Personal Income; also from Table SA25 Total Full Time and Part Time Employment. Washington, D.C.

US Census Bureau, Historical Income Tables – Households, Table H-8 Median Household Income by State: 1984 to 1998, www.census.gov/hhes/income/ histinc/ho8.html

US Census Bureau, Historical Poverty Tables, Table 21 Number of Poor and Poverty Rate, by State: 1980 to 2000, www.census.gov/hhes/poverty/ histpov/hstpov21.html

US Census Bureau, Statistical Abstract of the United States: Washington, D.C., various years.

PART IV
LIVING WITH CHANGING BORDERS

Living With Changing Borders

Barbara J. Morehouse, Vera Pavlakovich-Kochi and Doris Wastl-Walter

> The process of restructuring is not a pure mechanism of adjustment, but a politically contested and determined process enacted by governments and organizations. These practices are never abstract processes, but unfailingly manifest themselves on local, regional or national levels, and are in fact produced, contested and reproduced in the local, everyday life of human beings.
>
> (Paasi, 1996, p. 6)

The chapters in this section consider questions and issues arising in local border areas. Local-scale studies are essential, for political decisions taken at the supranational or national level generally lack consideration of local differences and concerns. The contributions presented here illustrate how border communities strategize and generally cope with border issues, in a search for policies and approaches appropriate to dealing with, and complementing, high-level decision-making. Through case studies drawn from selected border regions, the different ways in which border communities deal with issues of marginalization, economic underdevelopment, actual or perceived neglect by national centers, and demands for freer cross-border movements may be explored.

Experiences from the case studies presented here suggest that, while enforcement of boundaries and efforts persists in order to achieve stronger integration of border regions with the national core areas, efforts also exist to bridge borders and build partnerships with neighboring regions. As the studies presented here demonstrate, mechanisms and strategies not only vary from one location to another and among cultural traditions, but over time as well.

The first three chapters in this section examine how redefinition and reinforcement of boundaries affect local communities, and how local communities in turn influence these boundary-drawing activities. The fourth chapter brings us back to thinking about how links among global, regional, national, and local scales interact to produce particular results in particular places.

The boundary between Austria and Hungary reflects a long history of unification and separation. Wastl-Walter and Váradi consider the history of this boundary in terms of its role in shaping the cultural and physical landscapes of a

border region. The veritable abyss created by the heavily fortified and defended
Iron Curtain boundary, which existed from the 1950s until the early 1990s, severed
former ties between the two countries and between border residents. It also resulted
in a redrawing of the Hungarian landscape from one of human habitation to one of
fortified emptiness. Wastl-Walter and Váradi trace the fortunes of the areas
bisected by boundary drawing and redrawing, focusing particularly on impacts and
changes occurring in selected Hungarian borderland communities. Their findings
indicate that, while villages on both sides of the boundary line faced radical
changes, political evolution and local expectations have unfolded quite differently.
In Hungary, development of the lands on the border was recognized as essential to
prosperity; yet lack of appropriate legal structures and a dearth of entrepreneurial
individuals to take the lead posed large barriers. On the Austrian side of the border,
public and private investment has modernized the landscape while the Hungarian
side suffered from years of economic neglect and strong emigration. Ironically, the
fall of the Iron Curtain did not cause instantaneous, exuberant cross-border activity.
Decades of strong militarization of the border drastically reduced links among
relatives and friends, while time helped diminish cross-border excursions.
Especially on the Hungarian side, an influx of external funding and ideas is badly
needed to change deeply embedded structural divisions between Hungary and its
western neighbour. However, the emergence of Fortress Europe has reinforced the
old functionally divisive boundary with Austria, a situation that will not change
until Hungary achieves formal integration into an expanded European Union. As
Wastl-Walter and Váradi illustrate, this structural division has implications for
political, social, and cultural landscapes of this fraught borderland.

Janschitz and Kofler consider the border area where Italy, Austria, and Slovenia
meet. Taking a more explicitly cultural perspective, they note that the area has
historically been closely connected, based on common historical roots. This
'Three-Borders Area', they maintain, can be viewed as a multicultural living space,
one of only a few such examples in Europe. The authors use this area, where at
least three languages and several dialects are spoken, to explore the role of border
areas in European integration processes and to consider the ideas of a 'Europe of
border regions' and of a 'borderless Europe'. Reviewing the history of the area,
they note that, for much of history, the border itself was of only minor importance;
however, in the 20th century, boundaries took on increasing importance due to their
utility in differentiating 'we' from 'other'. In viewing the area as a multicultural
living space, Janschitz and Kofler observe that much of the commonality among
local residents traces back to the days when the area was a seamless part of the
multicultural Austro-Hungarian empire. By contrast, processes during the 1990s
swirling around political and economic socialization produced a new definition of
'we' and 'other', one that emphasizes otherness among residents of the three states.
The authors note that local residents do not view themselves as belonging to the
same community; only a few perceive the borderland as a cohesive social, cultural
and economic unit. At the same time, institutions and authority networks exist that
facilitate cross-border projects. These projects are usually financed by the

European Union, which leads the authors to an analysis of the role of European identity in the production of local border cultures.

Noting that currently there is a strong tendency to define European identity through political borders, only members of the European Union are considered. Places like Slovenia and Croatia are still excluded. Through identifying and examining specific transboundary projects in the Three-Borders area, Janschitz and Kofler link supranational, national, regional, and local perspectives to evaluate cross-border relations. They conclude that, over the decade of the 1990s, even though old boundaries may have been eliminated in Europe, new ones arose and existing boundaries were redefined. In fact, they conclude, even though common discourse refers to a Europe without borders and a Europe of regions, borders are now even more implicated in social and political construction and reproduction as multifunctional sites of differentiation. The Three-Borders area is part of this process for, even though there are many commonalties, each national sector still turns to its own national center rather than to its cross-border community members, and continues to reinforce notions of 'we' versus 'other' through invocation of boundary rules and functions. Actions on the part of local and regional authorities to foster cross-border projects and initiatives are needed to sensitize border residents to the possibilities for common resolution of shared economic, social and environmental problems. The authors conclude that only through elimination of borders from people's minds will the impacts of borders and boundaries be effectively reduced.

Barbič's survey of residents living along the Slovenia-Croatia border, localized in perspective and content, provides a view how the newly drawn boundary between Slovenia and Croatia has influenced daily life. The new border, she notes, has markedly changed economic and political relationships in the border region, particularly with regard to interactions between Slovenians and Croats. She focuses on the economic situation of Lower Sava region of Slovenia and Brežice municipality, which exists within a recently defined borderland with Croatia. She analyzes borderland residents' perceptions of the effects of the Slovenia-Croatia border on their everyday lives and cross-border relations. Her inquiry ranges from perceptions about changes in school attendance to transboundary travel and shopping patterns, transboundary conflict situations, environmental issues, quality of life, and cultural and national identity. She concludes that the newly created border has indeed affected local residents' lives. Residents must cope with new, complex cross-border regulations and procedures. They must strive to establish workable cooperative arrangements, and to overcome the many challenges associated with defining their borders in the context of global economic structures, and national and regional political contexts, as well as in terms of their own local experience. Defining 'we' versus 'other' in the context of shifting definitions of boundary functions is a challenge that local residents must meet. Residents must communicate inward toward their own national governments with regard to their particular needs and problems, and outward in order to cope effectively with the advantages and disadvantages of their border location. Barbič emphasizes that local governments have a crucial role to play in these forms of micropolitics. Her results indicate that open borders best address local needs and aspirations.

Pavlakovich-Kochi and Stiperski report the results of a survey of political and business representatives in Croatian communities located on the border with Slovenia. Their work provides a comparison to the view provided by Barbič. The study, which encompassed fifteen municipalities in northwestern Croatia, reveal that respondents consider cross-border relations between Croatia and Slovenia to be good, but that political change and the change in boundary function from an internal to an external boundary have caused problems locally. Perceptions about the frequency of border crossings before and after the drawing of the international boundary are somewhat mixed, with the majority noting that they believe cross-border visits by Croatian residents have declined since the boundary was created. They perceive trade between Croatia and Slovenia to have diminished as well. By the same token, respondents saw a decrease as well in the frequency of Slovenian crossings into Croatia. No conflicts are perceived to exist along the boundary. Notably, respondents perceive that life is better in Slovenia, due to factors such as job opportunities, entrepreneurial activity, and economic growth. This result is very similar to Barbič's findings with regard to Slovenian residents. Slovenians, as reported by Barbič, seem to be more aware than Croatians of smuggling activities. Notably, respondents believed cross-border cooperation was rare, though some activities involving officials on both sides of the border do occur, most notably cooperation in fire fighting. Most noted that some small percentage of the population also cooperated in the areas of sports, cultural events and social activities. Also notable was respondents' perception that the central government of Croatia was less concerned with development of the border region, relative to other areas of the country. The authors conclude that there are many similarities between the perceptions of Slovenian and Croatian border residents. They note, however, that changes in the national agendas of both states are being undermined by economic imperatives that exist at local and micro-regional levels.

Llera Pacheco's work in the El Paso-Ciudad Juárez (Paso del Norte) area of the US-Mexico border provides still another perspective on how local border relations may be studied and understood. Taking the concept of the 'urban growth machine' as his organizing framework, Llera Pacheco examines the activities of local actors who wish to create a new growth pole west of the existing transboundary urban conurbation. Working within their own local contexts, and operating from their own motivating factors, these actors have mounted a concerted effort to direct state and national-level investment toward infrastructure development and other activities needed to create a new trade-based city on a parcel of land in nearby New Mexico. Billed as a center for job creation and economic growth, the proposed city of Santa Teresa has been strongly supported by politicians in New Mexico as well as by local landowners and others who stand to benefit directly from the project. Likewise, on the Mexican side, certain individuals see large profits to be made from establishment of border infrastructure and other structures needed to support this transboundary growth pole. That the project has not yet been realized is due to many factors, including resistance on the part of families in Ciudad Juárez who believe the profitability of their enterprises will diminish if the project goes through as planned. Llera Pacheco concludes that both geographic location and the existence of interested and viable economic groups at the local level are required for such projects to move forward. The concept of a binational growth machine that combines global with local processes allows him to examine how interactions between and among federal and state interests, corporate capital, international banks, and entrepreneurially inclined and powerful individuals can surmount seemingly insurmountable obstacles to initiate interactions on major binational projects.

Morehouse and Salido address the issue of transboundary health care in the Arizona-Sonora border in a larger context of borderland geographies. They argue that, unlike borderland geographies of shopping, tourism, or commerce, geographies of borderland health care are produced within often-conflicting laws, rules, practices and expectations. While this may be typical of other border regions, the US-Mexico boundary is somewhat unique in that it marks a clear delineation of uneven development between the two countries. The patterns and practices associated with health care delivery and consumption in the US-Mexico border region reflect both a broader menu of choices as well as constraints not found in other places distant from the international boundary. The authors focus on what they see as a pivotal question: how transboundary spaces of health might be (re)produced in a way that minimizes the contradictions between international boundary politics and production of transboundary geographies of shared culture, values and knowledge. They argue that for this to occur, geographies of health must be explicitly recognized and articulated in local discussion of economic development strategies, education plans, community activism and other venues. The improvements need to be carried out carefully so as to include rather then exclude vulnerable populations. Specifically, federal and private-sector actors should be required to address inequities as part of their social contract. The authors conclude that the achievement of a humane integration of health services across the international boundary requires not only strengthening of cross-border linkages and cooperation of key entities, but a better understanding of border complexities, and active incorporation of local knowledge and concerns.

The chapters in this section illuminate the importance of local circumstances and how such circumstances filter and modify the decisions and definitions made at national and international scales. The chapters show the different ways in which factors such as personal experiences, common memories, and knowledge of local history may, in combination with educational, cultural, and economic conditions, shape local strategies and cross-border processes. The chapters also point to the increasing importance of economic motivation as an underlying force in cross-border interaction.

References

Paasi, A. (1996), *Territories, Boundaries and Consciousness: The Changing Geographies of the Finish-Russian Border*, John Wiley & Sons, New York.

Chapter 9

Ruptures in the Austro-Hungarian Border Region

Doris Wastl-Walter and Mónika M. Váradi

A Border Region in Transition

Theoretical and Methodological Approach

In this chapter we examine how people on a local level perceive and respond to geopolitical changes on the national and global level. In this way we can show region-specific responses to global challenges and understand the forces and values that support transborder cooperation. We can also reveal the discourses that lead to continuing separation. The case study examines the situation at the Austro-Hungarian border, where changes in the 20th century clearly show that borders are not ontologically pre-given but rather are socially and politically constructed in order to protect what is inside and to exclude what is outside. Borders also change: they change their place and they change their significance. Such big changes have been taking place in the Austro-Hungarian border region in the recent decades. In this chapter we will try to show how the border is being constructed by political actors on the international, national and regional levels, emphasizing changes in the location of the border and the most important ruptures that have occurred in regard to the meaning of the border, including reasons and consequences.

Our case study involves two small villages two kilometers from each other, Moschendorf on the Austrian and Pinkamindszent on the Hungarian side of the border.

The villages have a lot in common: the landscape and the potential for agriculture is the same. It is a flat, partly hilly region, and the same percentage (about 40 percent) of arable land and forests in the hills exists on both sides of the border, as meadows and pasturelands. Around 1900 the agrarian structure was also similar: the farmers had meadows, some grain fields, some wood and, in Moschendorf, some vineyards on the hills. The main income came from cattle breeding and dairy farming. Both villages had similar problems. Agriculture, under the existing land ownership and land use structure, could not support the population (as was also the case in many other parts of Central Europe at the time). To avoid famine, the population developed two strategies: a part of the Hungarian population migrated to Budapest, while many of the German speaking people emigrated overseas, mainly to the United States, but also to Argentina, Brazil and elsewhere.

In 1921, after World War I, an international border was delineated between the villages, although contact between the two villages was maintained until after the Second World War. When Hungary became part of the Council for Mutual Economic Assistance (COMECON), control of the border became much stronger. The Iron Curtain, with its mines and armed soldiers, eliminated any opportunities for contact that might have remained. After 1989, militarization on the eastern side of the border was given up, to be replaced by Austrian militarization after 1995, when Austria became a member of the European Union and became a party to the Schengen treaty. At this time, Austrian soldiers started to severely control the border to eliminate illegal immigration.

Commonalities still remain, however. For example, both communities have retained their agrarian character and both are still situated at the periphery of their respective states, in underdeveloped regions. We selected these areas as our case study sites because they are typical for this area in their remoteness and because their hopes have remained unfulfilled since the fall of the Iron Curtain.

We focused on two periods, the first being the years from the beginning of the 1980s to the 1990s, which was the time of the fall of the Iron Curtain. This work was carried out collaboratively between Hungarian and Austrian researchers (see Seger and Beluszky, 1993). The second research effort was undertaken about ten years later in the context of the project 'Border Discourse: Changing Identities, Changing Nations, Changing Stories in European Border Communities'. This project was part of the Fifth Framework Programme of the European Union, coordinated by Ulrike Meinhof, for the years 2000 to 2003 (see http://www.borderidentities.com; Meinhof, 2002).

The methods used for the empirical work carried out in the first period were mainly sociological and ethnographic, and included participant observation, questionnaires, and structured interviews. Discourse analysis was the primary method used in the second phase.

Historical Background

The Fall of the Monarchy in Central Europe

Over centuries this area has been part of the Austrian and later Austro-Hungarian Empire. With the constitutional change to a dual monarchy (Austro-Hungarian) in 1867, intensive industrialization and urbanization began. The different regions of the dual monarchy profited very differently from this development. The primary cities, such as Vienna and Budapest, had never before seen these types of innovations. Except for some of the other larger towns in Hungary, which experienced some development as well, Hungary remained an agricultural country, which translated into a poor and overpopulated country.

Eastern Austria (Burgenland) had always been part of the Hungarian half of the Austro-Hungarian Empire. To a large extent, it had the same agrarian socio-economic structure as the Hungarian area of which it was a part. However, the area was comprised of a different ethnic population mix, in that a German-speaking minority resided in the villages bordering the Austrian half of the empire. By contrast, in the towns, where state employees, teachers, officers and others lived, the population was mainly Hungarian. Most of the population was bilingual, or even trilingual if the local German dialect is defined as a separate language. Hungarian was the official state language and the teaching language, so the minority population spoke the local dialect, as well as German and Hungarian, while the Hungarian population spoke Hungarian and some German. (One of the frequent ways of learning the other language was the 'children exchange' whereby Hungarian boys and girls went to live with German-speaking families and vice versa.) This sharing of language promoted good knowledge of the other, as well as mutual understanding, cultural exchange and social networking. Thus, interethnic relations were quite close until 1921.

National Borders are Installed (1921-1948)

The international boundary between Austria and Hungary was installed in 1921, and was drawn, with some minor exceptions, along lines of language and ethnic division. In Burgenland, the official language was changed, and school lessons were now in German; Hungarian as the official language disappeared. This change resulted in a loss of knowledge and use of the respective other language among local residents.

Up to 1921, the two regions were linked to the central areas of Hungary. In 1921, they became border regions relative to the state to which each belonged. This fundamentally changed their situation, though local relations did not deteriorate. The installation of the border did not cause any displacements of population, social upsets or shocks because it followed in general the language divide. However, Hungary lost the German-speaking part of the local community while the German-speaking, formerly rural, border area lost its center. Important traffic connections were cut, meaning that each community had to build up its own independent infrastructure.

Border Crossing Relations and Trade

In absence of an alternative system of central places in Burgenland, the central places in Hungary continued to function as the economic and cultural centers of the whole region. This continued until the Second World War. As an example, Austrian families continued to send their sons to Hungary for higher education. New economic relations were established, with many families profiting. Some profited especially from smuggling. At that time the Austrian side was much poorer, and residents crossed the border to buy sugar or other goods for daily life in Hungary. For other things as well, such as clothes, the Hungarian towns were still the primary places to shop. With regard to smuggling, cattle were brought, for example, to Austria to be sold there. People in Hungary crossed the border to work illicitly in Austria. Those who had fields on the other side of the border could cross with a border pass. Social contacts also persisted for a long time. Much intercultural interaction, as well as good neighborly contacts, continued to exist until the end of the Second World War, at which point all contacts were severed. Thus, whereas the previous border had been permeable, traditional social and functional relations could be maintained, even if sometimes they were illegal, the new border was very impermeable.

The Division into Two Hemispheres (1948-1960)

After the Second World War, things changed dramatically, with different consequences for the two parts of the region. The newly built federal country, Burgenland, experienced a completely new geopolitical situation. It had always been a quite underdeveloped region, but had existed in the center of the strongly connected Austro-Hungarian Monarchy. Burgenland had only lost its historical relations little by little between the two wars. Now people found themselves on the eastern periphery of Austria, which became the outmost edge of Western Europe. The area was adjacent to the Russian zone of occupation, without any possibility of contact among former neighbors. As a result, development of agricultural structures and industrialization took much more time than in the other parts of Austria. Emigration remained an important survival strategy, with most of the migration flowing to the United States.

For the Hungarians, the shock was even worse than for the Austrians. The state border became a system border and its meaning and function went far beyond that of national boundaries, for it divided Europe and the world in two hostile parts. For Hungary the change meant that they were transformed from a region in the heart of Central Europe to one in the extreme periphery of the east, right at the edge of the Iron Curtain, which was erected in 1948.

The Iron Curtain was intended not only to protect the Warsaw pact states from the NATO states but even more importantly to keep people from the Eastern countries from leaving or making contact with the West. They were no longer allowed to contact their neighbor villages, which they could see from their homes, as the distance in the plain is only a little more than a mile. The 'technical border', with alarm systems and soldiers ready to shoot, enforced these rules from the 1960s until 1989-1990. For Hungarians it was only possible to go to the West if they possessed an invitation from relatives or if they could obtain a tourist visa. Travel abroad was limited to every three years until the late 1980s.

In place of the permeable border that existed from 1921 to 1948, the Iron Curtain was not only a physically but also a sociologically and psychologically menacing reality for the people who lived in this region, on both sides of the border. In the 1950s, land mines caused many accidents among humans and cattle in the area. The inhabitants, frightened, never went voluntarily in the direction of the border. Hungarians not only lost their fields in the area of the Burgenland, but also many fields along the border, which were taken out of production. In the vicinity of the community of Pinkamindszent, a 50-meter-wide border area was delineated, where they were only allowed to go and to cultivate their fields with special permission.

For those Hungarians who lived in the forbidden border area, in a zone extending about 20 kilometers along the Iron Curtain, the situation was severe. The border villages were not only closed on the western side to Austria but also to the rest of Hungary. The border zone became an isolated area where residents had to produce documentation to prove they had a right to be there. Even relatives were not allowed to enter the area except with special permission, which was difficult to get and took 30 days to obtain. No investments were allowed except for those undertaken by the military and the government; the intent was to depopulate the area. As a result, no modernization or industrialization took place. Such isolation had significant economic and demographic consequences. From the point of view of the people concerned, this meant that 'we became a forgotten community'; 'it was like a ghetto'; 'it was like a colony of lepers'. As a result of this peripheral status, the 1948/1949 emigration began. This movement of people out of the area irreversibly changed the demographic and social structure of the local society.

Autumn 1956: A Short Intermezzo

In the two months after the October 1956, revolution in Hungary, the border again became open and permeable. At that time, women from Pinkamindszent participated actively in cross-border trade. Looking back at that time, when they could visit the neighboring village again after eight years, individuals we interviewed revealed two different opinions about Moschendorf. Some remembered that, already at that time, Moschendorf was more developed with regard to infrastructure: 'the streets had all been asphalted', which in fact was not true and can only be interpreted as a projection, looking back from the situation in the nineties. Others remembered their perplexity about the poverty in the Austrian commune: 'My husband came back and said they are even poorer than we, they still wear the traditional pants (Zeughose)!'.

At that time, the Hungarian neighbor again became very close to the Austrian communes although only for a few days. During the revolution in 1956, many Hungarians took refuge across the border or took the chance to visit there, as we have seen above. A wave of helpfulness also emerged among the population from Moschendorf. But this period came and went very quickly and surprisingly. As strongly as the Hungarians had entered into the awareness of the population of Moschendorf, just as quickly did the people of Moschendorf forget them.

What followed was a period of decades of living side by side, separated by a barbwire fence, watchtowers, and patrolling border soldiers. From the Austrian side contact was reduced to a look at the Hungarian border soldiers. Very rarely did people simply exchange words over the border and if so, this only occurred with the soldiers. The inhabitants of Pinkamindszent remained hidden.

Modernization and Resignation (1960-1980)

From the 1960s onwards, in Burgenland as well as in Western Hungary, a restructuring of the traditional agrarian society began. This involved a large migration, and an increase in the number of commuters, which resulted in a change in the socio-economic basis of the households. Education and professional training became more and more important. However, in general, modernization in the two countries proceeded in different political and economic frameworks, producing great differences in quality and intensity.

Two specific aspects shall be examined below: the question of ownership and the structures of political power. Individual and community freedom and the personal property protection (i.e., the right of autonomous disposal of the personal property) have been very different in the two systems.

Socio-economic changes and rural exodus   During the 1960s and 1970s, Burgenland profited from the general economic development occurring in Western Europe. The nonagricultural jobs that were created locally were able to absorb those leaving agriculture to a greater extent than on the Hungarian side. Therefore emigration from the area was overall lower than was the case on the Hungarian side (see Table 9.1).

Table 9.1   Housing, population and age structure in Pinkamindszent, Hungary, 1900-2000

Census year	Number of houses/ apartments[1]	Total population[2]	19 years or less (%)	20-60 years (%)	60 years and over[3] (%)
1900	132	829	46.4	45.4	8.2
1910	135	783	44.4	46.4	9.2
1920	134	706	35.8	51.0	13.2
1930	138	699	37.2	51.9	10.9
1941	164	640	34.7	51.6	13.7
1949	151	659	24.6	59.8	15.6
1960	149	489	30.6	47.3	22.1
1970	136	403	28.0	45.0	27.0
1980	123	261	14.9	48.4	36.7
1990	107	197	15.2	43.1	41.7
2000	102	161	22.0	47.0	31.0

[1] 1900-1941: houses; 1949-2000: apartments
[2] 1900-1941: present population; 1949-2000: resident population
[3] 2000: 64 and over

Source: Census data.

Table 9.2 **Housing, population and age structure in Moschendorf, Austria, 1900-2000**

Census year	Number of houses/ apartments[1]	Total population[2]	19 years[3] or less (%)	20-60 years (%)	60 years and over[4] (%)
1900	175	928	45.8	47.1	7.1
1910	180	834	42.5	47.4	10.1
1920	189	894	45.0	42.7	12.3
1923	-	814	-	-	-
1934	-	745	-	-	-
1951	-	623	25.0	60.2	14.8
1961	-	586	25.1	62.5	12.4
1971	-	561	24.4	60.6	15.0
1981	158	469	23.5	51.4	25.1
1991	165	468	21.6	47.4	31.0
2001	161	463	20.3	47.7	32.0

[1] 1900-1920: houses; 1981-2001: apartments
[2] 1900-1941: present population; 1951-2001: resident population
[3] 1951-1971: 0-18 years
[4] 1951-1971: 65 and older

Source: Census data.

In Austria, changes in the agrarian structure have taken place in the absence of change in the legal framework governing ownership. This has meant that individuals often must look for another job, while keeping the farm as an additional occupation (sometimes the fields are sold and only the vineyards are kept). Sometimes this process has also meant a feminization of agriculture (the wife runs the farmstead and the husband works as a commuter in Vienna). In Hungary the sudden collectivization of agrarian production led to a total loss of autonomy among businesses and to dramatic changes for the individuals involved. In Burgenland the socio-economic changes had been accompanied by technical modernization of private farms, intensification of production, and substantial investment in infrastructure by the federal government, due to the fact that Burgenland was the least developed area of Austria. There have also been social changes that have implications the agriculture. For example, the heritage system has been changed. Instead of giving each child (now less numerous) a share of the farmstead, only one of them receives the farm; the others often receive a better education or a lot to build a house. However, although, until recently, many investments in agrarian production have occurred, it is probable that, with the succession of the next generation, additional farms will be given up.

In Hungary the collectivization of 1959-1960 took away the farmers' basis of existence. Although the farmers had brought their substance and their specific knowledge into the agricultural production cooperative, they saw the future of their children outside of agriculture and hence outside of the locality of the small communes. Even when they could make a small profit in the small private economic sector, they were not allowed, under the legal and economic strictures of socialism, to invest this money in modernizing their private farm. Instead, they invested all their spare money in private consumption, in professional development, and in providing a basis for existence for their children outside of the village. In this process, a change in the values and acceptance of socialist norms (discriminating against private agriculture) even by former farmers can be seen. Social ascent was no longer possible through increasing property ownership, but only through education and migration. Among those who remained very few people chose to commute to the urban centers because they lacked the infrastructure or means of transportation, unlike the situation in Burgenland. The dramatic increase of migration in the 1970s was accelerated by reforms in community structure. In 1970 many of the small villages had lost their autonomy and hence their relative economic and political independence.

Community, structural reform and autonomy   In several European countries, people tried to solve the problem of small and inefficiently working communities by amalgamating them. Such small communities also existed in Burgenland and western Hungary until 1971, when 181 villages were amalgamated. In Burgenland the loss of independence did not, however, have the same severe consequences as in Hungary. One reason for this disparity is the higher level of general economic development in Austria. Besides, Austrian regional policy tried to support and strengthen the periphery and border regions with special investments.

On the other side of the Iron Curtain the amalgamation, in the absence of further investments, only led to decline. Over the most recent decades, the border area received no investment (except for the military) because the central state could not invest there; further, the local population could not finance communal infrastructure through their own means.

The differences in public investment and prosperity between the two communities have an analogue in the private sector, particularly in the development of private housing. About 1990 in Moschendorf 30 percent of the houses were new and most of the others had been continuously modernized. In Pinkamindszent only 9 percent were new (from the prosperous period of the sixties) and 43 percent continuously modernized. Originally both areas had had ribbon-built villages along a main road with typical western *pannonian Streckhöfe* (stretched farmsteads). These had been modernized and transformed in Burgenland in the 1960s. In Hungary, no such rigorous transformation of the settlement occurred, due to lack of interest and emigration.

Until 1989, development on both sides of the border showed similarities in terms of loss of population and households. In 1990, some 197 people lived in Pinkamindszent, in 107 houses (Table 9.1). In Moschendorf, 468 people resided in 165 households (Table 9.2). The decline of the population was more dramatic in Pinkamindszent, where the population number has decreased by 75 percent since 1900. This led to an irreversible aging of the population: 42 percent were more than 60 years old. In Moschendorf, half of the inhabitants were lost and the percentage of those over 60 years was 31 percent, as of 1991.

Another similarity is the fact that agriculture had remained important: about 40 percent of the active population worked in the agricultural sector. In Moschendorf, the farms were privately owned, whereas in Hungary people were employed in agricultural co-operatives. Further, both communes had lost their political autonomy and had become part of a larger commune.

Both communes continue to be peripheral and economically marginalized settlements, although the situation has meant double marginalization for Pinkamindszent. An internal border separated the Pinkamindszent commune from the core area of Hungary. This status has led to social erosion and lack of a local elite. In Moschendorf, the possibility to commute (weekly) and the maintenance of the private farmsteads, as well as a quite strong social cohesion and presence of a local elite, has sustained the vitality of the commune. Notably, at this time, there were no more regular political or private contacts over the border, except for one family who has relatives there, and some accidental encounters.

Hopes and Deceptions after the Fall of the Iron Curtain

The Beginning of the Opening

After the fall of the Iron Curtain efforts to re-establish contacts with the neighboring community came mostly from the two mayors. They set up a provisory border-crossing post for one day in September 1990, and again about five years later. Events included were religious processions and church services for both communities.

The inhabitants of the Austrian village reacted quite differently to these events: '... the procession. That was very touching to me. First contact with the neighbors, with those you did not actually know before. That was somehow touching ... yet it is pity we could not understand them'. Although the opening of the border was initially combined with an interest in the Hungarian neighbors, curiosity soon disappeared: 'The first time an attraction. But later, that was all, I mean, there are just old houses and all, isn't it, nothing special down there'.

For people on the Hungarian side, whose freedom had been much more restricted before, the fall of the Iron Curtain had more meaning than to those on the Austrian side. The first opening of the border between Pinkamindszent and Moschendorf was especially important for the elder generation, who described it as an 'impressing' and 'moving' experience, 'a sudden feeling of freedom', as they remembered the border being open before, and had not believed that the Iron Curtain would ever be abolished. For the people in Pinkamindszent, the opening of the border was also combined with curiosity how their neighbors were living, and what their village looked like. But most of the inhabitants of Pinkamindszent only went for a walk in the neighboring village and returned, without talking or meeting anybody from Moschendorf. 'People there locked themselves up, they did not talk much with us.'

The mayors of both villages at the time planned to establish a permanent border crossing between Pinkamindszent and Moschendorf. However, because the road to the border post would have gone through the center of Moschendorf, massive protest on the part of Moschendorf inhabitants forced the community to launch a referendum. They decided against the permanent border post, so that now, in order to go to the neighboring community, which is only two kilometers away, one must make a 15-kilometer detour by car.

The border has been opened four times since then for a day, including once for a church fair and once when the fire brigades from Pinkamindszent received a fire engine as a gift from the neighboring community. 'I have given them a fire engine', the former mayor of Moschendorf remembered proudly. But the vehicle has stayed in a garage, without being used, because the fire brigades and the commune cannot afford the gas. In the hope that the border will be definitely opened, the commune of Pinkamindszent built a bowling alley, which they expected would be frequented by their Austrian neighbors. (It could not survive with only the income from local bowlers.) It was closed down and now houses a small community library. Nevertheless there were some people from Moschendorf who in the 1990s developed a superficial relationship with several people from Pinkamindszent. They dropped by from time to time and invited their acquaintances to a drink in the local pub. But the people from Pinkamindszent cannot even recall their names now, and it turns out that they have not visited for some years.

The mutual contacts, if such a thing even exists, have subsided. The driving forces on both sides are no longer active. The new leaders of the communities do not show much effort to make cross-border contacts. Benefits from any partnership, be it of economic or social character, are not visible to the inhabitants of Moschendorf. Instead, the language barrier is being pushed into the foreground as a justification for the lack of relations across the border.

Development at the Regional and Local Level after 1989, and Future Perspectives

Judgments about political evolution and expectations for their own localities were totally different in the two regions. While in Burgenland several groups made an economic profit and some others feared loss of their seclusion in Western Hungary, the opening of the border became the great hope. In both regions the border villages were confronted with a radical change. In Burgenland this led to a reevaluation of their geographical location in the periphery and the possibility of developing projects and serving new customers. In Western Hungary residents sought possibilities to pursue opportunities in a new economic system and a new market. But because the means of the local population were very restricted, the legal framework was lacking, and there were only a few optimistic and entrepreneurial persons in the region, development came to be based on small-scale, family-owned firms.

A total of 161 people lived in Pinkamindszent in 2000, fewer than ten years ago, still with a very high number of old widowers and older couples. In the village, people (especially men) work only in the agricultural co-operative, or commute to the nearby town, Körmend, where they work in blue- or white-collar jobs. All the investments that went to the region in the last 10 years bypassed Pinkamindszent. Some places have benefited from the activities of mainly foreign investors, who are bringing dynamic development linked with good international traffic accessibility along the main roads. Other places have been able to build on their prior status as economic centers. But these activities have not occurred in the peripheral and marginalized areas of the country. Demographic and social erosion of the local community could not be halted in the nineties, and although at the turn of the 21st century Pinkamindszent became politically independent again, civil society as well as the number of politically active citizens remains very restricted. There is a lack of an original political elite as well; the best proof of this is the fact that the mayor of the village is the owner of a second home, and lives most of the time in Budapest. The inhabitants of Pinkamindszent have, over the last ten years, experienced uncertainty about their existence; this loss of basic certainty is related to the systemic changes that have occurred and to enforcement of market economy principles.

For this village, stimulation can come only from outside. For that reason the issue of opening a border crossing is very important to the commune, regardless of whether, on an individual basis, people welcome it or not. Some people in Pinkamindszent, especially the mayor, hope that being located at the border, even without a crossing, could be an advantage in itself, over the long term. They reason that this beautiful, quiet and restful area could attract visitors. Relying on this vision, there is hope that the community may benefit from development as a tourism and recreation destination.

Indeed, today there is a noticeable though not brisk demand in the village. Austrians are among the few owners of second homes. The old castle and the old mill have been sold by the co-operative to a entrepreneur from Graz (Austria), who quickly began renovations. He is said to be planning to open an agricultural or tourist center. The Countess Ilona Erdödy, who now lives nearby in Austria, and her son, Count Mannsdorff-Pouilly, became entitled to 286 ha land in Pinkamindszent and the neighboring communes through legal restitution and purchase. The Count rented the right to hunt from the local landowners, as well as a barn for breeding pheasants. The family is also interested in some valuable real estate for tourism in the village. Until now the commune seems to be becoming more important for foreign hunting tourism, although the community and its residents have not really profited yet. Only those who sold their real estate to the foreigners received a direct profit. But people in the commune do not agree that the interest of foreign investors is an advantage; some wait and hope that their fields or house can be sold to them for a good price. Others despise the Austrian buyers altogether. All agree, however, that the selling of the castle and the mill was inevitable, because the co-operative had allowed them to decline and neither the co-operative nor the commune had the resources to renovate them.

It is still debatable and uncertain whether this vision, to be a destination for hunting tourism, would offer a possibility for success for the commune. The other, more probable development perspective would not change the basically dark, pessimistic views of the local people. This perspective envisions becoming a nice, quiet commune of second homes either for returning, or for retired former local people or other Hungarian or Austrian settlers.

In Moschendorf, the decline of the population may have ceased since 1995. Since that year Moschendorf has again become an independent commune. Recently, the weekly commuting to Vienna has become replaced, for some people, by a job in the nearby local centre Güssing. This allows them to live at home and participate in the local communal life during the week. To keep the local people in the village, the commune has built a youth club and a center for sports and culture, with the help of the European Union funds. But, despite all of this effort, the lack of jobs still forces many young people to commute to the big centers or to leave.

The near future of Moschendorf is viewed with mixed feelings. Agriculture is declining here in the border region since the Austria joined the European Union. Many part-time farmers have already leased their fields, the livestock has been sold, and the machinery, which was left over, is waiting in the back yard for a buyer from neighboring Hungary.

The emigration of the youth will continue, even though the responsible people of the community continue to make great efforts to make Moschendorf attractive through providing different kinds of activities. However, there is a little confidence on the part of the community management in these reinforced efforts to make the region and its natural beauty more attractive to tourists. A general perception is that the old people will remain in the village, while at the same time the local production base ('mom and pop' shops) will completely vanish.

The Influences of the EU in Burgenland after 1995, Skepticism towards EU-East Expansion

Since it became a member of the European Union in 1995, Austria has participated in the regional development programs of the EU. In the first step Burgenland as a whole was an 'objective 1' region during the period from 1995 to 1999. This was the only region of Austria so designated, which clearly shows that it has remained the least developed area of the country.

The large investments, however, were mainly made in the north of Burgenland, where the traffic routes from Vienna to Budapest had to be improved and where investors could be attracted (this area is within daily commuting distance of Vienna). People in our research area in the south expect some economic impulses for the region from a newly built biomass power station. For the period 2000-2006, Burgenland has again been designated an objective 1 region, again to decrease the area's marginality.

Within the scope of the community initiative called LEADER II, another EU program, the community of Moschendorf could see some small projects in the fields of tourism, culture, education, industry and agriculture, conducted together with neighboring Austrian communities. In addition to the common projects, every community has had its own project. The region is also included as a LEADER+-region for the period 2000-2006.

Cross-border activities have been restricted to construction and marketing of a bicycle road. This project was financed by funds from INTERREG and PHARE. Very few local people use this road for bicycling in their leisure time (given the rural and elderly local societies) and there is still very little tourism, so this effort to stimulate cross-border activity has not been very fruitful. Thus, the region could profit from infrastructure investment, supported by the European Union and the federal government. On the whole, however, people seem quite disappointed that development is so slow and has been very selective. The farmers in particular are very dissatisfied. They blame the European Union for the structural changes and the decrease in their income in recent years. 'Here the agriculture has collapsed all of a sudden when the EUcame. We had a stable behind (the house) full with cattle, but when the EU came, the decrease in prices was such that we had to give up agriculture. And so many others had too.'

On the other hand, since 1991 the soldiers of the Austrian army have been controlling the border. So, for local people, the border as a dividing line is still very real, and the mental impact of this militarization as a consequence of the EU-membership of Austria is much larger than cross-border activities like the bike road.

The entry of Hungary into the European Union is being anticipated very differently among the population of Moschendorf. The municipal politicians see a great chance to get out of their peripheral position, if they succeed in linking themselves more to the large Hungarian centers of Szombathely and Körmend, as used to be the case during the Austro-Hungarian Monarchy. The whole district is calling on the regional government of Burgenland to provide major infrastructure improvements, for example an extension of the roads to the east, or at least better connections in that direction.

The farmers in Burgenland see the end of their agricultural business if Hungary joins the European Union. What will remain on a family level will exclusively be self-supply, as long as the older generation is still able to carry on the farming activities. They anticipate that, in the end, there will only be a few large enterprises left, which will buy or lease all the fields.

The fear of cheap labor from former eastern areas is mentioned regularly as well. The only chances identified relate to establishing a higher qualification, through education, in order to be competitive with workers in the neighboring countries. One of the examples cited by interviewees is that of foreign workers who have taken jobs at the stone cutting operation in Moschendorf, where some workers from Hungary had been employed for several years.

The people in Pinkamindszent are not thrilled about entering the European Union. Their attitudes can be described in terms of uncertainty, skepticism and fear. This attitude is expressed repeatedly in interviews by comments such as 'I don't know', 'Even the wisest don't know' or 'I don't know what I should expect'. This is related to the already mentioned existential uncertainty and their pessimistic assessment of their own future perspectives. They are afraid that joining the European Union will result in worsened living conditions. Younger people think that, for their children, joining the European Union can bring more possibilities for jobs. Men who work in the co-operative are afraid that Hungarian agriculture could not be competitive within the Common Market.

Ten years after the fall of the Iron Curtain, people in Pinkamindszent no longer expect that the border crossing will be opened before accession to the European Union, as neither the Austrian nor the Hungarian government shows any interest. They hope that the European Union will perhaps financially support the opening of small border crossings. Now and then, someone expresses the hope that the Union will help Hungary to reach western living standards: 'If the Union perhaps will do us some good, then it should come, otherwise, otherwise not'. On the other hand, one can also see that, in this regard, people are poorly informed and that the news in the mass media do not contribute to a better understanding of the situation or the perspectives. It is, however, important that people in Pinkamindszent are conscious of the process of the EU expansion eastward, even if they cannot influence Hungarian accession.

From Geopolitical Ruptures to Mindscapes of Difference

The geopolitical changes and separation in this area manifest consequences also in the minds of the local people. In both villages the memories of common history get lost, and less and less people can remember, from their own experience, the time when the region was conjoined. Only a few family contacts over the border have remained more or less intensive over the decades, though these have been mostly restricted to the older generation. With the dying of these individuals, the relationships also die. Even worse, a thing that certainly has changed with the fall of the Iron Curtain is that fear has come into the lives of the people on both sides of the border. The fear comes with the uncertainty of their new lives. Regardless of whether the fear is realistic or not, people on both sides are concerned with security. Although the border is protected by the Austrian Army and a special Border Patrol, foreigners and refugees make it across every now and then. One of the repeated topics of local people is the memory of formerly open houses, doors, and entrances as a symbol of security and trust. Comparing current times to the years before the fall of the Iron Curtain, they always cite the fear of strangers and of crime nowadays. Other researchers at the Austro-Hungarian border region also report that one of the disadvantages in the view of the people living at the border in the selected communes is an increase in the criminal element.

Since the border is permeable again, and since strangers succeed in fleeing over the 'green border', old clichés about 'thieves' re-emerge or become mixed with new clichés. Thieves are today, just as between and especially after the wars when the border was passable, addressed in terms of 'them over there'. While it was the Hungarians then, now it's the 'Rumanians' or the 'Gypsies'. 'That's the Hungarian gypsies though ... or when they have gone away and a piece of clothing or anything is not there anymore, even they from over there say that you have to be aware of them, because they are evil. But other than that I have not had any negative experiences.'

Especially during the first visits after the opening of the border in 1989 in Pinkamindszent, old clichés seem to have been confirmed. The clean Moschendorf is opposed to the dirty Pinkamindszent, where old and scruffy open sewage ditches still exist, where the houses are shabby and 'not so civilized' as in Austria. But Austrian people make important differences about Hungarians: on the one hand there are the Hungarian people living in the border area, who are 'civilized, we have no problem with them', 'who are like us'. On the other hand there are the people who are living somewhere in 'deep Hungary', are maybe Roma, appear now and then as peddlers, and 'you have to be scared of them'. Austrian people are secure, feel protected, because the Austrian Army is there, and sometimes one finds a paradoxical nostalgia for the perfectly closed border: 'Today it would be better if the barbed wire had remained ... that all those would not have come along, the Rumanians, those from anywhere ...'.

Also in Pinkamindszent, as we observed, residents can identify the foreigners of whom they are afraid. They mostly mean the Roma, who come up and try to sell something. With regard to foreigners, they mean any kind of strangers, refugees. 'Many kinds of people move around. Who knows who is who, there, also in this eastern part how many people, from outside, how many come those "whatchamacallit"', and as one says, '... that they then would also come here and ... those kinds of Ukrainians and I don't know which kind of people. I am not happy that one admits all kinds of people. I say that finally even the Hungarians will be thrown out by them'.

Many people from Pinkamindszent had already been to Austria in the 1980s, before the fall of the Iron Curtain, but not in the neighboring village. Mainly women, organized by the church, went sometimes to Mariazell (a famous place of pilgrimage); others speak about one- or two-day shopping trips to Vienna or Graz (capital of Styria in Austria). Young men often went, in the early 1990s, from one commune to the other in Styria and the neighboring regions when there was a 'flea market'. But these trips did not produce close acquaintanceships, or friendships. In the commune, one cannot find any of the usual, typical border crossing activities: no one is working either legally or illegally in Austria, while shopping tourism, which was profitable in the late 1980s, seems to have ceased. Our survey revealed that most people do not even have passports.

To conclude, people from Pinkamindszent now have virtually no personal experience with Austrians. Their images and judgments about the other country and the people there relate partly to the differences they perceive, in favor of Austria. In the narratives you hear repeatedly that Austria is 'far ahead of us'; this is in reference to first impressions gained 10, 15 years ago, when they were amazed at the range of goods for sale, the infrastructure, the gas and sewage system, the 'fine asphalt streets' and 'even in the fields'. Always they emphasize the 'orderliness', the well-developed design of the villages, the cleanliness. 'There, there (in Moschendorf) yeah, one could hardly see any working people in the gardens or farms, but everything was straight. Here one worked still with the scythe, and there, yeah, since long they had used the lawnmower, everything was more orderly, even the grass there looked better.'

On the other hand their judgment about Austrians, which seems to be very common, is that they are 'not so very friendly, generous, hospitable', compared to the Hungarians, who 'would give even their last' and also to themselves in former times. It is said that compared to former times, as for instance the 1980s, the attitude of Austria and the Austrians towards Hungarians has changed. Austrian people 'don't esteem Hungarians very highly, they are afraid of Hungarians, because they are much further than we are. They are concerned about, in fact, about their jobs, about their all. If we go there, we will work for less'. This quotation shows how the small differences between 'we' and 'them' are formulated: a little feeling of inferiority towards the Austrians, who – in any respect except hospitality – are more developed than we are and who are, perhaps with some reason, distrustful, even hostile towards us.

On the one hand, their living at the border seems to have been a given, poorly reflected-upon fact. They argue they have felt many disadvantages related to the border situation. The border between Pinkamindszent and Moschendorf has been drawn again. While the Austrians show disinterest and indifference towards the Hungarians, they themselves feel discomfort and inferiority towards the Austrians, both without having real experience of each other. On the other hand, in both villages, the mental border seems to have moved more or less east or south: those living there are in the virtual hierarchy of societies and cultures below us, and if they want to rise, they are a potential danger for us and we are afraid of them. These images and judgments are crude, stereotypes, not supported by personal experiences, neither regarding the Austrians or Hungarians nor those 'from the East': both of their worlds are and remain foreign to people in both villages.

This nostalgia and incertitude finds its expression also in visions of the future. In ten years (this is uniform in both villages), it will not be very different from today. There will be even less people living in that area, there will be even more empty houses, the communities will have even more aged populations. Given the limited endogenous potential, any stimulation, especially on the Hungarian side of the border, is expected to come only from outside.

Conclusions

To summarize, we have found that the dividing effects of geopolitical decisions and discourses over decades had a strong impact on the mindscapes of people. Over the generations the commonalities are fading and becoming forgotten, and the international discourses of difference between East and West acquire a decisive importance on a regional and local level in an area where 'east' and 'west' have never existed in that way before.

The result is that past and recent changes in political and economic organization and power relations have strengthened the different cultural identities and the existing differences, thus creating new complexities and contradictions. No cross-border cooperation exists in this formerly well-interrelated and connected area. And even though the hopes that arose after the fall of the Iron Curtain could not be fulfilled, some still hope that with the EU-enlargement the old relations can be renewed again. But there are also undefined fears for the future on the part of the losers in the race toward modernization. For both villages, where a substantial development can only be introduced from outside, the doubts are quite realistic. The ruptures of the past century can only be smoothed out and overcome over the course of decades. For now, it even seems that the borders in the mindscapes of the region's residents are being pushed eastwards.

References

Baumgartner, G.; Kovacs, É. and Vari, A. (2001), 'A határmentisg paradoxonai: 'Besenyőantal' és 'Albrechtsdorf' 1999-2000' (Paradoxes of the border: 'Besenyőantal' and 'Albrechtsdorf' 1999-2000). (Manuscript)

Delaney, D. and Leitner, H. (1997), 'The political construction of scale', *Political Geography*, 16(2), pp. 93-97.

Dujmovits, W. (1975), *Die Amerikawanderung der Burgenländer*, Stegersbach.

Dujmovits, W. (1990), 'Südburgenland - Peripherie ohne Grenzen', in H. Alfons, (ed.), *Regionalentwicklung und Kooperation im Grenzgebiet Österreich/Ungarn*, Int. Seminar Stadtschlaining, Schriftenreihe Nr. 59, Bundesanstalt für Agrarwirtschaft, Wien, pp. 14-30.

Hardi, T. (1999), 'A határ és az ember – Az osztrák-magyar határ mentén élők képes a határról és a "másik oldalról" ' (The border and the Man – Picture of the People Living on the Austrian-Hungarian Border on the Border and on the 'other Side'), in *Elválaszt és összeköt- a határ*, pp. 159-191.

Jandrisits, W. (1992), 'Kooperationen über die Grenze. Zur wirtschaftlichen Situation im Grenzraum Burgenland/Westungarn', in: E. Müllner, (ed.), *Hart an der Grenze. Burgenland und Westungarn*, Verlag für Gesellschaftskritik, Wien.

Kocsis, K. and Wastl-Walter, D. (1993), 'Ungarische und österreichische Volksgruppen im westpannonischen Grenzraum', in M. Seger and P. Beluszky (eds.), *Bruchlinie Eiserner Vorhang. Regionalentwicklung im österreichisch-ungarischen Grenzraum*, Böhlau, Wien, pp. 167-223.

Kovacs, K. (1987), *Integráció vagy széttöredezés? Társadalomszerkezeti változások egy dunántúli aprofalu, Magyarlukafa példáján* (Integration or disintegration? Sociostructural changes on the example of a small Transdanubian village), MTA RKK Kutatási Eredményei 5, Pecs.

Kovacs, K. (1990), Urbanizáció alulnézetböl. Az utóbbi évtizedek társadalomszerkezeti változásal az aprófalvas régióban (Urbanization from bottom-view – the social-structural changes of the latter decades in a region of small villages), in *Ter - Idö - Tárdasadalom. Huszonegy tanulmány Enyedi Gyorgynek*, MTA RKK, Pecs.

Lang, A. (1992), 'Sichere Grenzen. Vom Eisernen Vorhang zum Assistenzeinsatz des Bundesheeres', in E. Müllner (ed.), *Hart an der Grenze. Burgenland und Westungarn*, Verlag für Gesellschaftskritik, Wien.

Leitner, H. (1997), 'Reconfiguring the spatiality of power: the construction of a supranational migration framework for the European Union', *Political Geography*, 16(2), pp.123-143.

Meinhof, U. (2002), *Living (with) Borders. Identity Discourses on East-West Borders in Europe*, Ashgate, Aldershot.

Nárai, M. (1999), 'A határ mente mint élettér. A határmentiség jelentősége az emberek életében' (Borderland as a Living Space), in M. Nárai and J. Rechnitzer (eds.) *Elválaszt és összeköt – a határ* (Separate and integrate- the Border), MTA RKK, Pécs-Győr, pp. 129-159.

Österreichisches Ost- und Südeuropa Institut, Abteilung Sozialwissenschaft (2000), *Die Österreichische West-Ostgrenze. Qualitative Rekonstruktion der 'mentalen' Grenzziehung seit 1989*, Endbericht, Österreichisches Ost- und Südeuropa Institut, Abteilung Sozialwissenschaft, Wien.

Schmidt-Schweizer, A. (1999), 'Motive im Vorfeld der Demontage des "Eisernen Vorhangs" 1987-1989', in P. Haslinger (ed.) *Grenze im Kopf. Beiträge zur Geschichte der Grenze in Ostmitteleuropa*, Wiener Osteuropa Studien 11, Verlag Peter Lang, pp. 127-141.

Seger, M. and Beluszky, P. (eds.) (1993), *Bruchlinie Eiserner Vorhang. Regionalentwicklung im österreichisch-ungarischen Grenzraum*, Böhlau, Wien.

Váradi, M. (1999), 'Pinkamindszent (Allerheiligen). Verlustgeschichte einer Grenzgemeinde. Ein alternativer Forschungsbericht', in P. Haslinger (ed.) *Grenze im Kopf. Beiträge zur Geschichte der Grenze in Ostmitteleuropa*, Wiener Osteuropa Studien 11, Verlag Peter Lang, pp. 141-157.

Váradi, M.; Wastl-Walter, D. and Veider, F. (2002) 'A végek csöndje. Határ-narratívák az osztrák-magyar határvidékrol', in: *Regio, Kisebbség, Politika, Társadalom*, 13. évfolyam, 2002. 2. szám, pp. 85-107.

Varga, É. (1999), 'Technische und mentalitätsgeschichtliche Aspekte des Eisernen Vorhangs an der österreichisch-ungarischen Grenze 1949-1957', in P. Haslinger (ed.) *Grenze im Kopf. Beiträge zur Geschichte der Grenze in Ostmitteleuropa*, Wiener Osteuropa Studien 11, Verlag Peter Lang, pp.115-127.

Wastl-Walter, D.; Váradi, M. and Kocsis, K. (1993), 'Leben im Dorf an der Grenze', in M. Seger and P. Beluszky (ed.), *Bruchlinie Eiserner Vorhang. Regionalentwicklung im österreichisch-ungarischen Grenzraum*, Böhlau, Wien, pp. 225-264.

Wastl-Walter, D.; Váradi, M. and Veider, F. (2002), 'Bordering Silence: Border narratives from the Austro-Hungarian border', in U.H. Meinhof (ed.), *Living (with) Border: Identity Discourses on East-West borders in Europe*, Ashgate, Aldershot, pp. 75-93.

Wastl-Walter, D.; Váradi, M. and Veider, F. (2003), 'Vieux Voisinages-nouvelles Chances? L'example de la microregion Moschendorf/Pinkamindszent', in *Identités transfrontalieres aux anciennes frontières entre l'Europe de l'Ouest et de l'Est*, Revue Géographique de l'Est, n° 2003/1-2 (tome XLIII).

Internet References

http://www.borderidentities.com

Chapter 10

Protecting Diversities
and Nurturing Commonalities
in a Multicultural Living Space

Susanne Janschitz and Andrea Ch. Kofler

Introduction

At the beginning of the 21st century Europe is characterized by cultural and ethnic patchworks divided by a net of political borders. But these borders do not always coincide with cultural and economic interests or needs. In the post-war period, when political and military blocs were established all over Europe, cultural links were cut off. During the past decade there has been a strong tendency to renew these links. Although frequently discussed and negotiated on the national level, this process primarily started in border areas. To date, successes are difficult to identify and the many different initiatives constitute merely a beginning.

As micro-units of a transnational form of living together, border areas have become a focal point for researchers, politicians and economists. In this regard the 'Three-Borders Area' between Austria, Italy and Slovenia is worth observing more closely. These three countries, or their provinces and federal states, have always been closely connected to each other because of common historical roots. Their economies, political decision-making processes and social patterns have had impacts on the people living on both sides of the border.

The Three-Borders Area can be defined as a triangle that symbolizes cross-border-cooperation projects and activities on different scales. First, there are several national relationships between Austria, Italy and Slovenia. National and even supranational questions concerning foreign trade, traffic, foreign policy or ecological problems dominate these contacts. The responsible partners (governments, governmental related institutions) are located in Ljubljana, Rome, and Vienna. At the federal state or provincial levels, regional planning strategies have priority. Regional headquarters and important institutions are located in Klagenfurt (Austria/Carinthia), Ljubljana (Slovenia) and Udine/Trieste (Italy/Friuli-Venezia Giulia). At the local level, the core Three-Borders Area includes only three communities: Arnoldstein, Austria; Tarvisio, Italy; and Kranjska Gora, Slovenia. Specific partnerships and cooperation activities exist among these communities (Gosar, 1991, p. 62). But, as the following research results show, other communities along the borders have already started to join cross-border-projects or at least have tried to develop local cultural initiatives.

The Three-Borders Area constitutes a multicultural living space by virtue of a shared history and material culture, as well as geographical proximity. There are only a few such examples in Europe, where three different cultures come together in one border area. Here, people speaking at least three languages as well as several dialects rooted in three different groups (the ancient Germans, the Romance peoples and Slavs) live together. The aim of this chapter is to discuss the role of border areas in European integration and expansion, through consideration of the ideas of a *Europe of Regions* and a *borderless Europe*. The aim is not to discuss multiculturalism, but rather do consider border areas as multicultural living spaces. Regional interests and goals associated with cross-border cooperation activities are discussed and explained from the perspective of the Three-Borders Area.

History

In the Three-Borders Area, not only three cultures but also different political and economic national and supranational systems have been coming together over time. For centuries the border itself was of minor importance; however, in the 20th century the function and meaning of the border changed frequently and served to demarcate *self* from *other*. In 1918, at the close of World War I, a political boundary line was drawn between Austria and the eastern neighbors to which it had been linked for centuries (Burkert, 1994, p. 15). The drawing of this new boundary led, in turn, to production of new cultural borders.

Before World War I, the Three-Borders Area belonged to the Austrian-Hungarian Empire. After the war, and during the following years, territorial rearrangements in Europe led to the establishment of the three independent states of Austria, Italy, and the SHS Kingdom. Founded in 1918, the Kingdom included parts of present-day Serbia, Croatia, and Slovenia; it was renamed the Kingdom of Yugoslavia in 1929. The post-World War I peace negotiations and aftermath influenced events in the immediate post-war years. The geographical locations of the boundaries caused many problems. Italy, for example, received parts of present-day Slovenia and Croatia, including Trieste and Fiume (Rijeka). The former boundary had been located east of the present boundary. The boundary between Austria/Carinthia and the SHS Kingdom/Slovenia also caused problems. Citing the right of self-determination of nations (after President Woodrow Wilson), the Slovenians wanted to annex southern Carinthian municipalities to the SHS Kingdom. These are, today, the Austrian municipalities with Slovenian speaking minority; Slovenian-speaking people constitute 3.5 percent of the Carinthian population (Österreichisches Statistisches Zentralamt, 1993). One may argue that the present borders were created with little regard for local/regional cultural and linguistic continuities but in the case of the border between present-day Slovenia and Austria at least several minority-protecting activities took place. For example, at the end of World War I, a plebiscite was held based on the results of the Miles

Commission. This international group was charged with defining the area to be included in the plebiscite. They accomplished this by looking for traces of German or Slavic languages in multilingual written and spoken forms such as names on gravestones and everyday spoken languages. The population in Carinthia south of the river Drau, the southeastern portion of Carinthia, were asked in October 20, 1920 plebiscite whether they wanted to stay with Austria or join the SHS Kingdom. The results, by a very narrow majority, favored staying with Austria. The peak line of the Karavanks mountain range was accepted as the political border (Seger, 1992, p. 227). However, it was only after World War II that the Slovenian-speaking minority on the Austrian side of the border was guaranteed minority rights. These rights have been very differently, and in many respects only minimally, realized.

Between 1920 and 1941, all three countries went through a number of drastic political changes. In the aftermath of World War I, changes also occurred in the cultural landscape, and technical infrastructure collapsed (Gosar, 1991, p. 61). By 1941, the northern part of the Kingdom of Yugoslavia, which had by that time dissolved, became part of the Third Reich and was called Süd-Steiermark (including the southern parts of Styria). Carinthia became part of the Ostmark. The boundary between present-day Carinthia and Slovenia played only a subordinate role during this time period. Since the end of World War II the boundary between Austria and Yugoslavia/Slovenia has followed the peak line of the Karavanks, while that between Yugoslavia/Slovenia and Italy was moved to the west. Since that time the Istrian peninsula, including the hinterland of Trieste, has belonged to Slovenia and Croatia, while the city of Trieste has remained Italian.

During the 40 years following World War II, several political and economic changes occurred, determining relations between the three neighboring countries and at the same time influencing the meaning and function of the boundary between Carinthia and Yugoslavia/Slovenia and that between Yugoslavia/Slovenia and Italy. This was the time when military and economic blocs as well as supranational organizations had begun gaining influence over national policies, including border policy. The Three-Border Area has always had a tripartite structure based on differences in political and social systems as well as economic conditions. This differentiation continued after World War II, when the three countries were subsumed into distinct supranational economic, military and political systems and organizations. The developments of the forty years since the war have had impacts on the flow of goods, people, capital, information, cultural links and common transborder interests as well as on activities in the core Three-Border Area.

Yugoslavia's boundary with Austria and Italy became a broken 'system border'; and Yugoslavia became a Communist country, though with significant differences from the other Iron Curtain Countries. The exterior boundary of the Yugoslav Republic served to separate the communist-oriented Yugoslavian state from the countries with western political and economic structures. Italy was a founding member of the European Union in 1952, while Austria joined the European Free Trade Association in 1960 and the European Union in 1995.

Economic matters dominated transborder policies between Austria and Italy, while relations between Austria and the Yugoslav Republic were influenced by the protective and defensive measures of the Yugoslav Republic.

Before 1991, the boundary between Italy and Austria was seen as a boundary line separating two countries participating in different supranational economic unions but relying on the same economic system. It was in the interest of Austria to protect the local economy by controlling imports by individuals from Italy to Carinthia. The boundary between Austria and Yugoslavia, on the other hand, was quite heavily guarded; border crossing involved strict checks of individuals and their travel documents. However it was the intention of neither Austria, nor Italy nor Yugoslavia to totally prevent border crossings. Today, after the downfall of Communism and the crumbling of Yugoslavia, the declaration of Slovenian independence on June 25, 1991, Austria´s admission to the European Union in June 1995, and finally the ratification of the Schengen Agreement, the Three-Borders Area is confronted with the fact that the borders have ceased being as open as they were previously. The borders between Austria and Slovenia, and between Italy and Slovenia, have been closed again, with respect to the free movement of people, goods and services, due to the fact that Slovenia is not (yet) a member of the European Union. The European Union is considering the country's accession but now, it remains for different programs of the European Union (Interreg-Phare-CBC) and for local populations and authorities to build up closer ties and/or intensify cooperation across the border (see Wastl-Walter and Kofler, 1999a/b).

Border Areas as Multicultural Living Spaces

Very often political borders are experienced as artificial barriers that disregard the mutual interests and relations of people living in border areas. Langer (1996, p. 332) points out that social relations and networks do not automatically end at the border and that state and society do not always correspond with each other. In border areas the population might be culturally and economically oriented towards its neighbors. They might feel themselves belonging much more to the other side than to the state they are part of. Friedmann (1996, p. 2) concludes that political borders are invisible lines, with extension but no width. The systems on each side of the border end at this line but in reality people, institutions and authorities carry attitudes, cultural elements, language and even norms across the border. A border area is a 'shifting terrain on which both the feeling of belonging to a local (region) and a cosmopolitan (Europe) reality, and a fluid perception of different cultural and national groups, can be developed more easily than within the national state' (Scartezzini, 1998, p. 262). Around the world border areas are characterized by different cultures living in the same place. The population on each side of the border is linked to the other because of history and cultural proximity. Such circumstances make it possible to distinguish between border regions where the populations of both the border area and the state have ethnic ties across the border from those where single ethnic groups are separated by a political border and from those where no minority lives next to the border. In this last case values, norms, language, music, attitudes or economic and political structures may be expected to be different (Wilson and Donnan, 1998, p. 14).

But why do we still speak of a multicultural Austrian-Hungarian Empire? Until 1918 everybody with different ethnic backgrounds could claim to be *Austrian* (Langer, 1999, p. 155). People living in the narrow, peripheral valleys of the present Three-Borders Area might have spoken a Slavic language, and might have had their specific dances and festivals but they felt themselves to belong to the Austrian-Hungarian Empire (Neèak and Zwitter, 1994, p. 173). Borders at that time were not meant to divide neighboring peoples. In comparison, Langer (1994, p. 66) points out that the borders between, for example, the Czech Republic, Slovakia and Hungary were established as a consequence of World War I and not because the people demanded them. These new borders not only cut off economic units but also ethnic relations. In Burgenland more than 40,000 Croats and approximately 10,000 Hungarians as well as thousands of bilingual or multilingual people were affected. In Carinthia, more than 30,000 Slovenian-speaking people were affected by the newly established borders (Baumgartner, 1995, p. 110).

Today the Three-Borders Area can be seen as a multicultural living space. Geographical, cultural and historical proximity foster communication and interaction. But due to political and economic socialization processes occurring over the past decade, the definition of the we and the other came to be underscored. Many people still tend to see the border as a dividing line. Those on the other side are supposed to be 'different' (Katschnig-Fasch, 1993, p. 43). This indicates that the cultural and social ties in the Three-Borders Area are not yet so strong that people 'take advantage of every opportunity to visit, shop, work, study or even live on the "other" side' (Martinez, 1997, p. 296). Few see the border area as a living and working area, as a social, cultural and economic unit. The area is mostly used and experienced for shopping and leisure time activities. People do not really feel themselves belonging to the same community based on common cultural or political experience yet. But what does exist, and will be described later in more detail, is institutions and authority networks that very often result in cross-border projects. These projects are usually supported financially by the European Union. This brings into the picture the role of border areas in the process of cultural harmonization within the European Union.

European Identity and the European Integration Process

European Identity

Due to European integration and unification processes, regionalism and culture have become very important sources of discussion and will in the future strongly determine European Union policies. In the 1980s an increasing number of official EU representatives have become aware of the necessity to consider cultural questions. In their view, arts, media, information, education, tourism, sports, and heritage should be regarded as part of 'culture'. Until recently European integration has involved little regard for cultural factors. Jean Monnet was supposed to have said that if he had been asked to begin once again with the European unification process, he would start with culture (Lübbe, 1994, p. 62). He was referring to common or similar elements in architecture, literature and language that occur everywhere in Europe (Lübbe, 1994, p. 67). Seton-Watson (1985, p. 15) argues that there 'is a European culture ... it exists, but it comprehends only those who can see and feel it ... it is simply the end-product of 3,000 years ... it is a heritage'. European Culture, in his view, refers to the Roman rule of law, the Greek ideas of art, philosophy and politics, the legacy of the military, the bureaucratic and the technical infrastructure of the ancient peoples that survives in modified versions, Christianity, and the early common experience of industrialization. Language and environment have been mentioned as two additional aspects. (There are more than forty languages, in three different alphabets, within Europe. Yet, although they have different roots, links between most European languages exist.) Finally, environmental and ecological influences need to be added (Wintle, 1996, p. 12).

Commonalities exist among the countries of Europe, and this supports the European Union's intention to create a common space. Although cross-border cooperation reaches back many decades, passages on cultural policy were missing in the Treaty of Rome, which established the European Market in 1957. The European Parliament first began emphasizing cultural features in the 1970s. In 1974 the Parliament passed a resolution to protect the European cultural heritage; their main interest was to establish a fund to guarantee financial help for the restoration of damaged monuments. In 1977 the European Commission declared that no common European cultural policy existed, only single actions such as the support of artists. As a consequence two cultural concepts (1982 and 1987) were passed. The concept of 1987 included the first mention of the creation of a European cultural area. The concept of 1992 revisited this idea. In a next step, a common community goal was declared: Europeans should be aware of their common culture but should not ignore the importance of their cultural diversity and especially the richness of their cultural heritage (Ellmeier, 1993, p. 11). In the Maastrich Treaty, Article 128 initiated several practical achievements in the field of culture. Today the European Union has clear advice for their cultural ideas and goals. Member States are encouraged to improve the knowledge and dissemination of the culture and history of the European peoples, to conserve and safeguard the cultural heritage of European significance as well as to support the non-commercial cultural exchanges (see http://europa.eu.int/en/record/mt/title2. html). Thus, culture has become a key dimension of the European integration process.

What might best describe European culture today is the slogan 'Unity in Diversity'. Diversity is understood in geographical (imagine the diverse heritages from Sweden to Italy) and genetic respects, based on a multicultural or pluralistic understanding of society. 'Unity in Diversity' reflects the attempt of the European Union to reflect diversities and nurture commonalities, especially in border regions (Zimmermann, 1998).

The problem today is that the tendency to define European identity through or because of political borders is very strong. Only the states participating in the European Union are taken into consideration when the characteristics of (an) European Identity are defined. But the question remains as to why Vienna, Graz, Klagenfurt (in Austria), Udine, and Trieste (in Italy) are part of this development while Maribor, Ljubljana, Krain, Nova Gorica (in Slovenia) or Zagreb (in Croatia) are excluded. We need to consider that, in the eighteenth and nineteenth centuries, it was not Klagenfurt (in Austria) but Ljubljana and Krain (in Slovenia) that served as the functional and cultural centers; Trieste provided the link to the sea for the Austrian-Hungarian Empire. In reality many doubt that 'this process toward a "borderless Europe" has also created the basis for a common European identity ...' (Scartezzini, 1998, p. 258).

Another problem is that people seldom identify themselves with a community in which roots and members are not known. Europe, as an idea and place of living, is too large-scale to be accepted and understood as a social space. Therefore, Vilfan (1994, p. 91) reminds us, a mega-culture can only be acceptable when regional diversities are underlined. In this understanding small units and communities should be fostered.

The results of a survey conducted between 1992 and 1996 in the borderlands of northeastern Italy, Austria, Slovenia, and Switzerland underline growing regional impacts. In this area, the feeling of belonging to a region has increased (Scartezzini, 1998, p. 264). At the same time the feeling of belonging to the EU has increased. Although spatial proximity plays a role in the peaceful perceptions the neighboring borderlands people have of each other, an open-minded attitude exists due to the existence of continuous contacts with the wider world (Scartezzini, 1998, p. 268).

Scartezzini (1998, p. 259) refers to the 'feeling of social and territorial belonging to a region which does not necessarily imply a political dimension, but simply the process of a socio-cultural determination of self-identity'. He emphasizes the crucial role of border areas/regions with regard to European cultural harmonization (Scartezzini, 1998, p. 261), noting that, in border areas, people are accustomed to living in two national realities. Borders are areas of economic interchanges and meeting points between different cultures and languages. These borders may shift in response to residents' spatial proximity, daily needs, and personal interests. People in border areas do not experience borders as fixed realities. Cultural borders in particular are permeable and mobile, depending on the degree of contacts across the border. Sometimes people perceive themselves to be more closely associated with the other than to the 'we' of their own nation state. Scartezzini states that border areas become 'bridges which unite, rather than barriers which divide'. It is here that people develop a 'feeling of belonging to a local (region) and a cosmopolitan (Europe) reality' (Scartezzini, 1998, p. 261). He concludes that people may live in a consciousness of overcoming nationally focused cultures, ideas, and goals as they develop cross-border understanding. Thus, residents tend to identify themselves with elements originally found across the border and to experience commonalities with those living across the international boundary. According to Martinez (1994, p. 12) this may lead to implementation of a new and independent binational micro-scaled system.

These systems or units (border areas or regions) are social constructs that can be experienced and realized through social, cultural, physical, and technical networks. They can be interpreted as patterns of relation and fields of interactions formed by social, economic and political actors (Danielzyk, 1998, p. 24). The actors are private persons living and working in a cross-border context, coping with given political and economic circumstances; but they are also institutions: universities, research centers, governments or private firms.

Cross-Border Cooperation Initiatives

The European Union regional policy contains a special and explicit focus on cross-border-interactions (including internal and external borders). The intent is to strengthen interactions in peripheral areas. The principles of unity and integration have always guided the initiatives of the European Union. In this context border areas represent micro-units that can be regarded as starting points for overcoming barriers and forming unities. In the 1950s border regions were referred to as *contact zones* for the first time. Due to their location close to international boundaries, these regions have very often faced poor prospects for development. Further, large differences exist with regard to the economic, political, social, and cultural characteristics of European border areas. On the other hand, the introduction of the single European market has facilitated the movement of borderlands from peripheral to more central status (Liberda, 1996, p. 32).

Europe has a long tradition of cross-border cooperation; such cooperation has intensified and become more institutionalized in recent years. In 1958 the first EUREGIO region, between Germany and the Netherlands, was established.[1] The driving force behind the establishment of this institutional arrangement was a desire to find common solutions for technical problems. Transboundary social, cultural, economic, and infrastructure questions, in the long run, remain within the purview of communal and regional territorial authorities (ÖROK, 1999/150, p. 271; Liberda, 1996, p. 37). In 1965, at the International Regional Planning Conference, the idea of a European association for border regions was discussed for the first time. In June 1971, the *Association of European Border Regions* (AEBR) was founded by ten border regions (http://www.aebr-ageg.de – Nov. 1999). Since 1979 the association has been an official observer at the European Council (http://ue.eu.int/en/summ.htm – Nov. 1999). It also supports the European Council in its effort to improve cross-border cooperation, and offers expert analyses as well as organizational assistance. An expert advisory group was set up to support design of cross-border programs for strategic economic development using methodologically sustainable principles. The association filters and analyzes problems currently occurring in European border regions and, in 1981, released a *European Charter for Border and Cross-Border Regions*. At the end of 1983, the AEBR assisted in the preparation of the first regional cross-border development programs. The aim is to support cross-border activities and to assist border and cross-border regions in articulating their problems, opportunities, tasks, and project interests to national and international authorities (http://www.aebr-ageg.de/agegbr/htm/abframnv.htm – Nov. 1999). The association also contributed its regional expertise to the design of the European Union INTERREG initiative.

The guiding principles for the Europe-wide INTERREG initiative on cross-border activities were laid down by the European Union 1990, although funds for border crossing pilot projects were provided for the first time in 1989. Fourteen pilot projects for cross-border co-operation were initiated with these funds. Financial support was granted for 31 operational programs under INTERREG I, (1990); in 1993, 59 operational programs were funded at EU internal and external boundaries under INTERREG II, which covered the period 1995 to 1999 (ÖROK, 1999/149, p. 20). The overarching goal of INTERREG I (1990-1994) was to support promotion of cross-border cooperation at the internal and external borders of the European Union. The field of operation was expanded under INTERREG II (1995-1999) to three primary areas: (http://www.inforegio.org/wbdoc/docoffic/commguid/intreg2_en.htm – Nov. 1999):

(a) INTERREG IIA was aimed at assisting development of cross-border co-operation in border regions;
(b) INTERREG IIB was designed to fill gaps in trans-European energy distribution networks;
(c) INTERREG IIC was intended to help develop transnational co-operation with regard to spatial planning.

INTERREG III covers the years 2000 to 2006. INTERREG IIIA supports cross-border cooperation, and has a strong focus on regional development in border areas.

In addition to the INTERREG initiatives, PHARE was introduced in 1990 to support non-EU countries.[2] With this program, the European Union began supporting initiatives along its borders with the Central and Eastern European Countries. The initial intent was to enhance cross-border cooperation in improving border crossings. In 1994 the PHARE-CBC- Program (Cross-Border Cooperation) was added to the basic PHARE structure (http://europa.eu.int/comm/dg1a/phare/ – Nov. 1999).

PHARE-CBC and INTERREG have common aims.[3] There are differences, however: PHARE-CBC promotes and supports interactions between the border regions of the European Union and its neighboring states in Central and Eastern Europe. INTERREG focuses on the internal and external borders of the EU member states (ÖROK, 1999/149, p. 20). PHARE-CBC acts as a mirror of the operational programs of INTERREG. From 1995 to 1999 coherence between the two programs was achieved (Wastl-Walter and Kofler, 2000).

Cultural Cross-Border Cooperation in the Three-Borders Area

An Analytical Framework for Cross-Border Cooperation Projects

Putting the wide variety of cross-border cooperation into an analytical framework requires that different characteristics be taken into consideration. These characteristics can be divided into two main categories.

First, cross-border cooperation activities can be classified by their spatial, organizational, and thematic context. The aim is to create a reference frame of data for similar projects that will enhance synergies and strengthen networks. In Europe, cross-border cooperation projects are implemented on different spatial levels. Financial and intellectual support for such cross-border projects is provided through the structural and regional policies of the European Union (e.g. INTERREG and PHARE-CBC). As mentioned earlier, different programs exist; their aim is to coordinate individual projects, which are actually implemented on a lower level. The interactions may be transnational, transregional, or local (carried out by local communes). The majority of the interactions, however, take place at the regional or community level, with organizations or associations taking responsibility for assuring successful bilateral cooperation. Frequently, however, lack of co-ordination between them causes problems. Folklore events, interchanges of cultural groups, and sports events organized by individuals or by groups continue to take place in the border regions. Furthermore, the organizational dimension must also be considered. Interactions on the intra-regional level require some sort of institutionalized networks and the acceptance of decision-makers. Contacts at the local and personal level tend to take place on a rather informal basis, and to some extent make up for the lack of organizational structure.

Project contents are mostly based on specific problem approaches. The restructuring of regions, economic development, as well as aspects of daily life and social life, determine cross-border cooperation interests and needs. Environmental and ecological questions, as well as infrastructure problems must also be considered. Cultural issues are gaining in importance as well.

Secondly, the project itself needs to be organized based on a *project-development-plan*. The plan should contain the project goals, target groups, measures, time schedule, and other such factors. This detailed plan is required to assure comparability and efficiency among individual project actions such as monitoring, evaluation, and control. Cross-border cooperation projects should be evaluated according the following considerations:

(a) *Goals and non-goals* must be developed; these help to define and differentiate the complex ideas and visions that exist at the beginning of most projects.

(b) At the beginning of a project it is important to define the expected economic, ecological, cultural and social benefits for the region. These are summarized as *results or outcomes*.

(c) The project should also have *impacts* on ways of thinking, on the creation of a local identity, and on the sense of place of the local population.

(d) *Measures* must be instituted in terms of necessary instruments, procedures, and actions required to realize projects and reach defined goals. Competencies and responsibilities are divided among stakeholders according to the different goals.

(e) The realization of projects very often depends on the *area* as well as on the *partners* involved. This needs to be discussed in a spatial and organizational context.

(f) *Financial aspects* (project costs, ways of financing, sponsors, stakeholders and their contributions) must be carefully worked out.

(g) Every project has a defined life span, and must stick to a defined *time*table. Further, project progress must be continuously monitored.

Some Examples of Cultural Cross-Border Cooperation Projects

Many ideas and initiatives for cross-border activities exist in the Three-Borders Area encompassing the common borderlands between Slovenia, Italy and Austria. But, due to the lack of detailed planning, partners or financing, only some of these ideas have been carried out as projects. The cross-border cooperation projects discussed below were selected because of their significance within a social and cultural context. Assessment of the chosen projects focuses on their perceivable cross-border effects, on the existence of cooperation or cooperative partners, and on regional economic impacts. These cross-border cooperation projects represent 'best-practice' examples in terms of organizational structure, cross-border networking, short- and long-term objectives, deep impacts on and the benefits for the region, social and cultural effects, and identification of the population with the projects and their results. The selected projects are classified according to their spatial, organizational, and thematic context, but are not ranked in terms of any order of importance. Detailed description of the most important features of each project (listed in the development plan) allows an analysis based of the specified variables. This classification does not include financial factors or the possibilities of financial support, although we recognize that these factors are very important for the implementation and carrying out of the projects.

Supranational Guidelines and the Implementation on the National Level

How can one describe cross-border cooperation activities on the national level? Throughout the world, states must cooperate on transborder economic or ecological issues. Such cooperation may be implemented based on foreign trade, transport, or ecological concerns. Cooperation in the Three-Border Area was first institutionalized through the Working Community Alpe-Adria organization (which includes regions of Austria, Croatia, Germany, Hungary, Italy, Slovenia and Switzerland). This organization was founded in 1978. Even before this time the area was characterized by friendly relations. Today, the participating partners are operating within the institutional framework of the working community, giving special attention to traffic, economic development, tourism, water management, cultural relations, and other such concerns (http://www.alpeadria.org/home6.htm – Nov. 1999).

While private initiatives have become an important aspect of the cross-border activities, the acceptance of the INTERREG-cooperation-program between Austria and Slovenia by the European Union in December 1995 should enhance transboundary governmental interactions. Within the last few years, the government of the Carinthia, in southern Austria, has begun to build a somewhat successful transboundary cooperation network. Meanwhile three large projects are in progress, focusing on tourism, regional development, and environmental preservation. Projects with an agricultural and industrial focus are in the planning stage. The State of Carinthia's planned expenditures, through the end of 1999, were about $7 million. Two-thirds of this amount was earmarked for overall economic development (including tourism); the rest was designated for addressing agricultural environmental preservation issues (ÖROK, 1999/149, p. 70).

Cooperation between Slovenia and Friuli-Venezia Giulia began in 1992 when Italy expanded the INTERREG I program to Slovenia. About $350,000 was guaranteed for new border-crossing, infrastructure, and agriculture products. In April 1997, INTERREG cooperation between Austria and Friuli-Venezia Giulia was established, with $3 million in financing. By fall 1997, the first projects, based on sectoral approaches, were developed. Project partners had to be identified and informed about the program and its possibilities. Several important problems needed to be solved during the implementation of the projects, mainly related to differences in the administrative, logistic (in this context especially concerning funding), and political frameworks of the respective states (Amt der Kärntner Landesregierung, 1996 and 1997a/b).

These examples illustrate the fact that, when talking about cross-border cooperation, financial and know-how frameworks are framed in terms of the supranational and national levels, while the actual activities take place at the regional and local scales and are initiated by communities or local interest groups.

Cultural Cross-Border Activities on the Regional Level

Some of the above projects are described in more detail below. These 'best practice' examples highlight the interest and need of people living in the Three-Borders Area to protect diversity while at the same time nurturing commonalities in their living space.

(1) By December 1996, seven Carinthian and three Slovenian communities had developed a cross-border cooperation plan for common marketing of cultural monuments and cultural events. Coordination and implementation of the project is the responsibility of the association *Kulturdreieck Südkärnten*, which was especially founded for this purpose. The main goals of the project are to increase the popularity of this cultural region, and to erase the *borders* from people's minds.

The cultural region, called *Südkärntner Kulturdreieck* (Cultural-Triangle Southern Carinthia), should increase people's awareness that they live in a unitary cultural region, and encourage them to keep in mind the positive aspects of living in a multicultural area. Local residents and tourists are both being targeted in the marketing effort. Local and regional print media as well as local radio stations are involved in the project, and serve as an important marketing platform. Folders, advertisements and posters emphasize the common-marketing strategies. The *Südkärntner Kulturdreieck* is also being marketed via the Internet (see http://www.suedkaernten.at). As a long-term measure, a *Guide to the Culture* of the *Südkärntner Kulturdreieck* will be published. The intent is to emphasize the uniqueness of this cultural region and to enhance transboundary cultural tourism activity. In addition to these marketing strategies, cultural facilities (e.g. museums, galleries, churches, castles etc.) have to be improved and restored, in order to increase their marketability as tourist attractions. Cooperation among galleries already exists, as does a well-organized network among the gallery operators. Exchange exhibitions are taking place in these galleries, accompanied by cultural events. Furthermore a *touring exhibition* between Carinthia, Slovenia and Friuli-Venezia Giulia has been planned. The idea of developing cultural trails, which link the most important cultural sites in the region and can be explored by car, bike or on walking tours has also been suggested (Zimmermann and Janschitz, 1997).

(2) The offer of new recreation and tourism attractions, in addition to natural attractions, is expected to generate a common interest in language and culture in the Three-Borders Area. Local agriculture, seen as a preserver of the cultural landscape, is included in this project for Cross-border Cultural Tourism. Tourist-packages have been specially designed to promote the specialties and characteristic features of the cross-border area. The packages are intended to benefit both tourists and the local population. All these activities are encapsulated in the slogan Specialties in the Center of three Cultural Landscapes. The Slovenian trade association, in cooperation with a management consultant, is responsible for the implementation of a further three-part project. Responsibility for coordination lies with the local Carinthian government. The three parts of the project include the following:

(a) Tourists are offered local meals in typical and traditional rural restaurants along alpine sightseeing roads. This involves a common, transboundary marketing strategy, the implementation of quality criteria for the cooperating partners and involvement of local agriculture. The revival of old, traditional meals and recipes, the use of local farm products, a quality seal for these products, and the organization of knowledge transfer among the cooperating restaurants is expected to guarantee a rise in quality and an increase in the importance of the Three-Border cultural region. Furthermore, the creation of tourist-packages, all-inclusive offers, routings tailored to specific target groups (car, biking, hiking trails), and a combination with cultural events are all part of the marketing effort.

(b) Old, historical railway-routes are expected to be reopened. Tourists will have the possibility of booking train-tours that include music events, dancing and/or culinary delights. Special events such as a horse-sledge tour or local sightseeing tours at the train stops are offered.

(c) The cultural particularities and the cultural diversity in the Three-Borders Area are to be promoted. The cultural trails, cultural events, music events, cultural products are presented in a regional cultural guide. This will, however, require enlargement of the existing offerings with regard to cultural activities and infrastructure. New special offers, such as a cooperation network between farmers to develop tourist-oriented opportunities based on local products have to be created. Such measures will provide new livelihood opportunities, and stabilization of the local economy (Zimmermann and Janschitz, 1997).

(3) Due to a redefined tourism understanding, a *Tourism Development Concept for the Three-Borders Area* organized around the idea of multiculturalism was adapted. The project encompasses a variety of cultural sites, social aspects, and natural resources that have both unified and divided the region in the past. It is an innovative effort, and is expected to strengthen transnational and cross-border connections in culture, economy, history, lifestyle, and environment. Achieved through implementation of a European style of sustainable tourism in border-regions and organized around common activities in this region, the initiative takes into account the interests of both present and future generations.

The project's slogan 'Unity in Diversity' emphasizes the goal of the endeavor. A number of different tourist opportunities and packages, organized around various themes, issues will be implemented through individual sub-projects (e.g. theme-trails, bike routes, winter sports, summer adventures, culinary delights etc.). The assembly of these cross-border tourism elements represents a future-oriented model of tourism – *sustainable border area tourism*. The project's measures include adaptation and improvement of the technical infrastructure, preservation of nature, and improvement of existing tourist structure and potential. Common marketing, development of information and cooperation structures, and production of new informational materials will help to increase the popularity of the Three-Borders Area. Beyond this, a central coordination, information and marketing platform can be achieved through the setup of a digital information system and the creation of a regional development office (Moritsch, Janschitz and Zimmermann, 1997).

(4) One of the most popular transborder cooperation projects in recent years was a coordinated bid for the Olympic Winter Games 2006. The three regions, united within the Three-Borders Area concept, applied for the XX Olympic Games; this initiative underlined a common desire and recognition of the need to grow together. The Olympic Games, organized around the idea of bringing together people in peace regardless their nationality and race, could have been mounted across national boundaries for the first time in history. The group's Winter Olympics slogan 'Senza Confini' ('Without Borders') which it used to promote the entire project, represented the idea of connecting sports, peace and

environment. In addition to the uniqueness of this event, the integration and cooperation between the countries and the will to commonly solve existing problems could have brought advantages to the region:

(a) The costs of the organization for the Olympic Games could have been divided between the three involved countries.
(b) Some 80 percent of the necessary sports facilities already exist in the area, as does a good technical infrastructure.
(c) The available resources in the region could have been used after the Games for a Skiing Experience without Borders.

Common marketing focusing on celebrating diversities while strengthening commonalities could have enhanced the popularity of the Three-Borders Area within Europe and worldwide: 'These will be the first Olympic Games which are "international", "border-crossing", and take place in a "Three-Borders Area"' (Regionales Bewerbungskomitee Kärnten für die Bewerbung um die Olympischen Winterspiele, 1997).

Local Perspectives on Cross-Border Activities

The oldest and most traditional form of exchange activities and events across borders are single, local ones. Although not supported by any professional or organizational framework, these exchanges have worked well. They are based on personal engagements, contacts, interests, and needs. Compared to institutionalized interactions, they have scarcely been affected by political or economic changes over the time. Due to their flexibility and to the needs, ways are devised to overcome barriers. The main goals of these local interchanges are to get to know each other, to communicate with each other, to exchange and share experiences, to come together for special events, to exchange local culture, and to keep old traditions alive. Such common interests underlie the activities of local associations such as choirs, folk-dance groups, small amateur theaters, local fire brigades, and sports clubs who organize events in the larger transboundary region. Activities include, for example, poets giving lectures in German and Slovenian, presentations of a *Village at the Border* in cooperation with the Slovenian Culture Club, transborder festivals of local folk music groups, and performances by choirs from Slovenia, Hungary, Croatia and Italy. Underlining official interest, the latter activity was honored with the Alpe-Adria-Signet. Local folk-dance clubs organize events or international folk dance festivals under the slogan 'Visiting Friends'. Farmer's markets are organized on a weekly basis, where products from the border area are sold (Baumgartner, 1994, p. 131).

These activities and events promote growing together among the local border populations, allowing them to overcome borders in their daily lives as well as protecting and widening linkages between people. It is also important to stress that the younger generation, in particular is attempting to keep such cultural traditions and exchanges alive.

Conclusions

In Europe borders were abolished, and new ones were established and subsequently redefined during the 1990s. The Three-Borders Area was affected by political and economic changes occurring at all scales from the local to the global. The fall of the Yugoslav Republic, the independence of Slovenia (in 1991), the accession of Austria to the European Union, and the ratification of the Schengen Agreement[4] brought changes in how borders influence everyday life, as well as cultural, social, economic, and political practices. Freer transboundary movement of goods, people, capital, and services has not affected all of Europe in the same way. Indeed, new barriers have arisen. Moreover, while Europe is currently dominated by the idea of a *Europe without borders* and a *Europe of regions*, new boundaries are being socially and politically constructed, and are being reproduced as multifunctional borders.

All over Europe different types of cross-border areas or regions currently exist. Today, we know that 'people along the border may have more in common with each other than with the citified folk of their respective heartlands' (Friedmann, 1996, p. 3). The Three-Borders Area, for example, is characterized by cultural commonalities based on common historical links. No significant differences exist in the way houses are built, churches are erected, people are dressed, or types of cars driven between Carinthia, Slovenia and the upper Italian area. German, Italian and Slovenian cultural elements are combined, as reflected in customs, architecture, literature, songs, names, fairy tales, and cultural landscapes. In this area the similarities are obvious; in fact, differences are greater between the Carinthian cultural elements and those of Vienna and Lower Austria.

Martinez (1997, p. 294) speaks of a cross-borrowing of language, religion, customs, traditions, holidays, foods, clothing, and architecture on the US-Mexico border. The problem in the Three-Borders Area seems to be that the local people in each country's portion of the border area tend to be oriented too strongly toward their national center. In many cases this orientation is related to prior political developments. Many people still deny any sense of cultural or geographical proximity, or of dependency. Different socialization processes might be one reason for this. One consequence of this is that people still tend to define their sense of 'we' and 'other' in terms of the political boundary. Only when it comes down to mutual interests does the perception of the border become very flexible and border-crossing self-evident.

Fortunately, there are signs of a growing consciousness of sharing a common or similar heritage of ideas and values. The projects and initiatives described above illustrate these developments. It is culture that structures space, as does the process of overcoming political and economic barriers (Häberle cited in Speiser, 1993, p. 230). Therefore, it is at the border where future initiatives should take place. According to Speiser (1993, p. 224), there are many transborder activities and transborder regions: there is not just one model, but many different models, each with its specific characteristics. Single agreements, common future concepts, and transborder activities and interactions that are based on individual interests or on established institutions can be seen as involving greater or lesser intensity in transboundary interactions. This is an area needing greater attention over the coming years. Local and regional authorities need to foster cross-border projects and initiatives aimed at sensitizing local population on each side of the border about how to work together in a common search for solutions to economic, social, and ecological problems. The examples discussed above suggest possible strategies for solving these problems: for example, reducing the economic gap through establishing a joint economic region (e.g. centered on tourism). A new form of living together without borders is the general idea of these projects, all of which are based on cultural elements. But only the disappearance of borders in people's minds will reduce the impacts of borders and the gaps within border regions over the long term.

Notes

1　They are considered as institutional as well as spatial units. Due to the different administrative structures of the individual member states of the European Union and their individual neighboring states, there is no common organizational scheme. In most cases, on both sides of the border, regional associations are made up of members who represent the local communes. Representatives of these different associations are forming a council called the EUREGIO-Rat (the Council of the EUREGIO). The purpose of the Council is to act as an advisory and coordinating organ concerning basic questions of regional border-crossing coordination. The ongoing business is dealt with either by one secretary that has been appointed by the parties on both sides of the border or by two managing directors, i.e. one from each side of the border. Teams of experts, appointed by the Council of the EUREGIO, are responsible for identifying the content of priority items (ÖROK, 1999/150, p. 271; Liberda, 1996, p. 37).

2　Financial support of projects on behalf of the EU corresponds to the amount contributed by the nation states. According to the priority of the programs, financing is derived from three structural funds (ERDF, EAGGF, ESF). The intent is (a) to assist both internal and external border areas of the European Union in overcoming the special development problems arising from their relative isolation within national economies and within the Union as a whole, in the interests of the local population and in a manner compatible with the protection of the environment; (b) to promote the creation and development of networks of cooperation across internal borders and, where relevant, the linking of these networks to wider Community networks, in the context of the completion of the single market in 1992; (c) to assist the adjustment of external border areas to their new role as border areas of a single integrated market; (d) to respond to new opportunities for cooperation with third countries in external border areas of the European Union and (e) to complete selected energy networks and to link them to wider European networks. (http://www.inforegio.org/wbdoc/docoffic/commguid/intreg2_en.htm – Nov. 1999). All regions along the internal and external borders, as well as those adjoining specific sea borders, may participate in the program.

3　PHARE (the Poland Hungary Assistance for the Restructuring of the Economies) was originally introduced to assist Poland and Hungary. At the beginning of the 1990s the program was expanded and started to include other Eastern European countries. Today the following states participate in the program: Poland (since 1989), Hungary (1989), Bulgaria (1990), Albania (1991), Rumania (1991), Estonia (1992), Latvia (1992),

Lithuania (1992), Slovenia (1992) The Czech Republic (1993 – Czechoslovakia joined PHARE in 1990), the Slovak Republic (1993), Macedonia (1996) and Bosnia-Herzegovina (1996). PHARE had by 1996 been extended to include 13 partner countries from the region (http://europa.eu.int/comm/enlargement/pas/phare.htm – Nov. 1999). The PHARE-Cross-Border Cooperation program for non-European Union members was established in 1994. It pursues almost the same objectives as the community initiative, INTERREG, through which the overall development of border areas within the European Union should be increased, their integration into the common market accelerated, and their peripheral status reduced. The PHARE-CBC program has been regarded as a fundamental part of the EU's pre-accession strategies (http://europa.eu.int/comm/dg1a/phare/programmetypes/crossborder/crossborder.htm – Nov. 1999). The main objectives of PHARE-CBC are (a) to help eligible central European border regions to overcome specific development problems stemming from their relative isolation within the national economy, while preserving the interests of the local population and respecting environmental concerns; (b) to encourage the creation and development of cooperation networks on both sides of the borders, as well as the forging of links between these networks and wider European Union connections; (c) to overcome large disparities in standards of living and growth at the European Union's external borders; (d) to accelerate the transformation process in the central European countries and their approximation to the European Union and (e) to contribute to the realization of 'bon voisinage' as recognized by the Stability Pact. In future the program is supposed to focus its attention on pre-accession strategies.

4   In 1974, several member states called for internal crossing privileges for cross-border passenger traffic. Many states would not consent to free passenger traffic due to security concerns at the time, and only agreed to relieve border controls. In 1985, France, Germany, and the Benelux states signed the first Schengen Agreement for the removal of controls on their common boundaries. The Schengen Agreement had two objectives: to relieve border controls in the short term and, eventually, to totally eradicate them. In June 1990, the second Schengen Agreement was developed on the basis of the long-term objectives of the 1985 agreement, and has since been signed by nine of the 15 EU member states. Its basic principles are defined in item two of the agreement. It provides for internal borders to be crossed without identity check and includes instructions for the control of external borders. It calls for the exclusion of people from countries that did not sign the Schengen Agreement and are not members of the European Union. As a result, member states must transfer certain responsibilities regarding security to other states. Germany, for example, must trust that Austria controls its external boundaries and limits illegal immigration. In addition, the Schengen Agreement requires a rearrangement of the right to housing and the responsibilities of police and customs officials (Achermann et al., 1995, p. 22, 51; Wastl-Walter and Kofler, 1999a/b).

References

Achermann, A.; Bieber, R.; Epiney, A. and Wehner R. (1995), *Schengen und die Folgen. Der Abbau der Grenzkontrollen in Europa*, Stämpfli, Bern/München/Wien.

Altermatt, U. (1999), 'Multiculturalism, Nation State and Ethnicity. Political Models for Multiethnic States', in H. Kriesi, K. Armingeon, H. Siegrist and A. Wimmer (eds.), *Nation and National Identity. The European Experience in Perspective*, Verlag Rüegger, Zürich, pp. 73-85.

Amt der Kärntner Landesregierung, Abt. 20 – Landesplanung (1996), 'EU-INTERREG-Projekt, Alpinkonzept und Landschaftsplan Petzen', Resümmeeprotokoll, Klagenfurt.

Amt der Kärntner Landesregierung, Abt. 20 – Landesplanung (1997a), 'Kurzbericht zum Umsetzungsstand des INTERREG-Programmes Österreich – Slowenien', Klagenfurt.

Amt der Kärntner Landesregierung, Abt. 20 – Landesplanung (1997b), 'Kurzbericht zum Umsetzungsstand des INTERREG-Programmes Österreich – Italien', Klagenfurt.

Baumgartner, H. (1994), 'Bildungs- und Kulturarbeit im Schnittpunkt dreier Kulturen', in K. Anderwald, P. Apovnik and R. Unkart (eds.), *Mehrheit und Minderheit – Eine gegenseitige Bereicherung?*, Kärnten Dokumentation, Band 11, Klagenfurt.

Burkert, G. (1994), 'Grenzenloses Österreich', in Bundesministerium für Wissenschaft und Forschung (ed.), *Grenzenloses Österreich. Symposium, April 1994*, REMAprint, Wien, pp. 15-21.

Danielzyk, R. (1998), *Zur Neuorientierung der Regionalforschung – ein konzeptioneller Beitrag*, Universität Oldenburg, Oldenburg.

Ellmeier, A. (1993), 'Kulturpolitik - Katalysator der (West) Europäischen Einigung? Aktionen, Hintergründe, Zusammenhänge', in Österreichische Kulturdokumentation, Internationles Archiv für Kulturanalysen (eds.), *EG-Kulturdokumentation*.

Friedmann, J. (1996), 'Introduction: Borders, Margins and Frontiers: Myth and Metaphor', in Y. Gradus and H. Lithwick (eds.), *Frontiers in Regional Development*, Rowman&Littlefield Publishers Inc., Lanham/London, pp. 1-23.

Gosar, A. (1991), 'Ansätze für eine komplementäre grenzüberschreitende Regionalentwicklung des Dreiländerecks (bzw. des Gail-, Save- und Kanaltales)', in P. Mandl und D. Wastl-Walter (eds.), *Regionalforschung von Grenzüberschreitender Bedeutung: Kärnten-Slowenien/Kroatien*, 22(1-3), Wien.

John, M. (1997), 'Skizzen zur Problematik der kulturellen und nationalen Identität in Österreich 1848–1937', in M. John und O. Luthar (eds.), *Un-Verständnis der Kulturen. Multikulturalismus in Mitteleuropa in historischer Perspektive*, Hermagoras-Mohorjeva, Klagenfurt/Celovec.

Katschnig-Fasch, E. (1993), 'Ursache und Wirkung einer Verleugnung' in H.L. Cox (ed.), *Kulturgrenze und nationale Identität*, Rheinisches Jahrbuch der Volkskunde, Bd. 30, 1993/94, Ferd. Dümmlers Verlag, Bonn, pp. 39-46.

Langer, J. (1994), 'Staatsgrenzen und Entwicklung', in Bundesministerium für Wissenschaft und Forschung (ed.), *Grenzenloses Österreich. Symposium, April 1994*, REMAprint, Wien, pp. 64-79.

Langer, J. (1996), 'Über riskante Verwerfungen in den Beziehungen der Österreicher zu ihren Nachbarländern', in Budnesministerium für Wissenschaft und Forschung (ed.), *Grenzenloses Österreich, Dokumentation 5*, REMAprint, Wien, pp. 331-343.

Langer, J. (1999), 'Last in, First out? – Austria's Place in the Transformation of National Identity', in H. Kriesi, K. Armingeon, H. Siegrist and A. Wimmer (eds.), *Nation and National Identity. The European Experience in Perspective*, Verlag Rüegger, Zürich, pp. 153-175.

Liberda, E. (1996), 'Regionalentwicklung in Grenzregionen: Eine Euregio als Regionalentwicklungsstrategie? Das Beispiel der Inn-Salzach-Euregio an der bayrisch-oberösterreichsichen Grenze', *Münchener Geographische Hefte*, 74, Passavia Universitätsverlag, Passau.

Lübbe, H. (1994), 'Europa – Einheit und Vielfalt. Kulturelle und politische Herausforderung', in M. Prisching (ed.), *Identität und Nachbarschaft: Die Vielfalt der Alpen-Adria-Länder*, Böhlau Verlag, Wien/Köln, pp. 63-77.

Martinez, O. (1997), 'Border people and their cultural roles: The case of the US-Mexican Borderlands', in P. Ganster, A. Sweedler, J. Scott and W. Dieter-Eberwein (eds.),

Borders and Border Regions in Europe and North America, San Diego State University Press, San Diego, pp. 293-299.

Moritsch, A.; Janschitz, S. and Zimmermann, F. (1997), 'Innovatives Tourismusbausteinkonzept Dreiländereck Italien, Slowenien und Österreich', (als Pilotprojekt für nachhaltige grenzüberschreitende Tourismusentwicklung in peripheren Regionen, Project Report, Klagenfurt).

Neèak, D. and Zwitter, F.(1994), 'Der staatliche Rahmen und die slowenische nationale Identität', in Bundesministerium für Wissenschaft und Forschung (ed.), *Grenzenloses Österreich. Symposium, April 1994*, REMAprint, Wien, pp. 173-178.

ÖROK Österreichische Raumordnungskonferenz (ed.) (1999a), 'Neunter Raumordnungsbericht', 150, Wien.

ÖROK Österreichische Raumordnungskonferenz (ed.) (1999b), 'Zwischenevaluierung der INTERREG IIA-Aussengrenzprogramme 1995-1999 in Österreich', 149, Wien.

Regionales Bewerbungskomitee Kärnten für die Bewerbung um die Olympischen Winterspiele Tarvisio 2006, 'Olympia-Bericht', Stand Jänner 1997.

Scartezzini, R. (1998), 'Social representations of northeast Italian border regions', in K. Glass, J. Kranjc and O. Luthar (eds.), *Grenzlandidentitäten im Zeitalter der Eurointegragtion*, Österreichische Gesellschaft für Mitteleuroäische Studien Verlag, Wien/Poznan, pp. 257-272.

Seger, M. (1992), 'Die Miles-Mission in Südkärnten 1919; eine regionale geographische Erkundung mit weitreichenden Konsequenzen', *Klagenfurter Geographische Schriften*, 10, pp. 227.

Seton-Watson, H. (1985), 'What is Europe, where is Europe? From mystique to politique', *Encounter*, 64-65 (July-August).

Speiser, B. (1993), *Europa am Oberrhein. Der grenzüberschreitende Regionalismus am Beispiel der oberrheinischen Kooperation*, Schriften der Regio 13, Dissertation, Helbing&Lichtenhahn Verlag AG, Basel/Frankfurt am Main.

Österreichisches Statistisches Zentralamt (ed.) (1993), 'Volkszählung 1991, Hauptergebnisse I Kärnten', Heft 1.030/2, Österreichische Staatsdirketion, Wien.

Vilfan, S. (1994), 'Kulturregion und Nation – Gemeinschaften und Gemeinsamkeiten', in M. Prisching (ed.), *Identität und Nachbarschaft: Die Vielfalt der Alpen-Adria-Länder*, Böhlau Verlag, Wien/Köln, pp. 91-115.

Wastl-Walter, D. and Kofler, A. (1999a), 'Dynamics of Local Cross-Border Activities between Carinthia (Austria) and Slovenia', in H. Eskelinen, I. Liikanen and J. Oksa (eds.), *Curtains of Iron and Gold. Reconstructuring Borders and Scales of Interaction*, Ashgate, Aldershot, pp. 213-229.

Wastl-Walter, D. and Kofler, A. (1999b), 'The Dynamics of Economic Transborder Cooperation between Austria/Carinthia and Slovenia', *Journal of Borderlands Studies*, XIV(2), Fall, San Diego. pp. 23-47.

Wastl-Walter, D. and Kofler, A. (2000), 'European Integration and Border-Related Institutions: A Practical Guide', *Journal of Borderlands Studies*, XV(1), Spring, San Diego. pp. 85-107.

Wilson, T. and Donnan, H. (1998), 'Nation, state and identity at international border', in T. Wilson and H. Donnan (eds.), *Border identities: nation and state at international frontiers*, University Press, Cambridge, pp. 1-31.

Wintle, M. (1996), 'Culture and Identity in Europe: Shared experience', in M. Wintle (ed.), *Culture and Identity in Europe. Perceptions of divergence and unity in past and present*, Ashgate, Aldershot.

Zimmermann, F. (1998), 'Multikulturalität im Europa der Regionen – theoretische Überlegungen und praktische Beispiele', *Arbeiten aus dem Institut für Geographie der Karl-Franzens Universität Graz*, Band 36, pp. 297-309.

Zimmermann, F. und Janschitz, S. (1997), 'Kultur im Dreiländereck Italien, Slowenien und Österreich – Möglichkeiten grenzüberschreitender Kooperationen in der Europäischen Union (INTERREG)', Project Report, Klagenfurt.

Internet References

http://europa.eu.int/comm/dg1a/phare/
http://europa.eu.int/comm/dg1a/phare/programmetypes/crossborder/crossborder.htm
http://europa.eu.int/comm/enlargement/pas/phare.htm
http://europa.eu.int/en/record/mt/title2.htm
http://www.aebr-ageg.de/agegbr/htm/abframnv.htm
http://www.alpeadria.org/home6.htm
http://www.inforegio.org/wbdoc/docoffic/commguid/ intreg2_en.htm
http://www.suedkaernten.at

Chapter 11

Perceptions of New Realities along the Slovenian-Croatian Border

Ana Barbič

Introduction

The collapse of the socialist systems of Eastern, Central and Southern Europe in the late 1980s and early 1990s, accompanied by the formation of new nation-states in the territories of former Soviet Union, Yugoslavia and Czechoslovakia, has resulted in a hardening of the once-soft lines separating bordering nations. The hardening is an outcome of the efforts of the individual states to protect their national territories. In the process, mutual cooperation and help across the formerly soft borderlines have been replaced by competitiveness between the bordering states. The simultaneousness of the integration of traditional states and the creation of new ones calls attention to the complexity of strategies of cooperation and separation, for these strategies not only reflect economic, but also political, cultural, and historical themes. Complementarity between conflict and co-operation among the neighboring states introduces specific dynamics into borderlands, stimulates or handicaps exchange, and enriches or impedes local life on both sides of a border.

Because the international border between Slovenia and Croatia had not yet been formally defined, minor cross-border conflicts and incidents had occasionally taken place and cooperation between the two neighboring states and between local borderland communities had suffered. Borderland residents still suffer the most from these conflicts. It is not coincidental that borderland research has concentrated on the problems of borderland residents along Slovenian-Croatian border. Research approaches and findings have introduced new dimensions and themes (Knežević-Hočevar, 1999; Kržišnik-Bukić, 1999) into 'traditional' cross-border research that has been concentrated mainly on the Slovenian-Italian and Slovenian-Austrian border (Plut, 1970; Klemenčič and Jeršič, 1972; Klemenčič, 1974; Pak, 1993).

This chapter examines the economic situation of Lower Sava region of Slovenia and the Brežice municipality, which constitutes a new borderland along the Slovenian-Croatian boundary. Specifically, the chapter focuses on borderland residents' perceptions of the effects of this new, international Slovenian-Croatian border on their everyday lives and cross-border relations.

Types of Relations in Borderlands

Territorial boundaries represent a demarcation line between nations and co-define their identities. Territorial boundaries have, through history, enabled nations to preserve their language as well as their natural and spiritual creations. At the same time, there have always been external influences that have brought new stimuli and new contents to national identities across the territorial borders (Connolly, 1996, p. 153). Although borderlands are typically viewed as peripheries of states (Maier and Schimak, 1997, p. 10) the borderlines themselves are foci of intensive processes of cooperation and separation. For this reason, borderland populations can develop varied forms of human relationships, while access to the foreign economy across the border increases employment possibilities and consumer choices (Martínez, 1994, p. 25). The existence and intensity of cooperation depend to a great extent on formal relations between the bordering states. However, through everyday experiences and comparisons, borderland residents easily identify (dis)advantages of life on both sides of the border.

Cross-border relations among borderland residents (economic, cultural, recreational, contacts with relatives and friends) are to a great extent determined by the relations between the neighboring states. The normative arrangements between the nation-states, as well as the overall political atmosphere, can either stimulate or hamper local cross-border relations, and can increase or decrease economical, boundary as a physical line may divide territories of the bordering states but it is seldom effective in completely interrupting cross-border movement.

From a theoretical perspective, there are three types of relations between borderlands (see Figure 11.1).

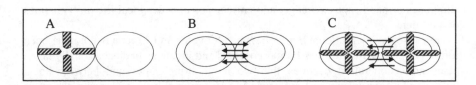

Figure 11.1   Types of relations between bordering states and borderland regions

Borderland Type A is characterized by the absence of any relation, either between the neighboring states, or among the borderland communities. The Iron Curtain is an example of this borderland type. Borderland Type B although is also characterized by a lack of relation between the neighboring states, but here borderland residents still find ways to maintain contacts and exchange goods. Borderland Type C, by contrast, represents open relations/cooperation between the neighboring states and among local communities and their residents in the borderlands' regions.

Transboundary relations among borderland communities are determined by relations among their respective nation-states. However, borderland communities are somewhat independent from the states, especially with regard to border residents' inventiveness in overcoming obstacles created by the boundary, and in taking advantage of different economic situations and/or conditions in the neighboring state. Thus, while borderland communities and residents must cope with problems arising from border situations, at the same time they can also take advantage of their border location. More generally, as a rule of thumb, the stronger the role of the boundary in delimiting the neighboring nation-states, the greater the difficulties are for borderland residents to engage in cross-border relations. Some of these relations may be of vital importance in their everyday lives.

The intensity of the frustrations caused by conflict and controversy in border areas depends on the ratio of advantages to disadvantages on either side of the border. In order to minimize frustrations, bordering states, which are sensitive to the situation of their borderland residents, often formulate specific rules for local cross-border relations. Among these arrangements, 'open border' polices have proven to be an optimal solution for local border-area residents. For example, an open border policy between Gorizia (Italy) and Nova Gorica (Slovenia) has been in effect since 1980. Today, the residents of both towns don't even perceive a boundary to exist between the two countries.

Open borders are especially useful for stimulating development in borderland areas, for such policies facilitate discovery and realization of numerous business opportunities, based on the comparative advantages/disadvantages that exist in the neighboring country. Because of the short distances, transport and trading costs are lower; more importantly, transparency in cross-border relations, based on personal contacts, enables direct social control in the borderland area (see Figure 11.2).

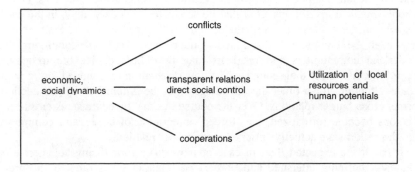

Figure 11.2   Conflicts/cooperation in the borderland area

Slovenia is now an independent state. As such, it shares borders with two European Union member states (Italy and Austria), with one state formerly located behind the 'Iron Curtain' (Hungary), and with one newly independent state

(Croatia). These borders have some similar characteristics, but also numerous areas of uniqueness, which are primarily related to their past history as international border areas (Bufon, 1998, pp. 1-2). Neighboring states and their borderland communities rule under different laws, and operate within different economic, social, political, and environmental conditions; they also pursue different development strategies. While laws and development strategies may not contradict one another, they may differ markedly in details that either facilitate or constrain cross-border relations. Efficiency in utilizing available opportunities and coping with obstacles depends to a great extent on the inventiveness and creativity of local border-area governments and local residents.

Economic cooperation between the neighboring countries/regions/residents may depend on specific opportunities the border offers for cross-border trade and for cross-border travel associated with making purchases and taking advantage of consumer-oriented goods and services available in the neighboring country. This kind of situation applies to borderlands where old, stable boundaries exist, across which cross-border economic and other cooperation has developed over a long period of time. By contrast, a newly instituted boundary line, at least at the beginning, typically severs relations, or reduces former practices and patterns of cooperation. Here, changed circumstances require development of a new basis for cooperation. Local production patterns, for example, have to be adapted to new demands and to the purchasing capacities of the neighboring citizens. Further, new production may need to be developed to meet newly emerging demands.

In the case of a border in transition (Barbič, 1998a) the normative frame for behavior/actions of borderland communities and residents is not defined at a detailed level. Here, achieving agreement about traffic and cooperation between the neighboring borderlands is essential for living along the border. Everyday activities of local residents that were formerly taken for granted, such as cultivating land on the other side of the boundary line or using nearby services (such as schools, medical institutions, etc.) that lie across the boundary, may, in the case of the new border context, be perpetuated only with great difficulty. Such activities may even be completely abandoned. Under these kinds of conditions, local borderland communities and residents may have little choice but to gravitate toward the interior of their country. The new orientation can, indeed, bring fruitful results although, for a time, the advantages may be diminished by the decline in former cross-border relations. Over the course of time, by contrast, as cross-border relations become formalized, the 'forced' integration of borderland communities into the nation-state actually enriches cross-border relations.

It has to be expected that, in case of new states formalizing an international boundary, defining interstate and borderland relations takes time. If the process takes too long, though, citizens and especially borderland residents may become impatient with their state officials and try to find their own solutions to local, transboundary problems. Such local cross-border relations tend to be limited to dealing only with the most essential problems of everyday life. It is, therefore, in the interest of borderland residents and local communities to elevate their problems to higher levels of government in order to accelerate interstate negotiations and to secure their own participation in this process.

For more than 70 years (1918-1991), the now-international border between Slovenia and Croatia constituted only an informal line of demarcation. This chapter is based on the findings of a research project entitled 'Border as a Factor of Cooperation/Separation of Borderland Residents along Slovenian-Croatian border in Brežice Municipality' (Barbič, 1998b). Based on a survey of 331 residents,[1] perceptions were gathered on the following topics: (a) local relations, (b) relations between neighboring states, (c) cross-border economic cooperation, and (d) similarities/dissimilarities between Slovenia and Croatia.

Four hypotheses were tested. First, after the boundary was implemented, relations between the two new states worsened much more than the relations between the borderland residents. Second, environmental conditions, as well as of work and life in the borderland, have in some aspects worsened; in other aspects things have become better, or have not changed at all. Third, borderland residents in Brežice municipality perceive the border with Croatia primarily as an obstacle for economic cooperation across the border. Fourth, borderland residents on the Slovenian side of the border are highly loyal to the state of Slovenia.

Study Area

Brežice municipality, together with the municipalities of Krško and Sevnica, form the Lower Sava region (see Figure 11.3). According to economic, social and demographic indicators, the region falls into the group of average developed regions of Slovenia, with a rather poor economy but with good development potential. Because at the time of this writing no data were available at either the national or regional scale, the economy of the Lower Sava region is evaluated here on the basis of partial indicators. Since Slovenia achieved independence, the Lower Sava region's economy, measured by gross value added per inhabitant, has been unstable. In 1991 the region's average gross added value per inhabitant was at 95.5 percent of the national average. In 1995, the proportion dropped to 68.8 percent then rose again in 1996 to 70.3 percent. The economic structure of the region in 1990's is not promising: the number of workers in industry is falling faster than the overall average for Slovenia, salaries are the lowest among Slovenia's regions, and the unemployment rate is higher than the Slovenian average.

In the Lower Sava region the inhabitants' economic power, measured in terms of average net income per inhabitant, is 12 percent below the average for Slovenia as a whole. On the bright side, some indicators are close to the national averages; these examples can be ascribed to the favorable treatment of agriculture in Slovenia and to the high level of informal economic activity developing along the newly drawn international boundary with Croatia.

The highest potential of the region lies in services (craft, tourism, retail trade, and transport), agriculture, and more generally in closeness to the border. Compared with other Slovenian regions Lower Sava has the highest employment rate in the private (mostly the service) sector, indicating considerable inventiveness among local residents in taking advantage of potential opportunities associated with living in the borderland.

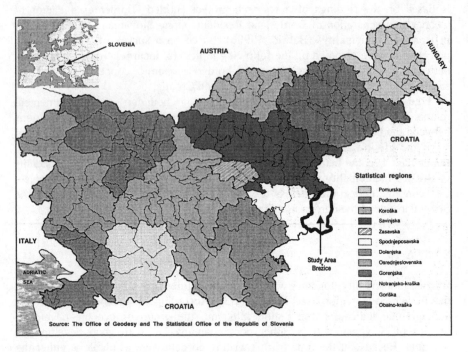

Figure 11.3   The study area within the Republic of Slovenia's statistical regions

Brežice municipality, with 24,724 inhabitants (1.3 percent of the population of Slovenia), is one of the largest of the 147 municipalities of Slovenia. The municipality has a higher proportion of active residents (49.4 percent) than Slovenia as a whole (48.1 percent), a higher proportion of agricultural population (15.6 percent, versus the Slovenian average of 7.6 percent), and a higher proportion of daily work commuters (23.8 percent versus Slovenia's average of 22.4 percent). In general, the population of the Lower Sava region is older than the average for Slovenia. The trend suggests that Brežice may face risks associated with an aging population. This trend may be offset, however, for recent data indicate that residents from other parts of Slovenia and from outside the country are moving to Brežice municipality.

The city of Brežice is situated 100 kilometers from Ljubljana, the capital of Slovenia, (Ljubljana has 350,000 inhabitants). By contrast, Brežice is only 40 kilometers from Zagreb (700,000 inhabitants), the capital of Croatia. Eighty percent of Brežice municipality's territory is within ten kilometers of the international boundary; this area includes 93 (81 percent) of the 109 settlements within the municipality. Some 20,000 (81 percent) of the 24,724 residents of the Brežice municipality live in these 93 settlements (Statistični letopis, 1997, pp. 55, 512).

An agreement on border cooperation between the Republic of Slovenia and Croatia was ratified by the Slovenian parliament in 2001 (Zakon o ratifikaciji sporazuma med Republiko Slovenijo in Republiko Hrvaško o obmejnem prometu in sodelovanju / Act of ratifying the agreement between the Republic of Slovenia and the Republic of Croatia on traffic and cooperation, Uradni list R Slovenije. Ljubljana, 31.7.2001, No. 63). Part of the agreement calls for the opening of 27 new local border crossings; this will not only release current pressure on international border crossings but will also revitalize relations which were cut off by the newly imposed international boundary (Podgoršek, 1997). The residents of Brežice municipality, as well as other borderland residents along the Slovenian-Croatian border, expect to be entitled to a special border-crossing pass under the new boundary rules.

Overall, during Slovenia's transition phase, Brežice municipality has experienced fewer problems with local economic restructuring. This has been the case even though other municipalities in the region have higher industrialization levels, and is related to current patterns of work emigration and daily commuting to work out of Brežice.

Among the three municipalities of the Lower Sava region, the municipality of Brežice has the best potential for economic and social development. Highly developed spa tourism at Terme Čatež, a 'wine route, through the vineyards of the area', and a summer resort area in the southern part of the municipality (predominantly owned by the citizens of Croatia) exemplify the area's dynamic tourism industry. In addition to tourism-oriented services such as new hotels and restaurants, locally oriented services such as retail trade, dentists, hairdressers, etc. encourage also cross-border development along the new international boundary.

The neighboring Croatian borderland has always been strongly linked with the economy of the adjacent Slovenian areas. Evidence of this fact may be found in patterns and intensities of daily and permanent migrations. The latter is evidenced in the ethnic composition of the border areas as well as in the provision of services on both sides of the border (Repolusk, 1999, p. 45). In the past, some Slovenian firms even opened branch operations on the Croatian side of the border in order to employ local Croatian labor. In general, before independence, Slovenian firms on the Slovenian side of the border typically employed workers from Croatia as daily work migrants; many of these migrants eventually moved to Slovenia permanently, affecting ethnic composition on both sides of the border. As indicated in Figure 11.4, the percentage of Croats within the total population of the Slovenian borderlands is much higher than the percentage of Slovenians in the Croatian borderlands (Repolusk, 1999, p. 37).

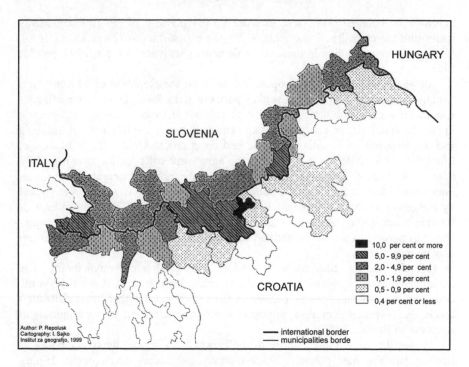

Figure 11.4   **The percentage of Slovenian residents within the Croatian borderland, and the percentage of Croatian residents within the Slovenian borderland municipalities (1991)**

The higher standard of living and better job opportunities on the Slovenian side of the border before independence, was due not so much to differences in the general level of economic development between Slovenia and Croatia as to the politics of polycentric development in Slovenia (Barbič, 1993). This had positive effects in the borderland. In spite of the fact that Slovenia is continuing with its polycentric development policy (The Law On Support of Comparable Regional Development of 1999), border regions along the Slovenian-Croatian border are now looking to increase internal cooperation and integration. According to Rejec Brancelj (1999),

> the participants of the recent regional planning workshop in Pokolpje (attended by 10 representatives of regional municipalities, nine representatives of state offices and seven experts) mentioned, among the comparative advantages of the region, the closeness of the border, a higher level of safety because of the new border, and cross-border cooperation. But by the same token, borderland isolation, on both sides of the border, was cited by respondents as an obstacle to local development. In defining the components/options of future development, the border was not even mentioned. (Rejec Brancelj 1999)

The practice among borderlands residents of distinguishing themselves on the basis of their nationality, defined by their state of residency, has increased in importance since the creation of two new states. There has always been a fluctuation in self-defined distinctiveness among local residents based on their national origin (Knežević Hočevar, 1999). This fluctuation has depended on the intensity of political, economic, social and cultural gaps between the neighboring countries. The new international border has intensified existing, nationally defined distinctions. By defining themselves as Slovenians or Croats, borderland residents stress the importance of international identity for themselves while at the same time expressing their loyalty to their own nation. A psychological explanation for the rise in importance of this nationalistic component of borderland residents' identity suggests that, in certain new situations, the hierarchy of the components in an individual's identity changes.

Borderlands Residents' Perceptions of the New Slovenian-Croatian Border

Relations between Slovenia and Croatia and Local Cross-Border Relations

The perception of local cross-border relations does not necessarily correspond with perception of relations between the neighboring states. Local relations are based on personal contacts and on mutual interdependency between the borderland communities, while relations between neighboring states are associated with political issues. The borderland, formally divided between two states' territories, operates as a region with a common or similar natural setting and with micro-level social arrangements. Therefore borderland residents' perceptions concerning their interrelationships are more favorable than their perception of relations between the two states. The perceptions of males and females are almost identical. The most frequently mentioned problems between the two states were the undefined borderline (78.6 percent) and political and economical problems (16.8 percent).

More than half of the respondents (total respondents 55.3 percent, male 54.4 percent, female 56.3 percent) stated that relations between the two states have worsened since independence; the second most common evaluation was that relations between the two states have remained the same (39.3 percent of total responses; male 39.8 percent, female 38.8 percent). Almost half (46.5 percent) of the respondents stated that their village or municipality was developing cross-border cooperation with regard to fire brigades, as well as in sports, culture, social events and hunting. Few respondents (12.7 percent) could identify a common problem that was in the process of being cooperatively solved. This could be explained by the fact that none of the eight investigated settlements is situated directly at the borderline so there are no 'twin' settlements. Although there is a willingness to cooperate, it will take some time until teamwork emerges and common problems are being solved collaboratively.

Cross-border school attendance was a common practice in the area before the internationalization of the Slovenian-Croatian boundary. Slovenian children would attend schools in Croatia and vice versa, mostly because of proximity and/or better transportation services. More than one in five respondents (23.3 percent) stated that the children from their village/municipality still attended school across the border in Croatia (men more often than women). Only 10 percent believed that Croatian schoolchildren currently attended school on the Slovenian side.

Frequency and Reasons for Border Crossings

Since independence, one-fifth (21.8 percent) of the respondents (20.5 percent of the male and 23.1 percent of the female) indicated that they have no reason to cross the border to Croatia. However, a large majority (78.2 percent) of respondents reported crossing the new border. It can be assumed that a majority of those who do not currently cross the border also did not cross prior to establishment of the international boundary.

Table 11.1   Frequency of border crossings

Frequency	All (%)	Men (%)	Women (%)
Almost every day	13.3	17.5	8.8
Almost every week	11.2	12.3	10.0
Almost every month	13.9	15.2	12.5
Several times a year	37.8	31.6	44.4
Never	21.8	20.5	23.1
No answer	2.1	2.9	1.3
Total	100.0	100.0	100.0
	(N=331)	(N=171)	(N=160)

Source: Survey 1996.

As shown in Table 11.1, men cross the border more frequently than do women. This can be at least partly explained by tradition. Typically, women's duties are typically limited to taking care of the family, the household and the children while men take the responsibility for business and outdoor matters. The new border does not seem to have changed this pattern. About half of the women cross the border with the same frequency, while only about 23.6 percent of interviewed women stated that they go to Croatia more frequently than before. It is obvious that the new border offers new challenges for border crossings to both genders, at least in Brežice commune. In the upper Kolpa valley, for example, frequency of cross-border contacts among those who had such contacts prior to creation of the international boundary has plummeted since the new boundary was formalized (Knežević-Hočevar, 1999, p. 139). Even more, in almost all life histories collected at the end of 1999 (Knežević-Hočevar, 1999; Kržišnik-Bukić, 1999), respondents stated that everyday life along the new international border was more difficult relative to conditions under the former 'soft' borderline.

The reasons why citizens of the neighboring states and particularly borderland residents cross the border are changing in accordance with economic measures instituted in the neighboring states, as well as changes in interstate economic cooperation. Cross-border cooperation, as well as national policies supporting such cooperation, depends strongly on the general political and economic situation in neighboring states.

Table 11.2   The reasons for border-crossings of Slovenian residents to the Croatian side

Reason	%
Purchase of goods for everyday use	18.5
Purchase of durable goods	10.4
Car purchase	2.3
Purchase of gasoline	4.6
Services	11.2
Consumption (Restaurants)	24.3
Holiday visits	14.3
Other reasons	46.7

Source: Survey 1996.

Almost half of all respondents (46.7 percent) mentioned reasons other than shopping and holiday visits as main motivations for crossing the new international boundary between Slovenia and Croatia (see Table 11.2). Among the other reasons most frequently stated for crossing into Croatia were visiting relatives or friends, maintaining business contacts and owning land in Croatia. With regard to goods and services available on the Croatian side, the most attractive to Slovenians was consumption of food (restaurant and food prices have been lower across the border); however, less than 25 percent of the respondents selected this alternative. Respondents were also asked about their perception of the reasons for Croatian residents crossing the border to Slovenia. Results in Table 11.3 reveal pronounced differences in perceptions of the reasons for border-crossings of Croatian residents to the Slovenian side.

For Croatian residents, according to the Slovenian residents' perceptions, shopping in Slovenia plays a more important role than shopping in Croatia does for Slovenian residents. For Slovenian consumers, shopping in Austria and Italy is far more attractive than shopping in Croatia due to competitive prices and the wide range of available goods (Wastl-Walter and Kofler, 1999b, p. 215). A relatively larger proportion of Croatian residents crosses the border during holidays than is the case with Slovenian borderland residents.

The advantages of cross-border shopping for Croatian borderland residents, however, have been reduced by the introduction of a 20 percent tax on all commodities brought into Croatia. This policy has been in effect since January 1998. The announcement of this tax prompted intense shopping by Croatian citizens in Slovenian shops at the end of 1997. On the other hand, Slovenian borderland retail dealers, shopkeepers and farmers were afraid that this tax would drastically reduce shopping activities of Croatian residents in Slovenia. This has encouraged them to keep their prices low and the range of choices high, in order to continue attracting Croatian shoppers to their stores. While Croatian merchants raised their prices due to the new import tax, the Slovenian border stores were thus able to remain competitive.

Table 11.3   Reasons for border crossings of Croatian residents to the Slovenian side, according to Slovenian residents' perceptions

Reason	%
Purchase of goods for everyday use	100.0
Purchase of durable goods	72.0
Car purchase	45.0
Purchase of gasoline	30.2
Services	28.7
Consumption (Restaurants)	16.9
Holiday visits	28.4
Other reasons	14.8

Source: Survey 1996.

Perceptions on Cross-Border Trade

Economic cooperation between neighboring countries/regions/residents depends on the specific opportunities a border offers for cross-border trade and visits for purchasing goods and consumption services. However, as noted above, this applies primarily to old and stable borders along with the cross-border economic and other cooperation have developed over a longer period of time. A new border, at least in the beginning, not only tends to sever or reduce former cooperation but also requires establishment of new grounds for cooperation under changed circumstances. Local production patterns have to be adapted to new demands and to the purchasing capacities of the local neighboring citizens. New form(s) of production must also be developed to meet newly emerging demands. A free trade agreement between Slovenia and Croatia (PDZRS, 1997), ratified in 1999, contributed a great deal to economic cooperation between the two states. Survey respondents, when asked about their perception of the amount of local manufacturing products being sold to Croatia, divided into two almost equal groups (see Table 11.4). While 39 percent believe that export of Slovenian goods to Croatia has decreased, 35.6 percent believe that an increase has actually occurred. By contrast perceptions about the level of sales of agricultural products to Croatia has been less optimistic. The majority (63.1 percent) of the respondents believed that the export of agricultural goods to Croatia decreased after independence. This kind of situation was observed in 1995, when a reduction in volumes of agricultural products (wine, meat, milk, vegetables and fruits) sold to Croatia, was characterized as a 'catastrophe' for the Slovenian borderland farmers (Barbič, 1995). Only processing firms, who developed their own wine and food, survived or expanded. Less inventive farmers found themselves in a rather poor economic situation. Since the chances for informal economic transactions (such as the direct selling of wine, fruits and vegetables), timber sales, and illegal seasonal employment have been diminished (Kukar, 1995, p. 22). With regard to tourism, about 39 percent of respondents perceived a drop in tourist visits; while only 20.5 percent believed that the number of tourists has increased since independence. Obviously these opinions depend on personal experiences and available information. The large number of 'no answer' responses indicates respondents' ready affirmation that they are not familiar enough with the situation to express a judgement.

Table 11.4   Perception of economic ties after the internationalization of the Slovenian-Croatian border

Economic exchange	Less than before	Same as before	More than before	Don't know	Total (%)
Export of manufacturing products from Brežice to Croatia	39.0	8.5	35.6	16.9	100.0
Export of agricultural products from Brežice to Croatia	63.1	6.3	8.2	22.4	100.0
Croatian tourists visiting Brežice municipality	39.0	23.0	20.5	17.5	100.0

Source: Survey 1996.

Perceptions about the Illegal Economy

The illegal economy is less transparent than legal economy for obvious reasons. However, rumors always emerge, especially when individuals suddenly appear to be doing very well economically and to display their high(er) economic status by driving new expensive cars and changing their lifestyle. When asked if they are familiar with illegal trade in their area, two-thirds (66.5 percent) of the respondents denied any such knowledge. About 20 percent answered, 'don't know', only 13 percent expressed knowledge about illegal economic trade among Brežice municipality residents. Among the illegal cross-border activities cited were smuggling of goods, including vehicles, and illegal employment.

Interestingly, although respondents who were aware of illegal ways to avoid legal obstacles for economic cooperation rarely admitted such knowledge to the interviewer, they were more forthcoming when asked about knowing individual residents on both sides of the border who were illegally trading with the neighboring state. Indeed, half of the respondents believed that there are individuals on both sides of the border illegally trading across the border, although only a few respondents identified the commodities associated with this trade (transportation of animals, domestic applications, transportation of people, gas, timber and weapons). According to the respondents, the illegal trade is taking place in villages, at informal border crossing points such as rivers, and at legal border crossing points during the night.

Perceptions about Cross-Border Employment

Legal and illegal cross-border employment is strongly related to specific situations in the borderlands. As the economic transformation process has unfolded, one of the biggest problems has been the high rate of unemployment. Differences in job opportunities, as well as chances for illegal employment, are key factors. However, borderland residents are increasing their resistance to illegal employment, for they believe that foreigners are taking their job, or the job of a fellow citizen.

Economic restructuring, privatization of formerly state-owned property, and newly emerging inventiveness in the private sector have shaken the working class of both countries. There has been poor correspondence between demand for and availability of suitable labor, causing employers to search elsewhere to find adequate workers. The neighboring borderland's population represents an excellent source of suitable workers, when favorable conditions exist, such as lower wages, higher worker motivation, and fewer employer obligations towards employees especially in the case of illegal employment. Cross-border employment conditions are not symmetrical along the Slovenian-Croatian border. This asymmetry provides the basis for why the majority of Slovenian residents surveyed (41.8 percent) indicated that they do not approve the employment of Croatian citizens in Slovenia, although they are in favor of the employment of the residents of Brežice municipality in Croatia (44.4 percent). Their disapproval of employing citizens from the other side of the border reflects their concern that the foreign workers may take over jobs that would otherwise be available to local residents. At the same time, the main reason other respondents approved the cross-border employment was the importance for a job-seeking person of obtaining a job.

There are two factors that contribute to illegal employment on either side of the border. First, medical and retirement contributions (21.9 percent of gross salary in Slovenia) are being decreased. Second, workers seek to avoid obstacles associated with legal conditions governing employment of foreigners. According to survey respondents, transboundary illegal employment indeed exists, although perceptions about this topic differ between Croatian citizens and residents of Brežice municipality. However, the high number of the respondents who responded by 'do not know' suggests that the topic is too sensitive to be studied in this kind of survey.

Perceptions on Cross-Border Conflicts

According to respondents' perceptions of cross-border incidents and of the effects of the border on the environment, the Slovenian-Croatian border in Brežice municipality can be described as a calm one. Only few respondents said they had witnessed or heard about a cross-border incident caused by either Croatian citizens or the state of Croatia (15.4 percent), or by Slovenian citizens and the state of Slovenia (7.6 percent). Among incidents cited as being caused by Croatian residents, smuggling and shooting were most frequently noted, followed by physical fights and car theft. Among incidents caused by Slovenian citizens, only a few were mentioned (smuggling, political problems).

Only few respondents mentioned interventions of either state into the territory of the neighbor. While 17.2 percent of the respondents are familiar with incidents of Croatia intervening into Slovenian territory, only 4.8 percent have noticed/heard about interventions of the state Slovenia into the territory of Croatia. Land takeover was mentioned in both cases.

Perceptions on the Effects of the New Border on the Environment

The effects of the border on the local environment seem to be of greater concern to the borderland residents than the cross-border incidents. More than half (56.2 percent) of the respondents expressed awareness of negative effects the border has had on the environment. Among those mentioned were effects generated by increased and poorly managed traffic (13.4 percent), an increase in the number of passengers crossing the border (11.3 percent), increased pollution (7.0 percent), and stronger official control/ larger number of policemen in the area (4.3 percent). Difficulties related to residents' cultivation of agricultural land owned across the border (9.7 percent) was cited by the borderland residents; also noted were negative effects on the local environment caused by the longer distances that have to be traveled to official border crossings in order to reach their lands.

Perception on Quality of Life

Borderland residents continuously compare their economic conditions and quality of life with conditions in the neighboring country. Although there are two arguments for favoring their own country (the loyalty towards their own country and poorer knowledge about the situation in the neighboring country) the respondents seem to be rather objective in their judgments. They favor Slovenia in all five aspects of life included in the questionnaire (see Table 11.5). At the same time, almost half of them admit that they don't know the situation in Croatia well enough to compare, for example, employment opportunities, conditions for entrepreneurial business activity, or the relative profitability of farming. Female and male perceptions differ only slightly, although two differences should be pointed out. First, more men tend to favor the situation in Slovenia than women and secondly, more women admitted to be uncertain about the relative speed of general development and general quality of life in the two countries. Women were either more cautious about stating their opinions, or less familiar with the situation in either of the countries.

Table 11.5   The comparison of Slovenia and Croatia in economic conditions and of life in general according to gender

	MALE				FEMALE				TOTAL			
	CRO	SI	Don't know	Total % N	CRO	SI	Don't know	Total % N	CRO	SI	Don't know	Total % N
It is easier to get a job	9.4	46.2	44.4	100 (171)	6.9	41.9	51.2	100 (160)	8.2	44.1	47.7	100 (331)
An individual as an entrepreneur has better conditions for running business	11.7	45.6	42.7	100 (171)	11.9	43.7	44.4	100 (160)	11.5	44.7	43.5	100 (331)
Farmers are better off/ farming is more profitable	11.7	45.6	42.7	100 (171)	15.6	38.8	45.6	100 (160)	13.6	42.3	44.1	100 (331)
General development is faster	19.9	62.6	17.5	100 (171)	16.2	56.3	27.5	100 (160)	18.1	59.5	22.4	100 (331)
The life of the citizens is better	1.5	83.6	14.6	100 (171)	3.7	76.3	20.0	100 (160)	2.7	80.1	17.2	100 (331)

Perceptions about Cultural Identity of the Borderland Residents

Although two countries typically share similarities in their natural environment and in the social characteristics of their borderlands, borderlines usually distinguish the territories of different nations in terms of distinguishing national characteristics and different cultural identities. Cross-border contacts (joint activities, employment, schooling) and especially mixed marriages soften the distinctiveness of national and cultural characteristics of the borderland residents while at the same time strengthening residents' need to identify themselves in terms of their citizenship.

In order to identify the level of distinctiveness of cultural identity on the Slovenian versus the Croatian side of the international boundary, respondents were asked to compare the residents of their settlement/local community with the residents across the border. The comparison involved 14 cultural identity characteristics.[2] Results indicate that residents on each side of the border are seen to differ most in terms of language, folk songs, and folk dances. Greater similarity was found with regard to folk arts, and to perceptions of honesty, diligence, respect for cross-border neighbors, spirit of entrepreneurship, and mutual help and co-operation. Respondents indicated that similarities were strongest with regard to food habits, manner of building houses, farming practices, and furnishing of interiors. Overall, neither big differences nor big similarities are perceived to exist among the borderland residents. Men and women do not differ much in their estimation of differences/similarities based on the 14 cultural identity characteristics.

Perceptions about National Identity

Before the creation of the international border the borderland residents developed a kind of common social group despite their different national identities (Croatians, Slovenians). After their formal separation residents have shifted their focus to differences between Slovenian and Croatian portions of the borderland. Differentiation is expressed in terms of standard of living, level of democracy, value of local currencies, and way of life in general (Knežević-Hočevar, 1999; Barbič, 1998b). The perception of differences has in the course of time widened due to several differences. One such difference is in the socio-political systems of the two states (including social security, and job opportunities). Others include the uneven speed of economic development (GDP, unemployment rate, loans for small entrepreneurs) and the different time frame established for inclusion of the two countries into European integration process.

Attachment of borderland residents to the state of Slovenia was tested by the following question: If you had the possibility to make a choice to live in Slovenia or in any of its neighboring countries, what would be our choice? The great majority (82.5 percent) of the respondents selected Slovenia as their preferred country to live in. Among the rest of the respondents, 8.5 percent choose Austria, 2.5 percent selected Croatia, 1.5 percent opted for Italy and 0.3 percent chose Hungary (4.8 percent did not make a choice). The relatively high proportion of respondents who favored other countries besides Slovenia (17.5 percent) can be explained in two ways. First, it is likely that Austria and Italy were selected because of their higher standard of living and because of the advantages of being member of the European Union. Second, it may be expected that Croatia and Hungary were preferred by residents of Croatian and Hungarian nationality or by those who are closely related to both states for other, personal reasons.

Conclusions

The new Slovenian-Croatian border has redefined life for borderland residents. In situations like this, new understandings of relations among local communities and residents of different nationalities need to be established. New boundaries also generate complicated cross-border procedures. These procedures can frustrate some borderland residents, prompting them to give up former cross-border relations and joint activities. Residents can either accept the border as an insurmountable obstacle, or they can take advantage of it by transforming it from an obstacle to an opportunity for new (economic) activities and new ways of engaging in mutual cooperation.

On one hand, cross-border cooperation and/or separation of borderland communities and their residents depend on general relations between the two countries. On the other hand, local governments have an extremely important role to play in identifying local problems, suggesting solutions, and initiating relevant cross-border actions to improve the quality of life of borderland residents. The problems faced by local borderland governmental entities are two-fold: first, they need to communicate with state authorities, informing them about the specific needs and problems of local residents and communities. Second, local borderland governments have to create their own cross-border micro-politics in order to enhance the advantages and minimize the disadvantages of their borderland situation. To realize the latter goal, local governments quietly and frequently tolerate illegal economic relations (illegal trade, illegal employment) while at the same time undertake actions to legalize these activities. In this sense, an 'open border' for borderland residents has been proved to be the best strategy to cope with the needs of the borderland communities and residents.

As far as the Slovenian borderland residents are concerned, relations between Slovenia and Croatia, as well as between local borderland communities, have worsened since the international boundary was formalized. Still, they do not perceive conditions as being dramatically bad. On the contrary, in spite of the high level of loyalty the Brežice municipality borderland residents display towards their nation-state, they utilize the economic advantages of their border context. Their loyalty to Slovenia and their knowledge about the situation across the border make them feel secure and rather objective with regard to their judgments about the situation on either side of the border. Although, according to the interviewers, the Brežice municipality residents were cautious in answering questions about illegal trading and illegal employment, they did not show any frustration.

The high number of those who gave a 'don't know' answer to some questions (mostly about the situation in Croatia) indicates a rather high degree objectivity and lack of prejudice toward their cross-border neighbors. In addition, there is definitely considerable willingness on the part of Brežice municipality and its residents (who do not approve of the broken relations that exist with neighboring Croatia) to engage in cross-border cooperation.

The socio-economic situation of Brežice municipality has definitely worsened since Slovenia gained its independence. The border has caused a reduction in economic exchange with neighboring Croatian communities, reduced the number of Croatian tourists (especially in the spa of Terme Čatež), and increased the unemployment. Contributing to the latter is the collapse of the Yugoslav army airport training center, in addition to transition-phase economic restructuring in Slovenia. Fortunately, formerly strong economic relations between Brežice municipality and Croatia, especially with Zagreb, have to some extent persisted even after independence. There are some indications that relations are slowly recovering, for residents on both sides of the border have not forgotten nor given up former habits in shopping, taking vacation and buying agricultural products directly from Slovenian farmers.

The stability of interstate relations, regulated by numerous mutual agreements accompanied by the stable and legally supported internal economic and political order of the neighboring states, is a reliable basis for good cross-border cooperation. Unsettled or ever-changing economic and/or political situations on either side of a border bring uncertainty into cross-border (economic) relations and represent a serious obstacle to building long-term economic plans. Slovenia and Croatia, as two newly emergent nation-states, have as their first need the formulation of their own body of legislation. Currently they are concerned only with the most urgent issues governing the relations with their neighboring states. At the same time, legal restrictions are affecting the free flow of commodities; these constraints are affecting borderland residents the most.

According to the respondents, the borderland residents' relations certainly have worsened after the independence, but not as much as relations between the two states, which still have several problems to solve. The majority of respondents voiced a preference for living and work conditions in Slovenia. Environmental conditions, and some aspects of life and work, have worsened while some have remained unchanged since Slovenian independence. In addition to these border influences, Slovenia is going through a difficult transition phase. The borderland residents of Brežice municipality perceive the border with Croatia as an obstacle to economic cooperation. Respondents are consciously or unconsciously overlooking opportunities for economic activities available at border. Few take advantage of the opportunities available.

The picture presented here of borderland residents' perceptions of issues related to the Slovenian-Croatian border is limited in that it only reflects data from Slovenia. Nevertheless, it provides at least some information relevant to decision-makers at the local and national levels. On the Croatian side, comparisons have been offered by Pavlakovich-Kochi and Stiperski (2004), who conducted a similar survey among the elected local officials and representatives of private establishments in Croatian municipalities along the Croatian-Slovenian border. Due to differences in the survey methodology, the findings cannot be directly compared, although they still provide insights that are extremely relevant here.

Findings related to the Slovenian-Croatian border can be compared with the possible effects of the forthcoming realization of EU Schengen agreement along the Slovenian-Austrian and Slovenian-Italian border. First, no border-crossing procedures, no matter how strict, can completely stop/break the cross-border relations that have existed for a long time. Second, due to borderland communities' and residents' initiatives and demands, the national-level compromises must be made in order to make life bearable for borderland residents.

State officials can learn much from borderland residents and local governments. Optimal policies for the development of the borderland, as well as policies aimed at neighboring states, need to be formulated. State officials can accomplish these tasks by drawing upon the experience of borderland residents concerning their ways of coping with border problems. If relations (economic, political, cultural) between the neighboring states are good, life in the borderlands flourishes. If, on the contrary, relations are bad, borderland residents and local communities are limited in the extent to which they can take advantage of their border position; their initiatives are frustrated. In such cases even internationally supported regional borderlands development programs (such as the European Union's PHARE Cross-border Cooperation Program) are only partly successful. Regional cross-border programs need to be incorporated into European integration processes not in the sense of automatically following general European patterns but by respecting regional specificities, some of which require targeted integration/cooperation strategies (Mlinar, 1996, pp. 974-979).

Notes

1   The survey was conducted in November 1996 with the support of the Brežice municipality, The University of Ljubljana Rector's fund, and the Republic of Slovenia Ministry for economic relations and development.
2   On a scale from 1 (the biggest difference) to 5 (the greatest similarity) points.

References

Barbič, A. (1993), 'Rural Development in the Time of Deconstructing One-Party Political Systems and Centrally Planned Economies', *Agriculture and Human Values*, Winter, 1, pp. 40-51.
Barbič, A. (1995), 'The socio-economic effects of the new Slovenian-Croatian border', Zbornik Biotehniške fakultete, Univerze v Ljubljani, No. 65, Ljubljana, Kmetijstvo, pp. 11-128.
Barbič, A. (1998a), 'Borders in Transition?', paper presented at the 94th Annual Meeting of the Association of American Geographers, March 25-29, 1998, Boston, Massachusetts.
Barbič, A. (1998b), 'Meja kot dejavnik sodelovanja in ločevanja obmejnih prebivalcev. Primer občine Brežice' (Border as a factor of cooperation and separation of borderland residents. The case of Brežice municpality), Univerza v Ljubljani, Biotehniška fakulteta (Poročilo o raziskavi/research report).
Bufon, M. (1998), 'Slovenia: A Central European Border Community', (paper presented at the 94th Annual Meeting of the Association of American Geographers, March 25-29, 1998, Boston, Massachusetts).
Connolly, W.E. (1996), 'Tocqueville, Territory, and Violence', in M.J. Shapiro and M.R. Alker (eds.), *Challenging Boundaries. Global Flows, Territorial Identities*, University of Minnesota Press, pp. 141-164.
Klemenčič, V. and Jeršič, M. (1972), 'Problemi socio-geografici della frontiera aperta', *Prospettive di efficienza numeri unici di sociologia*, Trento, 12(4), pp. 63-71.
Knežević Hočevar, D. (1999), 'Družbena razmejevanja v dolini zgornje Kolpe' (Social delimitations in the upper Kolpa river valey), Ljubljana, ZRC.
Kržišnik-Bukić, V. (ed.) (1999), *Slovensko-hrvaški obmejni prostor: življenje ob meji* (The Slovenian-Croatian Border Territory: life along the border), Ljubljana, Inštitut za mednarodna vprašanja, (Raziskovalno poročilo/research report).
Kukar, S. (1995), 'Siva ekonomija v Sloveniji - razlogi za njen razvoj' (The gray economy in Slovenia – some reasons for its development), in *IB revija*, Ljubljana, Zavod za makroekonomske analize in razvoj, no. 1-2-3, pp. 16-25.

Maier, K. and Schimak, G. (1997), *Cross-Border Planning Experience. A Joint Project of Austrian and Czech Universities at the Former Iron Curtain*, (paper presented at 11th AESOP Congress Planning Knowledge for the European Market, May 28-31, Nijnegen, Netherlands).

Martinez, O.J. (1994), *Border People: Life and Society in the US-Mexico Borderlands*, University of Arizona Press, Tucson & London.

Mlinar, Z. (1996), 'Obmejne regije in Evropa' (Borderland regions and Europe), in *Teorija in praksa*, Ljubljana, 33(6), pp. 973-988.

Pak, M. (ed.) (1993), 'Geografski aspekti obmejnosti in regionalnega razvoja' (Geographic aspects of border regions and regional development), *Dela 10*, Oddelek za geografijo Filozofske fakultete Univerze v Ljubljani, Ljubljana.

Pavlakovich-Kochi, V. and Stiperski, Z. (2004), 'The Croatian-Slovenian border: The local experience', in B. Morehouse, V. Pavlakovich-Kochi and D. Wastl-Walter (eds.), *Challenged Borderlands. Transcending Political and Cultural Boundaries*. Ashgate, Aldershot.

Plut, D. (ed.) (1970), 'Tromeja – obmejna območja Jugoslavije, Avstrije in Italije' (The three border area of Yugoslavia, Austria and Italy), *Dela 7*, Oddelek za geografijo Filozofske fakultete Univerze v Ljubljani, Ljubljana.

Podgoršek, V. (1997), 'Mejo s Hrvaško bo oživilo 27 maloobmejnih prehodov' (The border with Croatia will be revitalized by 27 local border-crossings), *Delo*, Ljubljana, June 3, p. 4.

'Predlog Zakona o ratifikaciji sporazuma med Republiko Slovenijo in Republiko Hrvaško o obmejnem prometu in sodelovanju' (The proposition of the Law about the ratification of the agreement between Republic Slovenia and Republic Croatia about local cross-border traffic and cooperation) (1997), *Poročevalec Državnega zbora Republike Slovenije*, Ljubljana, November 7, 1997, 52, pp. 25-88.

Rejec Brancelj, I. (1999), 'Regionalna planerska delavnica Pokolpje. Opredelitev razvojne problematike' (Regional spatial planning workshop Pokolpje. Identification of developmental problems), Črnomelj, April 20, (Poročilo/Report).

Repolusk, P. (1999), 'Opredelitev obmejnega območja med Slovenijo in Hrvaško ter nekatere njegove geografske značilnost', in V. Kržišnik-Bukić (ed.) (1999), *Slovensko-hrvaški obmejni prostor: življenje ob meji* (The Slovenian-Croatian Border Territory: life along the border), Ljubljana, Inštitut za mednarodna vprašanja, (Raziskovalno poročilo/research report), pp. 17-45.

Statistični, L., (1996), *1996* (Statistical Yearbook), Ljubljana, Statistični urad Republike Slovenije, p. 621.

Wastl-Walter, D. and Kofler, A. (1999), 'The Dynamics of Economic Transborder Cooperation between Austria/Carinthia and Slovenia', *Journal of Borderlands Studies*, XIV(2), pp. 23-47.

'Zakon o ratifikaciji sporazuma med Republiko Slovenijo in Republiko Hrvaško o obmejnem prometu in sodelovanju' (Act of ratifying the agreement between the Republic of Slovenia and the Republic of Croatia on traffic and cooperation), *Uradni list Republike Slovenije*, Ljubljana, 63.

'Zakon o spodbujanju skladnega regionalnega razvoja' (Law on supporting copatible regional development) (1999), *Uradni list Republike Slovenije*, 60.

Chapter 12

The Croatian-Slovenian Border:
The Local Experience

Vera Pavlakovich-Kochi and Zoran Stiperski

Introduction

The political independence of Croatia and Slovenia, achieved in 1991 in conjunction with their acceptance of free market policies, opened a window for reorientation of both states toward Central and Western Europe. At the regional and local levels, however, the proclamation of independence and redefinition of what was formerly an *internal* boundary into an *international* boundary changed conditions for the borderlands and for borderland residents.

In his study of Finish-Russian border, Paasi (1999) draws attention to a complex nature of interaction between national and local scales. He argues that in daily life on the local scale, the question of boundary becomes very concrete. Boundaries redefine questions of distance, well-being, culture, economics and administrative practices, and profoundly shape the social and personal spaces of border residents. Processes of re-territorialization and de-territorialization of borders, which are at the core of nation building and the changing role of state, present immediate and long-term implications for border residents.

Examples of re-territorialized borders after World War I and World War II have demonstrated how borders significantly reduce various 'flows' and disturb existing social practices that may gradually turn the border areas into what Martinez (1994) calls, alienated borderlands. The new borders tend to introduce not only new economic policies, but also new security and military practices, and discourses. Furthermore, the political separation of neighboring regions is capable of producing remarkable cultural and institutional differences. Because many of these changes are structural problems, their eradication is very difficult (Paasi, 1999).

For many residents and local enterprises in the newly redefined Slovenian-Croatian borderlands, the institution of a new international boundary resulted in an interruption of traditional labor and retail markets, cross-boundary land use, and kinship networks. Interestingly, these relationships between Croatian and Slovenian communities received little or no attention in the professional literature. It was only after the fact that these cross-boundary linkages attracted concentrated attention from practitioners and scholars. Indeed, the first statistics concerning the extent of pre-boundary commuting (Belec, 1993), long-established cross-border land ownership (Belec, 1994) and migration, together with changes in ethnic composition (Gosar, 1993), became available only after most of these cross-border interactions were already being affected by post-1991 restrictions.

The establishment of the Croatian-Slovenian international boundary is a relatively recent event. It provides an opportunity to explore the construction of reactions to a new border, how decisions at the national scale shape local people's perceptions and what kinds of adjustment processes are taking place in coping with new realities.

Slovenian researchers, most notably Barbič (1995; 1997) and Ravbar et al. (1995) were among first to examine the implications of the new international boundary from the viewpoint of the communities on the Slovenian side. In particular, Barbič's findings and the interpretation (1995; 1997) of a survey of more than 300 households in the Lower Posavje region on the Slovenian side of the Croatian-Slovenian border, serve as a point of departure for the study we discuss in this chapter. Our research was not designed to replicate the household survey on the Croatian side in order to find statistical similarities or dissimilarities between the two populations, but rather to provide general insights into perspectives shaped on the 'other' side of the border.

This study explores how local officials and business people in Croatia's border communities perceive the implications of a redefined boundary between Slovenia and Croatia, and how they incorporate and reproduce the new border at the local scale. Personal interviews were conducted with the representatives of 15 border municipalities during August and September 1997. The sample included elected local officials[1] and representatives of private establishments[2]. For the most part, the questions mirrored those asked in the survey of Slovenian communities (Barbič, 1997, Chapter 11), with a few minor exceptions where modifications were required to reflect the Croatian context.

Generalizations about Implications of the New Boundary

Barbič's work (1995; 1997), as well as that of several other authors (Ravbar et al., 1995; Klemenčič, 1993; Belec, 1994,) suggests a number of generalizations about the implications of the new boundary:

- The new Croatian-Slovenian boundary runs through spatially differentiated areas; the implications of the same boundary will differ, reflecting local and regional differences in economic development, degree of pre-boundary interdependency of labor and consumer markets, and marginality in relation to the respective national centers.
- A new boundary has become a greater barrier for every day life at the local level; new regulations (customs, passport control, import-export regulations) complicate everyday activities and pose a burden to the local population. The local population has had no control over decisions formulated at the highest (state) level, particularly in the beginning; thus, the boundary effect may be most strongly felt at the local level. Until the local population develops

strategies to cope with these boundary effects, cross-border activities will start to decline or even disappear, thus creating conditions for development of alienated borderlands.

• Yet the local-level informal ways to deal with regulations are easier to develop. Representatives of central and regional authorities who are located in remote areas may not be as stringent in their application of rules and policies as those who are physically located at the major border crossings. Thus, people and activities may transcend border barriers in ways not officially regulated or sanctioned in international agreements.

• The establishment of the new international boundary reinforces the marginal character of economically weak and sparsely populated areas. The pre-boundary connections that served local populations in coping with marginality (land ownership on both sides of the river, job opportunities, markets for local products, consumer goods) have been distorted. This has been coupled with severe economic recession and restructuring, as well as with a new national agenda – all of which limit or diminish expectations for near-term improvement in residents' current status.

• General marginality and less stringent regulations provide 'windows of opportunity' for some population groups that get involved in illegal trade and smuggling. Although these activities may be limited both in volume and space, they may provide an explanation for differences found in what otherwise appears to be the same environment.

• Border areas that had a higher degree of local economic interaction in the pre-boundary era, but must cope with a limited local economic base, face more severe implications from disruptions in the functioning of the local economic system caused by the establishment of the new international boundary.

• Cross-border cooperation (which replaces the economic integration phase of the pre-boundary era) depends to a large extent upon economic imperatives and the interests of the major local players. Past experiences (or inexperience) in dealing with the new economic (market economy), political (democracy) and ethnic (national, nationalistic and ethnocentric) contexts tend to profoundly influence the shaping of local outcomes in the process of rebuilding the cross-border economic system.

Study Area

The study area was limited to 15 municipalities in northwest Croatia: 10 municipalities ('općine') adjacent to the international border with Slovenia, and five municipalities located in the immediate vicinity of the international boundary[3] (see Figure 12.1). This is a relatively small area, but one that is spatially very differentiated. The central part is a sparsely populated rural area, with predominantly hilly topography along a narrow valley of the Sutla River. The municipalities on both sides of the boundary are underdeveloped areas, as judged by the standards of each country (Ravbar, 1999; Krevs, 2001; Klemenčič, 1993;

Feletar and Stiperski, 1996). On the Slovenian side, the Spodnje Posavje region (Brežice) is in a peripheral location relative to the major growth centers in Slovenia (Ljubljana, Maribor, Celje, Koper). On the Croatian side, with the exception of the Samobor area, the whole border zone is a periphery relative to both the Zagreb region and the national territory (Cvitanović, 1974). The main source of income for the majority of the local population is agriculture on small, fragmented fields and the small-scale raising of livestock, in combination with work in nearby manufacturing and service establishments. The landscapes on the Slovenian side (west of Sutla River) and on the Croatian side (east of Sutla River) resemble each other not only in terms of physical characteristics, but also in terms of land use and the way of life of the majority of population.

Figure 12.1   Study area: NW Croatia's border region

On the northern edge of our study area there are several local centers on each side of the border: Hum na Sutli on Croatia's side, and Rogatec with nearby Rogaška Slatina on Slovenia's side. These centers were developed on the basis of local resources (the glass industry in Rogatec and Hum na Sutli, and the health spa in Rogaška Slatina), together with the availability of cheap labor drawn from the surrounding rural area, particularly in the Hrvatsko Zagorje area of Croatia. Some local specialization was developed, along with professional skills (professional glass designers, hospitality services). Indeed, this used to be an integrated economic area, characterized by a local division of labor and sharing of resources (including land, water, and highways).

Krapina is the largest urban center in this northern part of the study area. Although it is not located directly on the border, and even though it is the administrative center for this part of the study area (i.e., the Zagorsko-Krapinska Županija region), which itself is largely adjacent to the border, Krapina is very much affected by the new border relationships. In terms of physical location, Krapina is closer to Slovenia than to the heart of Croatia. Nevertheless, the Krapina area has historically been oriented toward Zagreb, Croatia's capital and major economic center. Like other parts of Hrvatsko Zagorje, Krapina was a source of migrants to Zagreb as well as to other manufacturing centers (such as Germany and other west European countries). Post-1970s investments in housing (including weekend or recreational housing) reflect, to a large extent, investments facilitated by remittances generated by migrant workers and former residents. Krapina is located on the north-south axis that connects Zagreb and central Croatia with Austria via Ptuj and Maribor in Slovenia. This has been Croatia's principal link with Central Europe in the post-1991 period (see Pavlakovich-Kochi, chapter 5).

The southern 'edge' of the study area represents a relatively more developed region in the vicinity of Zagreb. Prior to the break-up of the former Yugoslavia, Croatian residents used to work on the Slovenian side. In particular, a joint project on the nuclear plant Krško attracted skilled and highly skilled labor from Zagreb. After independence, many lost their jobs; others took Slovenian citizenship and remained in Slovenia. By contrast, Slovenians did not work in large numbers in the Zagreb region, although the local economies in Brežice and Čatež depended upon proximity to Zagreb. A portion of Zagreb income used to spill across the border into Slovenia, primarily for recreation (for example at Čatež spa and at Slovenian hotels and restaurants). These activities have decreased in the post-independence era, although they are replaced with new functions, particularly new border retail systems.

With the exception of Hum na Sutli and Rogatec, there are no real border towns, or twin border towns, along the border as found in other places along international boundaries such as Gorizia-Nova Gorica on the Italian-Slovenian border, or the twin cities on the US-Mexico border. Historically, the Croatian-Slovenian border was not a significant barrier, allowing functional areas to develop around local functional nodes (Samobor, Brežice) in all directions, irrespective of the (then internal) boundary. The area corresponds broadly to the Posavje region around Brežice and the hilly region in Slovenia that extends northward, along the west side of the Sutla River.

Local Perspectives

Cross-Border Relations

Survey findings reveal that relations between Croatia and Slovenia are perceived as 'good', averaging 3.33 on a scale of 1 to 5, with 5 indicating the highest positive rating. Relations between residents on the local level are perceived to be even better, showing an average score of 4.2. The majority of the respondents believe that relationships among local people have remained the same, compared with the pre-boundary era; only a few (three of 15 respondents) believe that cross-border relations among the local population have deteriorated. As expected, nobody believed that the establishment of the new international boundary improved the cross-border relationships. The perceptions of the Croatian residents are, thus, similar to those on the Slovenian side, indicating that local cross-border relations are based on personal experiences and mutual dependence, while the relations between states are driven by political agendas (Barbič, 1997).

New Problems Caused by the Boundary

There is a general perception that a new political reality, together with the resulting change in the status of the Croatian-Slovenian boundary from internal to the international, have caused a number of problems for the local population. For example, the local Croatian population perceives the following as new burdens: the introduction of customs regulations; the unresolved status of Croatian residents' deposits in a Slovenian bank (the Ljubljana bank); the status of the bi-national nuclear plant in Krško; and continuing boundary disputes along other portions of the Croatian-Slovenian boundary.[4]

Frequency of Border Crossings

About half of the respondents believe that cross-border visits by the Croatian residents have declined relative to visitation levels during the pre-boundary era; another third believe that crossings have remained the same. Few believe that such crossings have intensified. This finding contrasts sharply with the perception of Slovenian residents, who believe that Croatians cross the border in larger numbers than before (Barbič, 1997). This may be partly influenced by the fact that the Slovenian survey focused on the Brežice area, the main shopping destination, while the Croatian investigation also included more isolated areas to the north. The main reasons mentioned for crossings by Croatian residents are shopping in Slovenian stores and working in their fields on the Slovenian side of the Sutla River.

Visits by Slovenian Residents

There is a general perception that Slovenian residents cross the boundary less frequently than Croatian border residents, and that crossings have declined in comparison with the pre-boundary era. According to survey respondents, in the past, when prices in local Croatian stores were lower than in Slovenia, Slovenian residents shopped more frequently on the Croatian side of the border. Now, since consumer prices are higher in Croatia, there is a perception that Slovenian residents are not motivated to engage in cross-border shopping, except for some limited services, to work in fields on the Croatian side, and to attend the Samobor fair, which remains the largest in the region. In three of the 15 surveyed municipalities, respondents stated their belief that no Slovenian residents cross into Croatia at all. Respondents in more than half of the surveyed municipalities noted that crossings seem to have decreased. Interestingly, these perceptions were not supported by the survey results on the Slovenian side, where more than 70 percent of the respondents indicated that they believed the frequency of border crossings was the same or higher relative to pre-boundary days (Barbič, 1997).

Conflicts along the Border

In the majority of the surveyed municipalities the perception is that conflicts do not exist. This may be more a reflection of 'official' statements than factual knowledge, however, since it is common for elected officials to portray the situation in their area in a better light than may actually be the case. Slovenian residents indicated greater awareness of incidents along the border, although judging from the relatively small percentage of those involved in or knowledgeable about such incidents, this segment of the boundary can be described as calm (Barbič, 1997). In general, the population on both sides of the border displays an awareness of the territorial disputes between Croatia and Slovenia in other border areas, but does not see the contests as affecting their area.

Perceived Difference between Croatia and Slovenia

All respondents except two articulated a general perception that life is better in Slovenia. With regard to specific economic aspects such as job opportunities, private entrepreneurship, and economic growth, the majority of respondents perceived that the situation across the border was better. The Croatian residents' perceptions resembled those of the Slovenian residents, who overwhelmingly perceived that the economic situation is Slovenia was better than across the border in Croatia (Barbič, 1997). Asked about human rights and democracy, the majority provided no opinion, either because they did not know the specifics, or because as elected officials they did not feel comfortable discussing those issues. Most of them, however, agreed that economic development in general, and the agricultural sector in particular, was better supported by official governmental policy in Slovenia. In general, Slovenia is seen as economically more developed, and overall, as a more modern country. At the same time, Croatian respondents commonly perceived that national feelings were very high and voiced their preference for living in Croatia despite the country's current economic difficulties.

Environmental Implications of the New Boundary

In contrast to the Slovenian residents, the respondents on the Croatian side did not see the establishment of the new international boundary, including issues associated with the border traffic and crossings, as particularly harmful for the environment on the Croatian side. An exception occurs, however, with regard to the border crossing at Bregana, which was built in the vicinity of the main water supply for the city of Samobor. This development has raised local concerns about water pollution due to increased traffic. Aside from the differences in survey methodology, the seemingly lower priority of environmental issues on the Croatian side may also reflect current economic difficulties in Croatia and the need to first solve the higher-priority problems of high unemployment and the bare survival needs of a large portion of population.

Trade between Croatia and Slovenia

Almost all government representatives noted that Croatia's exports to Slovenia declined after the establishment of the boundary. This is particularly true with regard to agricultural products that Croatian villagers used to sell in Slovenia. Of all perceptions about the implications of the new boundary, this one was the most commonly shared on both sides. Disintegration of the common currency system, new customs and border crossing regulations, a widening of the gap in incomes and well-being among the border population, economic recession, and transition to a market economy, have caused major disruptions in local trade. The majority of the Slovenian respondents reported that exports of agricultural goods to Croatia had drastically declined, causing a real catastrophe for farmers in the Brežice area (Barbič, 1995; 1997).

Plant representatives supported this general view of a declining trans-border trade, claiming that the Slovenian market was closed for products from Croatia. More than half of the surveyed plant representatives stated that their exports to Slovenia declined in comparison with the pre-boundary era; by contrast, only two of the representatives from Samobor-based firms experienced an increase in their exporting activity. It is interesting to note that the Croatian businessmen saw this situation partly as a result of an emphasis in Slovenia on the Slovenian-made products. However, a quick look at Slovenian retail establishments (for example in nearby Brežice) makes it very clear that many Slovenian-made products are cheaper than comparable products sold in Croatian stores. This goes a long way toward explaining the difficulties of exporting of Croatia-made goods to Slovenia's markets.

Although in the minority, some respondents saw new opportunities for cross-border trade on both sides of the newly internationalized boundary. The two surveyed companies in Samobor that reported an increase in their export activity to Slovenia specialized in custom-made products (air-conditioning and metal products) for large clients.

For many border residents, however, the new boundary made no difference. In about one-third of all surveyed municipalities the perception was that the border caused no changes, or the respondents had no opinion about the implications of the change in boundary status on cross-border trade. Similarly, about one-fifth of the respondents on the Slovenian side either provided no answer or were not aware of the situation (Barbič, 1997).

Underground Economy

Illegal import-export activities were known to exist along some segments of the border, on the Croatian side, even before the establishment of the international boundary. One of the surveyed officials noted the widely shared belief that about 30 percent of the population in the community was involved in the cross-border smuggling. This perception was based largely on visible display of sudden economic well-being, mostly expensive cars or other lifestyle manifestations unavailable to the majority of population. Slovenian respondents in the Brežice area seemed to be more aware of the illegal activity in their segment of the border; about a half of respondents believed that individuals on both sides of the border were involved in illegal trading (Barbič, 1997). On the Croatian side, this illegal activity is believed to involve importation of foreign cars, cigarettes, and other consumer goods that are unavailable in Croatia and in the neighboring countries of former Yugoslavia. On the Slovenian side, it was believed that the illegal trade involves livestock, household appliances, gas, timber, weapons, and undocumented immigrants (Barbič, 1997).

Cross-Border Tourism

Perceptions of boundary implications for Slovenian tourists visiting the Croatian side were divided between those who believed that the number of Slovenian tourists has decreased relative to the pre-boundary era, and those who saw an improvement in tourist flows. Among Slovenian residents, the majority believed that the number of Croatian tourists visiting the Slovenian side has declined (Barbič, 1997). While no official statistical data were available at the local level, a representative of the large Čatež resort[5] admitted that the number of visitors from Croatia (mostly from the Zagreb region) drastically declined after the new border was implemented.

The Labour Market

Residents on both sides of the border share a general perception that a relatively small number of Croatian residents, and an even lesser number of Slovenian residents, commute daily across the border. On the Croatian side it was noted that, in the pre-boundary era, many more Croatians commuted daily to jobs in Slovenia. Most of these commuters lost their jobs and returned to their communities in Croatia after Slovenian and Croatian independence, while others accepted Slovenian citizenship and stayed in Slovenia. Survey responses indicate that, of those still commuting daily (or weekly) to Slovenia, some are individuals possessing professional or other special skills; others are employed in low-paying jobs unattractive to Slovenian citizens. These changes, however, are not perceived as a result only of the political changes, but rather as related to the general economic restructuring process that has resulted from acceptance of free market policies, and to imminent downsizing of existing companies. Unlike the case in Slovenia, illegal employment of residents from the other side of the border is not an issue on the Croatian side, since there is practically no demand by Slovenian citizens for jobs in Croatia's firms.

Official Cross-Border Cooperation

Croatian survey respondents perceive official cross-border cooperation to be rare. However, some activities do exist that involve officials on both sides of the border, most notably cooperation between fire brigades. By contrast, almost one-half of all Slovenian respondents believed that border municipalities cooperated in sport activities, cultural events, and social events, although a relatively small percentage of residents were personally involved (Barbič, 1997).

Other Forms of Cross-Border Cooperation

Other forms of cross-border cooperation include participation in cultural and sports events, as well as hunting and fishing activities. In a little more than one-third of all municipalities on the Croatian side, common problems requiring some kind of cross-border cooperation also were identified. Currently, the most concrete project involves dealing with pollution of the Sutla River in the area of Hum na Sutli. Another example involves the operation of a tourist train, 'Atomček', that carries tourists from Atomske Toplice ('Atomic spa'), in Slovenia, once a week to Kumrovec, Croatia. Croatia's tourist officials promote this spa as an eco-village.

Participation in Schools

Survey results indicate that no Slovenian children attend schools in Croatia, while a relatively small number of children from Croatian villages attend school across the border, mainly from the municipalities of Djurmanec and Zagorska Sela. Respondents indicated that a larger number of children attended Slovenian schools in the pre-boundary era; these children came from the villages that had (and still have) a better connection with Slovenia than schools in Croatia. This general perception is similar to the perception of Slovenian residents regarding cross-border school attendance (see Barbič, 1997).

Perceived Similarities and Differences

According to Croatian survey respondents, the main perceived similarities between the Croatian and Slovenian sides of the border relate to food types and eating habits; the greatest perceived difference is related to language. This perception is mirrored in the responses obtained in the Slovenian survey (Barbič, 1997). Languages spoken in more isolated villages along the central and northern section of the study area share many similarities not found in the literary versions of Slovenian and Croatian languages.

Perception of Central Government Concern for the Border Region

Two-thirds of the respondents on the Croatian side of the border believed that the central government in Croatia was less concerned with the development of the border region than it was in developing other territories in the Republic. Only one respondent perceived that the border area received more attention that the rest of country. Most respondents saw improvements in physical infrastructure as the main factor in regional development. They particularly noted as imperative the need for improved accessibility to Zagreb, although some also noted they would like to see cross-border connections improved.

Comparison with Recent Findings

Several new studies were published after our fieldwork was completed (Klemenčič, 2001; Brečko-Grubar, 2001; Špes, 2001; Kves, 2001; Pak, 2001), all of them on the Slovenian side. All of these studies restated the importance of local context for social construction of the new boundary. Where pre-boundary practices were more intensive, the new boundary caused reduction in pedestrian crossings and vehicle traffic, as well as a limitation in the daily commuting of the labor force, reduction in out-shopping and other neighborly relations. The *de facto* restrictions and people's perceptions of border as a barrier were mostly related to new procedures involving new documents and border control. In other communities that used to be isolated from each other, the impacts of a new boundary were less noticeable.

The relationship between pre-boundary economic development and perceptions about the impact of the new boundary were documented in Špes' (2001) study of 1,200 households in four different sub-regions along the border with Croatia. In the most developed of the four sub-regions, Spodnje Posavje – which also was most dependent on ties with Croatia in the pre-boundary era – about 60 percent of residents expressed negative feelings about border impacts on their lives and the situation in their community. Their relation to the new border has been selective, however. Špes noted that, while for some residents the new border meant cutting off the employment income or restriction of communication with friends and relatives, for others the new border offered new employment in activities related to border maintenance and security such as border patrol and customs services.

Brečko-Grubar (2001) argues that, in border communities that already were among the least developed, the redefinition of the boundary as an international border did not have any particularly negative effects. This is because negative trends such as depopulation, out-migration and aging in agricultural households had already begun. Thus, she concludes, social changes in the late 1980s were more important than 1990s political changes that resulted in boundary redefinition. The immediate impacts of the new border in those communities were negligible because they were superimposed on socio-economic changes. However, in the long-term, the new boundary may have more pronounced impact.

Pak (2001) echoed this interpretation. He argued that a combination of border redefinition with economic restructuring caused a worsening of living conditions for border residents on both sides of the border. In the past the residents were able to improve their living conditions through transboundary employment, out-shopping, education and other modes of cooperation. As these transboundary interactions have come to be drastically reduced, the overall living conditions have worsened. Similarly, Krevs (2001) concluded that the worsening had less to do with the redefinition of the boundary than with the fact that these border communities were already marginally located with respect to major Slovenian urban centers. Further, they received little or no impetus from similarly less developed areas on the Croatian side (with the exception of Spodnje Posavje-Zagreb region).

Conclusions

In many ways, perceptions about the new political boundary do not differ very much between the Slovenian and Croatian sides of the border. The area has a long tradition of peaceful co-existence, and the new boundary is not perceived as creating reasons for territorial disputes. It is clear, however, that the changed agenda at the national level in each of the two newly independent states has undermined economic imperatives at local and micro-regional levels. Border residents indicated awareness that, although their portion of the boundary with Slovenia has been undisputed, many of the restrictions imposed on their cross-border movement are related to other disputes on the national level.

Empirical findings on the local scale further reveal that the impact of the new boundary, real or perceived, is selective. Communities that were linked more closely before the establishment of the new boundary obviously suffered more strongly from the new restrictions on flows. So did border residents whose social and personal spaces became first restricted and then reshaped by the new boundary. For other residents and communities with little or no links to the 'other' side, the implementation of the new boundary occurred almost unnoticed.

The findings also demonstrate that the boundary was ineffective in eliminating all cross-border activity. On the contrary, they show that residents at the local level eventually find ways to negotiate the border. The related transition to market economy, however, contributes to a fuzzy picture that overshadows the border effect in some places, while in others, underscores the border effect.

The border experiences of the 1990s, however, will soon face a new wave of testing. Since Slovenia has been identified within the first tier of new EU members, the border with Croatia will be reinforced as it becomes the new boundary separating EU and non-EU countries.

Notes

1 However, the elected officials and representatives of local governments ('načelnik' or 'gradonačelnik', i.e., the municipality mayor) were local residents who were born in the same municipality and who knew most of the other residents, by name, from childhood.
2 Interviews with representatives of private establishments were conducted in Samobor and Krapina, the two main urban centers in the study area.
3 Djurmanec, Hum na Sutli, Zagorska Sela, Kumrovec, Klanjec, Kraljvac na Sutli, Dubravica, Marija Gorica, Brdovec, Samobor, Krapina, Pregrada, Desinić, Tuhelj I Sveta Nedjelja.
4 Currently, Croatia and Slovenia have several minor border disputes in the Istria/ Žumberak-Gorjanci area.
5 Interview during a visit of the 1997 international conference participants.

References

Barbič, A. (1995), 'The Socioeconomic Effects of the New Slovenian-Croatian Border', *Research Reports*, 65, The University of Ljubljana Biotechnical Faculty, Ljubljana, Slovenia, pp. 111-128.

Barbič, A. (1997), 'Coping with new realities: The Slovenian-Croatian border', paper presented at the International Conference: Challenged Borderlands. Transcending Political and Cultural Boundaries, September 23-28, 1997, Klagenfurt, Austria.

Barbič, A. (2004), 'Perceptions of New Realities Along the Slovenian-Croatian Border', in V. Pavlakovich-Kochi, B.J. Morehouse, and D. Wastl-Walter (eds.), *Challenged Borderlands: Transcending Political and Cultural Boundaries*, Ashgate, Aldershot.

Belec, B. (1993), 'Prekomejna zemljiškoposestna pomešanost in zaposlovanje – primer obmejnih občin SV Slovenije s Hrvaško', *Dela*, 10, Department of Geography, University of Ljubljana, Ljubljana, Slovenia, pp. 73-82.

Belec, B. (1994), 'Differenzierung der Grenzgebiete mit Kroatien unter Berücksichtigung der Grundbesitzvermischung und Beschäftigung – Beispiel Nordostslovenien', in I. Crkvenčić, M. Klemenčić and D. Feletar (eds.), *Croatia – A New European State*, proceedings of a Symposium in Zagreb and Čakovec, September 22-25, 1993, University of Zagreb, Department of Geography and Spatial Planning, Zagreb, Croatia, pp. 166-172.

Brečko-Grubar, V. (2001), 'Geografska problematika naselja Dvori pri Movražu', *Dela*, 16, Department of Geography, University of Ljubljana, Ljubljana, Slovenia, pp. 193-202.

Bufon, M. (1994), 'Theory and Practice in Central European Border Areas: The Slovenian Example', in I. Crkvenčić, M. Klemenčić and D. Feletar (eds.), *Croatia – A New European State*, proceedings of a Symposium in Zagreb and Čakovec, September 22-25,

1993, University of Zagreb, Department of Geography and Spatial Planning, Zagreb, Croatia, pp. 173-182.

Cvitanović, A. (ed.) (1974), 'Geografija SR Hrvatske', 2, *Središnja Hrvatska – Regionalni prikaz*, Institut za geografiju Sveučilišta u Zagrebu, Zagreb, Croatia.

Feletar, D. and Stiperski, Z. (1996), 'The development and structure of the Croatian economy', *GeoJournal*, 38 (4), pp. 437-444.

Gosar, A. (1993), 'Nationalities in Slovenia – Changing Ethnic Structures in Central Europe', *GeoJournal*, 30, pp. 215-223.

Gosar, A. and Klemenčič, V. (1994), 'Current Problems of Border Regions Along the Slovenian-Croatian Border', in W.A. Gallusser (ed.), *Political Boundaries and Coexistence*, proceedings of the IGU Symposium, May 24-27, 1994, Basel, Switzerland.

Grozaj, K. (1997), 'Razvoj Krapine i okolice', paper submitted for B.A degree, Department of Geography, University of Zagreb.

Jurinjak, M. (1999), 'Značajke gospodarstva Krapinsko-zagorske županije 1994-1999', Hrvatska gospodarska komora, Županijska komora Krapina, Krapina, Croatia.

Klemenčič, M.M. (1993), 'Družbenogospodarski razvoj obmejnih območij v Sloveniji', *Dela*, 10, Department of Geography, University of Ljubljana, Ljubljana, Slovenia, pp. 127-134.

Klemenčič, M.M. (2001), 'Slovensko-hrvaška obmejna regija in njene funkcije v povezovanju med Hrvaško in Slovenijo in v luči europske integracije', *Dela*, 16, Department of Geography, University of Ljubljana, Ljubljana, Slovenia, pp. 7-16.

Krevs, M. (2001), 'Življenska raven prebivalstva slovenskega obmejnega območja ob meji s Hrvaško', *Dela*, 16, Department of Geography, University of Ljubljana, Ljubljana, Slovenia, pp. 105-118.

Martínez, O.J. (1994), *Border People*, The University of Arizona Press, Tucson, Arizona.

Paasi, A. (1999), 'Boundaries as Social Practice and Discourse: The Finish-Russian Border', *Regional Studies*, 33, pp. 669-680.

Pak, M. (2001), 'Regionalno razvojna problematika območja ob slovensko-hrvaši meji', *Dela*, 16, Department of Geography, University of Ljubljana, Ljubljana, Slovenia, pp. 29-38.

Ravbar, M. (1999), 'Posavje. Border Areas in Slovenia Along the Slovenian-Croatian Border', *Geographica Slovenica*, 31, pp. 71-87.

Ravbar, M. et al. (1995), 'Vloga in položaj posavske regije in njene razvojne možnosti' (The Role and Position of the Posavje Region and Its Development Possibilities), Inštitut za geografijo Univerze v Ljubljani, Ljubljana, Slovenia.

Špes, M. (2001), 'Odnos prebivalcev obmejnih območij Slovenije do slovensko-hrvaške državne meje', *Dela*, 16, Department of Geography, University of Ljubljana, Ljubljana, Slovenia, pp. 89-103.

Chapter 13

Transborder Urban Regime in the El Paso-Ciudad Juárez Region

Francisco J. Llera Pacheco

Introduction

The process of globalization in Mexico has produced important economic and political transformations in the role of public, private, and community actors. Globalization has forced the local politicians and land investors to establish alliances and to share the local land market with international investors. The case of San Gerónimo-Santa Teresa in the El Paso del Norte region (New Mexico-Texas-Chihuahua border) demonstrates how public-private cooperation transcends national boundaries and influences land development patterns in a border region. Regime theory suggests that public and private actors with economic resources, knowledge of local social transactions, and political power establish arrangements to influence the policy elaboration process within local governments (Stocker, 1996).

On the US-Mexico border, public-private cooperation has transcended national boundaries in pursuit of profits from bi-national land transactions. In this border context, public-private coalitions take advantage of both local and international factors to develop bi-national urban projects. The intention in this chapter is to answer three basic questions: 1) what are the characteristics of a bi-national urban regime, 2) what is the basis for public-private cooperation in the El Paso del Norte region, and 3) how are these binational coalitions perceived by local politicians, business community and community leaders.

A case study presented in this chapter, covering the San Gerónimo-Santa Teresa region on the US-Mexico border, demonstrates the presence of a bi-national urban regime in the El Paso del Norte region, and explains how actors within a bi-national urban regime modify the urban morphology of the US-Mexico border region. The San Gerónimo-Santa Teresa case study further demonstrates how a few actors with economic and political resources, on both sides of the border, merged their resources to promote bi-national urban projects on their land properties and to collect profits from the Mexican and American land markets. The San Gerónimo-Santa Teresa case study illustrates that bi-national cooperation emerges in those bi-national urban areas where there are powerful local regimes with political networks and common economic interests on both sides of the border. Furthermore, it demonstrates that bi-national cooperation, in the Ciudad Juárez-Santa Teresa border region, has been constructed based on the dominance of the PRI-clientelist regime over the Ciudad Juárez land market. Finally, it shows that the local groups in Santa Teresa and in Ciudad Juárez have established bi-national alliances based on their political and economic networks with local, state, and federal governments on both sides of the border and based on similar interests in promoting industrial growth and land accumulation. Four elements are necessary to differentiate a bi-national coalition from a local national coalition: the governmental context and the process of coalition formation, pro-growth advocacy, entrepreneurial attitude, and development of public policies.

Data from personal interviews with local politicians, land investors, and community leaders, on both sides of the border, support the arguments about the origin of public-private collaboration and the motivations for influencing policy elaboration in each city and in the region as a whole.

Study Area

The El Paso del Norte region presents a complex political geography because it encompasses urban land in three different cities, in three different states, in two countries. Each of the three cities presents different characteristics. Ciudad Juárez, Chihuahua, has a population of 797,697 inhabitants and is the second largest Mexican city along the US-Mexico border as well as the oldest urban center in the border region (INEGI, 1990; Martinez, 1982). El Paso, Texas has a population of 591,610 inhabitants and is the fourth major metropolitan center in Texas (University of Texas-El Paso, 1993). Finally, Sundland Park[1] has a population of 9,679 inhabitants and is the closest city to the Mexican border in New Mexico (City of Sundland Park, 1998). Overall, the El Paso del Norte region constitutes the second largest urban settlement along the US-Mexico border region with an estimated population of 1.3 million people and with a radius of economic influence of 200 to 300 miles encompassing parts of New Mexico, Texas and Chihuahua (El Paso Planning Department, 1988; INEGI, 1990).

The establishment of the maquiladora (foreign assembly) industries, in 1965, has not only been the most important economic driver within the region, but also the most important factor in increasing the demand for urban land on both sides of the border (Martinez, 1986; Schmidt, 1998; Stoddard, 1987a). This increase in demand for urban land among the three cities encouraged the emergence of different groups of investors competing to obtain the maximum amount of revenues from land development (Arroyo, 1993; Salas-Porras, 1987).

In the El Paso del Norte region, the most important economic engine during the last 34 years has been the promotion of industrial growth (Carrera, 1989; Martinez, 1986; Salas-Porras, 1987; Schmidt, 1998; Stoddard, 1987b). In the in the El Paso del Norte region more than half of the present urban growth was originated after 1960 when the foreign assembly industries arrived. The region experienced considerable urban sprawl and expansion during the 1960s because of this increase of industrial activity. This pattern has been reproduced and has increased in the entire region as more industrial and commercial activities have blossomed during the last thirty years.

The San Gerónimo-Santa Teresa project, which is the focus of this case study, is a private initiative to develop a new bi-national industrial city within the El Paso del Norte region (Harris and Lane, 1989). Santa Teresa, New Mexico, is a small community located within Doña Ana County, seven miles to the west of the twin cities of El Paso and Ciudad Juárez (Harris and Lane, 1989). Likewise, San Gerónimo is a new sector on the west side of Ciudad Juárez located along the boundary line between the state of New Mexico and the state of Chihuahua. The strategic location of Santa Teresa, close to El Paso and Ciudad Juárez, has attracted the interest of Mexican and American land investors to promote urban and industrial development toward this region of New Mexico.

The total area involved in the San Gerónimo-Santa Teresa project encompasses approximately 93,000 acres divided into 21,000 acres on the American side and 62,000 acres on the Mexican side (Conaway, 1988, Cruz, 1999a; García S., 1998). The purpose of the San Gerónimo-Santa Teresa bi-national project is to promote Santa Teresa as a service and retail center while San Gerónimo will be promoted as an industrial center (El Paso Times, 1992; Harris and Lane, 1989). In both San Gerónimo and Santa Teresa the concentration of land in the hands of a few landowners is a common characteristic and the most important incentive to develop this bi-national project (Cruz, 1999a; Pérez-Espino, 1990).

According to one of the main actors in the San Gerónimo-Santa Teresa project, Mexican President Adolfo López Mateos originally envisioned the project in the mid-1960s. His idea was to develop a new industrial complex on the US- Mexico border by taking advantage of the large amount of vacant land available for development in southern New Mexico, creating what he called a 'new village' between Mexico and New Mexico. He insisted that each side of the border should create its own framework with regard to responsibility and autonomy. The Texas government apparently did not like this idea; the reaction was understandable because Texas was the largest commercial partner of Mexico along the US-Mexico border. After López Mateos left the Mexican presidency, there was an impasse in the San Gerónimo-Santa Teresa project. However, when Miguel de la Madrid became the president of Mexico in 1982, he became interested in the Santa Teresa project, thus reviving its chances for success. At that time, Carlos Salinas de Gortari was the Minister of Budget and Planning. Salinas was also interested in this project, and when he became president, in 1988, he also supported the project. However, when Salinas was elected, he was dealing with negotiations over the North American Free Trade Agreement (NAFTA). His support of the San Gerónimo-Santa Teresa project faced tremendous opposition from many Mexican investors and economists who were more interested in negotiating projects with Texas.

The interest of the Mexican and the US federal governments in implementing NAFTA was important for local and political groups from Chihuahua and New Mexico in their effort to obtain political and economic support for this project from both governments (Monroy, 1999). The lobbying in Washington of Pete Domenici, a US Senator from New Mexico, to approve NAFTA also was important in obtaining Mexican support to develop the San Gerónimo area.

In general, the negotiations over the San Gerónimo-Santa Teresa project between public-private coalitions from New Mexico and Chihuahua have encompassed two different periods (Jiménez, 1989; Cruz, 1999). The first period, from 1986 through 1992, involved the conception and the materialization of this project. The second period, from 1998 to the present, encompasses the consolidation and development of the San Gerónimo-Santa Teresa project. During both periods, although different public and private actors have been involved, the same economic interest has been pursued: to collect profits from the industrial development of the San Gerónimo and Santa Teresa border region (Cruz, 1999; Jiménez, 1989; Monroy, 1999).

The first formal stage of promotion and development of the San Gerónimo-Santa Teresa bi-national project lasted from 1986 to 1992 and was largely driven by the political influence and economic power of two key actors on each side of the border: Jaime Bermúdez in Ciudad Juárez, and Charles Crowder in Santa Teresa (Jiménez, 1989; Ochoa, 1998). Jaime Bermúdez is the most important industrial developer in Ciudad Juárez and one of the most prominent members of the Revolutionary Institutional Party (PRI) (Aragón, 1997; Jiménez, 1989). In Santa Teresa, Charles Crowder has played an important role as the largest real estate investor in southern New Mexico and the owner of 21,000 acres of land and 110,000 acre feet of water rights in that area (Conaway, 1988; Segura, 1998).

In the San Gerónimo-Santa Teresa project Bermúdez and Crowder envisioned similar goals. Bermúdez wished to support industrial expansion in new locations within Ciudad Juárez, and Crowder wanted to develop Santa Teresa as the premier industrial city in New Mexico (Conaway, 1988; Jiménez, 1989; Old, 1985). Both Bermúdez and Crowder were aware of the limited industrial space in El Paso and the scarcity of water resources in Ciudad Juárez, and they knew that the location of Santa Teresa and San Gerónimo could guarantee enough water and land for the future industrial development of the region (Bermúdez, 1998).

Development of a Bi-National Urban Regime

On the US-Mexico border, national, regional and local actors share a history of cooperation. They also face mutual challenges associated with operating within a context in which interactions are between an advanced capitalist and a less-advanced capitalist country (Fernández, 1989; Guillén, 1992; Herzog, 1991). These local public-private alliances, on both the Mexican and US sides of the border, have their origins in a common interest in obtaining some type of economic benefit from land development.

A bi-national urban regime is defined as a public-private coalition led by dominant economic groups and land investors to influence the elaboration of land-use policies and land investments in bi-national metropolitan areas located along the US-Mexico border. A bi-national urban regime differs in several ways from the traditional urban regimes considered within the current urban literature. First, a bi-national urban regime pursues regional goals rather than local goals. Second, in a bi-national urban regime, every urban policy is designed to connect the outcomes produced in one urban context with the outcomes produced by a similar policy in a contiguous, but different urban context. Third, a bi-national urban regime incorporates private actors and different levels of government from the two countries to produce simultaneous urban outcomes, such as urban expansion or political decisions, in two different urban contexts. Finally, a bi-national urban regime is a larger urban regime that embraces local urban regimes from different national contexts.

A bi-national urban regime on the US-Mexico border can emerge when there are powerful local regimes characterized by political networks and common economic interests on both sides of the border. The case study discussed in this chapter shows that the local groups in Santa Teresa and the Ciudad Juárez clientelist regime share similar interests in industrial growth and land accumulation. The study also reveals how local groups in Santa Teresa rely on the better-developed political networks that connect the Ciudad Juárez clientelist regime with federal and state governments to promote the San Gerónimo-Santa Teresa bi-national initiative. This political involvement of the Mexican federal and state governments with the Ciudad Juárez clientelist regime has increased the confidence of the US federal government and the New Mexico state government confidence with regard to participating in the bi-national coalition.

On the US-Mexico border, urban, political and economic interdependency among Mexican and American border cities presents opportunities for use of urban regime theory to analyze international processes rather than local processes. This change in the scale of analysis of the process of public-private collaboration is the most important contribution of a bi-national urban regime concept to the current regime literature. Bi-national cooperation has occurred among public and private actors, but to a lesser degree than originally expected at the outset of this case study. In the El Paso del Norte region, findings indicate that demand for industrial land and the accumulation of land by a small number of land investors, on both sides of the border, has been a catalytic force in encouraging the formation of a bi-national regime. However, the development of this regime makes it clear that bi-national collaboration is not an inclusive, but an exclusionary process in which only a few actors with economic and political power are able to overcome the political and economic constraints imposed by the international boundary. Furthermore, as in other types of regimes, formation of a bi-national coalition in the San Gerónimo-Santa Teresa region highlights the role played by the local community, through local electoral processes, in guaranteeing the control and permanency of the coalition members in the local and state governments on both sides of the border. In particular, the permanency of the PRI in state and local governments has become the most important condition for the survival of the bi-national coalition.

As noted above, the emergence of a bi-national coalition differs from the emergence of local national coalitions in that local actors in a bi-national coalition must develop political and economic networks with varying scales of government from two countries. The process of bi-national collaboration in the San Gerónimo-Santa Teresa region is limited to only a few economic and political actors who possess large parcels of land, economic power, and political networks. These individuals not only can negotiate the agenda of one city, but they can have sufficient influence on local urban agendas in both national contexts. It is also important to note that pro-growth advocacy of the bi-national urban regime in the San Gerónimo-Santa Teresa border area is different from the pro-growth advocacy of the local national regimes because, in this bi-national regime, land development and the design of urban initiatives are not constrained by national boundaries. Further, in contrast to typical local coalitions, the bi-national coalition in this area displays a very aggressive entrepreneurial attitude because it is competing against other regions to attract foreign investments and because it is pursuing economic interests from two different land markets simultaneously. Finally, this case study illustrates that, in a bi-national coalition, development of urban policies in one national context influences policies across the international boundary.

The process of forming the bi-national public-private coalition has been distinct on each side of the border. In the US Paso del Norte area, the most important actors in the development of a bi-national urban project in the Santa Teresa region represent three type of groups: local land holders, the largest railroad companies in the southwestern United States, and New Mexico state and county politicians (Conaway, 1988; Fraizer, 1999; Simonson, 1998). The two largest land investors in the Santa Teresa area began formal development of Santa Teresa in the mid-1980s. Currently one of them owns the majority of the water rights (110,000 acres) in the region (Segura, 1998; Torres, 1998), while the other owns 21,000 acres of land and the largest industrial complex in the region (Segura, 1998; Torres, 1998). The three largest US railroad companies (the Union Pacific Company, the Southern Pacific Transportation Co., and the Burlington Northern Santa Fe Railroad Co.) have recently become involved in the development of Santa Teresa, due to its locational advantage. Their intent is to establish the largest transportation hub on the border for exports and imports moving between Mexico and the United States (Cruz, 1999; Fraizer, 1999; Zaragoza, 1997). New Mexico state politicians' interest in developing Santa Teresa has provided the opportunity to establish what they anticipate will be the most important industrial city in New Mexico and to stimulate creation of jobs and economic development in the state (Old, 1985; Simonson, 1998; Simonson, 1999).

In the Mexican portion of Paso del Norte region, the most important actors in the development of the San Gerónimo-Santa Teresa bi-national project include the five families that comprise the largest landholders in Ciudad Juárez, the most important industrial investors in Ciudad Juárez, and the PRI federal and state politicians (Cruz, 1999a; Medina, 1997; Monroy, 1999). Most of these landholders have accumulated land in San Gerónimo more with the intention of speculating on the future urban growth of Ciudad Juárez than with the intention of developing urban projects (Cruz, 1999a; Gutiérrez, 1999a; Linares, 1999a). However, the political and economic links of the San Gerónimo landholders with the largest industrial groups in Ciudad Juárez have encouraged them to target industrial growth as the development strategy for San Gerónimo (Cruz, 1999; Jiménez, 1989; Monroy, 1999; Pérez-Espino, 1990). In addition, the recent land acquisition in this region by one of the most important industrial developers in the State of Chihuahua and in Northern Mexico has reinforced the industrial orientation of San Gerónimo (Gutiérrez, 1999b). Finally, the involvement of the PRI federal and state governments in the development of San Gerónimo has been motivated by a perceived opportunity to gain more political support for the PRI and by a desire to support a project advocated by their most important economic contributors in Ciudad Juárez (Cruz, 1999; Gutiérrez, 1999a; Pérez-Espino, 1990; Pérez, 1999). The PRI federal and state governments' commitment of public funds to enhance transportation and other basic infrastructure in the San Gerónimo area will satisfy the needs of the largest landholders, as well as the goals of 'priista[2] community leaders' in the surrounding areas to promote introduction of basic services in exchange for political support for the PRI (Gutiérrez, 1999a; Pérez-Espino, 1990; Pérez, 1999).

The San Gerónimo-Santa Teresa bi-national initiative is the result of the presence of powerful groups of land investors with political connections and economic interests in Ciudad Juárez, Chihuahua, and Santa Teresa, New Mexico. In the San Gerónimo-Santa Teresa project, national and regional factors have combined to encourage bi-national alliances between land investors and politicians from the State of Chihuahua and the State of New Mexico. One of the land owners interviewed emphasized that regionally, the concentration of large parcels of land by a few local investors from both sides of the border and the interest of the State of New Mexico in promoting industrial development on its boundary with the states of Texas and Chihuahua created the conditions to concentrate economic resources and political power to develop this region.

In the El Paso del Norte region, the emergence of a bi-national urban regime has depended on the personal linkages of the local dominant land investors with politicians from the federal and state governments on both sides of the border, and on the desire of local and foreign economic groups to take advantage of the region's strategic location for industrial activities (Conaway, 1988; Crowder, 1998; Escanero, 1991; El Paso Times, 1992; Monroy, 1999).

Bi-national business interests might also be a major force driving the process of public-private cooperation. For example, the interest of the State of New Mexico in promoting industrial development in its border area with Ciudad Juárez has been an important engine for the emergence of the public-private coalition in Santa Teresa (El Paso Times, 1992; Old, 1985; Torres, 1998). This coalition of New Mexico state politicians and Santa Teresa land investors has targeted the development of the San Gerónimo-Santa Teresa bi-national industrial project as the primary growth pole for creating jobs and increasing the local tax-base on the southern New Mexico border (Escanero, 1991; Heilman and Watson, 1993; Simonson, 1998). Furthermore, the allocation of money by this public-private coalition in Santa Teresa has been important for the negotiation of common initiatives with Mexican authorities and economic groups (Cruz, 1999; Jiménez,

1989; Old, 1987; Simonson, 1999). The largest industrial groups in Ciudad Juárez, in particular, have been lured by the considerable US investment, $150 million, in industrial infrastructure within the Santa Teresa region (Jiménez, 1989; UACJ, 1998).

Although the political relationships of two principal actors in the United States and Mexico were important in bringing economic and political support to the region, other national factors also encouraged the federal governments of the US and Mexico to support the San Gerónimo-Santa Teresa project. New Mexico politicians capitalized on the interest of the Mexican federal government in establishing NAFTA with the United States and Canada; they obtained Mexican support for the San Gerónimo-Santa Teresa project in exchange for votes by the state's congressional delegation favoring approval of the agreement (Monroy, 1999; Pérez-Espino, 1990). According to El Diario, a local newspaper in Ciudad Juárez, in November 1994, in the middle of the negotiations to approve NAFTA, New Mexico Senator Pete Domenici negotiated with the Mexican President, Carlos Salinas de Gortari, to obtain 16 or 17 votes in favor of NAFTA in exchange for a highway to connect Santa Teresa with other close Mexican highways in Chihuahua. NAFTA was approved by a few votes and President Salinas kept his promise (Monroy, 1999). This negotiation allowed for the introduction of a transportation infrastructure and for the establishment of Mexican custom offices in San Gerónimo.

In the United States, political and economic pressure from the state of New Mexico to promote industrial development on its boundary with Ciudad Juárez and the strategic location of Santa Teresa for establishing the largest transportation hub in the region for exporting and importing industrial goods were important factors in convincing the US federal government to approve a new port of entry between Mexico and the United States in the San Gerónimo-Santa Teresa region (UACJ, 1998; Sánchez and Chavarín, 1995). In 1991, during the 10th Bi-national Reunion of Border Cities, the San Gerónimo-Santa Teresa project achieved formal bi-national recognition when the Mexican and the American federal governments approved the opening of a new border crossing point between Ciudad Juárez, Chihuahua, and Santa Teresa, New Mexico (UACJ, 1998). The primary rationale expressed by both countries was the economic impact expected from the San Gerónimo-Santa Teresa bi-national project. Local developers estimated the project would attract 360 industries, create 270,000 jobs and generate $543 million per year during the first 10 years (Escanero, 1991; UACJ, 1998).

In the El Paso del Norte region, a bi-national urban alliance has emerged as the result of the interests of local pro-growth coalitions in pursuing revenues from land development on both sides of the border (Schmidt and Lloyd, 1986). Two different types of public-private coalitions were responsible for developing the area. On the one hand, in Santa Teresa, an alliance was established between a developer and the New Mexico state government to promote the industrialization of southern New Mexico and develop the premier industrial city of New Mexico. The New Mexico state government had political and economical incentives for cooperating with the local developer to develop his 21,000 acres of land into the best-planned industrial city along the US-Mexico border. Together, the developer and the New Mexico state government invested, between 1982 and 1985, more than $100 million in planning, improvements, and buildings to encourage the development of Santa Teresa (Old, 1985).

In Ciudad Juárez, the key land-owning families have accumulated more than 62,000 acres of land in the San Gerónimo-Anapra area (Cruz, 1999; Figueroa, 1999). These families have traditionally supported the PRI in Ciudad Juárez and were confident that their relationships with the PRI local and state governments would aid in achieving their plans for urban development of San Gerónimo (Cruz, 1999; García J., 1998). The local and state PRI-affiliated governments have supported urban expansion toward the San Gerónimo area by promoting the formation of squatter settlements in the western sector of Ciudad Juárez, close to the San Gerónimo area (Arroyo, 1993c; Cruz, 1999a; García J., 1998; Pérez, 1999). This promotion has used 'clientelist practices',[3] in which PRI partisan leaders organized poor migrants to establish illegal neighborhoods in vacant parcels of land (Pérez, 1999; Linares, 1999b). This strategy has helped them justify the allocation of public investment and the introduction of basic infrastructure into this sector. (Jiménez, 1989; Pérez-Espino, 1990). However, the budget needed to develop the San Gerónimo area in 1986 was estimated at more than $250 million, making it difficult for the local and the state governments to achieve their urban development goals for San Gerónimo in one governmental term of six years (Jiménez, 1989).

The development of the San Gerónimo-Santa Teresa project is important for the economic development of the entire region. However, the Mexican part still has problems in introducing infrastructure. It seems that the development of the Mexican side will take a long time because it seems as if there are political groups not interested in supporting this project in Ciudad Juárez. In New Mexico, the public and private sectors are working and investing money together, but in Ciudad Juárez, the private sector is waiting for the government to invest public moneys to introduce infrastructure. This will delay the development of San Gerónimo.[4]

The large parcels of land encompassed by the San Gerónimo project and the considerable amount of money required for the development of this part of the border make the Mexican side the most important priority for the bi-national economic groups promoting this project (Jiménez, 1989; Pérez-Espino, 1990; Monroy, 1999). Acknowledging the relevance of San Gerónimo for the success of the bi-national project, from 1986 through 1992, PRI politicians in Ciudad Juárez worked together with politicians from New Mexico on urban and transportation planning, as well as in the development of economic strategies for San Gerónimo (Escanero, 1991). According to Jaime Bermúdez, although local politicians and land investors developed urban and economic strategies on both sides of the border, the favorable political conditions did not continue for the promoters of the San Gerónimo-Santa Teresa project in 1992. In this year, the National Action Party (PAN) won the state and the local elections in Chihuahua, for the first time. It introduced changes that were contrary to the interests of the public-private coalition supporting the development of the San Gerónimo area (Alvarado, 1997;

Linares, 1999c). In general, development toward San Gerónimo was neglected by
the new authorities for two reasons: to support the economic interests of the PAN
land investors in other areas of Ciudad Juárez, and to reduce the political power of
the PRI at the local level (Linares, 1999a; Pérez-Espino, 1990). An urban planner
in Ciudad Juárez stated that the most important barrier to the San Gerónimo-Santa
Teresa project was that the biggest developers from the PAN in Ciudad Juárez did
not have land near San Gerónimo. These groups will be the first to challenge urban
expansion toward San Gerónimo.[5]

In 1998, the Revolutionary Institutional Party (PRI) PRI recovered control of
the state government, but PAN retained control over the local government in
Ciudad Juárez. This situation has created a conflict between the two types of
interests within the Ciudad Juárez land market. On the one hand, the new state
administration headed by Governor Patricio Martínez expressed interest in
supporting the economic groups involved in the San Gerónimo-Santa Teresa
project. On the other hand, in Ciudad Juárez, the city government led by one of the
most important land developers from PAN, showed more interest in supporting
urban projects being carried out in various parts of Ciudad Juárez by PAN-
affiliated economic groups (Monroy, 1999). These conflicting positions have
created conflicts over the allocation of public investments and the selection of the
most appropriate areas for urban growth in Ciudad Juárez (Cruz, 1999b).

Recapture of the state government by PRI in 1998 has been important to the
continuation of the San Gerónimo-Santa Teresa bi-national project. After six years
of minimal activity on the Mexican side, landholders from the PRI are attempting
to complete the development of San Gerónimo. The new Chihuahua governor from
the PRI, Patricio Martínez, and New Mexico state Governor Gary Johnson, both
have expressed interest in accelerating the industrial development of Santa Teresa
and San Gerónimo (Gutiérrez, 1999b; Simonson, 1999). At the same time, local
economic groups in San Gerónimo have incorporated new land investors in order
to consolidate development of the area before the end of the administration of the
new Chihuahua state government in October 2003 (Gutiérrez, 1999a).

In Ciudad Juárez, the magnitude of the economic resources that will be
allocated by the state governments of New Mexico and Chihuahua to the San
Gerónimo-Santa Teresa area has been decisive in convincing the local government
to cooperate with state politicians and PRI land investors. However, the interest of
the PRI in gaining political support through this project has created some
disagreements between local PAN authorities and state PRI authorities about the
best way to develop San Gerónimo without providing either party with an electoral
advantage (UACJ, 1998). As Javier Ortíz, a mayor's advisor in Ciudad Juárez,
stated in a newspaper interview, 'The Ciudad Juárez local government recognizes,
more than ever, the pivotal role that southern New Mexico, especially the port of
entry of San Gerónimo-Santa Teresa will play for the development of the entire
region. Therefore, we have already been talking to officials from the New Mexico
state government, Doña Ana County and with private investors in the Santa Teresa
area' (Simonson, 1999).

The formation of a bi-national urban alliance to develop the San Gerónimo-Santa Teresa bi-national project has been possible because local economic groups have taken similar economic risks to pursue a costly and innovative urban project (Gutiérrez, 1999b; Old, 1985). Mexican and American economic groups have combined their political networks, on both sides of the border, to convince federal and state governments to support the San Gerónimo-Santa Teresa bi-national project. The economic and political support that local land investors obtained from the Mexican and American governments shows the capacity of this bi-national urban alliance to influence policies and decisions in national and state governments.

In 1998, the purchase of 48,352 acres of land by Eloy Vallina, one of the largest landholders in San Gerónimo, was an important factor in accelerating the allocation of public and private investments on both sides of the border, and in expediting negotiations between the New Mexico and the Chihuahua state governments to consolidate the San Gerónimo-Santa Teresa project (Cruz, 1999). Vallina is one of the most powerful entrepreneurs in Mexico and was an important contributor to the political campaign of the current state governor of Chihuahua, Patricio Martínez (Gutiérrez, 1999a).

Eloy Vallina's economic contribution to Martinez's campaign has been an important factor in obtaining the political and economic support of the state government to develop San Gerónimo. This support has been translated into the announcement of three important actions by the Chihuahua state government: the allocation of public investment to introduce basic infrastructure in the poor areas surrounding the San Gerónimo area; the construction of a border highway to connect San Gerónimo with Ciudad Juárez and other border locations along the Chihuahua-Texas boundary line; and the consolidation of the San Gerónimo-Santa Teresa project to create more jobs and economic development in Ciudad Juárez (Cruz, 1999b; El Norte, 1998).

The strategy of the local coalitions to accelerate the urban and industrial development in San Gerónimo and Santa Teresa seems to be to allocate the majority of their economic resources to the two most important urban ventures in this region: the Transportation Intermodal Hub in Santa Teresa that has the potential to make this area one of the most important distribution centers in the United States, and the construction of the Chihuahua border highway that will connect San Gerónimo with Ciudad Juárez and other border towns along the Chihuahua/Texas boundary line (Gutiérrez, 1999b; Freizer, 1999; UACJ, 1998). The Transportation Intermodal Hub in Santa Teresa is crucial to the plans of local land investors and the State of New Mexico to develop the most important distribution center on the US-Mexico border and to guarantee the future industrialization of Santa Teresa. The center is important to the development of Santa Teresa in that it will allow the three US railroad companies and Ferrocarriles de México (the Mexican Federal Railroad Company) to concentrate and distribute products having a value of more than $1.2 billion to the eastern, western, and northern sectors of the United States (Freizer, 1999; Gutiérrez, 1999a). The construction of this transportation hub will channel through Santa Teresa about 16 percent of the total exchange of products imported and exported between the United States and Mexico (Freizer, 1999; Gutiérrez, 1999a). Likewise, the construction of a border highway to connect San Gerónimo with Ciudad Juárez is important for the Mexican land investors to guarantee the incorporation of San Gerónimo into the Ciudad Juárez urban area and the expansion of industrial areas from Ciudad Juárez to San Gerónimo. Over the short term, the allocation of public and private investment in Santa Teresa will amount to $250 million to support the construction of the transportation intermodal center while, in San Gerónimo, the Chihuahua state government will allocate about $14 million to construct the San Gerónimo-Ciudad Juárez border highway (Freizer, 1999; Monroy, 1999).

The development of the San Gerónimo-Santa Teresa project will produce economic and political benefits for a few groups on both sides of the border. In Santa Teresa, industrial and commercial development will benefit the two most important local land investors: Charles Crowder and Christopher Lyons. The former will take advantage of his rights to large amounts of local groundwater and the latter will benefit from the majority of the industrial and commercial investments that are planned for his 21,000 acres of land (Segura, 1998; Torres, 1998; UACJ, 1998). Similarly, the three railroad companies interested in the Santa Teresa transportation hub, the Northern Santa Fe Railroad, Southern Pacific Transportation, and the Union Pacific Company, will also have the potential to benefit from transporting about 16 percent of the total exchange of imports and exports between Mexico and the United States (Freizer, 1999; Gutiérrez, 1999a). The creation of jobs and the industrialization of the border location of Santa Teresa may also produce political gains for the governing political party in the New Mexico state government, and particularly may strengthen the career of Governor Gary Johnson and the aspirations of the Senator Pete Domenici (Segura, 1998). Ramon Galindo, a former PAN city mayor in Ciudad Juárez, has observed that, in Ciudad Juárez, the development of San Gerónimo can possibly help the largest landholders in this region develop one-third of the land in Ciudad Juárez, and to obtain profits from industrial and commercial development. Moreover, the construction of the San Gerónimo-Ciudad Juárez border highway and the introduction of basic infrastructure from Ciudad Juárez to San Gerónimo will benefit other small and medium land owners who have already created the Committee for the Development of the West of Ciudad Juárez to obtain major economic benefits from the development of this region (Cruz, 1999; Pérez, 1999). In addition, the development of San Gerónimo will help federal and state governments obtain political support for the PRI in future elections (Cruz, 1999a; Pérez, 1999).

As this study shows, bi-national cooperation in the San Gerónimo-Santa Teresa region has only been attainable by a few actors on each side of the border, because the process demands access to both economic power and political networks at different levels of government in both countries. The process of bi-national cooperation, as manifested here, is different from the kind of public-private cooperation that occurs in a single national context because, in the bi-national context, policies on each side of the international boundary are designed, through cross-border cooperation to correspond with each other. Here the ultimate goal is to produce simultaneous outcomes in two national land markets. The limited number of actors capable of combining the necessary characteristics to achieve success makes the process of bi-national collaboration difficult to reproduce in border localities lacking powerful economic groups with local roots.

Overall, in the San Gerónimo-Santa Teresa border region, six main policy outcomes have been produced as a result of the activities of the bi-national coalition: a) prioritization, in the Mexican Paso del Norte area, of investment of public monies in industrial infrastructure rather than in addressing social needs; b) an increase in the value of land in limited areas close to the international boundary; c) urban sprawl; d) political conflicts between the local and bi-national coalitions over who would lead the process of industrial development; e) costly subsidies (more than $100 million) absorbed by the New Mexico state government to introduce infrastructure in Santa Teresa (Old, 1985) and interest on the part of the Chihuahua state government to subsidize transportation infrastructure (at a cost of $14 million) to develop San Gerónimo (Monroy, 1999), and f) empowerment of a small group of landholders who have invested in the Ciudad Juárez and Santa-Teresa-area land markets.

As part of this case study, individuals on both sides of the border were surveyed. The intent of the survey was to identify perceptions about the impact of the San Gerónimo-Santa Teresa bi-national coalition on the process of urban development in the El Paso del Norte region. Overall, the results of the survey and interviews show that the local actors on both the American and the Mexican sides of the El Paso del Norte recognize the formation of public-private alliances as a common local process. However, the way bi-national cooperation is established and developed in the El Paso del Norte region is still an unfamiliar process for the majority of the local politicians and land investors since few actors have the economic resources and the political networks to develop bi-national alliances.[6]

Implications for the Process of Policy Elaboration in the Region

In the El Paso del Norte region development of local and national policy reflects the interests of the powerful regional economic groups. On the one hand, at the national level, the economic success of the maquiladora industrial program promoted by Jaime Bermúdez and other local entrepreneurs in Ciudad Juárez and all along the US-Mexico border has favored, and will continue to favor, local groups on both sides of the border who wish to influence industrial regulation and the allocation of industrial infrastructure in the El Paso del Norte region. On the other hand, at the local level, the economic dependence of the local politicians on local economic groups has been essential to promoting profitable and innovative projects in the El Paso del Norte region. In this region, the political power of the local economic groups allows them to influence local policy, and to decide which projects will be supported at the local level. This capacity of the local economic groups to influence local decision-making processes has played, and will continue to play, an important role in supporting coordination of political and economic strategies, on both sides of the border, aimed at integrating the region into a single economic unit. Such integration is essential to the region's ability to compete successfully against other regions to attract foreign capital.

Finally, the global-scale tendency to encourage regional integration of different localities into unitary economic blocs will also be reproduced among the US-Mexico border localities, generating the emergence of different types of bi-national coalitions in the region. In the future, bi-national cooperation will become at once more common and complex within both the national and border-region contexts. At the same time, study of the process of policy elaboration and the formation of public-private alliances at the bi-national level will dominate the urban, political and economic literature. In this research, transferring urban regime theory to the study of the processes of public-private cooperation, such as the case study presented here, constitutes the first step towards explaining the origin of bi-national alliances on the US- Mexico border and elsewhere. However, more research will be necessary in other sub-regions and in other contexts to develop more systematic analyses and comparisons about the origin, reproduction and crisis of different types of bi-national alliances. With an increase in the number of bi-national studies, a new sub-discipline might be created, within the current border literature, concerned with cross-national alliances. Urban regime studies conducted on the US-Mexico border promise to provide a central theoretical reference point for guiding such research in other less integrated and interdependent contexts.

Notes

1　Sundland Park is the area in the state of New Mexico in which Santa Teresa is located and hereafter this chapter will focus solely on the targeted area for development: Santa Teresa.
2　Member of the Revolutionary Institutional Party (PRI).
3　Clientelist practices: In this document I compared 'clientelist practices' to those in which PRI political leaders offer the provision of urban land to poor people in exchange for political support to the PRI.
4　Interview with Ing. Manuel Ochoa, former Director of the Ciudad Juárez Chamber of Commerce and current employee at the El Paso Chamber of Commerce, El Paso, November 15,1998. (English translation).
5　Interview with Mtro. Salvador García, General Director of Espacio Urbano. Ciudad Juárez, Chihuahua.
6　Bi-national alliances: In this document I identify bi-national alliances as those arrangements that are only possible to be established between a few powerful local actors sharing not only common land investments and similar economic interests but also similar political networks with different scales of government on both sides of the border. The lack of these requirements for the majority of local politicians and land investors in Ciudad Juarez, El Paso and Sundland Park make it difficult for them to understand and to be involved in bi-national alliances.

References

Alvarado, I. (1997 September), 'Los enredos de Salbarcar', *El Diario De Ciudad Juárez*, p. 8 A.

Aragón, O. (1997 September), 'Los Feudos de Sur', *El Diario De Ciudad Juárez*, p. 8 A.

Arroyo, J. (1993 April), 'Los planes de desarrollo a la medida de ex-alcaldes', *El Norte De Ciudad Juárez*, p. 6 A.

Bermúdez, J. (1998), Grupo Bermudez, Personal Interview, Ciudad Juarez, Chihuahua.

Carrera R.J. (1989), 'Ciudad Juarez: punta de lanza de las transnacionales', in S.A.A.C. y J.C. Alejandra Salas-Porras (Coordinadores), *Frontera Norte, tan cerca de los Estados Unidos*, Nuestro Tiempo, Mexico, pp. 119-140.

City of Sundland Park (1998), *City of Sundland Park Land Use Committee*, Data Analysis Summary, Sundland Park, New Mexico (unpublished document).

Conaway, J. (1988 June), 'International city planned for border', *NewsCount Alburquerque Journal*, p. 1.

Crowder, C. (1998), Crowder Land Co., Personal Interview, Santa Teresa, New Mexico.

Cruz, J. (1999a May), 'Cinco Colonias, Cuatro Dueños', *El Diario De Ciudad Juárez*, p. 11 A.

Cruz, J. (1999b May), 'VETA DE ORO al poniente', *El Diario De Ciudad Juárez*, p. 8 A.

El Norte de Ciudad Juárez (1998 December), 'Paran otra venta de predio a Municipio', *El Norte De Ciudad Juárez*, p. 1 A.

El Paso Planning Department (1988), 'Economic Development in El Paso', *El Paso Plan*, El Paso, Texas, City of El Paso, pp. 1-8.

El Paso Times (1992 May), 'Developers pool cash for crossing', *El Paso Times*, p. 2 B.

Escanero, J. (1991 January), 'Santa Teresa captura inversiones extranjeras por 3 mil millones de dolares', *El Diario De Ciudad Juárez*, p. 2 B.

Fernández, A.R. (1989), 'The future of growth and policy', *The Mexican American Border Region: Issues and Trends*, University of Notre Dame Press, Notre Dame, Indiana, pp. 111-123.

Figueroa, L. (1999 May), 'Nuevo Mexico Impulsa el Viejo Camino Real', *El Diario De Ciudad Juárez*, p. 11 A.

Freizer, J. (1999), El Paso Planning Department, Personal Interview, El Paso, Texas.

García, J. (1998), Corett Federal Land Office, Personal Interview, Ciudad Juarez, Chihuahua.

García, S. (1998), Despacho de Planeación Espacio Urbano, Personal interview, Ciudad Juarez, Chihuahua.

Guillén, T. (1992), 'El PRI: Modernización política o cambio de elites. El caso de Ciudad Juárez de 1983 a 1986', *Política y Poder en la Frontera*, IV, Colegio de la Frontera Norte-UACJ, Ciudad Juárez, Chihuahua, pp. 7-14.

Gutiérrez, A. (1999a May), 'A la conquista de la frontera', *El Diario De Ciudad Juárez*, p. 10 A.

Gutiérrez, A. (1999b May), 'Las razones de Vallina', *El Diario De Ciudad Juárez*, p. 9 A.

Harris, C. and Lane, J. (1989), *The Harvard Santa Teresa Study*, A Report on the Urban and Land Development Studios, Harvard Graduate School of Design, Boston, Massachusetts.

Heilman, G.J. and Watson, D.J. (1993), 'Publicization, Privatization, Synthesis, Tradition: Options for Public-Private Configuration', *International Journal of Public Administration*, 16(1), pp. 107-137.

Herzog, L. (1991), *Where North Meets South: Cities, Space and Politics on the US/Mexico Border*, Center for Mexican American Studies, University of Texas, Austin, Texas.

Instituto Nacional de Estadistica Geografía e Informatica (INEGI) (1990), *XI Censo de Población y Vivienda*, Chihuahua: Resultados definitivos, tabulados básicos, México, INEGI.

Jiménez, F. (1989 February), 'El proyecto Santa Teresa: un negociazo para Bermúdez', *Semanario Ahora*, p. 113.

Linares, G. (1999a February), 'Los dueños: un puñado de apellidos', *El Diario De Ciudad Juárez*, p. 9 A.

Linares, G. (1999b February), 'Apuestas al Futuro: Las invasiones, el acaparamiento', *El Diario De Ciudad Juárez*, p. 8 A.

Linares, G. (1999c February), 'La expansión de la mancha urbana', *El Diario De Ciudad Juárez*, p. 9 A.

Martínez, O. (1982), *Ciudad Juárez: El Auge de una Ciudad Fronteriza apartir de 1848*, Fondo de Cultura Economíca, México.

Martínez, O. (1986), 'The Foreign Orientation of the Ciudad Juárez Economy', in G. Young (ed.), *The Social Ecology and Economic Development of Ciudad Juáre*, 1st. ed., Westview Press, Boulder, Colorado, pp. 141-153.

Medina, F. (1997 September), 'La nueva ciudad', *El Diario De Ciudad Juárez*, p. 6 A.

Monroy, E. (1999 May), 'Viejo Plan: La nueva ciudad del poniente', *El Diario De Ciudad Juárez*, p. 8 A.

Ochoa, M. (1998), El Paso Chamber of Commerce, Personal Interview, El Paso, Texas.

Old, J. (1985 February), 'Entrepreneur Charly Crowder developing hopes for new city', *El Paso Herald Post*, p. 5 A.

Pérez, R. (1999 June), 'Avala Estado Fraude: Gobierno, PRI y Lideres ofrecen a colonos tierras inexistentes', *El Norte De Ciudad Juárez*, p. 1 A.

Pérez-Espino, J. (1990 December), 'Despilfarro de dinero en un proyecto politico', *Semanario Ahora*, p. 54.

Salas-Porras, A. (1987), 'Maquiladora y burguesia regional', *Revista El Cotidiano*, Universidad Autonoma Metropolitana, 1, pp. 51-58.

Sánchez, A. and Chavarín, R. (1995), 'El tratado de libre comercio y la frontera norte de México', in J. Arroyo Alejandre (ed.), *Regiones in Transición: Ensayos sobre la integración regional en Alemania del este y en el occidente de México*, Universidad de Guadalajara, Guadalajara, pp. 325-331.

Schmidt, R., and Lloyd, W. (1986), 'Patterns of Urban Growth in Ciudad Juárez', in G. Young (ed.), *The Social Ecology and Economic Development of Ciudad Juárez*, Westview Press, Boulder, Colorado, pp. 23-47.

Schmidt, S. (1998), *En busca de la decisión: la industria maquiladora en Ciudad Juárez*, Universidad Autónoma de Ciudad Juárez/University of Texas at El Paso, Ciudad Juárez, Chihuahua.

Segura, J. (1998), Sundland Park City Mayor, Personal Interview. Sunland Park City, New Mexico.

Simonson, S. (1999 April), 'Area Mayors Join Chorus of Economic Unity', *El Paso Times*, p. 4 B.

Stoddard, E.R. (1987a), 'Historic Border Development in Mexico's Sociopolitical Milieu', in E.R. Stoddard (1987), *Maquila: Assembly Plants in Northern Mexico*, Texas Western Press, El Paso, Texas, pp. 1-16.

Stoddard, E.R. (1987b), 'Mexico's Border Industrialization: Policies and Development', in E. R. Stoddard (1987), *Maquila: Assembly Plants in Northern Mexico*, Texas Western Press, El Paso, Texas, pp. 16-27.

Stoker, G. (1996), 'Regime Theory and Urban Politics', in T.R. LeGates, and F. Stout (eds.), *The City Reader*, Routledge, London, pp. 268-281.

Torres, V. (1998), Director of the Office of Community Development, Personal Interview, City of Sundland Park, New Mexico.

Universidad Autónoma de Ciudad Juárez (UACJ) (1998), Base de Datos Hemerográfica (Unpublished work), Centro de Investigación y Posgrado-ICSA.

University of Texas at El Paso (1993*), Paso del Norte Regional Economy: socioeconomic Profile*, Texas Center for Economic and Enterprise Development, Institute for Manufacturing and Materials Management, El Paso, Texas.

Zaragoza, R. (1997 June), 'Ampliarán complejo industrial y comercial en Santa Teresa', *El Diario De Juárez*, p. 2 B.

Chapter 14

Transboundary Health Care and the Production of Space on the Arizona-Sonora Border

Barbara J. Morehouse and Patricia L. Salido

Introduction

Is it indeed true that disease knows no boundaries? Every day, all along the US-Mexico border, individuals cross in both directions to visit dentists, doctors, hospitals, pharmacies and providers of medical devices and supplies (Warner, 1997; Nichols et al., 1991). These flows have a long history, but have assumed even more significance in the contemporary context of globalization, pursuit of free trade, intensified privatization of health care, and increasing transboundary circulation of people, goods and information.

Given the rush of capital to appropriate the most lucrative elements of state-provided health care, critical questions arise about how the rather unholy alliance of state and corporate health care providers plays out in the everyday lives of individuals. There are spatial elements to this question, and nowhere are the changing geographies of health care coming into greater prominence than in the borderlands between nations and health care systems. Continuous vigilance is required to ensure that state policies and capitalist opportunism do not marginalize vulnerable populations, or take away options – such as crossing an international boundary for health services – that may be absolutely essential to their well-being. For this to happen, the ways in which social action produces and is affected by health care geographies must be brought to the forefront of local discourse. This spatial knowledge must be asserted in a manner that promotes transboundary community cohesiveness and produces strong borderland spatialities.

How transboundary spaces of health care might be (re)produced in a way that minimizes the contradictions between international boundary politics and production of local, transboundary geographies of shared culture, values, and knowledge is a pivotal question. We suggest that devolving authority to the local level for day-to-day decisions is important for assuring that changes and innovations in the health care arena include rather than exclude vulnerable populations, and support rather than undermine the state's responsibility to provide for the health of its citizens.

The spatialities of health care and the geographies of health on the US-Mexico border are complex, multilayered and dynamic; however, in the end it is how health care is provided and utilized by individuals and communities that matters. Assuring that equity and principles of compassionate care are not lost in the onrush of privatized health services requires an understanding of how geographies of health are produced and reproduced at all scales from the local to the international. In this chapter, we build a case for why these complexities should be introduced into policies and actions that empower individuals and communities with regard to establishing the rules, spaces, and practices associated with borderland health care delivery and consumption.

Borderland Geographies of Health and Medical Geography

Provision and utilization of health care services are longstanding elements in transboundary dynamics on the US-Mexico border. Through the location decisions and marketing efforts of providers and the utilization patterns of consumers, a complex and overlapping pattern of health care geographies has emerged. These geographies are an outgrowth of the juxtaposition of two very different health care systems, a high overall level of uneven development, and weaknesses in the health care systems of both countries. Globalization of health services as an element of international commerce, together with strong pressures to reduce health care costs to both the public and private sectors, bode changes in the US-Mexico borderlands. Promoting a borderlands politics predicated on community-based geographies of health holds promise for protecting vulnerable populations and stimulating further integration of binational border communities.

International boundaries influence the production and reproduction of particular kinds of geographies that do not typically exist in more distant locations, largely due to everyday opportunities for interaction and shared experiences. However, unlike borderland geographies of shopping, tourism, or commerce, geographies of borderland health care are produced within a context of myriad and sometimes conflicting laws, rules, practices, and expectations. This is nowhere more evident than on the US-Mexico border where a philosophy of private enterprise meets a state welfare structure. The border functions as the point of differentiation with regard to costs, approach to medical care, quality and accessibility of products and services, even hours of operation. In this context, the boundary marks a clear delineation of uneven development between the two countries. It serves as the locus for a broader menu of choices for consumers while at the same time influencing the geographical location of health services on both sides of the line. Thus the patterns and practices associated with health care delivery and consumption on the US-Mexico border reflect specific kinds of opportunities and constraints not found under other circumstances or in other places away from an international boundary.

Especially where communities are located in close proximity to each other on either side of the boundary, shared patterns of provision and utilization of health services contribute to the production of unique transboundary geographies of health that would not arise in the absence of the international boundary. This uniqueness may be traced in large part to the disparity in level of development between the two countries, but also reflects weaknesses in the health care systems and infrastructure on both sides of the boundary. At the same time, the political boundary continues to represent a powerful impediment to full realization of place-based geographies of health, which, as defined by Kearns (1993) and Kearns and Joseph (1993), reflect the value and role of places, and the ecological interactions between places and health.

Medical Geography, Geographies of Health, and the Social Construction of Space

Medical geography, focusing on 'the provision and location of health services and patient spatial behavior' (Earickson et al., 1989, p. 433), and studies associated with epidemiology constitute a longstanding topical area of interest. Over many years, medical geography has continued to make important contributions to society's understanding of the importance of concepts such as location and flow in conducting health and medical research.

More recently this orientation has been supplemented by the emergence of a new focus revolving around the notion of 'geographies of health' (Kearns and Gesler, 1998; Kearns, 1993; Kearns and Joseph, 1993). In keeping with a general trend in society toward focusing on health and how to maintain it, this approach focuses on how place and space are at least in part defined based on health-oriented activities, organizations, and institutions (see also Eyles, 1990; Jones and Moon, 1993; Moon, 1990; 1992; Moon, Gould and Jones, 1998). As Kearns (1993) clearly illustrated in New Zealand, where health care facilities also serve as important locations for the reproduction of community, the social production of health and the social production of space may interact in important ways in the formation of larger community relations and structures.

Geographical perspectives on the production of space provide a means for understanding some of the opportunities and constraints that contribute strongly to the patterns and processes of transboundary health care. The social production of space, as developed by Lefebvre (1991) and Soja (1989), further facilitates analysis and interpretation of these patterns and processes.[1] The social production of space may be productively applied to analysis of the production of boundaries and borderland spaces, which are intimately and inextricably embedded in the production of space more generally. This perspective allows analysis, at multiple spatial and temporal scales, of how space/spatialities come to be produced or challenged through everyday discourse and practice (deCerteau, 1984; Foucault, 1982) as well as through formulation and implementation of laws and policies (Morehouse et al., 1997; Morehouse, 1993). This broader approach to boundary and border studies is reflected in a wide range of publications (Newman and Paasi, 1998). The work of Paasi (1996) on the social production of nationhood, as well as boundaries and space is likewise germane to the perspective employed here.

The Arizona-Sonora Health Services Study

In this chapter, we explore the social construction of space from the perspective of health care and health services in the borderlands of the Mexican state of Sonora and the American state of Arizona. The chapter is derived from a collaborative study, Health Services in Arizona and Sonora: Opportunities for Transboundary Integration (Morehouse et al., 1997), carried out by researchers in Arizona and Sonora. The study, funded by the Arizona-Mexico Commission and the Comisión Sonora-Arizona, was designed to identify opportunities for private-sector business development in health services in the two-state region through development of a transboundary health services cluster (in part based on Porter's (1990) work on clusters). The study was one of a series of research efforts aimed at taking advantage of opportunities afforded under the North American Free Trade Agreement (NAFTA) by capitalizing on the economic strengths of the two states. The main goal of the larger effort has been to improve the competitiveness of the two-state region vis-à-vis the other US-Mexico border states.

The Arizona portion of the Health Services Study was carried out by a team that included a geographer, two public health experts, and two research assistants; the Sonoran portion was accomplished by a team that included two economists and two physicians, with assistance from other collaborators. The methodology used in the study was designed around written surveys of providers in both Arizona and Sonora, personal interviews with providers on both sides of the border, a series of two-hour focus group sessions attended by invited community members and local public and private health care providers, and intensive review of statistical data and previous studies. Because there was nothing in the questions posed that could conceivably compromise respondents, no human subjects clearance was required; however, confidentiality was maintained. Two reports emerged from the study. The first was the one mentioned above, Health Services in Arizona and Sonora: Opportunities for Transboundary Integration (Morehouse et al., 1997). The second, Arizona Border Community Health Indicators, evaluated available health status indicators and recommended a set of indicators that might be used to monitor health status in the Arizona border communities (Kunz et al., 1998); a parallel study of health in the Mexican border communities did not receive funding, and therefore was not carried out.

While we draw upon information and findings presented in these reports and on interactions among the members of the research team, we address the issue from a quite different perspective in this chapter. Here, we focus on using geographical perspectives and critical theory to how activities and policies associated with transboundary integration of health services in the two states might affect borderland geographies of health. The reason for this emphasis is concern that the North American Free Trade Agreement, combined with heightened pressures from globalization and internal demographic changes could have significant negative impacts on geographies of health in the US-Mexico border region.

Health Services and NAFTA

NAFTA provides an important structural basis for pursuing trade relations and economic integration among the three states. While not expressly covering health services, five chapters of the agreement have pertinence to health services as a form of commerce: Chapter XI (investment opportunities), Chapter XII (transboundary trade), Chapter XIV (financial services), Chapter XVI (temporary entry of business people into NAFTA member states), and Chapter XXVII (intellectual property). In addition, NAFTA provides for exceptions in areas where governmental activity falls outside of the agreement's definition of 'commerce'. Public health activities, health services operated by government organizations and public health regulations – including technology and facility regulation, food and drug safety, and qualifications for professionals – were among activities exempted when the agreement was formulated.

In recognition that many disparities exist in the health care systems of the three countries, the NAFTA framers proposed that negotiations on key issues take place among professional associations and the governments of the member states, with the goal of incorporating agreed-upon measures into the trade agreement. The framers anticipated it would take at least ten years for harmonization in the health care sector to be accomplished. It will probably, in fact, take much longer to achieve (for an excellent discussion of NAFTA and health services on the US-Mexico border, see Warner 1997; for insights into NAFTA and health care in Canada, the United States and Mexico, see Freeman, Gómez-Dantés and Frenk, 1995).

Economic asymmetries between Mexico and the wealthier United States and Canada pose a considerable constraint to development of integrated, borderless health services structures under NAFTA, as do differences in educational requirements for providers, licensure and permitting policies, health care financing mechanisms, and regulatory frameworks and practices. Lack of portability of health care plans among the member countries poses yet another impediment. Further, although transboundary health care has occurred for many years, and trade in medical equipment and supplies is likewise long-standing, deep differences exist among the health systems of the three countries (see Escárgzaga, 1997; Lamarche, 1995; Gómez-Dantés and Frenk, 1995; Clarke, 1996). One problematical area involves the health care structures in each country.

The US system revolves around private-sector provision of health services, with the public system covering the elderly and certain other vulnerable populations such as children living beneath the poverty level. At its best, the US system provides some of the highest-quality health care in the world; however, inequalities exist in access and quality of care among different segments of the population and between geographical areas. Those unable to afford private coverage and those with conditions considered uninsurable by the private sector are the most seriously affected. Also affected are those who are covered, but whose coverage excludes important elements such as low-cost access to prescription drugs. Lower-income US citizens covered by Medicare and Medicaid are among the chief populations in this category. Resistance to substantive change in the system among powerful segments of the population, notably corporations and small businesses as well as the health services industry itself, continues to stymie progress toward a humanitarian goal of universal coverage.

Private health services also exist in Canada and Mexico; however, the philosophical orientation of both countries revolves around a state commitment to provide universal health care to their citizens. Based on 1991 figures, 57 percent of health care funding in Mexico came from the public sector, and 43 percent from the private sector. By comparison, in Canada 72 percent of health care was provided by the public sector; 43 percent was funded by the public sector in the United States (Escárgaza, 1997).

Canada, faced with serious financial pressures on its health care system, has in fact tightened its previously generous national health policy on reimbursing care received outside of the country. At the same time, some providers in Canada have begun targeting their services and marketing activities to attract US citizens, a growing number of whom are seeking health care in Canada.

Within Canada, significant efforts are underway to reduce costs and social tensions associated with the country's health care system. The system, as designed, reflects the European-style, state-supported social welfare systems. Like the European systems, the Canadian system represents a response to the social impacts of monopoly capitalism. Yet, in recent years, strikes by medical professionals, and political debates regarding steep increases in costs of maintaining the system, have prompted heated discussions about the pros and cons of introducing private-sector coverage (Clarke, 1996).

Given that Canada's urban centers and population are heavily concentrated within 100 miles of the international boundary (McKinsey and Konrad, 1989), an opening of the country's health services economy to privatization would appear provide opportunities for growth in transboundary health services. At the same time, however, the public health system may be jeopardized by private-sector arrangements to the extent that those arrangements deprive the state system of needed revenues, personnel, and infrastructure.

Like Canada, Mexico is experiencing serious difficulties in financing its public health care system. Health reform, initiated in 1994 under the Zedillo presidency, opened the way to considerably more private-sector activity in health services, including marketing of insurance and managed care plans by Mexican and foreign firms, and full investment by foreign entities in Mexican hospitals and other facilities (Robles, 1999; Nigenda, 1999). Under the new structure, Mexican Ministry of Health plans call for limiting its health care delivery to the rural poor. The expectation is that private-sector health care plans will cover those urban and rural residents having adequate financial means to avail themselves of privatized health services (Nigenda, 1999), presumably through employer-provided or self-financed insurance. This is a significant change that bears close scrutiny. Under the new arrangements firms that have traditionally been required to pay into governmental health funds, whether or not they invested in private plans, will no longer have to do so if they can demonstrate they have invested in private coverage. This change will certainly have an impact on the total amount of funding available to maintain and operate the public health systems. As in the case of Canada and the United States, transboundary commerce in health services may give rise to class-based and geographical inequalities along with the benefits accruing to wealthier segments of the population.

Production of Health Care Geographies in the Borderlands

Crossing the border for health care may be seen as a tactic employed by individuals in their everyday lives to address their health needs, in reaction to the larger policy strategies employed at state and federal levels (deCerteau, 1984). These tactics and strategies contribute to the social construction of space in the border area, whereby tactics produce and are influenced by geographies of health that connect providers and consumers. At the state, federal, and (increasingly) international level, on the other hand, policies constitute strategies formulated in abstract space (see Lefebvre, 1991; Soja, 1989). In some areas, geographies associated with accreted practice and local community identity may be produced and reproduced as well. This appears to be the case, for example, among residents of the Douglas-Agua Prieta and Nogales Arizona and Nogales Sonora border areas (see Figure 14.1).

Geographies of health care on the US-Mexico border are characterized by many of the same contradictory forces that drive relations between the two countries more generally. On the one hand, people seeking health services and health services-related goods have a long-standing tradition of crossing the border in both directions, and providers on both sides of the boundary line have profited by the exchange (Warner, 1997; Nichols et al., 1991). Yet providers on the US side of the boundary continue to express concern about losses due to foreign nationals' inability to pay for the services they receive. The contradiction is an important element in the way geographies of health care are constructed in borderland communities.

Nonreimbursement for services such as health care may be a somewhat spurious issue. Hayes-Bautista and Rodriguez (1997), for example, observe that non-citizens, overall, pay significantly more in taxes than they receive in benefits. A 1991 study by Nichols et al. likewise concluded that it was doubtful that overall financial losses incurred by indigent foreign nationals exceeded gains for border health care providers. Mignella (1998) investigated the issue of losses incurred because of unreimbursed treatment of indigent undocumented aliens in private hospitals. These facilities are often caught in a legal bind between being required by federal law to treat all emergency cases they receive, and not being able to obtain federal or state reimbursement for the services provided, on the grounds that they are private rather than publicly funded or contracted entities. She concluded that a number of intervening factors, including lack of data on nationality of the patient, made it impossible to definitively determine whether or not overall costs to private hospitals are offset by revenues received.

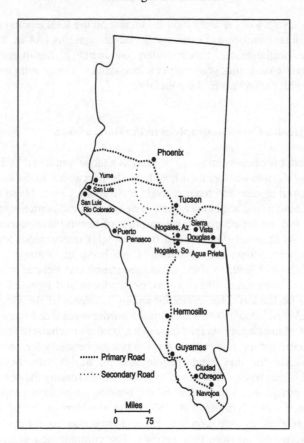

Figure 14.1 Communities addressed in the Arizona-Sonora health services study

Interviews with participants in the Arizona-Sonora Health Services study (Morehouse et al., 1997) and previous research (Nichols et al., 1991) indicated that hospitals and public health clinics in border communities and certain specialized services such as trauma units bear the greatest burden of unreimbursed care generated by border crossers from Mexico (see also Nichols et al., 1991). Again, because these providers are seldom able to determine the origins of their patients, quantitative data are scarce. One interviewee even commented that a threatened lawsuit based on discriminatory practices forced them to discontinue their practice of asking for the country of origin of their patients.[2] By contrast, as revealed in focus group sessions and personal interviews, other facilities within and beyond the border region actively market health care services in Mexico, even to the point of featuring package deals for commonly utilized services such as coronary bypass surgery.

The production of geographies of health care is both a product of and an influence on social actions and interactions. For example, a provider at a public health clinic in Arizona noted that his facility received many tuberculosis patients from several hundred miles away. Apparently an efficient word-of-mouth network operates among Mexicans in the southwestern portion of the state, indicating that this particular clinic provides good treatment. The provider observed that a discernible migration channel has been established that carries Mexican patients from the southwestern portion of the state to the facility. Thus a health care space is produced which, in turn, is influencing providers' expectations.

As illustrated below, significant differences in amount and quality of health care available indicate the extent of uneven development within and between the two countries (see Smith, 1984). Too, very different philosophies exist between the United States and Mexico about the nature of the relationship between the state and its citizens. The combination of these two factors operates to produce particular geographies in the borderlands.

Basic Health Care Statistics

In Mexico, public health care coverage is required under the country's constitution. Based on 1991 figures, some 89 percent of Mexican citizens had coverage either through one of the federal or state-operated health financing programs. While in theory, everyone is supposed to be covered, 11 percent of Mexicans lacked access to health services. In total, approximately 9 million Mexicans lack access to health services (Escárzaga, 1997). Even for those with access, the level and quality of health care provided varies significantly from one place to another, with the best services provided in the largest cities. Private-sector health care is available to those who can afford it. Only 1.3 percent of the population has private health insurance, but more than one-third of Mexicans obtain part or all of their care in the private sector. Further, it is not uncommon for physicians working in the public sector to also operate in the private sector.

In Sonora, 54 percent of the population is insured by federal or state health programs, and another 45 percent is covered by the Secretaría de Salud Pública (SSP), the country's Social Security system. On paper, only one percent of Sonorans lack coverage; however, as is the case nationally, inadequacies in the SSP system, particularly in poorer areas, means that acceptable levels of health care are not available to all. Most of these individuals live in belts of poverty and in indigenous settlements; some are excluded because they work in the informal sector and do not pay into any of Mexico's public health care programs. It remains to be seen whether reforms mentioned earlier in this article will actually improve coverage for these marginalized individuals.

In the United States, private health insurance and managed care plans are the main sources of financing for people below retirement age. The federal Medicare Medicaid and military benefits programs are the main governmental programs. According to US Census Bureau (1996) data, uninsured individuals account for 16.3 percent of the US population. Arizona, at 24.5 percent, currently shares with

Texas the lowest ranking in the country with regard to health insurance coverage (Arizona Daily Star, 1999a). Among those most likely to lack insurance were the working poor, and Hispanics. As will be discussed below, this latter group constitutes an important customer base for physicians on the Mexican side of the border.

A Brief Profile of Transboundary Health Services

Provision and utilization of health services in the US-Mexico borderlands are asymmetrical, and largely complementary (for an excellent analysis of health care on the US-Mexico border, see Warner, 1997). People regularly crossing into Mexico seeking some form of health service or product represent a broad cross section of the US population, as well as Canadians and other nationalities visiting the Southwest. Individuals cross into Mexico most frequently to obtain dental services, or to purchase pharmaceutical products. Some cross to have plastic surgery done, and sometimes to obtain vision care services and products. Lower cost is the major reason for crossing. Another common factor drawing consumers south is the greater convenience associated with longer business hours. Consultation with a Mexican physician is not uncommon, although in this case the consumers are primarily of Mexican origin. Their reasons for crossing may include a greater level of cultural comfort and ability to interact in Spanish, as well as cost.

An examination of the geography of transboundary health care provision and consumption in Sonora reveals a strong pattern of distance decay, with services oriented toward transboundary traffic located in close proximity to the international boundary (Nichols et al., 1991). Most notably, the number of providers speaking English or Spanish, respectively, drops off significantly outside the border communities (Morehouse et al., 1997). Fully 95 percent of dentists in the border communities indicated that they treated foreign patients, while only 69 percent of dentists in Hermosillo and Navojoa, both located far from the border, did so.

Individuals from Mexico who seek health care in the United States tend to be from more affluent segments of society (Homedes et al., 1992). Typically, they cross into the United States seeking a variety of services ranging from routine care, to highly specialized tertiary care and rehabilitation services. Some people also enter the United States to purchase pharmaceuticals, such as advanced cancer medications, not available in Mexico (Nichols et al., 1991; Warner, 1997; Morehouse et al., 1997). As mentioned above, some health care providers aggressively market their services to Mexican nationals. This, together with the commonly held perception among Mexicans that health services in the United States are much superior to those available in Mexico, contributes to a steady northward flow of patients, averaging perhaps 0.7 percent of all border crossings from Sonora to Arizona (Hopkins, 1992). In many cases, individuals cross for multiple reasons, health services being only one. Given an annual legal border-crossing rate into Arizona of about 22 million per year, this computes to more than 15,000 visits that at least in part are to obtain health services.

The US-Mexico Boundary in the Context of Health Care

Significant differences exist in the border crossing rules and procedures enforced by US and Mexican border agents; these differences have important implications for the production of transboundary geographies of health. It is not uncommon for US citizens who appear 'Mexican' to be stopped by US border patrol guards, even while travelling entirely within Arizona. Not surprisingly, the process of legitimately crossing into the United States is often even more stressful for Mexican nationals. The US Immigration and Naturalization Service (INS), for example, often requires Mexican citizens to provide multiple forms of documentation to prove that they have substantial roots in Mexico and are likely to return home after their visit. A participant in the Arizona-Sonora Health Services Study noted that the escalating demands of the INS agents for such proof caused a relative, who had long crossed into Arizona and paid in cash for health services, to switch to a provider in Mexico. It is unknown at this point how much lucrative business is lost by US providers due to these procedures, but if the providers are serious about profiting from integration of health services in the two countries, monitoring these trends could become necessary.

Viewed from another perspective, the availability of health services to Mexican nationals in US border health care facilities may provide an important 'safety valve' that alleviates pressure on the Mexican system to improve health services to border residents. The huge population growth in the Mexican border cities, fuelled by an increasing number of manufacturing and assembly plants, has not seen similar growth in health care provision. Further, US federal law, 42 USCS § 1395dd(a) and (b), requires that emergency stabilizing care be provided to everyone, regardless of ability to pay and regardless of legal status. In Sonora, sophisticated emergency care is not available in border communities, and the trip to Hermosillo, location of the closest Mexican facilities, is long. The combination of geographical factors, including health service location, transportation networks, and insufficient medical transportation services, operates to encourage border crossing for emergency care. The situation has significant implications for Arizona providers, who must often absorb the costs in cases when the bills are not paid.

Border providers advocated enactment of legislation to reimburse providers for emergency care delivered under federal law. As enacted, the legislation, 8 USCS § 1369, provides that each State or subdivision thereof that provides, through a public facility (including a non-profit hospital) or through contract with a facility, care to an illegal alien is eligible for Federal reimbursement of costs incurred and not otherwise reimbursed. Yet judicial and administrative interpretations of the statute have precluded private facilities from obtaining reimbursement (Mignella, 1998). Further, not everyone who receives care is an illegal entrant to the United States. In these cases, reimbursement is not even an option.

Intensified competition among health care providers in the United States, under restructuring associated with globalization and other competitive pressures, has increased firms' need to manage for bottom-line profitability and shareholder returns. This in turn intensifies concerns over how to restrict access by patients unable to pay the costs of their care. In the process, tensions have increased over who is empowered to participate in production of transborder spaces of health care, and what the rules governing the operation of the international boundary in structuring those spaces should be.

In contrast to the restrictive border crossing rules enforced by the United States, Mexican procedures generally require little beyond evidence of citizenship and vehicle insurance. Certainly Mexican border guards do not require voluminous proof of financial stability, nor do they habitually view people entering the country as potential parasites feeding on their social services. Interestingly, providers' policies of requiring payment up front before services are delivered shortcuts any potential problem of nonpayment. Anecdotal evidence collected during the Arizona-Sonora Health Services study, including stories of individuals having to scramble to scrape together the cost of emergency treatment, indicates that the kind of 'good samaritan' law enforced in the United States does not exist in Mexico. More generally, however, the revenue generated by sales of health services to US citizens constitutes a welcome infusion to the economies of border communities and to Mexican providers.

The above discussion has focused on geographies of health care utilization. As a side note, some mention must be made of structural factors affecting the transboundary activity of providers. Providers, unlike consumers, continue to experience strong barriers to transboundary professional practice; thus, their capacity to contribute to production of transboundary geographies of health remains quite limited. Differences in institutions governing medical education, licensure, and credentialing operate quite effectively to prevent practitioners from providing transboundary services. An addendum to NAFTA, Annex 1210.5, opens the possibility for negotiating common policies for recognizing licensed and certified professionals (Albro and Norton, 1997); however, such harmonization will require considerable time and careful negotiation.

Brief reviews of two borderland communities illustrate how transboundary spaces of health services and place-based, borderland geographies of health are produced in specific contexts, and how production of the one may facilitate or constrain production of the other.

Transboundary Environmental Health: The Case of Nogales, Arizona and Nogales, Sonora

Near the center of the Arizona-Sonora portion of the international boundary lies a pair of border communities with longstanding affinities: Nogales, Arizona with a population of just over 20,000 and Nogales, Sonora with an official population of around 130,000 and an estimated population of over 200,000 (see Figure 14.1). Today the two cities are harshly bisected by a high fence and by a border zone that is monitored on the US side by sophisticated surveillance technology and on both sides by armed border patrol agents. At the same time the two communities are linked not only by close social, economic, and cultural ties, but also by environmental pollution issues.

The physical geography of the two communities, collectively known as 'Ambos Nogales' is one of steep hills, arroyos, and increasing elevation as one travels southward. Due to the geology of the area, water generally flows northward from Nogales, Sonora to Nogales, Arizona. These flows can carry pollutants from maquiladora manufacturing and assembly operations as well as effluent from occasional breaks in the sewerage system. Much of the problem is associated with rapid population growth in Nogales, Sonora, stimulated by growth in the city's manufacturing sector. Today, there are more than 80 maquiladoras (manufacturing and assembly operations) in the city. Population growth has been accompanied by development of colonia settlements characterized by makeshift living structures that typically lack basic water and sewer connections (Varady and Mack, 1995).

Citizens in Nogales, Arizona have cited the occurrence of cancer and autoimmune disease clusters as evidence of the considerable threat posed to their community by inadequate water and sewerage systems in Nogales, Sonora and lax enforcement of Mexican environmental laws. Activists on the Sonoran side of the border cite these same inadequacies in articulating their concerns about community health and well-being. Mexican authorities have responded to the concerns by focusing on infrastructure development, including heavy investment in new well field development, associated delivery infrastructure, and improvements in their sewerage system.

During negotiations leading up to the 1993 signing of the border Environmental Cooperation Agreement, the Public Health Director for Santa Cruz County, of which Nogales (Arizona) is the county seat, persistently voiced local public health concerns associated with the flows of polluted waters from the Mexican side of the border. These concerns were somewhat buttressed by a study carried out between 1989 and 1993 by the University of Arizona's Udall Center for Studies in Public Policy. The research team identified pollution problems in some of the wells along Nogales Wash, the primary conduit for flows from Nogales, Sonora (Ingram et al., 1995). The study prompted further water quality studies by the Arizona Department of Environmental Quality and the International Boundary and Water Commission, as well as by public health researchers.

The story of the community's efforts to address its concerns provides a glimpse of how geographies of health in borderland areas come to be produced under conditions of tension among entities operating at different scales from the local to the binational. One of the most interesting elements of this story is that ordinary citizens of the community not only raised the issue, but also participated in research designed to translate their concerns into empirical results. Members of a group called Living is for Everyone (LIFE), under the direction of the University of Araizona researchers, surveyed their community to try to identify whether any or all of the three diseases they believed to be occurring at higher than normal rates in fact formed identifiable disease clusters that could be related to environmental contaminants (Varady and Mack, 1995). The very name of the group, as well as its mission, expresses the high value placed on sense of community and of place, and reveals the importance of understanding local dynamics from the perspective of geographies of health (Kearns, 1993).

The three diseases that the group tracked included multiple myeloma (a rare bone marrow cancer), systemic lupus erythematosus (SLE), and leukemia. Results of the survey eliminated leukemia; however, multiple myeloma and SLE showed up at levels markedly above expected levels. Between 1989 and 1993, 14 individuals were found to have multiple myeloma where five occurrences would have been expected; 26 people were found to suffer from SLE, where only four should have been found. The strong results prompted a more detailed study, the results of which were released late in 1994. Again there was strong evidence of abnormally high occurrences of both illnesses (for a full discussion of these events, see Varady and Mack, 1995).

Individuals participating in the Arizona-Sonora Health Services Study (Morehouse et al., 1997) provided insights into how the issue has subsequently unfolded. According to participants, several years ago the US Environmental Protection Agency (EPA) assigned an epidemiologist to further research the suspicious clusters of SLE and multiple myeloma occurrences in the community. In due time, the scientist completed his study and submitted the results to the EPA; however he did not, at that time, furnish the results to the local community. The EPA subsequently sent the report to Arizona Department of Environmental Quality but not to Nogales. Again, state strategy resulted in the community being kept out of the loop, based on the argument that the results could not be communicated until the Mexican government formally authorized release of the study.

In this example, international relations of power and concern for maintaining national sovereignty worked against local efforts to address community health issues in the context of everyday life. Local activism aimed to sustain a particular geography of health constructed of shared knowledge, experience, and concern. Local residents' conviction that they live under unacceptable levels of community health risk has only been deepened by the actions taken at the state and federal levels. The way in which the research results were handled has produced a fertile filed for local suspicion and resentment of outside authorities in both countries. Thus, the transboundary context of Ambos Nogales, reluctance to release public health information to local administrators and residents confounds efforts to work together to solve common problems. On the other hand, the two communities share the all too common borderland dilemma of being buffeted by the workings of international politics and have found ways to grapple with shared problems based on their long history of common experience and cultural ties. Activism in Nogales, Sonora to improve environmental conditions complements activism in Nogales, Arizona to identify the literal and figurative downstream effects of those conditions. In the process, a transboundary geography of health continues to be constructed and reconstructed through the everyday tactics of local residents.

Geographies of Health Care: The Case of Douglas, Arizona and Agua Prieta, Sonora

East of Ambos Nogales are the Arizona communities of Douglas and Bisbee, and the Sonoran communities of Naco and Agua Prieta (see Figure 14.1). In this area, the availability of health services in the Sonoran communities serves to some extent to make up for the lack of services on Arizona side. Indeed, southeastern Arizona is officially designated by the US government as a 'medically underserved area'. Likewise, the availability of hospital services on the Arizona side makes up, to some extent, for the lack of similar facilities in the Sonoran towns. The closest comparable facilities in Mexico are located in Hermosillo, a long way from the border. The opportunities and constraints posed by the existing patterns of location of health facilities in the area, together with the everyday behavioral patterns of providers and consumers, serve to (re)produce a distinctively transboundary spatiality of health.

Local focus group participants, representing the public and private health care sectors as well as community leaders, noted that individuals travel south to the Mexican border towns seeking dental care, medical care, behavioral health care and prescription medications. Mexicans travel north into Arizona communities primarily to obtain medical care or supplies of various kinds (Morehouse et al., 1997). Although issues persist, communities and individuals on both sides of the border benefit from the arrangement.

Dental Care

Focus group participants in the Arizona-Sonora Health Services Study (Morehouse et al., 1997) stressed the importance to the community of having access to Mexican dentists, due to a dearth of dentists on the Arizona side of the border. The option of using Mexican dental services is facilitated for some Arizona residents through insurance coverage that pays for services received from designated Mexican providers. For others, particularly those with limited means, access to less expensive dental care in Mexico is a key tactic for avoiding the high prices charged by Arizona providers. For some residents on the Arizona side who are of Mexican descent, culture and language play a role in decisions to utilize Mexican dentists. The interchange benefits Mexican dentists by providing them with a larger customer base and a larger income than they might otherwise have. The situation may also benefit Mexican border residents by increasing the number of providers in their area, although increased cost of care, induced by US-based demand and reimbursement arrangements, may pose constraints to utilization. For residents on the Arizona side of the border, dental costs may be lower, and there may be greater choice among providers. However, for those residents who do not choose to have their dental work done in Mexico, few local providers are available. Further, competition from lower-priced Mexican dentists, combined with low population numbers, decreases the ability of the area to attract additional providers. Thus the local geography of dental care is a lopsided one, characterized by relatively few providers on the Arizona side, and predominantly southward traffic to providers on the Sonora side.

Pharmaceutical Purchases

Like dental care, the spatiality of pharmaceutical purchases is largely characterized by north-to-south flows and a related predominance of pharmacy services south of the border. The southward tilt of the geographical space is largely the result of price differentials, for many products sell for half or less of the cost of the same product in the United States (Vogel, 1995; Morehouse et al., 1997). The ability to obtain products not available in the United States, or over-the-counter items that are only available by prescription, also attracts people to Mexican pharmacies.

Most pharmacies in the Mexican border communities are located close to the international boundary, have long business hours, and employ English-speaking staff. Interestingly, some of the demand for pharmaceuticals purchased in Mexico may be generated by prescription drug fads in the United States. According to one participant in a local focus group session, it is not unusual for people from out of town to ask residents where they can purchase things that have recently been in the news.

Similar to the case of dental services in the border area, competition from Mexican pharmacies seems to have discouraged growth of pharmacy services in Douglas and Bisbee. Indeed, there are only four pharmacies in the area. Like the space created by dental services, the geography of pharmacies is lopsided, with a marked tilt toward the Mexican side of the border.

Medical Care

A notably different pattern exists with regard to border crossing for medical care from physicians (Morehouse et al., 1997; Nichols et al., 1991; Homedes et al., 1992). In contrast to border crossers who purchase pharmaceutical products or seek dental care – and who may or may not be of Mexican heritage – people who cross into Mexico to obtain medical care are typically Hispanic in heritage, and are fluent in Spanish. Some of these individuals seek less-expensive care, or more convenient appointment times, while others prefer to interact with a physician steeped in the norms and expectations of Mexican culture. This latter case is important, for Mexican physicians tend to take a more personal approach to interacting with their clients. They may also prescribe medications more readily than their more cautious counterparts in the United States. For individuals who retain very close ties to their Mexican heritage, having the option to seek care in Mexico provides them with an important opportunity to reaffirm their connections with their culture. It would be a valuable addition to knowledge about transboundary community dynamics to examine the social dynamics associated with the intermingling of people from both sides of the border in Mexican physicians' offices, for such encounters may play a role in reproducing borderlands geographies of health.

Providers on the Arizona side of the international boundary have also been active contributors to the production of transboundary health care spaces. Some providers in the Douglas/Bisbee area (and elsewhere), for example, have offered package plans for selected medical procedures and services. These packages were specially tailored to attract Mexican customers, and give typical prices for the various packages. This availability of 'package deals' is not ordinarily available to Arizona customers, according to interviewees of the Arizona-Sonora Health Services project, in part due to rules imposed by health care insurers. Providers in the Bisbee/Douglas area who offer these packages have the explicit goal of capturing customers who would otherwise be likely to obtain these services in Tucson or Phoenix. The strategies of providers to maximize their clientele, and the tactics of consumers to satisfy their needs and preferences, results in an identifiable transboundary health care geography. The space is characterized by a compact area of interaction near the international boundary, with hospital services tilting the space northward, and dental and pharmacy services tilting the space southward. Physician services present a more complex geography based on cultural factors, health insurance arrangements of Arizona consumers, and other variables.

Geographies of Compassionate Health Care on the Border

Another manifestation of transboundary health care geographies may be found in the production of compassionate space. Here, providing care regardless of a person's station in life, ability to pay, or other characteristics is paramount. It is a contested area of activity, for balancing patients' well being with providers' concern for finances is tricky even in the best of circumstances, and even more problematical when an international boundary is involved. US providers (especially hospitals) on the border bear a disproportionate share of unreimbursed care. One study found that border providers reported uncompensated and reduced-fee care at more than $860,000, while Tucson providers reported a bit more than $564,000 (Nichols et al., 1991).

Such services are often related to emergency situations such as trauma, childbirth, and neonatal care. Here, uneven development plays a role, for communities on the Mexican side of the boundary typically lack high-quality emergency facilities and equipment. Long distances to qualified hospitals located in major population centers far from the border, and poor transportation and communication connections to those facilities compound the dilemma. Clearly, travelling a mile or two across the border from Sonora to Arizona in an emergency is preferable to making a journey to a hospital in Hermosillo. The motivation to cross to the United States for care is enhanced by commonly held perceptions that care in the United States is of better quality than that available in Mexico.

Recently, a joint effort was undertaken by two hospitals in Tucson and health care authorities in Mexico to address the high costs these facilities were experiencing due to unreimbursed care for newborns. The result is the recent opening of a modern neonatal treatment facility in Agua Prieta, Sonora across the border from Douglas, Arizona. Plans also call for improvement in emergency transportation so that patients can be rapidly transferred by air to hospital facilities in Hermosillo, Sonora (Arizona Daily Star, 1999b).

In addition to people who arrive on their own, US facilities also bear the burden of unreimbursed costs for treating injured and ill people delivered to their doors by the Border Patrol agents and others. Given that US law forbids these facilities from refusing emergency stabilizing care to anyone, the providers find themselves with few means of recompense. Arizona has never passed an initiative like the infamous Proposition 187 in California that banned delivery of government services – including health care – to non-residents, but issues associated with unreimbursed care continue to prompt some providers to call for actions to filter these patients from their case-loads. Most notable is the 1996 federal Welfare Reform Act, which has actually served to aggravate the problem by setting parameters for care of non-residents everywhere. In essence, non-residents are barred under the Act from receiving services from providers who receive federal funding, except in the case of clear emergency. As a result of the Act, patients without means to pay are being pushed even more onto those facilities that are most heavily involved in public health care.

Among the facilities most heavily affected by problems of unreimbursed care are the border facilities that are the sole provider for their area, and those that focus on publicly provided care for low-income people. These facilities are caught in a double bind, for not only are they required to turn away all illegal entrants except for obvious emergency cases, they are also unable to identify the citizenship status of their patients. As one Arizona-Sonora Health Services Study participant noted, it is not unusual for patients to give false residence information. Another interviewee noted that a threatened lawsuit, charging discrimination, prompted their facility to discontinue its practice of asking patients for their country of origin. Several representatives of hospitals stressed that they do not have any acceptable avenue for obtaining, much less effectively verifying such information.

US citizens in Mexico have much less protection in case of emergency health or injury crises, and it is not untypical to hear of people who were forced to produce significant amounts of cash before care was rendered. A recent case in the Mexican border state of Baja California illustrates the differences in policy between the two countries. In this case, a man was injured in an automobile accident and was transferred to a medical facility in Ensenada. There, doctors determined that the man needed immediate medical attention in the United States. However, Mexican authorities required that the family post a $2,300 bond[3] and pay $4,700 for emergency care and helicopter transport. His transfer to a US hospital was delayed 18 hours, and the man subsequently died of his injuries (Arizona Daily Star, 1999c).

The contrast between the policies of the two countries regarding emergency care strongly suggests that the differences may be more a matter of degree than intent. On both sides of the border, the providers and the government may define 'compassionate care' and its geographies, but it is the patients themselves who bear the ultimate risks. At the same time, efforts to establish a national-level system for reimbursing local unreimbursed transboundary health care costs thus far remain unsuccessful.

Conclusions

Transboundary geographies of health care are not characterized simply by a geographical region specified in some economic development plan or a set of governmental rules. Rather, the decisions, behaviors, values, and preferences of health care providers, health insurers, consumers, and regulatory authorities interact to produce multiple and overlapping geographies of health.

Strong differences exist between and within states and localities on both sides of the border. For Arizonans and others north of the international boundary, lower cost, cultural compatibility, convenience, treatment philosophy, and in some cases, opportunities for alternative forms of treatment contribute to the production of distinctive geographies of transboundary health care. Like Mexicans seeking health care in the United States, US citizens typically pay out-of-pocket for services they receive in Mexico, and their expenditures contribute substantially in some cases to providers' revenues. Insurance arrangements exist in some parts of the borderland that allow Mexican providers to serve insured US clients. With Mexico's recent efforts to reform its health care system and to introduce privatization into some parts of the system, it is likely that additional insurance arrangements will emerge that cover care received by Mexicans in the United States.

Focusing on the Arizona-Sonora region, the geographies of health care produced by Mexicans seeking services in the United States are generally larger, stretching as far as Tucson and Phoenix, than those produced by US citizens seeking services in Mexico. In this latter case, the space of health services does not extend beyond the border communities, except for some instances of service provision in Mexican tourist areas. However, the international boundary, which remains very visibly in place both materially and metaphorically as a line of strong political and cultural differentiation as well as of state sovereignty, poses constraints to realization of fully developed borderland geographies of health as part of a larger process of sustaining local places. Further, these transboundary geographies are highly susceptible to changes in the expectations, discourses, and practices of both providers and consumers. The resulting pattern is a complex mosaic of constantly shifting spaces. This observation leads to the posing of two questions.

The first question is, how might a better understanding of geographies of health improve the overall health and well-being of border residents? There is a strong need for continuous vigilance to ensure that state policies, constructed in abstract space, and capitalist opportunism that is focused on profits derived from delivery of health services, do not marginalize vulnerable populations. Instead, federal and private-sector actors should be required to redress inequities as part of their social contract.

For this to occur, geographies of health must be explicitly recognized and articulated in local discourse to promote community cohesiveness. For example, issues surrounding production of geographies of health should be routinely incorporated into discussion of education plans, economic development strategies, old-fashioned boosterism, faith-based community activism, park and playground development, and in other venues. Perhaps a greater awareness would be generated of the intimate connections between health care availability and accessibility, individual and community well-being, economic and personal development, and human-environment interdependencies. If such discussions were to be pursued by people from both sides of the border, working together toward common ends, communally valued transboundary geographies of health could be effectively produced and defended.

The second question (related to the first) is, how might transboundary spaces of health care be (re)produced in a way that minimizes the contradictions between international boundary politics and production of local, transboundary geographies of shared culture, values, and knowledge? Certainly devolution from the federal to the local level of authority over day-to-day decisions is important, for Washington, D.C. and Mexico City are too far removed from borderland communities to understand the dynamics, issues, and needs of these localities. Establishing boundary-spanning health care insurance and managed care arrangements, and developing transboundary communication mechanisms for providers are important. Also important is improvement in cooperative emergency care arrangements, reimbursement mechanisms, and patient referral structures. Thus, improvements should be carefully carried out so as to include rather than exclude vulnerable populations. The improvements should also be done in a manner that supports rather than undermines the State's responsibility to provide for the health of its citizens. Under such conditions key linkages among entities might be strengthened and a critical mass might be built to achieve a humane integration of health services across the international boundary (Morehouse et al., 1997).

In line with the above recommendations, continued context-specific research on the patterns and practices of transboundary health care provision and utilization are required in order to assess the effects of the above changes on providers and consumers, and on borderland communities. Such research becomes even more important with regard to monitoring the effects of globalization on health services provision and consumption, and tracking the effects of continuing changes in the structure of health services at the national and state level within the United States and Mexico.

NAFTA poses its own questions with regard to geographies of health in the borderlands. Opportunities for making profits from private-sector health services undoubtedly exist, and would benefit providers with the resources and savvy to compete in international markets. Further, to the extent that the agreement exerts a positive influence on income, employment, and access to goods and services more generally, the array and quality of health services available in Mexican border cities should improve. Whether this increases or decreases opportunities for private-sector health services on the US side of the border remains open to question, unless these providers can establish profitable collaborative agreements with their Mexican counterparts. Also open to question is whether development of health services in Mexico would raise prices, thus excluding even more people than is the case today. In addition, the introduction of more open competition among the three signatory countries could pose threats to vulnerable populations in all three countries, both in terms of reducing levels of publicly funded care available, and closing off less-expensive alternatives such as travelling to areas offering lower-cost services. Economic development under NAFTA could exacerbate existing occupational and environmental health threats associated with manufacturing and assembly operations in Mexico, given continued resistance to policy designs that incorporate humanitarian concerns into broadly defined geographies of health.

On the other hand, based on existing asymmetries associated with uneven development, there is potential to develop low-technology facilities such as chronic care institutions and nursing homes in Mexico that cater to retired US and Canadian citizens. Many US and Canadian retirees already live in Mexico. Changes in the rules governing payment for health services under Medicare and Medicaid to allow treatment in Mexico would likely enhance this trend. In these cases, new transboundary geographies of health would be produced. Ensuring benefits for all involved, rather than only for the more well-off expatriots at the expense of (undoubtedly mainly female) Mexican care providers would require a substantially greater commitment to social justice than has occurred in the past.

Looking Forward

The spatialities of health care and the geographies of health are complex, multilayered and dynamic. Any set of borderland health policies based on a simplistic perception that health services occur on a uniform plane of abstract space is sure to founder on the particularities of place and local production of space. A richer and more workable vision of borderland geographies of health would focus on the concurrent (re)production of community and individual health in multiple settings, based on the overlapping and sometimes contradictory needs, motivations, and desires of local providers, consumers, community leaders, and government agencies. In this vision, the relative power (or lack thereof) of the different players to influence the making of these geographies must be recognized and addressed in order to assure that equity and principles of compassionate care are not lost in the process of developing health services.

The process of producing boundaries and borderland geographies, particularly as it occurs at the local level, gives rise to a more general but provocative set of issues. Understanding the complexities of borderland geographies of health is essential to devising better health policies and delivering better services to borderland residents. This in turn requires active incorporation of local knowledge and concerns, and informed analysis of the social production and reproduction of space in the context of border health delivery and consumption practices.

Acknowledgments

The research project that inspired this chapter was funded through the Arizona-Mexico Commission and the Comisión Sonora-Arizona. Special thanks to Susan Craddock and the anonymous reviewers for their constructive comments on earlier versions of this work.

Notes

1   Advocating, from a Marxist perspective, for a science of space, Lefebvre emphasized that descriptions and cross-sections of space might allow for compilation of inventories of things that exist in space, or might even generate a discourse on space. However, they 'cannot ever give rise to a knowledge of space' (1991, p. 7; emphasis in original). He identifies ideal space, i.e., that having to do with mental categories, as separate from real space – the space of social practice. Each of these two types of space 'involves, underpins and presupposes the other' (p. 14). Thus, understanding social space must be understood as a process and as a social product, rather than as a naively given, abstract backdrop to social process. Indeed, 'every society – and hence every mode of production ... – produces its own space' (p. 31). Lefebvre identified a 'conceptual triad' for understanding the production of space. This triad includes spatial practice, which includes production and reproduction in the context of specific locations and spatial sets. Spatial practice 'ensures continuity and some degree of cohesion', wherein the cohesion 'implies a guaranteed level of competence and a specific level of performance' (p. 33; emphasis in original). According to Lefebvre, a society's spatial practice 'secretes that society's space; it propounds and presupposes it, in a dialectical interaction' (p. 38).

2   Recently warnings by two Tucson hospitals that they would have to close their trauma units due to financial stresses identified insufficient reimbursements from medical insurers and health maintenance organizations and unreimbursed care provided to non-citizens as the primary problems. The issue remains unresolved, though both hospitals received a fiscal-year 2001-2002 infusion of funds from the Arizona Legislature to ensure the continued operation of their units. The issue is significant, for these are the only top-level trauma units in all of southern Arizona.

3   Mexican law requires that, if involved in a traffic accident considered to be criminal, foreigners must post a bond in order to leave the country.

References

Albro, K. and Norton, K. (1997), 'Cross-border collaboration in medical practice', in D.C. Warner (ed.), *NAFTA and Trade in Medical Services between the US and Mexico*, pp. 187-249.

Arizona Daily Star (1999a), 'Arizona at bottom on health insurance', October 4, 1999, p. 1A.

Arizona Daily Star (1999b), 'UMC, TMC help babies at border', September 21, 1999, p. 3B.

Arizona Daily Star (1999c), 'Mexico demands cash; injured American dies', September 7, 1999, p. 4A.

Clarke, J.N. (1996), *Health, Illness, and Medicine in Canada*, 2nd ed., Oxford University Press, Toronto, New York and Oxford.

deCerteau, M. (1984), *The Practice of Everyday Life*, University of California Press, Berkeley.

Earickson, R.J.; Greenberg, M.R.; Lewis, N.D.; Meade, M.S. and Taylor, S.M. (1989), 'Medical geography', in G.L. Gale and C.J. Willmott (eds.), *Geography in America*, Merrill Publishing Company, Columbus, pp. 425-450.

Escárzaga, E.F. (1997), 'Los sistemas de servicios de salud de Estados Unidos, Canada y Mexico, ante los nuevos enlaces de la salud transnacional: analisis comparativo', *Journal of Border Health*, II(2), pp. 10-26.

Eyles, J. (1990), 'How significant are the spatial configurations of health care systems?' *Social Science and Medicine*, (30)1, 157-164.

Foucault, M. (1992), 'The subject and power', *Critical Inquiry*, 8, pp. 777-795.

Freeman, P.; Gómez-Dantés, O. and Frenk, J. (1995), *Health Systems in an Era of Globalization: Challenges and Opportunities for North America, Institute of Medicine*, Board on International Health, Washington D.C., in collaboration with National Academy of Medicine, Mexican Commission for Health Research, Mexico City, Mexico.

Gómez-Dantés, O. and Frenk, J. (1995), 'NAFTA and health services: initial data', in P. Freeman, O. Gomez-Dantes and J. Frenk (eds.), *Health Systems in an Era of Globalization: Challenges and Opportunities for North America, Institute of Medicine*, Board on International Health, Washington D.C., in collaboration with National Academy of Medicine, Mexican Commission for Health Research, Mexico City, Mexico, pp. 97-111.

Hayes-Bautista, D.E. and Rodriguez, G. (1997), *Immigrant use of public programs in the United States, 1996*, Center for the Study of Latino Health, UCLA School of Medicine, Los Angeles, California.

Homedes, N.; Chacón-Sosa, F.; Nichols, A. W.; Otálora-Soler, M.; LaBrec, P.A. and Alonso-Vásquez, L. (1992), 'The role of physicians and dentists in the utilization of health services at the Arizona-Sonora border', *Monograph*, 31, March 1992, Southwest Border Rural Health Research Center, College of Medicine, University of Arizona, Tucson, Arizona.

Hopkins, R.G. (1992), 'The economic impact of Mexican visitors to Arizona', *Monograph*, September 1992, Economic and Business Research Program, College of Business and Public Administration, University of Arizona, Tucson, Arizona.

Ingram, H.; Laney, N.K. and Gillilan, D.M. (1995), *Divided Waters: Bridging the US-Mexico Border*, University of Arizona Press, Tucson, Arizona.

Jones, K. and Moon, G. (1992), 'Medical geography: global perspectives', *Progress in Human Geography*, 16(4), 563-572.

Jones, K. and Moon, G. (1993), 'Medical geography: taking space seriously', *Progress in Human geography*, 17(4), 515-524.

Kearns, R.A. (1993), 'Place and health: towards a reformed medical geography', *Professional Geographer*, 45(2), 139-147.

Kearns, R.A. and Gesler, W.M. (eds.) (1998), *Putting Health Into Place: Landscape, Identity, & Well-Being*, Syracuse University Press, Syracuse, NY.

Kearns, R.A. and Joseph, A.E. (1993), 'Space in its place: developing the link in medical geography', *Social Science and Medicine*, 37(6), 711-717.

Kunz, S.; Driesen, K.E.; Baum, M.F. and Morehouse, B.J. (1998), *Health Services: Arizona Border Community Indicators*, Border Health Foundation and Arizona-Mexico Commission.

LaMarche, P. (1995), 'Challenges to health systems in North America', in P. Freeman, O. Gomez-Dantes and J. Frenk (eds.), *Health Systems in an Era of Globalization: Challenges and Opportunities for North America*, Institute of Medicine, Board on

International Health, Washington D.C., in collaboration with National Academy of Medicine, Mexican Commission for Health Research, Mexico City, Mexico, pp. 71-79.

Lefebvre, H. (1991), *The Production of Space*, translated by Donald Nicholson-Smith, Basil Blackwell, Oxford.

McKinsey, L. and Konrad, V. (1989), 'Borderlands Reflections: The United States and Canada Borderlands', *Monograph*, Series No. 1, Canadian-American Center, University of Maine, Orono, Maine.

Mignella, A. (1998), 'Legal aspects of US-Mexico border health issues', National Law Center for Inter-American Free Trade, part one, August, 1998.

Moon, G.; Gould, M. and Jones, K. (1990), 'Conceptions of space and community in British health policy', *Social Science and Medicine*, 30(1), 165-171.

Moon, G.; Gould, M. and Jones, K. (1998), 'Seven up – refreshing medical geography, an introduction to selected papers from the Seventh International Symposium in medical geography', *Social Science and Medicine*, 46(6), 627-629.

Morehouse, B.J. (1993), 'Power relationships in the spatial partitioning and natural resource management of the Grand Canyon', Ph.D. dissertation, Department of Geography and Regional Development, The University of Arizona, Tucson, Arizona.

Morehouse, B.J.; Driesen, K.; Kunz, S.; Salido, P.L.; Taddei, C. and Santillana, M. (1997), *Health Services in Arizona and Sonora: Opportunities for Transboundary Integration*, Arizona-Mexico Commission, Phoenix, Arizona.

Newman, D. and Paasi, A. (1998), 'Fences and neighbours in the postmodern world: boundary narratives in politicial geography', *Progress in Human Geography*, 22(2), 186-207.

Nichols, A.W.; LaBrec, P.A.; Homedes, N.; Geller, S.E. and Estrada, A.L. (1991), 'Utilization of health services along the US-Mexico border', *Monograph*, 23, April 1991, Southwest Border Rural Health Research Center, College of Medicine, University of Arizona, Tucson, Arizona.

Nigenda, G. (1999), Remarks, conference proceedings, Arizona-Sonora Health Services Conference: Organizing for a Healthy Economy, January 15, 1999, pp. 10-12. Office of Economic Development, The University of Arizona, Tucson Arizona, and Border Health Foundation, Tucson, Arizona.

Paasi, A. (1996), *Territories, Boundaries and Consciousness: The Changing Geographies of the Finnish-Russian Border*, John Wiley and Sons, Chichester and New York.

Porter, M.E. (1990), *The Competitiveness of Nations*, The Free Press, New York.

Robles, J.N. (1999), Luncheon remarks, conference proceedings, Arizona-Sonora Health Services Conference: Organizing for a Healthy Economy, January 15, 1999, pp. 18-19. Office of Economic Development, The University of Arizona, Tucson Arizona, and Border Health Foundation, Tucson, Arizona.

Smith, N. (1984), *Uneven Development: Nature, Capital and the Production of Space*, Blackwell, Oxford.

Soja, E.W. (1989), *Postmodern Geographies: The Reassertion of Space in Critical Social Theory*, Verso, London.

US Census Bureau (1996), Supplement to Current Population Survey, http://census.gov.ftp/pub/hhes/hltins/cover95asc.html.

Varady, R.G. and Mack, M.D (1995), 'Transboundary water resources and public health in the US-Mexico border region', *Journal of Environmental Health*, 57(8), 8-14.

Vogel, R.J. (1995), 'Crossing the border for health care: an exploratory analysis of consumer choice', *Journal of Borderlands Studies*, X(1), pp. 19-44.

Warner D.C. (1997), *NAFTA and Trade in Medical Services Between the US and Mexico*, Policy Report No.7, Lyndon B. Johnson School of Public Affairs, University of Texas, Austin.

PART V
EPILOGUE:
IMPLICATIONS FOR POLICY-
AND DECISION-MAKING

Epilogue:
Implications for Policy- and Decision-Making

Bruce A. Wright and Vera Pavlakovich-Kochi

> Above all, good decision-making requires continual reappraisal in the light of what is learned from action already in progress.
>
> (Baker, 1999)

In the last 20 years all regions have been challenged by profound political shifts, emergence of 'new' economy and continuing globalization. What makes it particularly challenging for border regions is that in addition to what every other region must do in adjusting to these new conditions, border regions must also do it in collaboration with the region(s) on 'the other side'. This not only increases the number of decision makers, but also increases the heterogeneity of the decision-making body, and complexity of the decision-making process. This may, as numerous examples have shown, become complicated by questions of national sovereignty, historical baggage and cultural identities.

The material presented in this book suggests a number of key points that need to be included in policy- and decision-making concerning border regions.

'Regionalized' decision-making In spite of competition for investment, tourism and other activities between the two sides, it is argued that due to interconnectedness, virtually anything that increases economic activity on one side of the border can result in some increased activity on the other through a variety of cross-border flows. Thus, from an economic perspective, transborder consultation-coordination mechanisms must be formed in order to realize potential economies of scale, manage spillovers effects and lower transportation costs.

Need for flexibility In response to constantly changing constellations of power relationships, economic processes and cultural imperatives, degree of flexibility should be built into policies at all levels.

Understanding complexities of borderland geographies Issues surrounding production of borderland geographies must be explicitly recognized and articulated in local discourse. In particular, production of borderland geographies should be routinely incorporated into discussion of education plans, economic development strategies, provision of health services, community activism, and other venues.

Incorporation of local knowledge   State officials can learn from borderland residents' experiences and local governments' practices. By drawing upon the local experience in coping with border issues, policy- and decision-makers can more successfully develop optimal policies.

Importance of catalyst   In supporting coordination of political and economic strategies on both sides of the border it is essential to recognize the capacity of the local decision-making process. Importance of local-level cooperation and ties assures continuation of cross-border cooperation despite changes in institutional organizations.

Context-specific approach   Regional cross-border programs need to be incorporated into integration process not in the sense of automatically following a single model, but by respecting regional specificities, some of which require targeted integration/cooperation strategies.

Recognizing historical experience   In regions with strong impacts of periods of political divisions and economic stagnation/isolation, the importance of outside, higher-level decision-making bodies (national and supranational governments) should be recognized.

Building comprehensive policy frameworks   Although many decisions deal with short-term solutions, long-term policies must address region's structural problems. In particular, under conditions of asymmetric interdependence, state-sponsored projects could generate positive results if existing asymmetries are used in intelligent ways.

Monitoring context-specific effects   Continued monitoring of effects of globalization and tracking the effects of continuing changes in regional structures is needed. In particular, vigilance to ensure that state policies, constructed in abstract space do not marginalize vulnerable populations needs to become an integral part of the decision process.

As new constellation of economic forces, politics and culture unfolds, and new modes of cross-border interactions develop, Oscar Martinez (1994) reminds us about one of rather persistent truths:

> The border is predictable and unpredictable; it divides and unifies; it repels and attracts; it obstructs and facilitates. (Martínez, 1994, p. 305)

References

Baker, V. (1999), 'Water science and policy in the Southwest', 1999 University of Arizona Faculty Community Lecture Series, Tucson, AZ, April 28.

Martinez, O.J. (1994), *Border People: Life and Society in the U.S.-Mexico Borderlands*, The University of Arizona Press, Tucson.

Index